High School to Employment Transition:

Contemporary Issues

Edited by
Albert J. Pautler, Jr.

 Prakken Publications, Inc.

Library of Congress Catalog Card Number: 93-86908
ISBN: 0-911168-88-5

Permissions

Permission to use "A Proposal for Making Transition from Schooling to Employment an Important Component of Educational Reform" by Kenneth B. Hoyt granted by the Youth Policy Institute. The work first appeared in *Future Choices*, Vol. 2, No. 2, Fall 1990.

Permission to use "The Effects of Part-Time Work Experience on High School Students" by Bassem N. Kablaoui and Albert J. Pautler granted by Human Services Press. The work first appeared in the *Journal of Career Development*, Vol. 17, No. 3, Spring 1991.

Dedicated to
Marilyn J. Pautler

Contents

Part IV: What Might Be Done

Special Section

Acknowledgments

This book results from the efforts of all those people who have taken the time to contribute one or more chapters, as well as those from Prakken Publications who supported and produced the final product.

The idea for the book was that of the editor, who prepared the prospectus and shared it with publisher George F. Kennedy and other Prakken Publication staff members.

This book would not have been possible without the scholarship of the many writers who have contributed a chapter. Their only reward is the personal satisfaction of seeing their efforts appear in print. Thanks to all of you folks.

My special thanks are due to Susanne Peckham of Prakken Publications for editorial assistance in the preparation of the final manuscript. She and others from Prakken were most helpful in supporting my idea for a book of this nature and for editorial and production support.

The book is dedicated to my best friend, wife, and the mother of our four children, Marilyn Pautler. She has been a very strong supporter of my work and efforts over many years. Many thanks, Lynn.

My special thanks also go to Sally Claydon for many drafts of letters, outlines, and related items. Thanks, Sally, for assisting me in this project.

Introduction

The issue and discussion of school-to-employment transition experiences of youth is not new. In 1976, the National Commission for Manpower Policy published a collection of policy papers titled *From School to Work: Improving the Transition*. The first chapter in that book was written by Paul E. Barton and titled, "Youth Transition to Work: The Problem and Federal Policy." You will note that the first chapter of this book, "Odyssey of the Transition from School to Work 1960-1990," is also by Paul E. Barton.

The ideas of Kenneth B. Hoyt influenced my decision to use "employment" instead of "work" in the title of this book. The use of the word "work" may convey the message to high school students that schooling is not work. Therefore, I chose the title *High School to Employment Transition* as the most appropriate title.

The interim report on the School-to-Work Transition project of the William T. Grant Foundation greatly influenced my decision to seek a publisher for this selection of chapters. The 1988 report *The Forgotten Half: Non-College Youth in America* focused attention on those high school graduates who are not likely to attend college. What things about the group of young people who finish their formal education upon graduation from high school make them unique? The second chapter in this collection, Atelia Melaville's "Forgotten No More: The Contribution of the William T. Grant Foundation Commission Reports on Non-College Youth and the Transition from School to Employment," helps to set the work of the Grant Foundation's Commission on Work, Family and Citizenship in focus.

Organization of the Book

As you will note in the table of contents, the book has four parts. The decision to place chapters in particular parts of the book and the order used were arbitrary on my part. The user can choose to read the chapters in any order that suits his or her needs and desires at a given time. No attempt was made to sequence the flow of material from chapter to chapter.

Part I includes several chapters that provide background on school-to-employment transition.

Research reviews related to the theme of the book can be found in Part II. Articles dealing with national studies, research reviews, and experiences of high school graduates in finding employment appear in this part of the book.

In Part III, program analysis and reviews on a variety of topics dealing with school-to-employment issues can be found. Included are chapters on special-needs and at-risk students. You will notice that a chapter on transition experiences of students planning to attend college also appears in this part.

The section that deals with suggestions regarding what might be done, Part IV, includes proposals for improving the awareness of people to the plight of the so-called "forgotten half" in America. Selections deal with curriculum, guidance, and partnerships, as well as the reform movement.

A special section concludes the book with two resource lists developed by Charles R. Doty that readers may find helpful in their own efforts to improve the school-to-employment transition experiences of high school graduates.

How You Might Use This Book

This book can be used in college-level courses dealing with school-to-employment transition experiences of high school graduates. I hope the book will find its way into programs that prepare guidance counselors for their role in counseling high-school-age students.

Though not a book on the curriculum, *High School to Employment Transition: Contemporary Issues* should be a resource to those planning curriculum for the high school. The major concern of most high schools is to direct students to college. The one exception to this may be vocational high schools. This book deals with what can be done to direct equal attention to students not planning to continue their formal education beyond high school.

This book should be a timely addition to the literature on school transition theory. It should serve as a reference to those interested in the school-to-employment experiences and practices of high school graduates. Where *High School to Employment Transition* is used in a formal college or staff development course, assigned readings can be given by the instructor followed by guided review, analysis, and discussion.

About the Authors

The authors of the chapters were all requested by me to prepare their papers for the book. As indicated earlier, in the Acknowledgements section, their only reward is the personal satisfaction of seeing their scholarship in print in this book. I have appreciated the opportunity to work with the writers, and I appreciate all of their efforts to develop a first-class work.

Contributors

PAUL E. BARTON is director of the Policy Information Center at Educational Testing Service. Prior to that position, he served as president of the National Institute for Work and Learning. He was a member of the U.S. Department of Labor's Policy Planning Staff and also worked for the U. S. Bureau of the Budget, in the Executive Office of the President (now the Office of Management and Budget). His publications address the areas of the school-to-work transition, youth employment and unemployment, income maintenance programs, and education.

CLIFTON P. CAMPBELL is a professor in the Department of Technological and Adult Education at The University of Tennessee and is an international consultant. He has 29 years of experience in education and training, including instructional, administrative, and managerial positions in the U.S. and abroad. He has written numerous publications dealing with human resource development issues. His most recent research and writing focus on performance-based training.

URSULA CARGILL graduated from high school at age 15 in 1979 and received the foundation of her academic training in Nassau, Bahamas, where she was granted an Associate in Arts degree in Business Administration from the College of the Bahamas. She then went to Baltimore, Maryland, where in 1983 she received Bachelor of Science degrees in Business Administration and Management from Morgan State University. In 1985, she received a Masters of Business Administration at Morgan State. She is actively pursuing a Ph.D. in Educational Administration at the State University of New York at Buffalo. Ms. Cargill plans to work in the administration of higher education

institutions. She has participated in the private sector, working for major corporations, which included Ford Motor Company. Her Ph.D. research has focused on student retention strategies in higher education, as she believes that retention of students (like customer loyalty in the private sector) is significant for the future stability of higher education.

GERALD D. CHEEK is professor and head of the Department of Technological and Adult Education, College of Education, The University of Tennessee, Knoxville. His teaching experience spans 29 years and includes secondary education, technical education, teacher education, and industrial training. Dr. Cheek has extensive experience with both developing countries and the private sector in establishing training programs for economic development. He currently is interested in finding more effective ways to form linkages between vocational-technical education and the private sector.

DOUGLAS R. COCHRANE is a research associate for the Consortium of Urban Issues at State University College at Buffalo and a doctoral candidate at the State University at Buffalo in Social Foundations, Comparative Education. He holds an M.S. in Student Personnel Administration from State University College at Buffalo and a B.S. in Marketing from Rochester Institute of Technology. He was recently one of four students recognized by the ACPA Gerald L. Saddlemire Outstanding Graduate Student Award, and one of eight students to win an honorarium and presentation through the ACPA Graduate Student Paper Competition. He is currently coauthoring a series of three articles introducing total quality management to the not-for-profit/

human services sector. He is also involved in work in the inner city.

GEORGE H. COPA is Professor and Chair in the Department of Vocational and Technical Education at the University of Minnesota, Twin Cities Campus. He has twenty-five years of professional work in vocational education. Recently, he completed a three-year project for the National Center for Research in Vocational Education on the subject matter of vocational education; a two-year effort on new designs for the comprehensive high school is now underway. Prior to this work, he completed a program of research on the purpose, practice, and future directions of secondary vocational education. He has served as president of the University Council for Vocational Education and the American Vocational Education Research Association. He coauthored the chapter on vocational education in the AERA *Handbook on Curricular Research* (1991) and the *Encyclopedia of Educational Research* (1992). Forthcoming is a chapter on vocational teacher education in *A Knowledge Base for Teacher Education*, to be published by the American Association of Colleges of Teacher Education.

LAWRENCE M. DERIDDER, a former chair of the Department of Educational and Counseling Psychology at the University of Tennessee at Knoxville, retired in 1986 as professor emeritus. For three years he was involved as a consultant to Tennessee's Comprehensive Career Development Program. His current research emphasis is on preventing and reducing the number of at-risk students.

CHARLES R. DOTY, is a graduate advisor in the Vocational and Technical Program, Department of Theory, Policy and Administration, Graduate School of Education, and Pre-Student Teacher Coordinator, Office of Teacher Education, Rutgers–The State University of New Jersey. Perspectives for writing for this book include having a father who was a coal miner (seeing men removed from coal mine shafts after mine explosions) as well as being a farm laborer, part-time bank teller, part-time construction worker, high school teacher, vocational teacher educator and administrator at

two universities, married (once), and father of two children who are presently in the transition stage.

KENNETH GRAY is an associate professor and the professor in charge of vocational and industrial education at The Pennsylvania State University. Before joining the faculty at Penn State in 1987, Dr. Gray served as superintendent of schools for the Connecticut Vocational Technical School System. He is currently a member of the Pennsylvania Council for Vocational Education. Dr. Gray has conducted research and published widely on a variety of education-for-employment issues. He holds degrees in economics, counseling psychology, and vocational technical education. He has been a Ford Fellow and recently was awarded the prestigious Harold Silvius Outstanding Scholarship Award.

JAMES P. GREENAN is professor and chair of Vocational Education at Purdue University, West Lafayette, Indiana. He received his Ph.D. from the University of Minnesota's Department of Vocational and Technical Education. His programmatic research focuses on generalizable skills and special-needs populations. His instructional interests include research methods, program evaluation, leadership development, and special-needs learners. He has held several national and state leadership positions in a variety of professional associations. Dr. Greenan collaborates with local education agencies to improve and expand school-to-work transition programs for youth and adults.

ROBERT R. HANSON, is a teacher educator in the Technological and Adult Education Department at The University of Tennessee. For three years, he served as director of the Tennessee Comprehensive Career Development Project. His major goal is to promote career education and pre-vocational experiences for all youth.

KENNETH B. HOYT is University Distinguished Professor of Education at Kansas State University. He has served as president of the National Career Education Association and the American Personnel and Guidance Association. Prior to his present university appointment, he was employed by the University of Maryland, the University of Iowa, the U.S. Department of Education, and Embry-Riddle Aeronautical University. He is the author of many books and manuscripts dealing with career education, guidance, and vocational education.

BARBARA A. HUDDLESTON-MATTAI is associate professor of Social Work at the State University College at Buffalo. She received a Doctorate of Social Work degree from U.C.L.A, an M.S.W. from Atlanta University, and a B.S.W. from Tennessee State University. Her twenty-one years of social work experience are focused on urban and rural families with particular emphasis in African-American families. She is currently involved in work among African-American social workers and African-American clients, and teen parents. Dr. Huddleston-Mattai has published in several journals.

BASSEM KABLAOUI received his Ph.D. from the University of Buffalo in the area of Educational Administration. His research has focused in the area of school-to-employment transition and its relationship to school curriculum.

W. JOHN KOZINSKI earned a B.S. in Education from SUNY College at Buffalo in 1969. He then taught industrial arts in the Buffalo public schools for 16 years. In 1973, Canisius College awarded him an M.S. degree in Guidance and Counseling. He also earned a Professional Diploma in Educational Administration (CAS—Certificate of Advance Study) in 1976 from State University of New York (SUNY) College at Buffalo. In 1987, SUNY-UB granted him an M.S. degree in Educational Administration. Since 1984 he has worked as a guidance counselor at Burgard Vocational High School in Buffalo, New York. Mr. Kozinski resides in West Seneca, New York, with his wife and four children.

PHILLIP MARRON has worked as a high school industrial arts teacher, a middle manager in private business and industry, and currently he is a school business administrator in Livo-nia Central School District in New York. His interest in worker recruitment, training, and retention has led him to investigate school-to-work transition as his dissertation topic at the State University of New York at Buffalo, where he is a candidate for an Ed.D. in Educational Administration.

ATELIA I. MELAVILLE served as Research Associate at the William T. Grant Foundation Commission on Work, Family and Citizenship from 1986 to 1992. She has written several articles and reports on youth and service delivery issues and presently is a senior associate at the Center for the Study of Social Policy in Washington, D.C.

P. RUDY MATTAI is professor of Educational Foundations at the State University College at Buffalo. He received Ph.D. and M.Ed. degrees in the Social Foundations of Education and International and Comparative Education from the University of Pittsburgh, an M.A. in Sociology of Religion from Pittsburgh Theological Seminary, and a B.A. (Hons) from the University of the West Indies, Jamaica, West Indies. He does extensive work and is published in the area of education among Africans in the diaspora. He currently directs a Consortium in Urban Issues, which is a forerunner of the Center for Multidisciplinary Applied Research in Urban Issues.

ROBERT C. NICHOLS, a 1954 Ph.D. graduate of the University of Kentucky, is professor of Educational Psychology in the Graduate School of Education of the State University of New York at Buffalo. He is Director of the Quantitative Analysis Laboratory, and has served as chair of the Department of Educational Psychology. He teaches in the areas of individual differences, measurement, and statistics. Before coming to Buffalo in 1968, he was director of research at the National Merit Scholarship Corporation, where his research addressed the identification of talented students and the role of higher education in their personal development. From 1976 through 1982, he served on the National Planning Committee for *The National Longitudinal Study of the High School Graduating Class of 1972* and for *High School and Beyond*.

DAVID L. PASSMORE is a professor of Vocational Education at the University Park campus of The Pennsylvania State University and is affiliated with Richard A. Swanson Associates of St. Paul, Minnesota. He has served on the faculties of the University of Massachusetts/Amherst and the University of Northern Iowa and as director of occupational research at National Technical Institute for the Deaf. He held a one-year appointment as the Carnegie Visiting Scholar in Maternal and Child Health at the Harvard School of Public Health, where his research on the epidemiology of injuries was sponsored by the Centers for Disease Control. Dr. Passmore's current research involves integrating training efforts with economic development plans. He teaches courses in research methods, data analysis, educational planning, and thesis planning to graduate students in vocational education at Penn State. He served as editor of the *Journal of Industrial Teacher Education* and on the editorial boards of *Human Resources Development Quarterly*, *School Review*, and *Accident Analysis and Prevention*.

ALBERT J. PAUTLER, JR., a 1967 Ed.D. graduate of the State University of New York(SUNY) at Buffalo, is professor of educational administration in the Graduate School of Education at SUNY-Buffalo. Prior to his present position he was a professor at Rutgers University in New Jersey and a high school teacher of electronics in New York State. He is the author of some 50 published articles and 12 books. Previous to this one, his most recent book was *Vocational Education in the 1990s: Major Issues*, published by Prakken Publications. His research and publications are in the area of school-to-employment transition, career education, curriculum design, and educational administration.

VIRGINIA H. PEASE is currently a graduate research assistant at the University of Minnesota, Twin Cities campus, in the Department of Vocational and Technical Education. She received her M.B.A. and bachelor's degree in secondary education from the University of Wisconsin at Madison. While at the University of Minnesota, she coordinated a National Center for Research in Vocational Education research project that looked at new ways to integrate academic and vocational education in comprehensive high schools. Earlier, she worked in partnership with numerous employers in the areas of workplace literacy, work readiness, and computer applications. Her teaching experience in secondary school in Wisconsin included mathematics, computer applications, and special education.

LISA B. PENKOWSKY is an English teacher who is currently a research assistant for the Department of Teacher Preparation and Special Education at the George Washington University. She is the assistant editor of the journal for *Career Development for Exceptional Individuals*. She received her B.A. in English at the University of Maryland at College Park and her M.Ed. at the George Washington University.

CLARENCE H. PREITZ is a professor in the Department of Secondary Education, University of Alberta, Edmonton, Alberta, Canada. He holds life membership in numerous national and international professional organizations concerned with technology and vocational education. One of his major research interests is apprenticeship training.

DAVID J. PUCEL is a professor and the head of the Division of Industrial Education, Department of Vocational and Technical Education, University of Minnesota. He received his B.S. from the University of Wisconsin-Stout in 1962, his master's degree from the University of Illinois in 1963, and his Ph.D. from the University of Minnesota in 1966. Since that time he has conducted numerous research studies and written extensively on curriculum in training and vocational education. He has consulted with representatives of 13 different countries on the design of curriculum and the development of educational systems. He has written or co-written four texts on curriculum. Dr. Pucel currently serves as the consulting edi-tor of a basic skills series for workplace success.

MICHELLE SARKEES-WIRCENSKI has a background in both special education and vocational education. She is the past president of The National Association of Vocational Education Special Needs Personnel. Dr. Sarkees-Wircenski currently teaches undergraduate and graduate courses in trade and industrial education and training and development in the Department of Occupational and Vocational Education, University of North Texas.

HARRY SILBERMAN is professor emeritus at UCLA, and he continues to teach courses on education and work. He was chairman of the National Commission on Secondary Vocational Education, which published *The Unfinished Agenda: The Role of Vocational Education in the High School* in 1984. He has conducted research on instructional technology and has published journal articles on the educational effects of work experience. He edited *The 1982 NSSE Yearbook on Education and Work*. He received an outstanding service award from the American Vocational Association in 1987.

DAVID W. STEVENS is director of the University of Baltimore's Regional Employment Dynamics Center and a research professor in the Department of Economics and Finance. He is currently investigating the employment and earnings histories of former students in high school and community college vocational-technical education programs. This research is sponsored by the Congressionally mandated National Assessment of Vocational Education and is being conducted through the auspices of the National Center on the Educational

Quality of the Workforce at the University of Pennsylvania. He is a member of the Senior Scholars Panel affiliated with the center. Through the center's auspices, he will soon attempt to design and test a practical way to routinely monitor the flow of trainees who emerge from the increasingly diverse sources of skill competency enhancement in the United States.

LYNDA L. WEST is a professor in the Department of Teacher Preparation and Special Education at the George Washington University. Dr. West earned her Ph.D. in education at the University of Missouri-Columbia. She served as Director of Missouri LINC, a statewide resource center that provides technical assistance to state and local educational agencies seeking to improve career, vocational, and transition programs for students with special needs. She was formerly a teacher of at-risk students in the Missouri public schools. She is a published author and public speaker, and she is a teacher trainer.

JERRY L. WIRCENSKI has experience in vocational special-needs education and trade and industrial education. He currently teaches undergraduate and graduate courses in trade and industrial education and training and development in the Department of Occupational and Vocational Education, University of North Texas. Dr. Wircenski also serves as coordinator of the interdisciplinary master's degree in corporate training and development at the university.

Part I:

Background

1

Odyssey of the Transition
from School to Work
1960–1990

Paul E. Barton

The United States entered the decade of the 1960s without great concern for either a youth employment problem or the quality of young people's transition from school to work. No such preoccupations had beset the nation since the Great Depression, when a massive Civilian Conservation Corps and National Youth Administration provided jobs and education to millions of American youth.

New Frontier

There was youth unemployment that caused concern from time to time after World War II, but it was generally thought to be linked to overall unemployment and recessions. There had been a bad recession in 1958, and a sluggish recovery. And by the fall of 1960, when presidential campaigning was in full swing, those who watch such matters closely knew the country was entering another recession. President-elect Kennedy took that problem with him to a post-election retreat at Palm Beach, Florida, where orders were issued to prepare remedies. What emerged from the administration, almost immediately on taking office, was a proposed Youth Employment Act with three parts: a Youth Conservation Corps (modeled on the old Civilian Conservation Corps), a Neighborhood Youth Corps (modeled on the old National Youth Administration), and a youth training program.

The training title was submerged in the Man-power Development and Training Act of 1962; the other two titles were finally to get Congressional approval after they were merged into the Economic Opportunity Act of 1964. That was basically the structure for federal youth employment programs until the enactment of the Comprehensive Employment and Training Act.

The period of the early to mid-1960s was one in which almost the entire concern was with expanding youth-training-type opportunities for what came to be called the "disadvantaged," in the Job Corps, the Neighborhood Youth Corps, and under Manpower Development Training Act programs. And if the Neighborhood Youth Corps was mainly jobs, the training value was stressed in the rhetoric, and new improved models were developed that gave greater emphasis to training and basic education. On the school side, the major concern lay with high school dropouts and convincing youth to stay in school. The best known phrase was "social dynamite," used by James Conant to describe the dropout situation. There was also a renewed interest in vocational education, resulting from a presidential commission and an amended law in 1963, which will be discussed more fully below.

New Federal View
in 1967 and 1968

As the economy threw off the plague of frequent recessions and sluggish recoveries which started with the end of the 1957 recession, the employment of youth increased, as employment grew for all ages. Now, the more fundamental, underlying situation was revealed. Youth employment was advancing, but the World War II baby boom was rolling into the job market, and the youth unemployment rate was not receding as it should. The Department of Labor's Policy Planning Staff[1] took a deeper look.

What it found from relatively brief review was an underlying structural problem that was not going to yield to only aggregate economic growth. The ratio of youth to adult unemployment had been steadily worsening. More ominous still, the unemployment rate for black youth (almost exactly the *same* as for white youth in the late 1940s[2]) was steadily deteriorating relative to that of white youth. The public employment service wasn't doing much for youth who were in the process of leaving the schools, and education and manpower[3] agencies at all levels mainly ignored each other. Something was wrong, but it would take some work to find out what it was, in the detail necessary for action. The problem called for cabinet-level and presidential attention.

The annual manpower message of the president was initially drafted in the Department of Labor, and Secretary of Labor Willard Wirtz recommended that the youth situation, in these new structural terms, be a major part of that message. The White House agreed. President Johnson spoke of five new directions for manpower policy in his 1967 Manpower Message to the Congress. The first of these was that "we must bridge the gap between education and work." He said that "we pay too little attention to the two out of three young people who do not go on to college and the many others who do not finish." He called for a broader concept of apprenticeship, more opportunities for stu-

dents to learn about work in education programs, and a system in which education and work experience are brought together.

To achieve these results, Johnson directed the Secretary of Labor and the Secretary of Health, Education, and Welfare (HEW) "to make a thorough study of the relationship between . . . learning and earning in America," and to consult state education and employment agencies, local boards of education, business, labor leaders, and others.

The joint study by Labor and HEW was carried out, and submitted to the White House by Secretary Wirtz and Secretary Gardner. The study was summarized in a chapter in the 1968 *Manpower Report of the President*. It began by saying that an intensive review of the youth situation has led to concern "over the adequacy of the entire range of institutions that normally serve as bridges between school and work." What had emerged by now was a new conception of the youth situation which required improvements in the youth jobs transition as well as providing remedial education and training. (There was no competition between the two; they were considered complementary.) Discussions among Labor, HEW, and the White House led to a decision to translate the recommendations into an administration program. The recommendations were for:

- Joint programming between the local school and manpower agency to expand work experience, provide youth counseling, and job placement
- Increasing the involvement of employers
- A move toward year-round school operations to accommodate more work experience
- Scholarships and loans for those pursuing work-oriented educational programs
- A volunteer service foundation for additional bridges between education and work

"Earning and Learning" Act Proposed

The actual drafting of the legislation took place in the Department of Labor, under the direction of Phillip Arnow and in collaboration with Grant Venn, who headed vocational education in the Office of Education in HEW;

---

[1] A small staff of a half-dozen people, reporting to the Secretary of Labor. The office was created and directed by then Assistant Secretary Daniel Patrick Moynihan.

[2] A fact first disclosed in 1964, using previously unpublished data, in *One Third of a Nation*, a report of the Commission on Manpower Conservation, created by President Kennedy.

[3] A name later changed; "manpower" agencies became "employment and training" agencies.

the resulting draft Earning and Learning Act of 1968 was sent to the Bureau of the Budget (now the Office of Budget and Management) for White House clearance. However, an unexpected hitch developed. While high-ranking HEW officials had been involved in the effort, and the report to the White House had been signed by both the Secretary of Labor and the Secretary of Health, Education, and Welfare, an objection was raised in HEW. Now, late in the process, HEW opposed this separate legislation and favored folding it into the Vocational Education Act.

In the ensuing negotiations, this separate bill was rewritten to become part of the administration's proposed amendments to the Vocational Education Act. In final passage, these provisions became Part D, Exemplary Programs and Projects, of the Vocational Education Amendments of 1968.

The Secretary of Labor had testified in support of these "learning and earning" proposals, closing his testimony in this way: "Until now, the concern has been with attempting to pick up the pieces resulting from the failure of these institutions to do their jobs. By and large, it has only been possible to identify the individuals who are already out of school and have not been able to make their way in the employment world. There has been some success in this, in the Neighborhood Youth Corps, in the Job Corps, and in MDTA training. And it is clear that such efforts will continue to be necessary for some time to come. But there is no satisfaction in merely treating failures of the system. The causes of those failures must be ferreted out and the institutions that are involved must be restructured. This is without doubt a harder proposition; one that takes longer and requires a resolve that does not crumble in the face of hard—and frequently resisted—decisions."

This new Part D of the Vocational Education Act was the broadest charter ever written in federal legislation dealing with the school-to-work transition. It started with a statement of purposes, which were "to stimulate, through federal financial support, new ways to create a bridge between school and earning a living for young people . . . and to promote cooperation between public education and manpower agen-

cies." Since the legislation was administered solely by HEW, the Department of Labor no longer involved itself, after having taken the initiative to get the legislation in the first place. And while there were leading figures in the practice of vocational education who put great emphasis on creative implementation of this broader charter (Grant Venn and Gene Bottoms, for example), it was only a small eddy in the river of vocational education, which continued to concentrate almost wholly on teaching job skills in the public classroom. But it was not an unimportant beginning, and served purposes described later.

The Princeton Conference

The legislative effort did not seem overwhelmingly successful, so the decision was made to assemble a broadly representative group to explore the whole youth transition situation and to make policy recommendations. A conference was held in May 1968 at Princeton University, jointly sponsored by the Department of Labor; the Department of Health, Education, and Welfare; the Manpower Policy Task Force; and Princeton's Woodrow Wilson School and Industrial Relations Section.

Its purpose was summarized as being "to discuss the roles and responsibilities of schools, private enterprise, trade unions, voluntary agencies, and various levels of government in development of better bridges between school and work for non-college-bound youth." The attendees were approximately 60 experts from education, business, government, unions, and associations. Background papers were commissioned to provide a briefing for the participants. They provided perspectives that considerably enlarged understanding. A few illustrations are provided below:

- Hugh Folk analyzed youth unemployment in terms of the "disorganization of the youth labor market," and he provided the first accounting of employment policies which excluded youth from regular entry jobs.
- Joseph Zeisel inquired into why the U.K. had lower youth unemployment rates and concluded it was because the U.K. had comprehensive vocational guidance and placement programs, as well as a

larger role for apprenticeship and other formal on-the-job training programs.

- Franz Groemping provided a comparison of the transition services and arrangements among nine countries. A multitude of examples added up to the stark conclusion that the U.S. did relatively very little to facilitate the transition.
- Rupert Evans made the point forcefully in his presentation that the emphasis in American education is on preparing youth for *further education*–high school, college, graduate school–rather than on preparing them for exits into the employment world.
- Garth Mangum concluded that the school-to-work transition process of the American manpower development system provided reasonable preparation for employment to less than half of those who transverse it, and that about one million a year could profit from a "second chance."

After two days of deliberation and debate, the Princeton symposium called for:

- More occupational counseling
- Better prepared counselors
- More and better packaged occupational information
- Occupational exploration in the school curriculum
- Closer contact between school counselors, manpower agencies, and employing institutions
- Much more reliance on cooperative-education-type approaches
- A closer liaison between schools and employers
- Review of the effects of college entrance requirements on high school curriculum
- More resources to schools to improve their facilitating role
- A call to employers to review their hiring criteria and recognize their strategic role
- An emphasis on special "training status" wages in collective-bargaining contracts rather than a youth differential in the minimum wage
- A federal role of initiator or catalyst

The Johnson administration ended with having given a new dimension to the youth issue, as well as having defined it in such a way as to make it the responsibility of local as well as federal government, and private as well as public institutions.

The First Nixon Administration

While very little actually materialized from the Labor Department in these four years, there was considerable interest and a major proposal prepared. Secretary of Labor George Shultz agreed with the analysis of the youth transition problem of the previous administration, and discussed it in testimony and speeches very soon after taking office. The assistant secretary of labor for policy, Jerome Rosow, ordered a major presentation assembled by the policy staff. While there was a new assistant secretary, there was continuity at the staff level, and the analysis and presentation was completed. It was made before Secretary of Labor James Hodgson and his top staff. He ordered that it be prepared jointly with HEW and Commerce, for presentation to the White House. The joint presentation was completed, but about the time it was being scheduled for a meeting of the cabinet, Secretary Hodgson departed from the cabinet to become an ambassador, and the effort collapsed.[4] Such is the fate of many policy initiatives in Washington.

A very significant development did get under way, however, within HEW. Commissioner of Education Sidney Marland had surveyed the condition of the general track in the public high schools and found it inadequate as preparation for work. This is the story of "career education."

Career Education

While there are some antecedents to the development of the term *career education*, it began, for all practical purposes, with the late Sidney P. Marland, when he became commissioner of education, heading the U.S. Office of Education, in 1970. Marland's views were tending in this direction in the late 1960s as he served as superintendent of schools in Pittsburgh, Pennsylvania. He was aware of James

---

[4]But the underlying analysis was available when President Ford made his important speech at Ohio State University in 1974.

Conant's conclusion in *Slums and Suburbs* that a need existed for a smooth transition from school to employment, at whatever age and level a young person left the education system. Marland came to his new post with a conviction that the education system had a responsibility to help all students with achieving "useful and satisfying" employment, parallel to "intellectual and academic effectiveness."

The precipitating event was a call from the White House asking that a proposal be developed to enlarge the federal role. The concept was called *career education* and Sidney Marland launched it early in 1971 during a speech before the National Association of Secondary School Principals in Houston, Texas. The chief state school officers agreed to use the $18 million of discretionary funds in the Vocational Education Act to get it off the ground, funds that included the appropriations for the Part D Exemplary Projects title, previously described.

In effect, career education was the implementation of the 1968 legislation described above. Part D funds continued to be the funding source along with funds allocated by the National Institute of Education, until a statutory base for career education was secured in 1974. That year, in the amendments to the Elementary and Secondary Education Act, Congress included career education, in Section 406. These funds were for demonstrating effectiveness, not for implementation. The next legislative step was the Career Education Incentive Act of 1978. However, the executive branch refused to request funding, and appropriations fell far short of authorization.

Sidney Marland's efforts as commissioner of education were continued for a period of time after he left that position as chair of the Career Education Advisory Council, which played a role in getting the 1978 legislation enacted. The driving force behind career education was to become (and remain) Kenneth B. Hoyt, after he took over direction of federal efforts in the Office of Education early in 1974. The small amount of federal funds was supplemented by Hoyt's energy and leadership, expressed in his extensive work with leaders in each state, as well as through speeches and prolific writing.

The career education legislation was re-pealed by Congress in 1981, at the urging of the administration. It played no role in the education reform movement of the 1980s.

No attempt will be made to capsule the concept of career education, which evolved and broadened in its application to elementary, secondary, and postsecondary education. Writing in 1981, Kenneth Hoyt said he abandoned the one-sentence definition he had in 1977 and, in a monograph in 1978, he published a definition that required three printed pages. It was a school-based effort to make education serve better in preparing youth for careers, but it also aimed to fulfill broader purposes of reform in education, drawing on the world of reality and experience to increase motivation to learn. While the federal leadership role is gone, considerable support and influence remains in a network still led by Kenneth Hoyt from his academic position at Kansas State University, where he is University Distinguished Professor. Said Hoyt in 1992: "I am more optimistic about career education's future today than I have been at any time since the federal career education legislation was repealed in 1981."

Experience-Based Career Education

While the *experience-based career education* (EBCE) program rose out of career education activity, it became a development separate from the nationwide effort described above. It was a model undertaken by the National Institute of Education (NIE) in a research-based program development exercise. Four regional education laboratories developed models, prototypes developed and operated by the labs. Originally, EBCE was called the *employer-based model*, and it called for the radical approach of having an alternative school system operated by employers within the place of employment. What came to pass was more a school-based system in which experience at the employer site was integrated into the instructional program. Thus, the name change to experience-based career education.

The program's objectives were to advance learning in general, to improve oral and written communication skills, and to reduce the dropout rate. The experience aspect was not to be at the expense of academic achievement.

After operation and evaluation by the labs, the model was replicated, and by about 1984 it was operational in 156 school districts. Evaluations continued, and by 1984 there were 80 or so separate evaluations. Unexpectedly, in addition to results related to the central objectives, there were also academic gains relative to the achievement of control groups.

The NIE support and monitoring was withdrawn in the early 1980s; the result is that there is no longer a federal role, and no longer a central source of information about these 156 sites. It is a lesson in how hard it is to sustain the development and operation of such national programs, even when the development is careful, testing thorough, evaluations emphasized, and success attained–and even with about a dozen years of federal involvement. In this era of renewed emphasis on work-based learning and improving the transition from school to work, the EBCE experience should be revisited.

Collaboration and Community Councils

Meanwhile, an avenue for improving the school-to-work transition, which had its roots in the work of the Labor Department in the 1960s, was going down a parallel track, but with points of intersection with career education. Shortly after leaving his post as Secretary of Labor, Willard Wirtz became president of a new nonprofit organization, the National Manpower Institute (NMI). NMI emerged from a conference board undertaking, had strong roots in the business community, and had a board of trustees with members from business, unions, and education, chaired by John Dunlop, who later became Secretary of Labor. The idea of *collaboration* among these three sectors to improve the transition became the central principle behind the efforts of NMI, and, after it changed its name, the National Institute for Work and Learning. NMI took some time to plan its agenda, and published it late in 1975 in a book called *The Boundless Resource: A Prospectus for an Education Work Policy*, by Willard Wirtz and the National Manpower Institute.

A central recommendation of this book was the creation, in each community, of a community education work council, composed of representatives of the three institutions represented on the NMI board of trustees, plus local government representatives and other interested citizens. This resulted, beginning in 1976, and formally running until 1980, in the Work-Education Consortium involving 33 communities, funded by the U.S. Department of Labor, and led principally by the National Institute for Work and Learning (NIWL), but also, for a dozen of these councils, by the American Association of Community and Junior Colleges. Leadership in activities also continued to be provided by the National Association for Industry-Education Cooperation, led by Donald Clark, an organization still active today.

These groups established a process of collaboration, emphasized the shared responsibility they had for improving the transition, and tried to open and maintain communication between industry and the schools. They hammered out programmatic approaches as well.

By the early 1980s, the last systematic effort was made by NIWL to track these council efforts. At that time more than 150 such councils existed. On a state-wide basis, they were strongest in California, led by the Industry Education Council of California. They went under several different names. Private industry councils (PICs), under the Comprehensive Employment and Training Act, were created in the late 1970s, and some of these collaborative efforts became a base to build from (in Lexington, Kentucky, for example).

Vocational Education

Established by federal legislation in 1917, federal government initiatives have largely shaped the reach and approach of the vocational education system. While most of the dollars spent are now state and local, the federal role remains very large in shaping direction. The last 30 years have seen vast change and enlargement of this system. It began with a federal commission report in 1963, and each five-year reenactment has been significant in shaping the present system. Vocational education has both strong supporters and vocal critics. There is little question that, from sheer magnitude alone, it has been the largest institutional force in the last three decades in the public school side of preparing youth for the employment world. Whatever one's views about its efficacy, it is a force that must be reckoned with.

It cannot be reckoned with adequately in a few short paragraphs in this broad review of the happenings of three decades. I asked James (Gene) E. Bottoms, who has spent an illustrious career in vocational education, to distill the major developments. Below, I have either paraphrased him or quoted him directly:

1. **Creation of institutional capacity**
   In 1960, the nation had very limited capacity to prepare youth and adults for employment. That capacity began to be built as a result of new 1963 federal legislation. A network of area vocational and technical schools was created, and vocational and technical education expanded in the junior and community colleges.

2. **Emphasis on special populations**
   Beginning with the 1963 legislation, and continuing with enactments in 1968 and 1976, the vocational education system concentrated on enlarging the access of special population groups, through earmarking federal dollars. This generally meant minority youth and adults. While access was in fact enlarged, "accommodation became the mode" instead of serving these groups with "quality and excellence." According to Bottoms, the emphasis on accommodating rather than educating special population students through vocational programs had become, by the late 1970s, the central driving force of vocational education.

3. **Separating secondary and post-secondary programs**
   Beginning in the 1970s, with virtual completion in the 1980s, was the administrative separation of vocational education at the secondary and postsecondary levels. This separation was cemented in recent vocational education legislation.

4. **Return to academics**

In vocational education's era of accommodating special populations, it drifted more and more toward training, and away from education. Beginning with the 1984 legislation and continuing with recent amendments, the effort is beginning to reconnect vocational and academic education. We are moving to a focus "where the vocational labs will be used, not only to teach skills, but also as an extension of the language arts, math, and science classes in high school."

As the 1980s closed, new promise came in linking secondary and postsecondary study in what are called "Tech-Prep" or "2+2" arrangements, a system given prominence by the work of Dale Parnell, who was until recently the president of the American Association of Community and Junior Colleges. What is envisioned is a four-year program with the last two years of high school carefully articulated with a two-year program leading to an Associate Degree from a community college.

While the federal government has initiated the major new directions for vocational education, the last several years have brought state-led reform in linking vocational and academic studies, with the objective of moving vocational students towards the achievements attained by those bound for college. The Vocational Education Consortium, organized by the Southern Regional Education Board, has experimental schools in 13 states, and it is expanding to a total of 17. The students are assessed periodically using the tests of the National Assessment of Educational Progress to see if targets are being reached. This 17-state initiative aligns the system with the broader educational goals that were set for the year 2000.

Retreats and Advances in the 1980s

In the 1970s, policy toward youth was going down two tracks with regard to the school-and-work relationship. Emerging from the 1960s was a concern for high school dropouts and disadvantaged youth and minority students. There grew to be substantial programs that combined education, training, work experience, and job placement for these youth, initiated with the war on poverty and the employment and training arms of the U.S. Department of Labor. These "second chance" efforts–the Job Corp, the Neighborhood Youth Corp, Urban League programs, 70001, Operations Industrialization Centers of America, and private industry councils–were remedial in nature, for those who had not made it in the mainstream system. They were "targeted" programs in which eligibility required meeting criteria that described being disadvantaged. While the federal policies and budgets of the early 1980s were not kind to these second chance programs, they did survive in the transition from the Comprehensive Employment and Training Act to the Jobs Partnership Training Act. And programmatically they gained strength through the flowering of private industry councils, which had a majority of representatives from business, and the competent participation of the National Alliance of Business.

But they were, nonetheless, remedial programs. Another path beginning to be cleared in the 1960s was a concern with prevention, through improving structures and relationships that were not serving well for the half or more of high school graduates trying to move from classroom to workplace. During the 1970s, these fledgling efforts coexisted with the remedial approaches. But it came to pass that efforts that were not narrowly targeted were not looked upon with favor either by federal or foundation funders.

Collaborative efforts of the "council" type waned, although many continued to do good work and the National Association for Industry-Education Cooperation continued to bring them together. The Career Education Act was repealed in 1981. The Employment Service's Cooperative School Service, which went into high schools to counsel high school seniors and take their job applications, was essentially abandoned.

If one believed the diagnosis that our whole arrangement for the school-to-work arrangement was in serious disrepair, this decade was one of a failure to move forward, after only a few baby steps had been taken in the previous decade. But a diagnosis had been made, and an agenda set forth.

There is one significant exception. The general education reform movement of the 1980s did begin to deal with the low levels of achievement in the American school system. Among the many things wrong in the school-to-work transition arrangements, one important one was the low academic achievement of too many high school graduates. Employers were saying this, at the same time that they emphasized other deficiencies in students' employment readiness. The Education Excellence Movement was beginning, with the report of the National Commission on Excellence in Education, appointed by Secretary of Education Terrell Bell and reporting in 1983, contributing to this important aspect of institutional reform.

School-Employer Partnership

The local councils nurtured by Willard Wirtz and Donald Clark were a formal means of bringing schools and employers together. They represented attempts to build new institutional relationships that were durable. Beginning in the early 1980s, a variety of *business-school partnerships* rapidly formed. It was a decade of partnerships, though the partnerships tended to be ad hoc.

The most ad hoc of all was (and is) the adopt-a-school movement, which became ubiquitous across the landscape. There are probably more than have ever been fully counted, but those that were carefully planned and had staying power were likely in the minority. However, they have shown a desire and willingness on the part of the employer community to help in improving education.

The education-work councils concentrated on building bridges from school to work. The partnerships usually were formed to improve education generally, and they scattered their efforts over the whole of the education scene. It is hard to say what this has amounted to or what role these efforts will play in the future.

A promising example of community-wide collaboration emerged in the Boston Compact, and although buffeted by the winds of deep and long lasting recession, it remains a promising model. Schools promise to make high school graduates employable. Employers pledge to hire the graduates. There are staff in the school to provide counseling and help with the transition. The National Alliance of Business has made efforts to spread this approach to other cities.

One promising approach to lasting change is that of the academies that exist in the public school system but have the sponsorship and involvement of a whole industry within a metropolitan area.

An old form of partnership, cooperative education, now involves about 600,000 high school students. It has received little attention in recent decades, and although it requires intense cooperation and coordination between schools and employers, we have few means of monitoring that system. Even annual data on enrollments are hard to come by.

The recent past has seen a considerable amount of employer interest and involvement in education. Yet it is hard to see lasting changes that bring the institutions of education and work together in any way resembling a system for the school-to-work transition. Nevertheless, employer involvement and interest is one positive development of the 1980s.

Summing Up

This chapter offers a too-compressed chronicle of efforts to diagnose and improve the school-to-work transition in the United States over the last three decades. It has not tried to chronicle the nature of changes in the economy and the labor market that have affected the transition's context. Most observers would say that these changes have exposed, ever more glaringly, the deficiencies in American arrangements, particularly those for the "forgotten half" who do not go to college, in a label placed on the problem by the W.T. Grant Commission in a report issued a few years ago.

Those deficiencies were already apparent to the analysts in the Department of Labor by the mid-1960s, and to the participants in the Princeton Conference in 1968. A total diagnosis of the transition shows that:

- The only blazed trail is through postsecondary education.

- The secondary school system prepares more for continuation of schooling than for exit.
- There is a lack of access of high school graduates to good jobs in good firms until they "ripen" to the age of 21 to 25 (even for jobs that only require a high school education).
- There is a failure to bring a labor market agency into the transition picture to work with the schools and the students.
- The apprenticeship system has dwindled in size, and does not serve youth 16 to 18.
- The demands of the workplace may well be rising in some sectors relative to what many high school students are receiving.

Considering those characteristics, the sum total of progress in restructuring the transition is meager. In some areas, we have regressed rather than progressed.

Thus, this is an odyssey of some promising beginnings that did not, for the most part, continue. It leaves a stage on which a few props put into place in the first several acts have been removed, and if the play is to go on there must be new actors, new dialogue, and an audience more ready to listen.

This story is of the past. Fortunately, there are a few new actors with some good lines. New scripts have emerged in the W.T. Grant Commission report *The Forgotten Half*, in the *America's Choice* report, and in the work of the Secretary's Commission on Achieving Necessary Skills. The work proceeds in the "work-based learning" approaches of the Department of Labor, initiated by its able former Assistant Secretary, Roberts Jones, in the work to improve vocational education in the Department of Education, in the now broader agenda of the National Alliance of Business, in the analyses of the American Society for Training and Development, in the attempts to spread the Boston Compact, and in the youth apprenticeship demonstration projects of Jobs For the Future and the Council of Chief State School Officers. As this book goes to press, new proposals are about to be forwarded to Congress by Secretary of Labor Reich and by Secretary of Education Riley. It remains to be seen whether this will be as ho hum to audiences in the 1990s as somewhat similar lines proved to be in recent decades. If so, the price of admission is bound to be higher later. But the stage is now set for some major advances and there is cause for optimism.

Author's Note

My own involvement with the events described above present both an advantage and a disadvantage. The advantage is personal memory of events and relationships between events that are not otherwise found in history books. The disadvantage is also personal memory, in that it takes away from balance that might have resulted from an investigation by a disinterested historian.

I held the position at the U.S. Bureau of the Budget that dealt with the original legislation on the Neighborhood Youth Corp, the Job Corp, and the Manpower Development and Training Act. I later did work for the task force that wrote the Economic Opportunity Act of 1964; was on the Labor Department policy planning staff that made the analyses described at the outset; helped write the Earning and Learning Act draft legislation; helped bring about the Princeton Conference; helped write the Exemplary Projects title of the Vocational Education Act of 1968; directed the staff work for the volume The Boundless Resource: A Prospectus for an Education Work Policy *by Willard Wirtz and the National Manpower Institute; helped launch the Community Education Work Councils; testified before Congress on the 1978 Career Education Act and on youth unemployment, wrote a lot about school-employer partnerships, and had modest involvement with the work of the American Vocational Association in its legislative efforts in the early 1980s. After this reasonably full disclosure, the sources and supplemental reading are described below.*

The "New Federal View" of 1967-1968 is spelled out in the Manpower Report of the President *for those two years.*

The results of the Princeton conference appear in The Transition From School to Work, *published in 1968 by the Industrial Relations Section at Princeton University.*

The origins of career education are described in Career Education: A Proposal for Reform, *written by Sidney P. Marland, Jr., and published in 1974. A comprehensive description of what it developed into can be found in* Career Education: What It Is and Where It Is Going, *written by Kenneth B. Hoyt and published in 1981. Also, I corresponded with Sidney Marland and Kenneth Hoyt in preparing this manuscript.*

The information on experience-based career education came from correspondence with Harry Silberman, who was involved in designing it, and from a paper I prepared for the Committee for Economic Development in 1984, published subsequently as "Employers and High Schools: The Fit Between Working and Learning," in Business and the Public Schools, Peabody Journal of Education, *1986.*

Community Education Work Councils were proposed and described in a book published in 1975, called The Boundless Resource: A Prospectus for a Education Work Policy, *by Willard Wirtz and the National Manpower Institute. The work of such councils is described in the three volumes authored by Gerald Gold, et al., resulting from the Industry-Education-Labor Collaboration Project, and published by the National Institute for Work and Learning in 1981.*

The summing up of what happened to vocational education in this 30-year period was provided to me in a letter from James (Gene) E. Bottoms, who watched these developments as a leader in vocational education, and who participated in them as executive director of the American Vocational Association from 1977 to 1985.

A recent review of school-business partnerships can be found in Business Impact on Education and Child Development Reform, *by P. Michael Timpane and Laurie Miller McNeill, Committee for Economic Development, 1991.*

As the decade of the 1990s began, my own assessment of the state of affairs was described in From School to Work, *a policy information report published by the Policy Information Center at Educational Testing Service in Princeton, New Jersey.*

2

Forgotten No More:
The Contribution of the William T. Grant
Foundation Commission Reports
on Non-College Youth and the Transition
from School to Employment

Atelia Melaville

In a Different Voice:
The Guiding Principles
Behind the Reports

In 1986, the William T. Grant Foundation established a 19-member Commission on Work, Family and Citizenship, also known as the Commission on Youth and America's Future. In the midst of a wave of school reform efforts, its charge was "to evaluate current knowledge, stimulate new ideas, increase communication among researchers, practitioners, and policymakers and, thus, help our nation chart a better future for youth."

According to *A Nation At Risk* (National Commission on Excellence in Education, 1983), the 1983 report which focused much-needed attention on the effectiveness of public education, our country's standing and ability to compete in a global economy is being seriously undermined by "a rising tide of mediocrity" in the academic preparation of American students. Reports by the Committee for Economic Development and the Carnegie Forum on Education and the Economy, among others, contributed to heightened public awareness of the need for school reform. At the same time, studies that focused on teenage pregnancy and youth unemployment

began to draw the public's attention on the "casualties of adolescence."

Against this problem-oriented view of youth, the Grant Foundation commission was launched "to speak in a different voice." Under the leadership of Harold Howe II, former U.S Commissioner of Education during the Johnson administration, a set of principles soon evolved that helped shift the commission's focus away from the narrowly defined academic issues of the school reform debate toward broader considerations of society's role in helping young people meet their full potential. Only by creating a new set of attitudes toward and a new compact with young people, the commission argued, could America begin to create better futures for individual youth and, in turn, for the country. At least five principles emerged that guided the commission's inquiry and gave shape to its recommendations.

1. *Schools are only one of the institutions responsible for assisting youth to become all that they can be.* While underscoring the importance of schools as a central institution in young people's lives, the commission rejected "school bashing" and the premise that inadequate schools are to blame for all the difficulties our young people face. Instead, it con-

tended that employers, public and private human service providers, community-based institutions, parents and families, and every level of government all have a part to play in helping young people succeed—in life, not just in school. Looking beyond schooling to education, the commission advocated the need for lifelong learning and recognition of the value of work—both paid and unpaid—not only as an economic necessity but as a major avenue to personal fulfillment and civic participation.

2. *Understanding the complexities of how young people succeed requires interdisciplinary inquiry.* Young people's accomplishments are a function of the overlapping and often interdependent opportunities and obstacles they experience in their families, in their communities, at work, and in school. Over the past decades, research on youth issues in each of these domains had been growing, but the results were fragmented and disparate. The commission knew that studying school failure, youth unemployment, substance abuse, or premature pregnancy in isolation—research on "small pieces of large problems"—too often missed the connections among the conditions of young people's lives that together can increase or diminish chances of success.

The commission's composition reflected this understanding. It assembled business and union leaders, academics in the social and behavioral sciences, state policymakers, and advocates who each brought a special lens to bear on the needs of youth. More than two dozen working papers in a broad range of youth-related fields and disciplines increased the variety of perspectives and breadth of research and practice knowledge the commission was created to synthesize. Established scholars were asked to consider key issues and research findings that would help to shed light on what young people need to succeed, as well as the obstacles that stand in their way. To add to the discussion and insights generated by the authors, each paper included a commentary (or two) written by another expert conversant in the same set of issues.

3. *Greater attention to the strengths of young people and their interdependence with adults is needed to balance the emphasis on how young people fail and the ways in which they are different than adults.* By looking "with renewed respect at youth, where they stride as well as where they stumble," the commission hoped to discover how best to strengthen connections and shared values among young people and adults. Adolescents are not only preparing for the future—and experiencing serious obstacles in the process—they are *already* playing important roles in our families, communities and work force. Young people need our help—and we need theirs. Mutual interdependence—a give and take relationship based on rights and obligations—the commission argued, is central to a productive relationship between young people and adults and the foundation of a caring and participatory citizenry.

4. *It is never too late to make a difference.* The commission approached youth issues from a life-span, intergenerational perspective. It vigorously supported early and timely prevention, whenever possible, believing that the "multiplier effect" of years of positive development is unquestionably the best insurance against the many risks of adolescence. The panel did, however, reject the sometimes assumed corollary that the human capacity to change and to tap one's full potential is largely spent by age five or six. There are many points of intervention, the commission reasoned, when support and help can make a vital difference in a young person's ability to succeed. Academic transition periods are especially stressful because they frequently coincide with other physical, emotional, and social developmental changes. Moving from middle school to junior high, deciding on postsecondary education and making the crossover between school and employment are some of the many points at which many young people need a helping hand. Young people—and the parents and other adults on whom they rely to meet their basic needs—can and do respond to flexible and appropriate assistance offered when it is needed.

5. *Adolescents, despite the similarities of age and time of life are, first and foremost, individuals with unique talents, temperaments, and learning styles.* While acknowledging its responsibility to define a core set of opportunities and supports likely to be of universal value to all youth, the commission consistently stressed the dif-

ferences among individuals and groups of young people. In a working paper written for the commission early in its deliberations, Melvin D. Levine, professor of pediatrics at the University of North Carolina at Chapel Hill made this point in policy terms:

> At the same time that we are becoming increasingly aware of adolescent disengagement, we are learning more and more about the ways in which these young people differ from each other and, therefore, have unique requirements that may or may not be met by the resources we offer them. By understanding the sources and manifestations of variations among adolescents, it is likely that we can derive policy that is more flexible and, therefore, more likely to result in a higher yield of young adults who are ready for work, for family membership, and for citizenship.(Levine, 1988, p. i)

The commission consistently underscored the importance of identifying differences among individuals and groups, the necessity of responding to them flexibly and creatively, and the potential of many kinds of variation as strengths to be exploited and celebrated.

What the Data Showed

The commission's two major reports (William T. Grant Foundation Commission on Work, Family, and Citizenship, 1988), and more than two dozen background papers and follow-up documents, drew a picture, not so much of "a nation at risk" but of the possibilities and promise of young people who need a fair chance to succeed. One major finding was that *in every state across the country, communities are looking for and finding innovative ways to better prepare young people to meet the demands of tomorrow.* For these creative efforts to make a difference in the lives of many—not just some—youths, they must be examined and evaluated. America's future depends on the successful contributions of all our young people and our society's willingness to help them make the transition to adult roles and responsibilities. Efforts must be made to adapt, extend, and coordinate what research and evaluation tell us works.

A more sobering finding, and *perhaps the commission's most lasting contribution*, was its discovery of the extent to which so many of our young people must make the transition to adulthood *with only minimal assistance and preparation.* This group, the nearly half of all 16-24 year-old youths who are not likely to go on to college, the commission called "the forgotten half." For this large group, economic and social prospects appear increasingly grim.

During the course of its study, the commission directed its attention, first, to how young people make the transition from school to work and, second, to the roles young people play in their families, in their communities, and as parents themselves. It asked: (1) what are the obstacles that deter older youth in their efforts to become productive workers, parents, and citizens, and (2) what can be done to lower those hurdles and enable more young people to meet their potential?

As facts and data were accumulated, it became increasingly clear that young people have been rocked by seismic shifts in three of society's most fundamental institutions—work, family, and community. Today's youth, far more than their parents and grandparents, have had their opportunities and expectations brought up short by: (1) economic declines caused by a shift from a manufacturing to a service-based economy, the loss of unionized wages and full-time jobs, and slowed productivity and growth; (2) changes in the structure of families that have rapidly increased the proportion of single-parent families even as economic factors have increasingly required a second paycheck to maintain their standard of living; and (3) a growing absence in neighborhoods and communities of "the ties that bind"—relationships with caring adults that open doors to young people and provide them with a source of information and values that can help them find their way in the larger world.

Compounding these findings was an even more disturbing set of income data. Together, they documented clearly the uncertainties and insecurities that have become part of too many young people's lives. Particularly hard hit were young parents. For example:

- The percentage of 20- to 24-year-old males with real earnings able to support a family of three above the poverty line dropped by nearly a quarter between 1973 and 1986–from 58.3 percent to 43.8 percent. Among blacks, the decline was more than twice as great.

- During the same period, families headed by a 20 to 24 year-old experienced a 27 percent decline in income while all American families lost only about 1 percent. Among female-headed single-parent families, the loss of income was 32.4 percent. Young black families, both married couple and single parent, lost 46.7 percent, nearly half of their income.
- Home ownership among married household heads under 25 with children decreased from 38.9 percent in 1973 to 29.1 percent in 1987.

Every young family expects to have to "pay its dues"–to experience some financial struggle as its earning power slowly grows. But the gap in income between today's young families and the rest of America reported by the commission widened by nearly a third over the last two decades. In 1967, the median income of young families was equal to about 77 percent of all American families. By 1986, that proportion had fallen to only 52 percent.

In its final report, the Grant Foundation commission reported that many young families were on the brink of disaster. Thirty-three out of every 100 young families had already fallen below the poverty line–a rate three times the 10.9 percent poverty rate of all American families. The most recent analyses available using 1990 data show no improvement in the poverty rate and a decline in median incomes of all young family heads from $20,665 in 1989 to $18,844 in 1990. Today, a child in a family headed by a parent younger than 30 is one-third less likely to be living in a home owned by his or her family than a child just a decade ago (Johnson, Weill, & Sum, 1992).

Instead of confidence in greater opportunities and a progressively better standard of living than their parents enjoyed, the future promises many young families a sharply abridged version of the American Dream. According to the commission, young men and women now entering adulthood can expect to earn 25 percent less throughout their lifetimes than the generation that preceded them. The earnings patterns are particularly bleak for non-college-educated youth. Regardless of race or ethnicity, workplace earnings and years of schooling are highly correlated. So, while young college graduates lost six percent of their earnings during 1973 and 1986, young males between the ages of 20 and 24 with only a high school education took a 28 percent cut. During that 17-year period, those with no high school diploma or GED degree reeled under a 42 percent decline in purchasing power.

Of course, some good jobs with substantial earnings potential do exist. But increasingly they are lodged at the high end of the wage/skill continuum and they are far fewer in number than those clustered at the low skill, low wage end. Without postsecondary training to acquire specialized skills, the commission concluded, young men and women simply will not be able to compete for those positions that offer a decent family wage, health and other insurance protections, and the promise of someday owning a home.

In exploring the adequacy of existing opportunities for youth who need this kind of training, the commission found a profoundly troubling discrepancy in the value our society attaches to the current and potential contribution of nearly one-half of all our young men and women. Those who go on to college routinely benefit from combined public and private subsidies that total more than $20,000 over four years. Yet young people whose talents and interests require other forms of education and training besides an academic degree–or those who simply have never been encouraged or enabled to aspire to college–are helped very little.

Why does this disparity exist? America depends on the success of this half of our youth every bit as much as on the achievements of its college-educated youth. But only about 5 percent of the students eligible for job training under the Job Training Partnership Act actually receive it, and then only for about four months–instead of years. All told, members of the forgotten half receive about one-tenth the support available to their college-going peers.

Non-college youth who have less than adequate support for necessary education and training are left with inadequate employment opportunities. They are chalked up as failures even though the vast majority work hard to make it on their own and to help others along the way. Consider the following:

- By age 25, approximately 86 percent of non-college youth have earned a high school diploma or a GED equivalent.
- Fully three-quarters of all high school seniors work between 16-20 hours per week and nearly one-third of all high school students hold part-time jobs in any given week.
- According to the Grant commission final report, young people also contribute an estimated minimum of 250 million hours of voluntary service to their communities each year through local, state and federal service programs. (Updating those figures, a recent national survey by the Independent Sector notes that more than half (58 percent) of all American teens 14 to 17 years old volunteered during 1989. Their contributions totalled 1.2 billion hours of formal volunteer time and translated into a dollar value of $4.4 billion.) (Independent Sector, 1990, p. 10)

If young people are America's future, the commission reasoned, common sense, as well as a sense of equity and fair play argue for the creation of many more pathways to success for *all* our young people. Non-college youth who have been kept at the back of the queue and whose ability to move forward has been steadily eroded need this attention most of all.

Rediscovering the Paths Less Traveled: Recommendations of the Final Report

The commission's recommendations for helping young people find purpose, direction, and opportunities for success were predicated on a single caveat: Business and government leadership must simultaneously launch spirited and determined efforts to reinvigorate the national economy. Many more career-ladder opportunities must be created for well-prepared, entry-level workers to contribute their talents at a family wage. If not, the commission

warned, efforts to create better futures for individual youth and, in the process, to reverse a troubling national decline in international economic competitiveness, will continue to be stymied. These commitments, however, must go hand in hand with comprehensive efforts to build on young people's talents and capacities and to prepare them to prosper as workers, parents, and citizens. The commission advocated a multiple strategy including (1) creating closer relationships among young people and adults; (2) expanding access to coordinated and community-based services, supports, and service-learning experiences; and (3) extending and improving employment and training opportunities and policies.

Strategy No. 1: Enhance the quality of youth-adult relationships.

The commission found that a majority of young people want and need the companionship and guidance of adults. Relationships with caring adults help young people cope with the risks of growing up and develop a realistic sense of competence. Parents are the most influential adults in young people's lives but single parenthood and divorce, absent fathers and attendant economic difficulties, increased work outside the home by both parents and teenagers, and conflicting and hectic schedules make it harder than ever for families to bear the full responsibility for helping children navigate the passage to adulthood.

Recognizing that other institutions must do more to enable families to adjust to a changing world, the commission recommended *greater consideration of public efforts to ease the financial strain of raising a family, enhanced private sector attention to the needs of working parents, and expanded community efforts to strengthen relationships among young people, their parents, and other adults.* Initiatives the commission recommended for a closer look included:

- Tax policy proposals to aid families; for example, an increased personal exemption and expanded earned income tax and child care tax credits
- Pro-family workplace policies, including provision for flextime, family leave, com-

pensatory time, and child care that recognize the parenting responsibilities of male, as well as female, employees and the needs of parents with older, as well as younger, children

- Full implementation of existing child support laws
- Expanded fatherhood programs that include employment and training opportunities as well as parenting and family planning education
- School-based efforts to develop parent participation strategies, policies, and activities that are responsive to the needs of working parents and developed in concert with them
- Public and private efforts to create quality after-school programs and community-based learning experiences for older children and adolescents
- Opportunities sponsored by churches, schools, businesses, and community agencies where young people and adults can work together on a one-to-one basis to achieve goals both groups care about

Strategy No. 2: Expand community supports and extend opportunities for service by all young people.

Families are essential to young people. So, too, are the communities where they and their parents live. Families depend on communities as a source of friends and neighbors, for recreation, educational and cultural opportunities, and for help and support in solving specific problems. Too often, however, communities offer far less than what youth and families need. The commission vigorously recommended that *many more localities consider promising strategies to create comprehensive and coordinated access to developmental, preventive, and remedial services*–the hallmark of responsive communities. Localities were urged to consider:

- Developing periodic profiles of local youth needs–such as "state of the child" reports to provide accurate information for state and local planning
- Experimenting with innovative funding mechanisms–such as trust funds, bonds, and special levies, to finance comprehensive service delivery

- Cooperative efforts to use libraries, schools, and other community facilities to house safe and constructive learning experiences for young people before and after school, on holidays, and on weekends all year long

In addition, the commission noted that every community is enriched by the diversity of its youth and has a corresponding obligation to pay careful attention to young people with special needs. The final report highlighted four groups in each case, *emphasizing the importance of beginning with efforts that strengthen the family's capacity to care for young people.* To support the most fragile families, the commission strongly advocated the widespread adoption of family preservation models and long-term case work. In addition:

For youth with disabilities the commission recommended:

- Aggressive enforcement of all existing legislation protecting their civil rights
- Increased support of programs to help young people make the transition to independent living
- Hiring incentives for employers and restructured benefits packages including health insurance to enable people with disabilities to work
- Greater inclusion of youth with disabilities in community organizations along with greater involvement of adults with disabilities as mentors and role models

For young people who have run away or who are living in foster care the commission advocated:

- Similar attention to independent living models, and added-chance employment, training, and life skills planning
- Decriminalization of running away and improved national data collection on runaway and homeless youth

For the "truly disadvantaged," those living in the most concentrated pockets of urban poverty, the commission called for:

- Comprehensive, flexible, individualized, and long-term services, including multiple, added-chance opportunities for education, employment, and training. These should begin early in life and be available to any family member who needs assistance.

Communities also provide a larger arena in which young people can learn the lessons of civic participation, leadership and responsibility. As important as it is for young people to know that help is there when they need it, it is when they are asked to lend their idealism and energy to help others that they are most likely to acquire respect for themselves and a stake in their community. The commission strongly advocated that *schools and communities instill an ethic of service to others* by:

- Incorporating elective, credit-bearing service opportunities into the general curriculum *or* by requiring community service as a requirement for graduation
- Increasing broad public and private support for community-based service opportunities and youth corps initiatives which integrate service with job training and education
- Building a network of existing state and local private sector organizations into a nationwide youth service federation

Finally, since voluntary, privately supported, youth-serving agencies, large and small, play an important part in providing young people with these experiences but often operate without the aid and recognition of the larger community, the commission recommended *greater support for youth-serving agencies,* including:

- A formal study to identify cooperative strategies to help youth-serving agencies strengthen their capacities to serve young people
- Inclusion of specialized training in youth work in undergraduate and graduate programs in education, social work, counseling, and related disciplines

Strategy No. 3: Extend and improve employment and training opportunities.

If "work is the backbone of an individual's life, providing the underpinning for a respected place in the adult world," the commission wrote, "a productive economy with a qualified, well-trained workforce is the marrow that sustains a country and its citizens." The commission urged state and local leaders in business and government to *improve the quality and quantity of education, training, and employment opportunities for the non-college bound.* Specifically, they recommended:

- Creating local *compacts* among schools, communities, and employers to reward students for educational accomplishments with job opportunities and support for additional education and training
- Giving greater attention to cooperative education, internship, apprenticeship, work-study, and other forms of hands-on, experiential learning to ease the school-to-work transition
- Exploring incentives for businesses to expand employment and training efforts, including renewed consideration of targeted jobs tax credits and tax abatements, favorable business loans, and zoning ordinances and other subsidies to encourage job development in high unemployment areas
- Opening more opportunities to non-college youth by employer development of alternative hiring criteria; for example, a performance test or trial employment period in lieu of a strictly academic credential
- Developing local education funds or foundations to strengthen school and business partnerships and to improve the quality and public understanding of the schools' mission
- Joint efforts by the U.S. Departments of Labor and Education to encourage partnerships among employers, unions, businesses, and the states designed to create a more effective school-to-employment transition

Finally, the commission recommended the Fair Chance: Youth Opportunities Demonstration Program. This proposal was envisioned as an effort to stimulate the development of a comprehensive, integrated system of education and training for all youth. Using federal funds, Fair Chance would create a state-approved, locally administered national demonstration to increase access to education, training, and support services to youth in targeted neighborhoods. The opportunities would be designed to meet the full range of educational needs and preferences, including two- and four-year college education, vocational-technical or career training leading to a certificate or diploma and skills training, remediation, and counseling primarily for the unemployed.

From Rhetoric to Action: Commission Follow-Up Activities

What did the commission achieve? Just before the commission began its work in 1986, an article was published in *The Brookings Review* that served as a cogent reminder of the pitfalls the commission hoped to avoid. In describing what it called "commissionitis," the article pointed out that national commissions, despite their numerous virtues, can do very little to overcome the fragmented way public policy is developed in the United States. They frequently have very minimal power, virtually no authority, and less accountability. As a result, commissions often overstate problems to capture attention, and they propose lofty ideals and "pie-in-the-sky" remedies that have very little to do with what is possible in the real world.

Five years after its publication, there is little evidence that the commission overstated the plight of non-college youth. More than ever, the data show young people lost in a free-fall of declining earnings and expectations. At the same time, public discussion about young people's need for a more effective transition from school to employment, and consideration of a variety of youth employment and training policy measures, including community service, reflect a new awareness of what young people need to succeed as workers, family members, and citizens.

The commission well knew that no single initiative in a country as diverse in geography, resources, and interests as the United States would be able to reverse single-handedly the trends identified in the *Forgotten Half* reports. It is not surprising that the progress that has been made is far less than that needed. But the increased dialogue about young people's role in society that has occurred should not be underestimated. At least in part, this renewed attention is attributable to the commission's persistent and pragmatic efforts to create an environment–particularly at national and state

levels–in which thought and action on the key elements of its reports could germinate, take root, and grow.

Realizing the short-term impact and limited shelf life of even the best reports, the foundation directed the commission staff to build on the momentum generated by the *Forgotten Half* reports in an extended, but clearly time-limited, period following their publication. This "follow-up" activity used the commission's visibility, neutral and well respected standing in many youth-serving sectors, and access to a small, but flexible pool of resources to share information among policymakers and practitioners on the issues of the forgotten half. Equally as important, it sought to increase collaboration and partnership among key policy, research, and membership organizations. By helping groups identify a common agenda, the commission follow-up worked to ensure a continuing focus on the multidimensional aspects of the school-to-employment transition and the full range of supports and opportunities young people and their families need. A firm belief of the commission–and a central idea of collaboration–is that no single partner can take sole credit for what a group was only able to achieve by acting together. But in effective partnerships there is always enough credit to share. In this spirit, along with its numerous partners acting with and on behalf of young people, the commission can look with pride to many accomplishments during its follow-up period. Some of the activities in which the commission has played a leadership role include:

- *Stimulating research and experimentation on the features of an effective school-to-employment transition system.* The commission follow-up initiated a first-of-its-kind national conference in 1990 on "Youth Apprenticeship–American Style" co-sponsored by three dozen national organizations. The conference attracted more than 300 practitioners, policymakers, business leaders, union representatives, researchers, and others to explore apprenticeship as one of several strategies to create a "better fit" between work and learning. More than 60 practical examples of other major approaches were later described in *States and Communities on the Move: Policy Initiatives to Create A World-Class Workforce*, which was published by the commission with 14 co-publishers to meet the burgeoning need for practical, experience-based information.

- *Encouraging timely and informed debate on school restructuring.* The commission published *Voices from the Field: 30 Expert Opinions on America 2000–The Bush Administration Strategy to 'Reinvent' America's Schools* soon after the president's plan was released in 1991. More than 30,000 copies have been used to spark debate in school districts, in college classrooms, and in national and regional conferences on education policy.

- *Advancing practice and research in collaborative strategies to improve comprehensive services for children and families.* In 1989, the commission convened the first meeting of the Education and Human Services Consortium, a coalition of more than two dozen national membership organizations, advocacy, and policy groups with a shared interest in improving delivery of services to children and families. Since then, well over 100,000 copies of four monographs in the consortium's *Series on Collaboration* have been distributed across the country to help communities more effectively coordinate available resources.

- *Expanding opportunities for youth service.* The commission follow-up offered technical assistance and substantive comment in the creation of the 1990 National and Community Service Act and helped found the District of Columbia Service Corps, the first youth service learning program in the nation's capital.

As important as each of these accomplishments is and as valuable as the many resources the commission has developed have been, perhaps the most lasting contribution to which the commission can point is the least tangible. As a result of the commission's work, the term *the forgotten half* has entered the policy, research, and media vernacular. This addition to America's collective vocabulary has enriched our ability to understand all young people and to consider new directions that will benefit not just youth but society in general. The acid test—not of the commission, but of our country's future—will be whether or not we choose to attend to the issues of equity, fairness, and mutual obligation to a shared future that the young men and women of the forgotten half remind us of—and that we forget at our own peril.

References

Independent Sector. (1990). *Volunteering and giving among American teenagers 14 to 17 years of age: Findings from a national survey.* Washington, DC: Author.

Johnson, C., Weill, J. D., & Sum, A. M. (1992). *Vanishing dreams: The economic plight of America's young families.* Washington, DC: Children's Defense Fund.

Levine, M. D. *The difference that differences make: Adolescent diversity and its deregulations.* (1988). Washington, DC: William T. Grant Foundation Commission on Work, Family, and Citizenship.

National Commission on Excellence in Education. (1983). *A nation at risk: The imperative for educational reform.* Washington, DC: U.S. Government Printing Office.

William T. Grant Foundation Commission on Work, Family, and Citizenship. (1988). *The forgotten half: Non-college youth in America* and *The forgotten half: Pathways to success for America's youth and young families.* Washington, DC: Author.

3

Expectations
for Entry-Level Workers:
What Employers Say They Want*

David L. Passmore

"The great battles of the future are to be commercial rather than military. . . . We are pitted against the world in a gigantic battle of brains and skill with the markets of the world, work for our people, and internal peace and contentment as the prizes at stake."

Does this passage sound like it could have appeared recently on the op-ed page of a major newspaper? That's not the case—these economic battle lines were drawn early in this century by Elwood Cubberly (1909, pp. 49-50), America's quintessential cheerleader/historian of education. The prospects and stakes for the potential economic war that Cubberly described led industrialists, legislators, and the public to support educational reforms and innovations designed to build the "brains and skill" of America's work force. The rise of the American industrial education movement was one result (Gray, 1980).

Cubberly's call to battle appears so current to us today because hardly a week passes during which we fail to see it presented in some form in our popular media and professional publications. And while the picture of each educational crisis seems unique, something about each one is also strangely familiar.

*Preparation of this paper was supported by Penn State's Institute for Research in Training and Development, Lord Corporation of Erie, PA, and The Ben Franklin Partnership of the Commonwealth of Pennsylvania.

Each call to battle is drawn using models with archetypal faces, framed by new and, at the same time, old economic facts, and tinted by the dark and frightening hues of impending doom. However, we all recognize the common theme when it surfaces: Our economy is going to hell in a hand basket; education is the root cause of this problem as well as the most likely instrument for its solution.

The theme recurs with regularity. For instance, the Soviet Union's launching of the Sputnik satellite whipped our fears of losing our competitive edge to Communism into a frenzy of educational change and spending. And, when everyone started complaining that we were losing our will to work, career education was reinvented from the ashes of previous school-to-work innovations and reforms. If nothing else, the career education movement revitalized the educational publishing industry by creating a demand for new textbooks at all educational levels that infused career information into the teaching of every school subject. Then, just as we were taking a breather, we experienced a literacy crisis. In fact, educational crisis seems to be our stable state.

In the remainder of this chapter, I will first examine a recent crisis defined by perceptions of the tensions between the low educational accomplishments of our nation's students and our urgent economic imperatives. Second, I will review four analyses of employers' expectations for their workers and their schools. I would have had a simpler, but more technical, task if I had chosen to report the number and kinds of workers our economy requires to sustain our current gross national product or a larger one. The production and consumption of goods and services—the flow of money between producers and consumers—create jobs. Econometric models of production, consumption, employment, and education are used commonly to calculate this type of information (see Passmore, 1979, 1990). Rather, I have chosen to examine the perceptions, tastes, preferences, and attitudes held by employers related to what they want in an entry-level worker.

A Recent Crisis

A crisis issued recently from the juxtaposition of our economic prosperity with the possibility of our competitive failure. First, consider the facts. The economy of the United States is a powerful job machine. It produced 16 million new jobs between 1982 and 1987, more than 2.5 times the number generated by six other major industrialized nations. In 1987 alone, 3 million new jobs were created, and 2 million workers were added to the labor force. The unemployment rate dropped below 3 percent in some areas of the country, and the proportion of the population working rose to a record high of 61.9 percent. The ability of the fertile U.S. economy to bear new jobs is remarkable given its chronic and severe federal budget deficits, unfavorable balances of foreign trade, diversion of capital to finance corporate mergers and acquisitions, and high labor costs. So, where's the crisis? Some say it looms in the future.

Belief is widespread among government and business leaders that the decaying quality of the work force jeopardizes continued growth of jobs, expansion of living standards, and competitiveness in the world economy. Educators are never short of radical critics, government pundits, academic squinters, and public-spirited captains of industry who will measure the dimensions of a crisis and assert their own solutions for them. For example, Elizabeth Dole (1989, p. 1), a former Secretary of Labor, claimed that young people "simply don't have

the education and skills needed to survive in today's work force. . . . America's work force is . . . unready for the new jobs, unready for the new realities, unready for the new challenges of the nineties." David Kearn, speaking as chairman and CEO of Xerox, charged that "American schools are flunking the job of education of the work force" and that some high school graduates can "barely read their own diplomas" (Bureau of Labor and Management Relations [BLMR], 1989, p. 10). Kearn reminded us that students who drop out of school cost the economy $240 million in lost earnings and taxes over their lifetimes. Little wonder that former-Secretary Dole described this problem as "the American dream turned nightmare" (BLMR, 1989, p. 3).

The school achievements of American students compare unfavorably with the achievements of students in most of the countries that are our economic competitors. A Stanford University professor, Thomas Rohlen, noted that "the upper half of Japan's high school students possess knowledge and analytic skills equivalent to those of the average American graduating from college" (quoted in Melville, 1990, p. 16). Analysts claim that our students watch too much television, read infrequently, attend school too few days each year, consume conspicuously, and can perform addition only with the aid of a calculator. One of every 10 adults is estimated to be illiterate. A majority of high school seniors cannot even calculate their own lunch bills or write letters to seek employment.

These educational deficits are likely to become more problematic for our economy. According to *Workforce 2000*, a government commissioned report (Johnston, Packer, & Associates, 1987), vast changes in work and in the work force will affect the U.S. economy until the end of the century. In particular:

- *The structure of employment will change.* Service industries will grow, while employment in manufacturing industries will decline.
- *Demographic groups traditionally less likely to participate in the labor force, and those with less access to education, will form an increasing share of the work force.* Women, blacks, and people of Hispanic or Asian

origin will comprise approximately four of every five workforce entrants. Approximately 600,000 immigrants will enter the country, and two-thirds of them will want to work. Fewer young people will enter the labor force due to declining population growth rates. White males will leave the labor force in record numbers due to retirement and death.

- *Skill requirements will escalate.* Education and training beyond high school will become a necessity for most jobs. Demands for sophisticated language and mathematics skills will double as compared with current levels.

Carnevale, Gainer, and Meltzer (1990) contend that the effects of technological advances and competitive necessities already are evident in the demands for more competent, adaptive, and literate workers. For example, secretaries are evolving into information managers. Bank tellers market financial services and furnish portfolio consultation for individual customers. Auto mechanics work less like grease monkeys and more like computer operators and clinicians. X-ray technicians are no longer merely "bone photographers." They also operate sophisticated computerized axial tomographic and magnetic resonance imaging equipment. Construction workers use lasers rather than pocket rules to make precise measurements. Many analysts have noticed this upscaling of job requirements for some time. For example, in an aged research finding that could stand as a leitmotif for our current workforce crisis, Walker (1958, p. 113) concluded from a study of technological change in a steel mill that:

> What was called for in the new mill was skill of a different *kind*: skills of the head rather than of the hand, of the logician rather than the craftsman, of nerve rather than muscle, of the pilot rather than the manual laborer, of the maintenance man rather than the operator. (emphasis in original)

Some analysts may question whether technological improvements in an economy actually increase skill requirements (cf.: Bailey, 1990, pp. 4-8 and pp. 39-42; Berg, 1970; Braverman, 1974; Freeman, 1976; Rumberger, 1981). However, the force of conventional wisdom and popular opinion dictate that the skills of the new American workforce are on a direct collision course with the skill demands of the future economy. The sharp contrast of dismal predictions for future worker skills with expectations for more complex, more demanding jobs caused editors at the *Wall Street Journal* to wonder in a headline, "Smarter Jobs, Dumber Workers—Is that America's Future[?]" (*Wall Street Journal Reports*, 1990, p. R1).

In response to concern about the effects of inadequate worker skills on productivity, three-quarters of our nation's largest employers provide remedial instruction in basic skills that they assert our elementary and secondary schools fail to teach. Consortia of companies work more directly with schools. One consortium, the Boston Compact, teams 600 companies with the Boston public schools to try to improve student attendance and reading levels. Similar partnerships have been formed in other cities—Albuquerque, Cincinnati, Indianapolis, Louisville, Memphis, San Diego, and Seattle, to name just a few.

Another response, however, has been to shape public perception to stimulate public action. For example, the National Issues Forums Institute conducted numerous town meetings on the topic, "Regaining the Competitive Edge: Are We Up to the Job?" Chrysler Motors sponsored a five-part public television program, "The Crisis in American Education: Can Our Schools Keep America Competitive?" Public service announcements about improvements needed in education now appear during late night and early morning television time slots. Corporations place full-page ads in major newspapers containing such warnings and slogans as "This business of global competition is really kids' stuff" (Ashland Oil) and "We're just about to lose our future scientists" (Pfizer). Political satirists and cartoonists skewer American workers for their low skills, American schools for their low performance, and American culture for its malaise in the light of competitive threats from abroad. Publishers have opened a new niche containing lamentations over the most recent crisis in our economic and educational systems (e.g., Doyle, 1989; Schlossstein, 1989; Union Carbide, 1989; W. T. Grant Foundation, 1989). This activity has set the stage for an airing of issues and for building coalitions, but the downside is that it also has resulted in finger pointing, calls for isolationism, scapegoating, and, in some cases, increased racism.

Four Studies of Employer Perceptions

Many opinion polls and surveys have been conducted regarding employers' beliefs about the quality and improvement of education. Some of these studies occurred at the national level and others at regional or local levels. All seem to start with the assumption that employers have something valid to say about these issues and that educators and policymakers should consult employers about these issues to maintain a customer focus. I have chosen to review four studies of employer perceptions of requirements for entry-level workers out of the many that are available on the basis of their prominence in the public eye.

Fortune/Allstate Study

During early 1989, *Fortune* magazine and Allstate Insurance commissioned a study among 1,000 CEOs (41 percent of whom responded to a questionnaire) to explore corporate executives' beliefs about the American public educational system (Lieberman Research Inc., 1989). Most of the responding CEOs were highly critical of the American public education system. Most believed that it represented one of our nation's biggest problems. CEOs rated the quality of Japanese and British systems of public education higher than that in the U.S. Only the educational system of the Soviet Union ranked lower than the American system, and that was not by a large margin.

Approximately two-thirds of the responding CEOs asserted that their companies had difficulties hiring employees because of basic skills deficiencies of job applicants, and that finding potential employees with adequate basic skills was tougher than in the decade preceding the survey. Further, this hurt their productivity and international competitiveness.

Many CEOs reported that their companies made efforts to help the American public educational system by offering summer and part-time jobs to students; providing career or job counseling to students; and donating time, money, and personnel to schools. CEOs overwhelmingly endorsed improving schools by increasing student motivation; getting parents more involved with students; making teachers more accountable for student performance; placing more emphasis on reading, writing, and math; and raising academic standards. Clearly, the CEOs preferred potential employees who are motivated, have basic skills, and have met higher performance standards. It is interesting to note that none of the responding CEOs suggested increasing emphasis on vocational, skill-oriented, or career-oriented education.

ASTD Analysis

The Employment and Training Administration of the U.S. Department of Labor and the American Society for Training and Development (ASTD) conducted an analysis of the skills employers seek in potential employees (Carnevale, Gainer, and Meltzer, 1990). Although ASTD provided few methodological details to allow evaluation of the quality of their research, some interesting conclusions were drawn. According to ASTD, many employers reported that they value the academic triumvirate—reading, writing, and computation—but that they also want much more. In addition, they prefer employees who know how to learn; can communicate, especially through listening and oral communication; are adaptable through creative thinking and problem-solving skills; possess effective personal management skills; have interpersonal, negotiating, and teamwork skills that make them effective work-group members; and can influence others to act through leadership skills. ASTD reported that employers prefer to conduct their own technical skills training, but only with employees who possess basic skills.

Harris Education Research Center Study

Funded by the Pew Charitable Trusts and in cooperation with the Committee for Economic Development, the Business Roundtable, the National Educational Goals Panel, and the National Council on Education Standards and Testing, the Harris Education Research Center (HERC) assessed the views of employers, higher educators, the public, recent students, and parents regarding American education. The study was also designed to allow direct comparison between the assessments of students and parents of the quality of education with assessments held by people who employ or further educate graduating students.

HERC (1991, p. 5) described the results of its survey as "a compelling and distressing look at American education today." HERC found alarm among employers and educators over the failures of our educational system. Employers clearly felt that their new hires out of high school were borderline in terms of their functional literacy, their capacity to express themselves, and their basic functional skills. Most of all, employers rated their recent hires out of high school as having little in the way of capacity for effective concentration on tasks and creative or skillful application of their minds to work challenges. At the same time, employers were upset about needing to provide remedial education because they felt that they could be only marginally successful in fulfilling what was originally society's charge to the public schools.

On the other hand, students and parents thought that their schools were doing just fine. The average gap between the positive ratings of education given by employers and those given by students and their parents was no less than 40 percent among students and 35 percent parents. HERC (1991, p. 14) found that:

> The reality gap is striking and alarming. To put it succinctly: the current crop of students and their parents are deluding themselves. This points up the real necessity of enlisting and informing America's students and parents about what employers...expect. It also means...that students and schools need to be made aware of what standards are demanded. Until this gap is closed, little progress can be made in ensuring that America has a truly educated work force.

SCANS Report

The U.S. Department of Labor Secretary's Commission on Achieving Necessary Skills (SCANS, 1991) was asked to examine skills required to enter employment through interviews with business owners, public employers, union officials, and line workers. As with the ASTD study, details of the methodological approaches used by SCANS to reach its conclusions are available only in rough outline.

The SCANS study report identifies five major competencies and three foundation areas that are required for entry-level job performance. Competent workers, according to the SCANS study, can allocate resources; have good interpersonal skills; can acquire, use, and communicate information; understand the socio-technical systems of work; and can work with a variety of technologies. The SCANS report is one of the few national reports calling for school reform that indicates that technical skills are important for entry-level workers. The technical skills uncovered by the SCANS study, however, go far beyond machine or process operation. They include selecting appropriate technologies for the task at hand, along with maintenance and troubleshooting of technologies.

SCANS asserts that basic skills, thinking skills, and personal qualities form the foundation on which the five broad competencies are built. Basic skills include reading, writing, arithmetic, mathematics, speaking, and listening. Thinking skills include creative thinking, decision making, problem solving, abstract visualizing of problems, knowing how to learn, and reasoning. Desirable personal qualities include individual responsibility, self-esteem, sociability, self-management, and integrity. SCANS estimates that one-half of young people in the U.S. leave school without the knowledge or foundation required to find and hold a good job.

What Do We Know, and What Should We Do about It?

The potential for economic disaster seems real enough in both the short and long term, as anyone who has reviewed our current economic situation can conclude. Also, it is clear that employers hold very certain opinions about the quality of education in the United States and about its improvement. However, it is difficult to know what to do with these two facts.

Choices among strategies for improving economic performance are difficult. We are confronted by an array of trade-offs. For instance, should we push our resources toward improving education for work? Or, would limiting immigration yield as much improvement in employment and earnings as expensive educational projects requiring a long lead time and with improved effectiveness. Would strategies to improve the balance of trade produce as much return on investment as would improving our public education system? These, and many other policy questions, remain. And, however well-intentioned employer statements about educational improvement may be, I believe that they hold little substance for debate about allocating resources among education and other activities for improvement of the economy.

Why do we seek and value opinions about education and training offered by employers more than we do any other received opinions? We may believe that "business sense" qualifies the opinions as practical. We may feel that business success is a little like receiving a Purple Heart: Worthy action is due its praise. We may want to focus on those we have identified as our "customers." Let me be clear about one thing, though: We are really talking about raw power here.

I believe the reason we stand at attention when an employer's perception of educational needs is delivered is an outcome of particular and fundamental economic relationships. First, employers have the jobs and money, for which workers trade their time, skill, knowledge, and effort. In most labor markets, workers need employers more than employers need workers. Second, employers represent a social class that often is wealthy and well connected politically. In a society that is materialistic, hedonistic, and impressed by consumption and the trappings of prosperity, many captains of industry stand high on the pedestal of success. I assert that the respect we hold for employers' perceptions of requirements for entry-level workers is based on the deference we accord them as people who can buy and sell us and

our hopes. In fact, many of us aspire to *be* them.

In short, I believe that employers' perceptions of requirements for entry-level workers are interesting—and, at certain stages of educational planning are worthy and necessary. However, I do not believe that they are definitive or sufficient for establishment of policy to guide public investment in education for work. That is, of course, what we lack, a clear national policy on education for work.

Such a policy would address some largely vacant areas. A few questions for starters:

- Who should pay for education that contributes to economic production? One general principle is that those who benefit should pay. We need a clear delineation of the nature and locus of benefits of public investment in education for work. Is the public paying for education and training programs that provide returns only to employers and stockholders, or are the marginal social benefits to additional investment in education and training so great that additional public investment is shrewd? Could employers reap additional benefits if they increased their already large expenditures on education and training by shouldering additional job training and retraining? Remember, it costs money to make money.

- For what reasons do we invest in education and training? Economic? Social? For instance, why do vocational education programs in cosmetology maintain student enrollments beyond their labor market justifications? Is this just poor planning? Or, is it possible that activity-based education is good instruction and, therefore, is a route to student motivation to achieve education as *method* in developmentally appropriate education?

- How can we justify potentially duplicative investments in, for instance, school-based vocational education, community-based training programs, and customized job training for employers? Is this just poor coordination? Or, do these programs actually serve different educational needs?

These matters go far beyond the scope of this short chapter. My major aim has not been to outline useful policy for education for work, but to consider the role of employers' perceptions of policies and practices. In conclusion, I believe that, for the most part, employers' opinions provide little guidance for these important educational policy decisions.

References

Bailey, T. (1990, May). *Changes in the nature and structure of work: Implications for skill requirements and skill formation.* Berkeley, CA: University of California at Berkeley, National Center for Research in Vocational Education.

Berg, I. (1970). *Education and the great training robbery.* New York: Praeger Publishers.

Braverman, H. (1974). *Labor and monopoly capital: The degradation of work in the twentieth century.* New York: Monthly Review Press.

Bureau of Labor and Management Relations, U.S. Department of Labor. (1989). *Productivity and employment: Challenges for the 1990's* (Bureau of Labor and Management Relations Report No. 132). Washington, DC: U.S. Government Printing Office.

Carnevale, A. P., Gainer, L. J., & Meltzer, A. S. (1990). *Workplace basics: The skills employers want.* San Francisco: Jossey-Bass.

Cubberly, E. (1909). *Changing concepts of education.* Boston: Houghton-Mifflin.

Dole, E. (1989, October 26). *State of the workforce address.* Speech delivered to the State Teachers and Principals of the Year ceremony, Washington, DC.

Doyle, D. P. (1989). *Endangered species: Children of promise.* New York: McGraw-Hill.

Freeman, R. (1976). *The overeducated American.* New York: Academic Press.

Gray, K. C. (1980). *Support for industrial education by the National Association of Manufacturers: 1895-1917.* Unpublished doctoral dissertation, Virginia Polytechnic Institute and State University, Blacksburg, VA.

Harris Education Research Center. (1991). *An assessment of American education: The views of employers, higher educators, the public, recent students, and their parents* (Study No. 912061). New York: Louis Harris & Associates.

Johnston, W. B., Packer, A. H., & Associates. (1987). *Workforce 2000: Work and workers for the twenty-first century.* Indianapolis: Hudson Institute. (ERIC Document Reproduction Service Number ED 290 887)

Lieberman Research Inc. (1989). *Business response to education in America: A study conducted among the largest U.S. companies.* New York: Time Inc. Magazine Co.

Melville, K. (1990). *Regaining the competitive edge: Are we up to the job?* Dubuque, IA: Kendall/Hunt Publishing Co.

Passmore, D. L. (1979). Uses of interindustry analysis in planning education for work. *Journal of Industrial Teacher Education, 17* (1), 7-24.

Passmore, D. L. (1990). Economic development and employment. *Journal of Technical and Vocational Education, 1,* 1-19.

Rumberger, R. (1981). *Overeducation in the U.S. labor market.* New York: Praeger Publishers.

Schlossstein, S. (1989). *The end of the American century.* New York: Congdon and Weed.

Secretary's Commission on Achieving Necessary Skills, U.S. Department of Labor. (1991). *What work requires of schools: A SCANS report for America 2000.* Washington, DC: U.S. Government Printing Office.

Union Carbide, Corporate Task Force on Education. (1989). *Undereducated, uncompetitive USA.* Danbury, CT: Author.

W. T. Grant Foundation, Commission on Work, Family, and Citizenship. (1989). *The forgotten half: Pathways to success for America's youth and young families.* Washington, DC: Author.

Walker, C. (1958). Life in the automated factory. *Harvard Business Review, 36,* 111-119.

Wall Street Journal Reports: Education. (1990, February 9). *The Wall Street Journal,* pp. R1-R36.

4

The Educational Reform Movement and School-To-Employment Transition of Youth

James P. Greenan

Educational reform has been a major topic of discussion throughout society in the United States for the past decade. Educational programs and their outcomes have been key items on several economic, social, and political agendas. Many of these agendas have been manifested in numerous federal and state initiatives, commission reports, research studies, and local initiatives over the past 10 years. The educational reform movement has had and will continue to have significant implications for school to employment transition (Pautler, Gergely, Sarkees-Wircenski, Greenan, & Oakey, 1992). This chapter will examine several significant educational reform initiatives and reports derived from general education, vocational education, and the business/industry sectors; identify the salient features and recommendations of the reports; discuss the implications of the educational reform movement for school-to-employment transition programs; and offer recommendations to improve and enhance programs.

Educational Reform Initiatives

One of the first "modern" reports was offered by Adler (1982) in *The Paideia Proposal: An Educational Manifesto*. It was addressed to parents, teachers, school board members, university/college educators, elected public officials, employees, minority groups, labor leaders, military leaders, and American citizens in general. Adler stressed the need for reform to educate *all* persons, develop thinking/problem-solving skills, recognize all kinds of learning and instruction, promote common learning and curriculum, and focus on the importance of teachers and principals in the learning process. Implicit in Adler's manifesto was that educational access and equity must apply to all persons. A variety of educational contexts, teaching styles, learning methods, and instructional materials should be employed. A major theme was the suggestion that all students should attain core knowledge and skills, such as reasoning skills. Administrators—especially principals—must assume a new and dynamic role in collaboration with teachers in the instructional process.

A Nation at Risk, one of the most frequently cited reports, was published by the National Commission on Excellence in Education (1983). This report focused on the need to enhance high school graduation requirements through the "new basics" (English: four years; mathematics: three years; science: three years; social studies: three years; computer science: half a year); raise university admission requirements; establish more "rigorous and measurable standards" for student academic performance; make a longer school year and day and use them more efficiently and effectively; improve teacher preparation and the teaching profession; create effective educational leadership; and request public fiscal support. The report clearly identifies a prescription which defines a core of *basics*, presumably for all students. These new basics are believed to better prepare students for a college education by providing more *academics* with higher standards for success. Does this suggest that a student may receive a more well-rounded education, or does it suggest a more intense study in a particular area of the curriculum?

Boyer (1983), in *High School: A Report on Secondary Education in America*, insisted on the need to clarify educational goals and objectives; develop written and oral language skills; identify a core of common learning, or core curriculum (literature, history, mathematics and science, foreign language, the arts, civics, non-Western studies, technology, the meaning of work, and the importance of health); focus on the transition to work and continuing education; adopt the new Carnegie Unit (public service); improve the teaching profession; improve instruction and learning; use new technology; make flexible use of resources, programs, facilities, and funding; promote effective leadership from principals; emphasize articulation among elementary, junior high/middle school, high school, higher education, and the private sector; and encourage public commitment to school improvement. Boyer's emphasis is clearly on the reform of mission, curriculum and articulation, transition, service, teacher preparation, instructional innovation, instructional technology, resources, and educational leadership.

Goodlad (1984), in *A Place Called School*, focused on the problems of the use of time and teachers, curriculum (balance, content, ability grouping, and tracking), instruction (innovation, exemplary models, leadership), organization (articulation of elementary and secondary education, selecting and preparing school principals, staffing elementary schools, schools within schools), and teacher education (incentives, programs). Goodlad cautions against the problems of curriculum tracking, and emphasizes the need for well-rounded and articulated curriculum. Teachers and administrators must assume a major role in instructional innovations within a variety of organizations.

The Unfinished Agenda, published by the National Commission on Secondary Vocational Education (1984), studied several areas of vocational education; cited several needs; and formulated practical recommendations related to program access, educational equity, curriculum, teacher recruitment and preparation, standards and accountability, articulation, leadership, business, labor, community, and field-based learning. This report was a proactive response by the vocational education community. The commission included an interdisciplinary group of individuals from the public and private sectors. A variety of recommendations were offered to local and state education agencies to improve the adequacy, quality, and effectiveness of vocational programs.

Parnell (1985), in *The Neglected Majority*, emphasized the need for a student-centered curriculum, greater structure and substance in educational programs, articulation in educational programs, connectedness between educators and the real world, continuity in learning, a larger range of program choices, and lifelong learning. Parnell strongly advocates articulation between secondary and postsecondary education which translates into 2 + 2 and tech prep programs.

Some reports have focused on the sociological impact of education and work on the individual and family. Based on the key trends that will shape the advent of the twenty-first century workforce, Johnston and Packer (1987), in *Workforce 2000*, strongly suggested that policymakers and educators must identify strategies to stimulate balanced world growth; accelerate productivity increases in service industries; maintain the dynamism of an aging workforce; reconcile the conflicting needs of women, work, and families; integrate black and Hispanic workers fully into the economy; and improve the educational preparation of all workers. The William T. Grant Foundation Commission on Work, Family, and Citizenship (1988), in its report *The Forgotten Half: Pathways to Success for America's Youth and Young Families*, recommended state-administered, federally funded programs intended to increase access to and equity in education and training programs that provide financial aid, counseling, and support services; cooperative arrangements; and baseline outcomes with a variety of performance measures in a wide range of education and training opportunities such as university, vocational, career, and remedial education. The commission pointed to the roles and responsibilities that state and federal agencies should assume relative to the support of the individual and families to receive access to and equity in educational and training programs. The keys appear to be public support, the principle of equal opportunity, support services, interagency cooperation, common outcomes, assessment, and a variety of program options.

Carnevale, Gainer, and Meltzer (1988), in *Workplace Basics: The Skills Employers Want,* indicated that employers want prospective employees to possess several key skills and attributes: knowing how to learn; reading, writing, and computation; listening and oral communication; creative thinking and problem-solving; self-esteem, goal setting/motivation, and personal/career development; interpersonal, negotiation, and teamwork skills; and organizational effectiveness and leadership. The authors are very prescriptive regarding what school curriculum should include and what should be taught. A series of issues related to assessment, planning, intervention, evaluation, and personnel preparation are required to give employers what they want. However, this report does offer contributions to make curriculum more functional.

The Commission on the Skills of the American Workforce (1990), in its report *America's Choice: High Skills or Low Wages,* recommended that new national educational performance standards should be established for all students and be achieved by age 16; states should be responsible for assuring that all students achieve an "initial certificate;" states should develop and finance alternative learning environments and programs for students who cannot achieve the initial certificate; the existing community college/technical school system should be improved and expanded and provide technical and professional education certificates and associate's degrees for the majority of students and adult workers; employers should provide support and incentives in the continuing education and training of workers;

and a system of federal and state employment and training boards should be established in collaboration with "local leadership." The commission clearly recognizes the need for strong technical education complemented by general education, lifelong learning, and functional assessment and performance standards.

The Secretary's Commission on Achieving Necessary Skills (SCANS) (1991), in *What Work Requires of Schools: A SCANS Report for America 2000,* proclaimed that all American high school students must develop a new set of competencies, knowledge, and foundation skills in areas that include: (a) resources (student identifies, organizes, plans, and allocates resources), (b) interpersonal (works with others), (c) information (acquires and uses information), (d) systems (understands complex interrelationships), and (e) technology (works with a variety of technologies). The curricula represented by these skills and competencies are quite different from the traditional three R's. These are more closely derived from the workplace. However, do these skills complement or replace traditionally valued curricula?

In 1991, the United States Department of Education, in *America 2000: An Educational Strategy,* outlined six "national education goals":

1. All children in America will start school ready to learn.
2. The high school graduation rate will increase to at least 90 percent.
3. American students will leave grades 4, 8, and 12 having demonstrated competency in challenging subject matter including English, mathematics, science, history, and geography; and every school in America will ensure that all students learn to use their minds well, so they may be prepared for responsible citizenship, further learning, and productive employment in our modern economy.
4. U.S. students will be first in the world in science and mathematics achievement.
5. Every adult American will be literate and will possess the knowledge and skills necessary to compete in a global economy and exercise the rights and responsibilities of citizenship.
6. Every school in America will be free of drugs and violence and will offer a

disciplined environment conducive to learning.

The president and governors set some clearly defined goals. However, it will be absolutely essential for all states to delineate these goals to form specific objectives, forward plans, and measurable outcomes. Fiscal support from the federal and state governments will be necessary to achieve these goals.

The Carl D. Perkins Vocational and Applied Technology Education Act of 1990 has been viewed as a congressional mandate to the field of vocational education. Jennings (1991) suggested that due to the failure to improve education in the United States over the past decade, as called for in myriad educational reform reports, vocational education is being challenged to be a participant rather than an observer. Essentially, vocational education, through the act, will respond to the reform movement by integrating academic and vocational education, will focus on tangible outcomes and results, will serve economically and academically disadvantaged youth and adults, and will give local education agencies more accountability and increased authority through program evaluation and assessment. Further, Asche (1991) described four major areas of educational reform that included: (a) national goals, testing, and accountability, (b) school or parental choice, (c) teacher education and certification, and (d) site-/school-based management. He noted that although these areas apply to all of education, currently they have special significance for vocational education programs.

In summary, several themes have emerged in these and other educational reform initiatives. The major theme clearly is in the area of curriculum. Many initiatives call for a definition or redefinition of the mission, goals, and objectives of education and the curriculum. Specifically, reform calls for common learning and core curriculum. Student-centered, private-sector-centered, and functional curricula also are called for in the initiatives. Reports have indicated the need for more emphasis on basic skills, generic skills, technical skills, workforce skills, and literacy skills. Some reports point to the need to extend and more efficiently use the school year and day. Extending

the school into the community by requiring students to perform public service is also part of curriculum reform. Articulation between and among elementary, middle/junior high, and senior high schools is necessary in areas of curriculum, assessment, instruction, and evaluation.

A second major theme is educational leadership. Most often, initiatives stress the important roles of principals and teachers in effecting educational reform. They are viewed as central to ensuring school improvement.

A third major theme is educational access and equity for all youth and adults. All persons must have access to the full range of programs, and they must receive the necessary support services to ensure their success in school and in the transition into the workplace or higher education. This idea focuses especially on special needs populations such as disadvantaged, disabled, limited-English-proficient, and minorities. However, only a few initiatives appear to have addressed specific issues and problems related to work, women, and families. The same is true of social problems in schools such as substance abuse and violence that also impact school-to-employment transition of youth and adults.

A fourth major theme is the improvement of learning and instruction, the primary function of education. The practice of teaching must be improved through better planning, assessment, instructional delivery, and evaluation. Learners must be offered the opportunity to learn in a variety of environments conducive to their success. Instruction should use a variety of methods appropriate to individual learners. Opportunities for lifelong learning within the schools and in the private sector are essential.

A fifth major common theme is standards. Standards related to the assessment of student knowledge and skills, criteria for high school graduation, and college admission, and exit criteria are issues in essentially all educational reform initiatives. Standardized assessments and performance standards to measure educational outcomes such as technical competencies, academic skills, and work readiness are called for in many reports. Increasing the high school graduation rate in the nation is a common outcome in educational reform.

Standards related to admission to, performance in, and exit requirements in teacher preparation programs are also highly visible in many educational reform initiatives. Accountability is prevalent in the discussions related to standards. Elected officials, boards of education, administrators, teachers, students, and community leaders must all be accountable in their roles in effecting educational reform. School personnel must be accountable towards the youth and adults they serve.

A sixth major theme that has emerged in educational reform is funding and resources. Many commissions and authors, while calling for major changes in educational systems, also realize the necessity for federal and state governments and local communities to support schools with the required fiscal and nonfiscal resources to bring about the changes. In addition, the effective use of resources is also recognized. For example, initiatives call for school personnel to make greater use of technology to assist in teaching and learning. Interagency cooperative arrangements are necessary to make maximum cost-effective and cost-beneficial use of the limited amount of resources that will likely be available. A major commitment and investment in education is necessary for the United States to compete and lead in the global economy.

A seventh theme to emerge is teacher preparation. Many educational reform initiatives point to the need to attract and retain the best people in teaching. In part, many reports suggest that this can be done by improving the nature of, environment of, and incentives in the education profession. Admission, curriculum, and outcome standards are major issues. New models for preservice and inservice education are needed. The creation of meaningful relationships between colleges of education and the schools (e.g., professional development schools) will improve the preparation of teachers and serve the needs of schools.

Implications of the Educational Reform Movement on School-to-Employment Transition

The major themes that have emerged through the educational reform movement over the past decade will continue to impact on school-to-employment transition programs, the effects of which will highly impact the vocational education discipline. Vocational education, along with other disciplines and agencies, will continue to play a major role in the school-to-employment transition process. This process includes entry into vocational programs, instructional, and support services, as well as exit of youth and adults from vocational programs into the workplace, higher education, and/or continuing (retraining) education. Accordingly, vocational education will be impacted by the educational reform movement in ways that attempt to improve and expand the transition process. Specifically, vocational education will be affected in areas that include curriculum, assessment, planning, instruction, and evaluation.

Curriculum

The vocational education discipline must examine and evaluate its curricula in relation to where it has been, where it is, and where it needs to go. This will require collaboration with other academic disciplines, the private sector, and community leaders. Based on the results of educational reform initiatives and research within the vocational education field, future curricula will need to be increasingly functional and student-centered. Programs will need to be less job-specific and more occupationally based. Vocational education curricula should include and integrate generalizable skills (Greenan, 1983), and basic and higher-order academic skills (Greenan, 1990; Greenan, Jarwan, & Munn, 1992). These studies clearly illustrate the concurrent importance of essential skills among vocational programs and between vocational programs and occupations in the workplace (see Table 1, pages 36-39, and Figure 1, pages 40-43). These studies also provide some evidence of the instructional involvement of vocational education in these skills, as well as the skill levels of youth in vocational programs and as they enter the workplace. The recommendations offered include:

- Basic mathematics, communications, interpersonal relations, reasoning, general occupational, and job-specific skills are very important in T&I programs and

Table 1—Generalizable Skills Curriculum (continued on next page)

Mathematics Skills

Whole Numbers
1. Read, write, and count single- and multiple-digit whole numbers
2. Add and subtract single- and multiple-digit whole numbers
3. Multiply and divide single- and multiple-digit whole numbers
4. Use addition, subtraction, multiplication, and division to solve word problems with single- and multiple-digit whole numbers
5. Round off single- and multiple-digit whole numbers

Fractions
6. Read and write common fractions
7. Add and subtract common fractions
8. Multiply and divide common fractions
9. Solve word problems with common fractions

Decimals
10. Carry out arithmetic computations involving dollars and cents
11. Read and write decimals in one and more places
12. Round off decimals to one or more places
13. Multiply and divide decimals in one or more places
14. Add and subtract decimals in one or more places
15. Solve word problems with decimals in one or more places

Percent
16. Read and write percents
17. Compute percents

Mixed Operations
18. Convert fractions to decimals, percents to fractions, fractions to percents, percents to decimals, decimals to percents, common fractions or mixed numbers to decimal fractions, and decimal fractions to common fractions or mixed numbers
19. Solve word problems by selecting and using correct order of operations
20. Perform written calculations quickly
21. Compute averages

Measurement and Calculation
22. Read numbers or symbols from time, weight, distance, and volume measuring scales
23. Use a measuring device to determine an object's weight, distance, or volume in standard (English) units
24. Use a measuring device to determine an object's weight, distance, or volume in metric units
25. Perform basic metric conversions involving weight, distance, and volume
26. Solve problems involving time, weight, distance, and volume
27. Use a calculator to perform basic arithmetic operations to solve problems

Estimation
28. Determine if a solution to a mathematical problem is reasonable

Table 1 (continued)

Communications Skills

Words and Meanings

1. Use plural words appropriately in writing and speaking
2. Use appropriate contractions and shortened forms of words by using an apostrophe in writing and speaking
3. Use appropriate abbreviations of words in writing and speaking
4. Use words appropriately which have the same meaning as other words but are spelled differently
5. Use words correctly which sound the same as other words but have different meanings and spellings
6. Use words appropriately which are opposite of one another in meaning
7. Use appropriate word choices in writing and speaking
8. Add appropriate beginnings and endings to words to change their meaning
9. Punctuate one's own correspondence, directives, or reports

Reading

10. Read, understand, and find information or gather data from books, manuals, directories, or other documents
11. Restate or paraphrase a reading passage to confirm one's own understanding of what was read
12. Read and understand forms
13. Read and understand short notes, memos, and letters
14. Read and understand graphs, charts, and tables to obtain factual information
15. Understand the meanings of words in sentences
16. Use a standard dictionary to obtain the meaning, pronunciation, and spelling of words
17. Use the telephone and look up names, telephone numbers, and other information in a telephone directory to make local and long distance calls

Writing

18. Review and edit others' correspondence, directives, or reports
19. Compose logical and understandable written correspondence, directives, memos, short notes, or reports
20. Write logical and understandable statements, phrases, or sentences to accurately fill out forms

Speaking

21. Speak fluently with individuals or groups
22. Pronounce words correctly
23. Speak effectively using appropriate behaviors such as eye contact, posture, and gestures

Listening

24. Restate or paraphrase a conversation to confirm one's own understanding of what was said
25. Ask appropriate questions to clarify another's written or oral communications
26. Attend to nonverbal cues such as eye contact, posture, and gestures for meanings in others' conversations
27. Take accurate notes which summarize the material presented from spoken conversations

companies and, therefore, should be included in all secondary T&I curricula and integrated into instruction.

- Higher-order mathematics, science, and computer technology knowledge and skills should be included and integrated into the individual programs and occupations that require them.

- Secondary T&I education curriculum should focus on new and emerging technical areas identified in the world of work including computer, electronics, computer-aided design/computer-aided manufacturing, computerized numerical control, robotics, and laser-related programs/occupations.

Table 1 (continued)

Interpersonal Relations Skills

Work Behaviors

1. Work effectively under different kinds of supervision
2. Work without the need for close supervision
3. Work cooperatively as a member of a team
4. Get along and work effectively with people of different personalities
5. Show up regularly and on time for activities and appointments
6. Work effectively when time, tension, or pressure, are critical factors for successful performance
7. See things from another's point of view
8. Engage appropriately in social interaction and situations
9. Take responsibility and be accountable for the effects of one's own judgments, decisions, and actions
10. Plan, carry out, and complete activities at one's own initiation

Instructional and Supervisory Conversations

11. Instruct or direct someone in the performance of a specific task
12. Follow instructions or directions in the performance of a specific task
13. Demonstrate to someone how to perform a specific task
14. Assign others to carry out specific tasks
15. Speak with others in a relaxed and self-confident manner
16. Compliment and provide constructive feedback to others at appropriate times

Conversations

17. Be able to handle criticism, disagreement, or disappointment during a conversation
18. Initiate and maintain task-focused or friendly conversations with another individual
19. Initiate, maintain, and draw others into task-focused or friendly group conversations
20. Join in task-focused or friendly group conversations

- Curricula should increasingly emphasize general knowledge and skills while retaining those necessary job-specific components to meet the needs of the labor market adequately.
- Increased state and local commitment and revenues are needed for T&I program expansion and improvement.
- Local T&I programs should systematically and formally assess students who complete programs to determine if they have attained the necessary entry-level skills and knowledge for the workplace.
- The skills and knowledge areas that are generic and, therefore, "basic" within and across secondary T&I programs, need to be disseminated and integrated within the context of T&I programs and for the occupations that students are preparing to enter.
- Preservice, inservice, and graduate education programs should include the concepts, skills, and knowledge identified to improve the preparation of vocational and T&I teachers.
- Since the generic skills identified are likely a concern of education in general (i.e., K-12), long-term solutions will require enfranchisement of and input from educators in all disciplines.
- Further research needs to be conducted to develop curriculum standards, outcomes, and proficiencies for each (and all) secondary T&I education programs (Greenan, Jarwan, & Munn, pp. 36-38).

In addition, vocational curricula should integrate workplace literacy skills as proposed by Carnevale, Gainer, and Meltzer (1990). Further, vocational education curricula must include and update the specific technical skills and knowledge required in different and similar careers, occupations, and jobs. These kinds

Table 1 (continued)

Reasoning Skills

Verbal Reasoning

1. Generate or conceive of new or innovative ideas
2. Try out or consciously attempt to use previously learned knowledge and skills in a new situation
3. Understand and explain the main idea in another's written or oral communication
4. Recall ideas, facts, theories, principles, and other information accurately from memory
5. Organize ideas and put them into words rapidly in oral and written conversations
6. Interpret feelings, ideas, or facts in terms of one's own personal viewpoint or values
7. State one's point of view, opinion, or position in written or oral communication
8. Defend one's point of view, opinion, or position in written or oral communication
9. Distinguish between fact and opinion in one's own and in others' written and oral communication
10. Identify the conclusions in others' written or oral communication
11. Identify the reasons offered by another and evaluate their relevance and strength of support for a conclusion
12. Compile one's own notes taken on several written sources into a single report
13. Compile ideas, notes, and materials supplied by others into a single report
14. Carry out correctly written or oral instructions given by another
15. Observe another's performance of a task to identify whether the performance is satisfactory or needs to be improved
16. Ask questions about another's performance of a task to identify whether the performance is satisfactory or needs to be improved

Problem Solving

17. Recognize or identify the existence of a problem, given a specific set of facts
18. Ask appropriate questions to identify or verify the existence of a problem
19. Enumerate the possible causes of a problem
20. Use efficient methods for eliminating the causes of a problem
21. Judge the credibility of a source of information
22. Identify important information needed to solve a problem
23. Identify others' and one's own assumptions relating to a problem
24. Generate or conceive of possible alternative solutions to a problem
25. Describe the application and likely consequences of possible alternative problem solutions
26. Compare the application and likely consequences of alternative problem solutions and select a solution that represents the best course of action to pursue

Planning

27. Sort objects according to similar physical characteristics including shape, color, and size
28. Estimate weight of various objects of different shapes, sizes, and makeup
29. Estimate length, width, height, and distance between objects
30. Use the senses of touch, sight, smell, taste, and hearing
31. Set priorities or the order in which several tasks will be accomplished
32. Set the goals or standards for accomplishing a specific task
33. Enumerate a set of possible activities needed to accomplish a task
34. Determine how specific activities will assist in accomplishing a task
35. Select activities to accomplish a specific task
36. Determine the order of the activities or step-by-step process by which a specific task can be accomplished
37. Estimate the time required to perform activities needed to accomplish a specific task
38. Locate information about duties, methods, and procedures to perform the activities needed to accomplish a specific task
39. Locate information and select the materials, tools, equipment, or other resources to perform the activities needed to accomplish a specific task
40. Revise or update periodically plans and activities for accomplishing a specific task

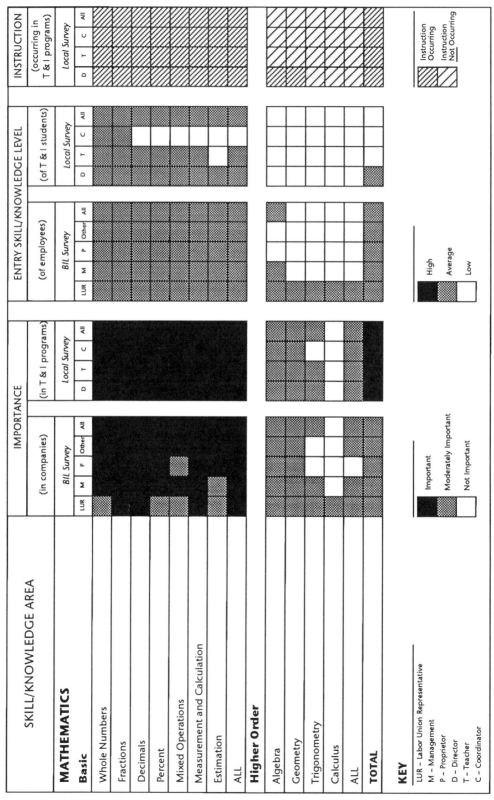

Figure 1—Importance of skills and knowledge in companies and T & I education programs, entry skill and knowledge levels of employees and students, and occurrence of skills and knowledge instruction in T & I programs (continued on next page)

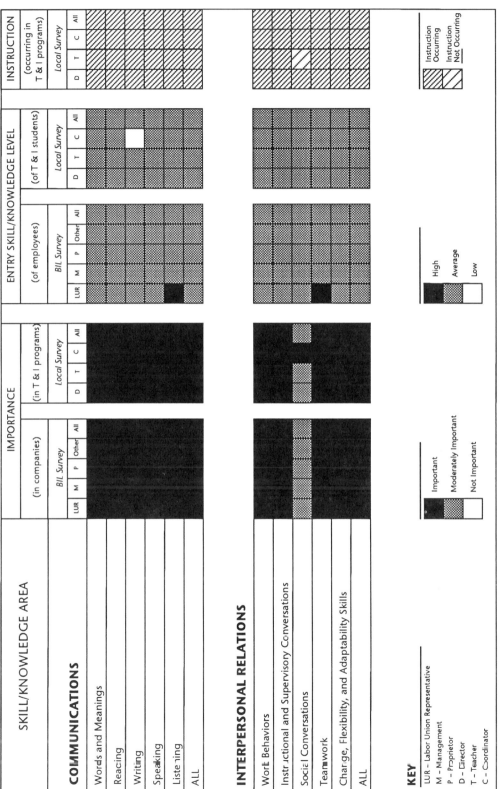

Figure 1 (continued)

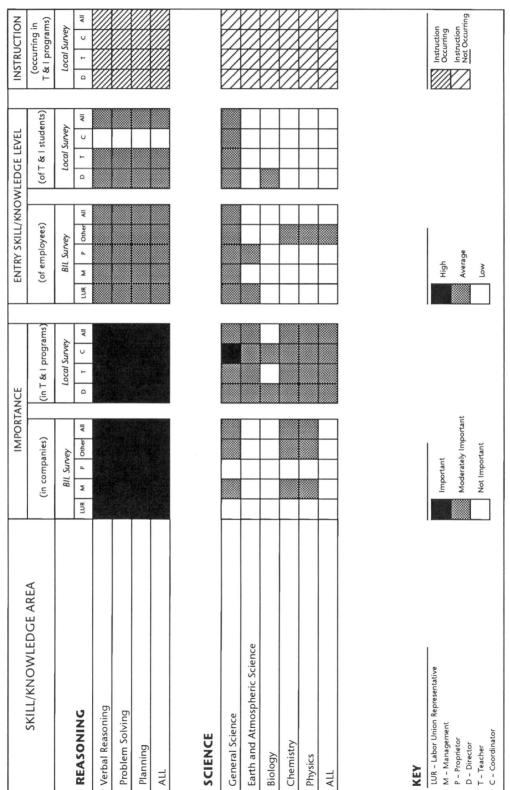

Figure 1 (continued)

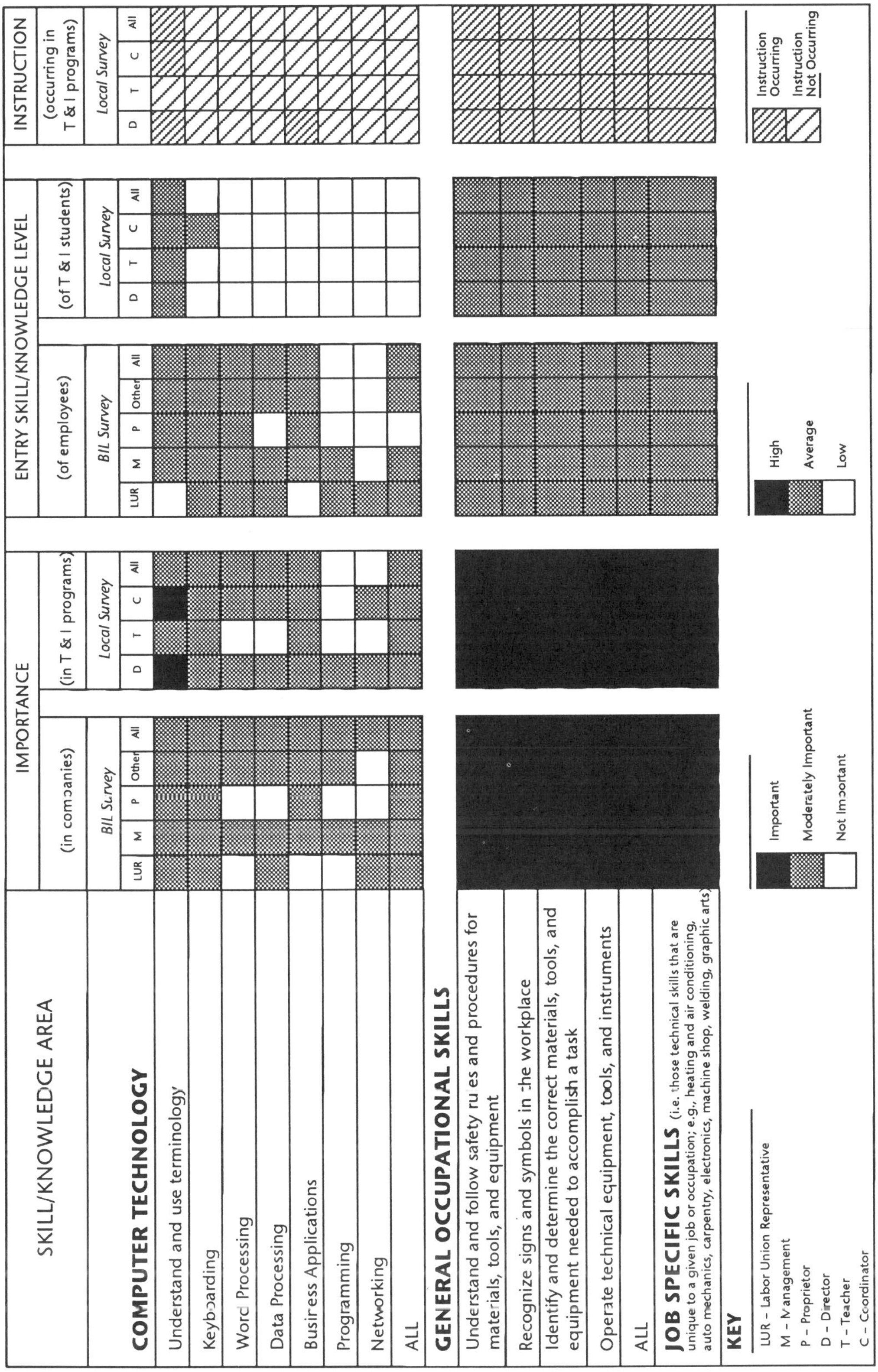

Figure 1 (continued)

SKILL/KNOWLEDGE AREA

IMPORTANCE
- (in companies) BIL Survey: LUR, M, P, Other, All
- (in T & I programs) Local Survey: D, T, C, All

ENTRY SKILL/KNOWLEDGE LEVEL
- (of employees) BIL Survey: LUR, M, P, Other, All
- (of T & I students) Local Survey: D, T, C, All

INSTRUCTION (occurring in T & I programs)
- Local Survey: D, T, C, All

COMPUTER TECHNOLOGY

- Understand and use terminology
- Keyboarding
- Word Processing
- Data Processing
- Business Applications
- Programming
- Networking
- ALL

GENERAL OCCUPATIONAL SKILLS

- Understand and follow safety rules and procedures for materials, tools, and equipment
- Recognize signs and symbols in the workplace
- Identify and determine the correct materials, tools, and equipment needed to accomplish a task
- Operate technical equipment, tools, and instruments
- ALL

JOB SPECIFIC SKILLS (i.e. those technical skills that are unique to a given job or occupation; e.g., heating and air conditioning, auto mechanics, carpentry, electronics, machine shop, welding, graphic arts)

KEY

LUR – Labor Union Representative
M – Management
P – Proprietor
D – Director
T – Teacher
C – Coordinator

Importance:
- Important (High)
- Moderately Important (Average)
- Not Important (Low)

Instruction:
- Instruction Occurring
- Instruction Not Occurring

of skills and knowledge should be consistent with those required in initiatives such as 2+2 and tech prep programs. Vocational curricula must not remain static and must be updated on a formative basis.

Assessment

All education disciplines including vocational education have been charged to evaluate the outcomes of their programs. Vocational education and other school-to-employment transition programs have been challenged (i.e., mandated) to assess accurately, reliably, and validly the generalizable, academic, workplace literacy, and technical skills of youth and adults. Assessments are to be curriculum-based, functional, and prescriptive. They should be related to specific performance standards (criteria) and outcome measures. The Perkins Act specifies that each state shall establish and implement statewide core performance standards and measures for secondary and postsecondary vocational programs within the first two years of the act. Annual program evaluations will be based on the core performance standards and measures. The core standards and measures will include:

- Academic achievement (basic and higher order skills)
- Occupational competency and skill attainment
- Student retention; course, program, and certificate completion rates; and high school graduation rate
- Program and school attendance
- Placement rates into employment, higher education, and/or the military
- Instructional and support services for special needs populations to ensure access and equity
- Employee satisfaction (e.g., wages, benefits)
- Employer satisfaction (American Vocational Association, 1990; Sarkees-Wircenski & Wircenski, 1992; Hoachlander, 1991)

Those in the vocational education field will spend a considerable effort, therefore, to develop performance standards and measures, implement the standards and measures, and evaluate the standards and measures to assess the adequacy, quality, and effectiveness of its programs.

Planning

Vocational education and other school-to-employment transition programs need to become more efficient and concise in planning activities, given the growing demands on resources, an increase in special populations to serve, and anticipated reduction in federal and state fiscal support for programs. Planning activities should be based more on labor market needs and data (Feichtner, Apolloni, & Olivier, 1992). Curriculum updating and assessment revision activities may be based on such needs and data. Public/private partnerships and effective interagency agreements among education agencies will help to ensure more efficient use of limited resources and nonduplication of efforts. Program planning activities should also focus on individuals, particularly individuals who require special instructional services to make the successful transition from school to work or to continuing education.

Instruction

Vocational education and other school-to-employment transition programs must ensure access and equity for all youth and adults. Individuals, including those from special populations, should have a variety of program and career options. Admission criteria must recognize the special needs of individual students. Individualized initiatives and support services need to be available to persons who require them. A variety of learning environments and instructional methods that are matched to the learning styles and characteristics of individual learners should be available. Programs must also consider the special needs of the adult learner and the notion of lifelong learning. In addition, vocational educators must identify and use effective methods to integrate academic content into their programs. They also need to take the initiative to work with other academic disciplines and assist instructors from them to make applications of the theory and knowledge of their subjects. Vocational and other instructors, therefore, must collaborate on ways to assist learners to successfully make the transition from high school to the workplace with marketable and saleable knowledge and skills—or into higher education with the knowledge and skills necessary to complete a technical certificate, associate degree, or bachelor's degree.

Evaluation

Vocational education personnel are being held increasingly accountable in regard to the processes and products of their programs. State and local program personnel and their evaluations will be required to specify performance standards, measures, criteria, and outcomes. Evaluation activities are to relate directly to program objectives and curriculum. Vocational personnel will need to become proficient in evaluation planning, design, instrument development, and interpreting evaluation results. Evaluation results must be used in program planning, decision-making, and resource allocation. Essentially, vocational educators are required to evaluate the adequacy, quality, and effectiveness of their programs.

Summary

Indeed, much attention has focused on the education profession over the past decade. The emphasis has primarily related to curriculum, leadership, access and equity, improvement of learning and instruction, standards, funding and resources, and teacher preparation. These themes and issues apply to all education programs; however, they have particular importance and implications for vocational education and other school-to-employment transition programs. The implications of the reform movement on vocational education appear to be particularly related to curriculum, student assessment, program planning, instructional delivery, program evaluation, and teacher preparation. If vocational education responds proactively to the challenges facing it over the next decade, there is little doubt that the field will thrive and be recognized and complimented for its contributions to educational change. However, if vocational educators ignore the challenges or respond by reacting to the challenges in traditional ways, there is little doubt that vocational education will be viewed as offering minimal contributions to educational reform and the school-to-work transition process. The mandates are clear, the tasks are awesome, and the stakes are high. Are we ready, willing, and able to respond proactively to the challenges? I believe we are!

References

Adler, M. J. (1982). *The Paideia proposal: An educational manifesto.* New York: MacMillan.

American Vocational Association. (1990). The AVA guide to the Carl D. Perkins Vocational and Applied Technology Education Act of 1990. Alexandria, VA: Author.

Asche, M. (1992). Education reform and vocational education: Review with implications for research and development. *Journal of Vocational Education Research, 16*(3), 1-34.

Boyer, E. L. (1983). *High school: A report on secondary education in America.* New York: Harper & Row.

Carl D. Perkins Vocational and Applied Technology Education Act. (1990). P. L. 101-392.

Carnevale, A. P., Gainer, L. J., & Meltzer, A. S. (1990). *Workplace basics: The skills employers want.* San Francisco: Jossey-Bass.

Commission on the Skills of the American Workforce. (1990). *America's choice: High skills or low wages!* Rochester, NY: National Center on Education and the Economy.

Feichtner, S., Apolloni, T., & Olivier, P. (1992). Designing local plans for programs based on labor market information. *The Journal for Vocational Special Needs Education, 14*(2, 3), 46-53.

Goodlad, J. I. (1984). *A place called school: Prospects for the future.* New York: McGraw-Hill.

Greenan, J. P. (1983). *Identification of generalizable skills in secondary vocational programs: Executive summary.* Springfield, IL: Illinois State Board of Education, Department of Adult, Vocational, and Technical Education.

Greenan, J. P. (1990). *Review and assessment of secondary trade and industrial education curriculum: Executive summary.* Indianapolis, IN: Center for School Improvement and Performance.

Greenan, J. P., Jarwan, F. A., & Munn, K. B. (1992). The status and needs of secondary trade and industrial education curriculum: A state and national study. *Journal of Industrial Teacher Education, 29*(3), 21-38.

Hoachlander, G. (1991). Designing a plan to measure vocational education results. *Vocational Education Journal, 66*(2), 20-21, 65.

Jennings, J. F. (1991). Congressional intent. *Vocational Education Journal, 66*(2), 18-19.

Johnston, W. B., & Packer, A. H. (1987). *Workforce 2000: Work and workers for the 21st century.* Indianapolis, IN: Hudson Institute.

National Commission on Excellence in Education. (1983). *A nation at risk: The imperative for educational reform.* Washington, DC: U.S. Government Printing Office.

National Commission on Secondary Vocational Education. (1984). *The unfinished agenda: The role of vocational education in the high school*. Columbus, OH: National Center for Research in Vocational Education.

Pautler, A. J., Gergely, D., Sarkees-Wircenski, M., Greenan, J. P., & Oakey, J. (1992). Educators and industrialists talk about the school-to-work transition. *School Shop/Tech Directions, 51*(8), 29-31.

Parnell, D. (1985). *The neglected majority.* Washington, DC: The Community College Press.

Sarkees-Wircenski, M. D., & Wircenski, J. L. (1992). Performance standards and measures for vocational education programs: Meeting school reform through vocational programs. *The Journal for Vocational Special Needs Education, 14*(2&3), 28-32.

Secretary's Commission on Achieving Necessary Skills. (1991). *What work requires of schools: A SCANS report for America 2000.* Washington, DC: U.S. Department of Labor.

U.S. Department of Education. (1991). *America 2000: An educational strategy.* Washington, DC: Author.

William T. Grant Foundation Commission on Work, Family, and Citizenship (1988). *The forgotten half: Pathways to success for America's youth and young families.* Final report. Washington, DC: Author.

Part II:

Research Reviews

5

The National Longitudinal Studies:
A Window on the
School-to-Employment Transition

Robert C. Nichols

Several years ago, an agricultural statistician told me about his work with a data base that contained extensive information about every cow in New York state. He was using these data to study the relationship of pedigree and developmental history to milk production. When I expressed envy of his data resources, he said with astonishment: "But you are in education. You have millions of children attending thousands of schools for long periods of time. You must have fabulous data!" Sadly, I responded, "I hate to tell you, but you know a lot more about your cows than we do about our children."

Of course, we do know a great deal about the children attending our schools at any given time. We know how much they differ in achievement and occupational aspirations, as well as how these differences are related to home background and to the characteristics of their schools. Yet, although certainly helpful and informative, snapshot analyses have not been able to answer the most fundamental questions because they lack the important time dimension. Education and the transition to adult roles is a process that takes place over a long period of time, and to study this process there is no substitute for long-term longitudinal data in which the same students are assessed repeatedly.

This is not a new insight. Educators have long lamented the lack of longitudinal data, yet

adequate studies have been slow in coming. This seems to be because of the way educational research is organized and funded. Research funding tends to be small scale and short term; the academic reward system does not encourage prolonged data-collection projects; and the unpredictability of researchers' careers makes long-term projects tenuous.

As a result, all successful educational longitudinal studies have been mounted by stable bureaucracies that have been able to overcome these difficulties. The first was *Project TALENT,* started in 1960 by the American Institutes for Research with funding from several government agencies. It survived staff turnovers and funding uncertainties to collect longitudinal data over a 14-year period. With TALENT providing an illustration of the value of timely longitudinal data, the U.S. Congress charged the National Center for Education Statistics with conducting the *National Longitudinal Study of the High School Class of 1972* (NLS-72). This was followed in 1980 by *High School and Beyond* (HS&B), and then by the *National Education Longitudinal Study of 1988* (NELS:88). The last two of these studies are still collecting data, and both conducted major follow-up projects in 1992.

A major goal of all four of these projects was to study the transition from school to adult roles. Thus, they sensibly began with high school students and followed them

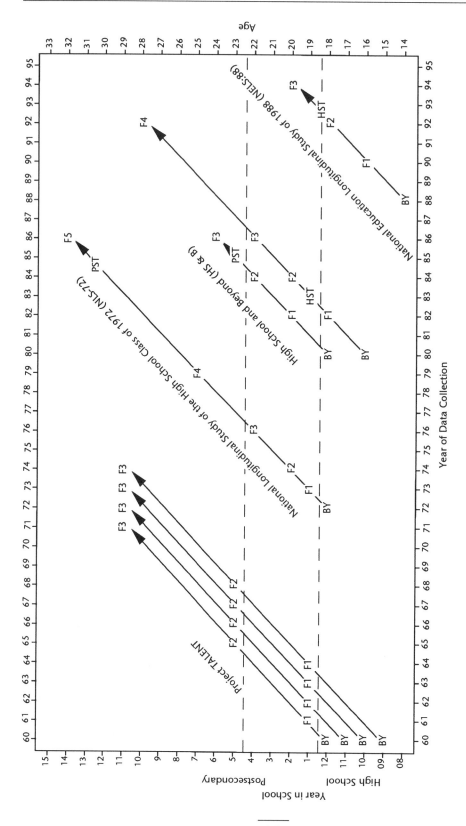

Figure 1—Schedule of data collection for the four major educational longitudinal studies. BY = base year data collection. Fn = follow-up number n. HST = high school transcript. PST = postsecondary education transcript. All data collection took place in the spring, with the exception of the Project TALENT follow-up surveys, which were conducted in the fall.

through postsecondary education, if any, into the world of work. Figure 1 shows the schedule of data collection for the four projects.

Four Major National Longitudinal Studies

The four major longitudinal studies span the four decades from the 1960s through the 1990s. Thus, together they form an integrated data resource that can provide information about the development of individual students as they grow older and about changes that occur over time in the educational processes.

Project TALENT

Project TALENT was the brainchild of John C. Flanagan, who directed the successful program to develop a selection system for Air Corps pilot trainees during World War II (DuBois, 1947). One of the goals of Project TALENT was to apply the pilot-selection methodology, on a grand scale, to predict performance in a wide variety of civilian occupations and activities (Flanagan, et al., 1962).

To provide adequate samples of respondents in small occupational categories, about five percent of the students in high school in 1960 were included in the study. All students in grades 9 through 12 of a national probability sample of 987 high schools were tested in their schools in spring 1960. The approximately 400,000 participants completed a two-day battery of 60 ability tests, personality and interest inventories, and a detailed biographical questionnaire. (It is daunting to consider that this massive data-collection effort was begun when data-processing technology was in its infancy.)

All participants were followed up by mail 1, 5, and 11 years after their expected high school graduation, as shown in Figure 1. A planned 20-year follow-up was abandoned for lack of funding. Response rates to the mail questionnaire varied from more than 60 percent for 1960 twelfth graders followed up one year after high school to about 20 percent for 1960 ninth graders followed up 11 years after high school. In general, response rates fell off slightly each year. To overcome the problem of non-response bias, special surveys of representative samples (usually about 2,500 cases) of

non-respondents to each follow-up were conducted.

The possibility of conducting follow-back studies was an added benefit of the large sample. About 5 percent of any occupational or other group, in the age range that was in high school in 1960, would be members of the Project TALENT sample. Data could be retrieved for identified cases to study the distinctive early characteristics of the target group. It is surprising, considering the power of this methodology, that no follow-back studies have, so far, been conducted.

Now that the participants in Project TALENT are about 50 years old, this may be an opportune time to conduct a new follow-up to collect a lifetime career history. A series of follow-back studies would also yield valuable information about long-term career development.

The National Longitudinal Study of the High School Class of 1972

As the federal government expanded its involvement in financing higher education in the 1960s and 1970s, Congress authorized the National Center for Education Statistics to collect timely information about the role of postsecondary education in the transition from school to employment, and the National Longitudinal Study of the High School Class of 1972 began. In spring 1972, a national probability sample of about 19,000 seniors from 1,070 public, private, and church-affiliated high schools participated in the base-year survey. Each student completed a 104-item questionnaire and a 69-minute test battery. Due to a late start of data-collection, an additional approximately 4,500 members of the sample could not be tested in their schools and were given the questionnaire only. All participants were followed up 1, 2, 4, 7, and 14 years later, as shown in Figure 1. Through persistent tracking of non-respondents, response rates of about 90 percent were achieved.

High School and Beyond

Two conflicting purposes emerged in the design of the High School and Beyond survey. It aimed to replicate NLS-72 as closely as possible to study temporal changes in the process of transition from school to employment.

But changes in design were also desirable to collect important new data and to correct deficiencies that were discovered in the implementation of the previous study. As a result, HS&B involved two cohorts of participants: sophomores and seniors.

The senior cohort was very similar in instrumentation and design to NLS-72, which freed the sophomore cohort to incorporate desirable changes. The major purpose of beginning in the sophomore year was to include a more complete sample of the age group, which would include high school dropouts. The earlier base year, however, also opened up the possibility of studying changes that occurred during the last two years of high school, and the instruments for the sophomore cohort were designed with this purpose in mind. The sophomore tests included curriculum-specific content in writing, mathematics, science, and civics that would be sensitive to differential school learning, while the senior cohort largely repeated the NLS-72 tests, which were designed to measure aptitude.

A national probability sample of about 1,000 high schools was drawn and 36 seniors and 36 sophomores were randomly selected for the study in each school. The realized sample sizes were about 30,000 sophomores and about 28,000 seniors. The entire sophomore sample was retested in their schools two years later as seniors, with special efforts made to track transfers, dropouts, and early graduates. About half of each cohort was then selected, with over-sampling of groups of special interest, for the post-high-school follow-ups that were conducted mainly by mail according to the schedule shown in Figure 1. Persistent tracking of non-respondents yielded completion rates of about 90 percent.

The National Education Longitudinal Study of 1988

The valuable analyses of educational experiences and school effects that were stimulated by the HS&B sophomore cohort led to an expansion of the within-school portion of the next longitudinal study, which began in 1988. NELS:88 started with the eighth grade and emphasized the collection of data related to the process of secondary education in addition

to data relevant to the school-to-employment transition.

Twenty-four students were randomly selected from each of a national probability sample of 1,052 schools. The resulting sample of about 24,000 eighth-grade students completed a questionnaire and took curriculum-based achievement tests in reading, mathematics, science, and social studies, which used item overlapping methods to measure ability and its growth between eighth and twelfth grades. In addition, a parent of each student completed a questionnaire, and each student was rated by two teachers, who also provided information about classes in which the student was enrolled.

Similar data were collected two and four years later when the students were sophomores and seniors, except that the parent questionnaire was omitted from the sophomore assessment. Thus, the data collected in the early years of NELS:88 was designed primarily for the study of the process of schooling during the high school years. These data will provide valuable background information when the focus of the study shifts to the transition from school to work in the post-high-school follow-ups.

Access to Data from the National Longitudinal Studies

The Project TALENT data were originally considered to be proprietary, which limited the number and variety of analyses that were done. The capable people on the Project TALENT staff had neither the time nor the diversity of interest that was needed to do justice to the mass of valuable data that they collected. After the timeliness of much of the data had faded, a data bank was formed through which qualified researchers could specify analyses to be done or obtain copies of parts of the data (Wise, McLaughlin and Steel, 1977). After the last follow-up, a public-use file was released that contained all data for a representative sample of 4,000 cases, all of whom responded to the eleven-year follow-up. This public-use file is now available from the Inter-university Consortium for Political and Social Research.

NLS-72 was a relatively modest undertaking compared with Project TALENT, yet it was subjected to more intense analyses and yielded more useful information than did its more ambitious predecessor. No doubt, this is partly due to the remarkable advances in computing technology that were taking place at the time. Another important factor, however, was the fact that the NLS-72 data were in the public domain, freely available to all, in conformity with a new standard for public access to data collected with public funds.

Each of the HS&B data collections was publicly available as soon as it was ready for analysis, which contributed to their use. Another stimulus for analysis of the HS&B data was the study of public and private schools, funded as part of the initial data-collection contract (Coleman, Hoffer, and Kilgore, 1982). This controversial study attracted attention to the data and provided motivation for additional analyses.

It seems likely that NELS:88 will make even more significant contributions to knowledge than have the preceding longitudinal studies because of its broader focus. This rich data collection will attract researchers interested in the process of secondary education in addition to those concerned with postsecondary education and the transition from school to employment.

Data tapes and user's manuals for NLS-72, HS&B and NELS:88 are available from the National Center for Education Statistics. As an indication of the astonishing advances in computing technology, the entire data-sets for HS&B and for NELS:88 have recently been released on CD-ROM disks that will fit in a coat pocket. A policymaker with these disks in his or her personal computer can get rapid answers to an almost infinite variety of questions, such as: "How many women who attended rural high schools and who had one or more children were employed full time two years after high school graduation?"

Some Findings Concerning the Transition

There have been many analyses of the four major longitudinal studies, the majority of which involve some aspect of the school-to-employment transition. For example, Taylor, Stafford, and Place (1981) reviewed 279 reports of analyses of the NLS-72 data, a rate of about 40 reports per year in the 6 years after the first follow-up data were available. A bibliography accompanying the HS&B third follow-up user's manual (National Center for Education Statistics, 1987) lists 276 reports through 1985, a rate of about 50 per year following the base-year data collection.

Studies might be grouped in a number of ways, and the following rough categorization is intended merely to give an idea of the range of topics that can be studied with these data:

- Individual differences in a variety of personal characteristics of high school students and how these variables relate to student background, school environment, and post-high-school aspirations and achievement.
- Differential effects of schools on student achievement and other outcomes.
- Access to postsecondary education, including changing patterns of college attendance, race and sex differences, financial aid, and delayed entry.
- Performance in postsecondary education, including choice of major, persistence, transfer and withdrawal.
- Labor force participation, career aspirations, and achievement as a function of student background, cognitive ability, and educational experience.
- Studies of methodological issues involved in large-scale longitudinal research.

High School Graduation

For most students, graduation from high school is the major starting point in the sometimes-prolonged transition from school to employment; however, about 15 percent of the male and 13 percent of the female members of the sophomore cohort of HS&B had dropped out of school at the time of the first follow-up. Peng (1985) reported that the dropouts tended to be low in school grades, socioeconomic status, and test scores. At the first follow-up, about 60 percent of the male dropouts were working full time and about 30 percent were looking for work. The female dropouts were about evenly divided among three activities: working, looking for work, and full-time homemaking.

The 86 percent of the members of the sophomore cohort of HS&B who were still in school at the first follow-up were asked to describe the main activity that they expected to occupy their time during the year after graduation. Figure 2 shows that about one-third planned to work full time, another third planned to attend a four-year college or university, and the bulk of the remaining third planned to enter some other form of postsecondary education. These are short-term plans expressed in spring of the senior year of high school, and yet the shading of the columns of Figure 2 shows that many of these plans did not work out during the following fall. About a third of those planning to enter a four-year college and about half of those planning full-time work actually ended up doing something else. The majority of those with other plans did not engage in their planned activity.

It seems clear from these results that many high school seniors change their plans at the last minute, no doubt in response to the many reality factors that confront them as they leave the protected high-school environment.

Career Choice

The dubious nature of many high-school seniors' plans for the short-term raises questions about the stability of long-run career plans. In the base year and in each follow-up, HS&B students were asked to write in the job that they expected to hold at age 30. Then, they were asked to classify that job into one of 17 major occupational categories. Figure 3 shows the percentage of respondents indicating a job in each category as seniors in high school and four years later, separately by sex. A notable feature of the figure is the large proportion of students aspiring to a professional career (between 35 and 40 percent), a far larger proportion than will eventually occupy jobs in professional areas. Although the over-preference for professional careers was reduced somewhat

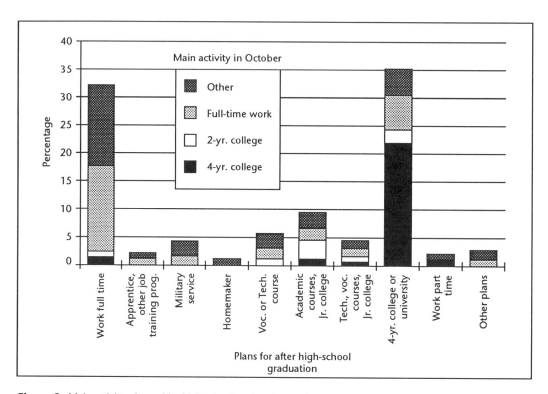

Figure 2—Main activity planned by high school seniors for the year after high school graduation. Shading of the columns indicates actual activity in October following graduation from high school. Data are from the first and second follow-ups of the HS&B sophomore cohort. Case weights were employed to yield population estimates for 1982 graduates.

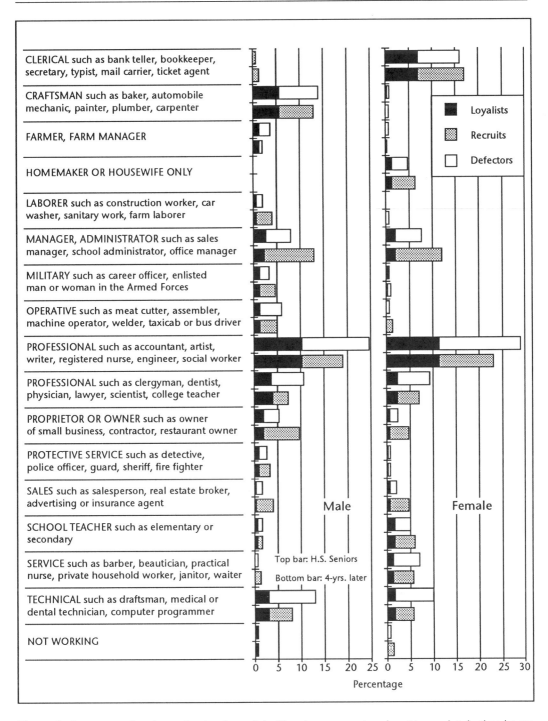

Figure 3—Percentage of students planning to work in 17 major career categories at two points in time by sex. The top bar for each career category shows the percentage planning to enter the career as high school seniors. The bottom bar for each category shows the percentage planning to enter the career four years later. Those who indicated a career in the same category at the two time points (loyalists) are shown in black. Those who initially indicated a career in the category and subsequently changed to another category (defectors) are shown in white. Those who shifted into the career category from another category (recruits) are shaded. Data are from the HS&B first and third follow-ups. N = 5,187 males and 5,772 females (high school dropouts were excluded).

four years after high school graduation, the proportion still seems excessive. Perhaps this merely reflects the operation of market forces in a capitalist economy. The more rewarding careers are oversubscribed, allowing the market to select the most appropriate candidates for the higher status jobs.

Detailed analysis of these data is beyond the scope of this chapter, but they provide a good example of the unique potential of longitudinal data. The repeated expressions of career choice by students about whom a great deal is known provide an opportunity to study the process by which students are sorted into the various career fields during the years of transition from school to employment. Figure 3 shows that the size and composition of the fields change as students move from one field to another. Students who are recruited into one field must defect from another, while others remain loyal to their initial choice. By comparing the ability, socioeconomic status, sex, race, and other characteristics of loyalists, recruits, and defectors in each career category over the several two-year periods covered by

the HS&B data, analysts could piece together the process by which the final size and composition of each field is determined.

Entry into Postsecondary Education

Figure 4 shows how the rate of entry into the major categories of postsecondary education has changed over 21 years. Perhaps the most remarkable feature of the figure is how similar the entry rates were for the three years and the two sexes. The figure does show, however, the rapid growth of two-year colleges during this period and the dramatic increase in college attendance by women. While the college enrollment rate for women in 1961 was only three-fourths that for men, by 1982 the college enrollment rate for women exceeded that for men.

An interesting recent analysis of the NLS-72 fifth follow-up (Adelman, 1991) sheds further light on the sex-equity issue, and it demonstrates the power of long-term longitudinal data. Although women were more likely to persist in higher education, and tended to obtain higher grades than did men, their average

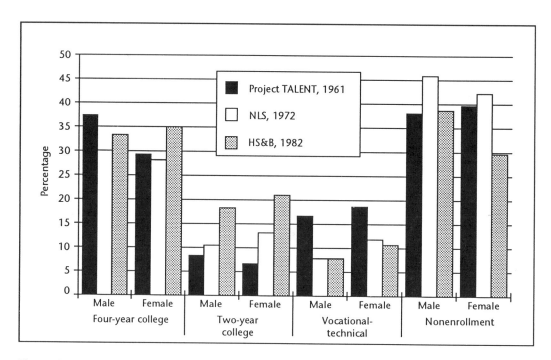

Figure 4—Enrollment of recent high school graduates in postsecondary education by type of institution by sex by year of high school graduation. The percentages in the four enrollment categories add up to 100 for each sex in each of the three years. Data are from Clowes, Hinkle, and Smart (1986).

earnings and occupational status at age thirty-two fell considerably below those of their male counterparts.

The Role of Ability and Socioeconomic Status

Figure 5 shows the rate of enrollment in a four-year college or university by ability and socioeconomic quartiles. One might argue that it is desirable for the most able students to enroll in four-year colleges and universities, since they may benefit more from the college experience and may perform better in the more responsible jobs to which a college degree often leads than would students of lower scholastic aptitude. One might further argue that it is undesirable for socioeconomic status to be a factor in college attendance, since it unfairly handicaps able students from the lower social classes and serves to perpetuate the existing socioeconomic hierarchy. Since 1960, such reasoning has led to large-scale government programs to broaden access to higher education by greatly expanding public colleges and universities and by providing schol-

arship and loan assistance to students based on financial need. We can now ask what changes have occurred in college enrollment patterns since these programs were instituted.

Figure 5 contains good news and bad news. The good news is that the relationship of ability to college entry was about twice as strong as was that for socioeconomic status (SES), although there was still a strong association of socioeconomic status with college entry at every ability level. The bad news is that the relationship of college entry to socioeconomic status and ability has not noticeably changed over the 21-year period for which data are available. In 1961, the lowest SES quartile had a little less than half the college-entry rate of the highest SES quartile at each ability level. The same was true in 1972 and again in 1982. While the relationship of SES to college entry has not decreased, as one might hope, neither has the relationship of ability to college entry increased, as one might also hope. The social and economic factors that produce these relationships must, indeed, be very stable, persistent, and strong. Alexander,

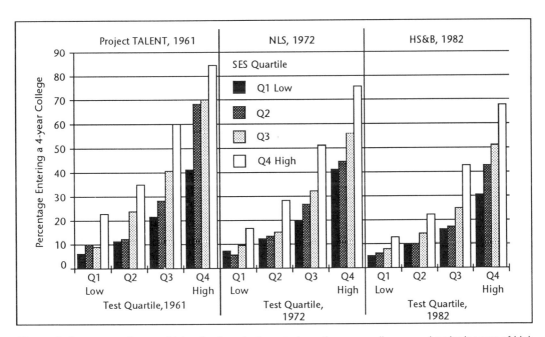

Figure 5—Percentage of recent high school graduates entering a four-year college or university by year of high school graduation by cognitive-ability test quartile by socioeconomic-status quartile. Project TALENT data are from Schoenfeldt (1966). NLS 72 data are from Peng (1977). HS&B data were calculated by the author. Both Schoenfeldt and Peng reported results separately by sex, but, since the relation of ability and SES to college attendance was remarkably similar for the two sexes, they were averaged for this chart.

Pallos, and Holupka (1984) investigated these relationships more extensively using NLS-72 and HS&B data.

The decline in college enrollment in 1972, which can be seen in both Figures 4 and 5, was cause for concern when it was reported by Peng (1977), and Figure 5 shows it continuing through 1982, although Figure 4 does not. The difference between Figures 4 and 5 appears to be due to the inclusion of students who delayed entry to college in Figure 4. To be comparable to the 1961 and 1972 data, only students who entered a four-year college immediately after high school graduation were included in the 1982 data in Figure 5.

The decline in college entry shown in Figure 5 cannot be interpreted directly as a reduction of interest in higher education, because it does not include the dramatic increase in enrollment in two-year colleges that occurred during this period. In fact, the increased availability of two-year colleges may be a major factor in the decline of the rate of entry into four-year colleges. There also seems to have been an increased tendency for delayed entry into higher education after high school graduation. The lower response rate of the Project TALENT follow-ups may also have inflated the college entry rate for 1961, since students in college may be more likely to return questionnaires. The response rate was 45 percent for the first follow-up of eleventh-grade students that was used for the Project TALENT results (Schoenfeldt, 1966), while the response rate for NLS-72 and HS&B was about 90 percent.

Racial Differences

One of the surprising findings of NLS-72 was that when test scores were taken into account blacks were more likely to enter college than were whites (Thomas, Alexander, and Eckland, 1979). Figure 6 shows this finding and indicates that the higher college attendance of blacks persisted and became more pronounced through 1982. Figure 6 also shows that Hispanics had gained parity with whites in 1982. These findings go against the popular stereotype of lower performance levels of minorities. The generally lower average test scores of blacks and Hispanics tends to obscure the academic performance of talented minority students. This suggests that studies of minority performance, which are becoming increasingly popular, should always take test scores and other factors into account when comparing the performance of the various groups.

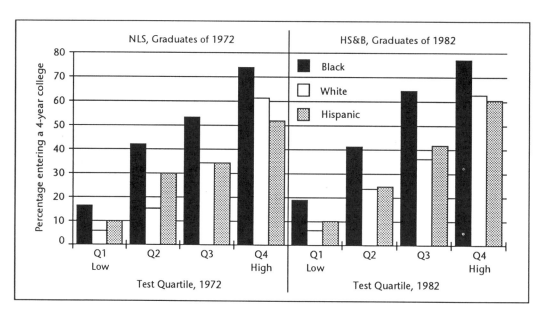

Figure 6—Percentage of recent high school graduates entering a four-year college or university by year of high school graduation by cognitive test quartile by racial/ethnic group. Data are from Clowes, Hinkle, and Smart (1986).

Characteristics of Groups of Students in Different Post-High-School Activities

An indication of the forces that sort high school graduates into various activities can be obtained by studying differences among groups engaged in different activities on variables measured before high school graduation. Figure 7 shows the mean T-scores of five groups, formed on the basis of post-high-school activity, on selected variables of interest. There were substantial differences among the groups on all variables, ranging from 1.4 standard deviations for test scores to 0.4 standard deviations for parental supervision. Students attending four-year colleges had the highest average score and students in the "other" classification had the lowest average score on all variables studied. The first three variables show that the groups differed most on ability, then on socioeconomic status, and on high school grades. The next three variables show the partial relationships of ability, controlling

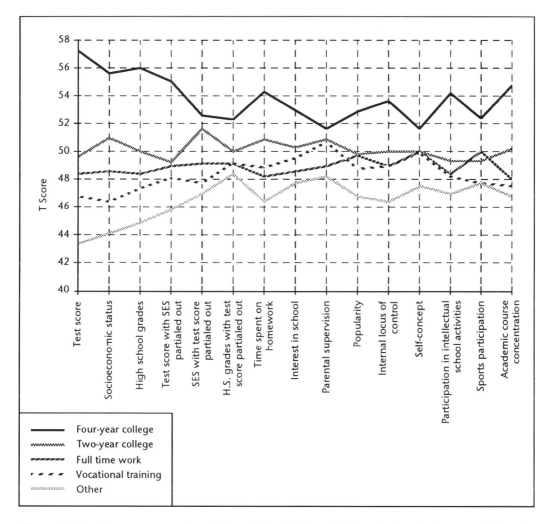

Figure 7—Mean T-scores on several variables of interest of recent high school graduates grouped by major activity after high school graduation. T-scores have a mean of 50 and SD of 10 for the total sample. Data are from the first follow-up of the HS&B sophomore cohort, when the students were seniors in high school. Grouping by post-high-school activity is from the second follow-up. Numbers of cases are approximately: Four-year college: 3,250; Two-year college: 1,800; Vocational training: 775; Full-time work: 3,500; Other: 2,100. Differences among groups were statistically significant (p < .01) for all variables, using case weights and allowing for design effects. The four-year college group was highest and the other-activity group was lowest on all variables.

for SES, and of SES and grades, controlling for ability. Although smaller than for the uncontrolled relationship, all of these partial relationships were highly significant statistically, indicating that each of the three variables differentiated among each group independent of the others. It is interesting to note that, on these three important variables, students who entered vocational schools after graduating from high school were, on average, about 0.2 standard deviations below those who began full-time work.

The other variables included in Figure 7 were selected to show that students engaged in different post-high-school activities differed significantly on almost every variable that is available in the HS&B data-set. This suggests that there is an active sorting process involved in the transition from school to employment that selects different kinds of students into different post-school roles.

Conclusion

The data presented in this chapter are intended to illustrate the sort of information about the school-to-employment transition that can be obtained from the national longitudinal studies. The large, nationally representative samples, the broad diversity of data collected, the parallel studies conducted at roughly ten year intervals, and, most important, the longitudinal perspective, combine to provide a data resource of great depth and power. Although they have been analyzed in many ways by talented researchers, there is much more that can be done to exploit these valuable data. Those interested in the transition from school to employment should be familiar with this large and varied national resource.

References

Adelman, C. (1991). *Women at thirtysomething: Paradoxes of attainment*. Washington, DC: Office of Educational Research and Improvement, U.S. Department of Education.

Alexander, K. L., Pallos, A. M., & Holupka, S. (1984). *Consistency and change in educational stratification: Recent trends regarding social background and college access*. Baltimore: Center for Social Organization of Schools, Johns Hopkins University.

Center for Education Statistics. (1987). *High School and Beyond 1980 sophomore cohort third follow-up (1986): Data file user's manual*. Washington, DC: U.S. Department of Education.

Clowes, D. A., Hinkle D. E., & Smart, J. C. (1986). Enrollment patterns in postsecondary education, 1961-1982. *Journal of Higher Education, 57*, No. 2, 121-133.

Coleman, J., Hoffer, T., & Kilgore, S. (1982). *High school achievement: Public, Catholic and other private schools compared*. New York: Basic Books.

DuBois, P. H. (Ed.) (1947). *The classification program*. (AAF Aviation Psychology Program, Research Reports. Rep. No. 2.) Washington, DC: U.S. Government Printing Office.

Thomas, G. E., Alexander, K. L., & Eckland, B. K. (1979). Access to higher education: The importance of race, sex, social class, and academic credentials. *School Review, 87*, 133-156.

Flanagan, J. C., Dailey, J. T., Shaycoft, M. F., Gorham, W. A., Orr, D. B., & Goldberg, J. (1962). *Design for a study of American youth*. Boston: Houghton Mifflin.

Peng, S. S. (1977). Trends in the entry to higher education: 1961-1972. *Educational Researcher, 6*, No. 1, 15-19.

Peng, S. S. (1985). High school dropouts: A national concern. Paper presented at the Education Commission of the States' Forum on Youth Policy, Washington, DC, March 8, 1985.

Schoenfeldt, L. F. (1966). Post-high-school education. In J. C. Flanagan & W. W. Cooley (Eds.), *Project TALENT: One year follow-up studies*. Pittsburgh: University of Pittsburgh.

Taylor, M. E., Stafford, C. E., & Place, C. (1981). *National Longitudinal Study of the High School Class of 1972 study reports update: Review and annotation*. Washington, DC: U.S. Department of Education, National Center for Education Statistics.

Wise, L. L., McLaughlin, D. H., & Steel, L. (1977). *The Project TALENT data bank handbook*. Palo Alto, CA: American Institutes for Research.

6

Research Review of School-to-Employment Experience

Harry F. Silberman

Numerous reports have expressed concern over the low skill levels of young people entering the labor force. The National Commission on Excellence in Education (1983) blamed schools and called for tougher academic standards as a solution to the problem. The National Commission on Secondary Vocational Education (1984) called attention to the role of vocational education as the unfinished agenda in raising the productivity of the work force. More recently, The William T. Grant Foundation's Commission on Work, Family, and Citizenship (1988) focused on the "forgotten half," the 20 million non-college-bound youth who are ill prepared for labor force entry. The commission called for a more coherent system to assist these people in the school-to-employment transition. Its report recommends that schools provide youth with pre-employment training and monitored work experience, including cooperative education, internships, apprenticeships, youth-operated enterprises, and community service opportunities.

The W. T. Grant Commission seeks to change vocational education's emphasis to broad general education purposes rather than specific job preparation. It recommends guaranteed employment for youth who work hard and acquire skills while they are in school. It also calls for more career guidance and special tutoring by school volunteers who serve as mentors for young people. The recommendations are intended to enhance job quality—not just job opportunities—for young people.

Other studies also emphasize the plight of the forgotten half. In an evaluation of National Longitudinal Data, McPartland (1986) found that the role of school accomplishment is surprisingly unimportant for the low-level jobs usually filled by recent high school graduates. Another follow-up study of 742 employed high school graduates in Michigan (Saginaw Public Schools, 1989) found that most of them were in relatively unskilled jobs, half in personal services industries. Alsalam and Nevzer (1989), in a study of 825,000 high school graduates who went to work immediately after leaving school, found that work-bound youth receive less employer training than either college-bound youth or youth who already had some college experience. Most entry-level jobs for high school graduates are in the secondary labor market, which comprises low-paying jobs without career ladders that are clearly inferior to those in the primary labor market (Doeringer & Piore, 1975). Reich (1991) notes that highly paid elite professional and managerial workers are "quietly seceding" from the less fortunate majority, withdrawing from public schools, neglecting public investment, and refusing to finance social programs that would aid those less skilled individuals whose living standards have been cut by foreign competition.

Not surprisingly, entry-level jobs for college graduates pay considerably higher wages than jobs for high school graduates—for example, 70 percent more in 1986 (Murphy & Welch, 1989). College graduates had an average of $300,000 more in career earnings than high school graduates (Patrick, 1988).

Bachman, O'Malley, and Johnston (1978) in a longitudinal study of males in the U.S., found that group differences were remarkably stable over an eight-year period. Boys from higher socioeconomic backgrounds had higher cognitive ability, got better grades, had higher aspirations in school, attained higher levels of education, subsequently attained higher job status when they went to work, and had higher levels of self-esteem as adults. Preferred attributes seemed to go together, and those who scored highest on a dimension at one point in time were likely to score highest at later points in time. While the analysis failed to find strong effects of differential high school quality on student outcomes, it did suggest that the assumption of responsibilities such as employment, marriage, and paternity may result in positive social outcomes such as reduced delinquency, drug use, and aggression, and increased self-esteem. McClelland (1990), using a social reproduction theory, described the process by which disadvantaged high school seniors aspiring to high-level positions are sorted out after graduation. Early educational progress and changes in occupational expectations show a process of cumulative disadvantage. Willis (1977) described how working class youth resist attempts by schools to help them achieve middle class status. He showed how the rebellion of poor and working class children against school authority prepares them for working class jobs. A job is just a job, from their viewpoint. There is no need to prepare for it.

Work and Family

Commission reports often focus on the effects of schooling on the transition to employment and overlook the influence of a broader set of community institutions, such as work and family, which may have an important impact. Families that lack coherence, and work settings that exploit the worker may indirectly retard the school-to-work transition. In this section, work and family factors will be considered.

Some youth get off to a bad start, do poorly in school, become delinquents and drug abusers, and as adults are either unemployed or underemployed in the secondary labor market. The Panel on Youth (1973) hypothesized that young people are too isolated from positive adult role models, that much of the delinquent behavior of youth is due to the influence of delinquent peers. The panel recommended alternative forms of education for youth, involving greater interaction with adults, such as supervised work experience. Children would be expected to work alongside adults, to discover their own abilities and prepare for a more productive adulthood. Of course, the nature of the work that students observe, and the quality of their own work assignments, would have to be redesigned for educational purposes, since experiences at work are often unfulfilling, dehumanizing, and alienating (Gil, 1991).

It has also been hypothesized that problem youth are more likely to come from large families in which there is more competition for limited resources, such as space to study, parental attention, and available jobs (Elliott, Huizinga, & Menard, 1989). Zajonc (1986) presented evidence that the declining achievement test scores of youth are attributable to the effect of family birthrate patterns on intellectual growth rather than on the declining quality of schooling. The literature consistently demonstrates that positive adult interactions and high adult-child ratios enhance children's personal, intellectual, and social development (Lande, Scarr, & Gunzenhauser, 1989). Yet, the trends continue for increasing numbers of single-parent households, and for greater numbers of mothers to be in the labor force. More than half of the mothers of children under one year of age are in the workforce.

How parents are treated at work not only affects their health (Karasek & Theorell, 1989), but it also affects the growth and development of their children. If work does not provide sufficient time and funds for families to provide adequate care for children, those children may not benefit from school programs. If adults are ill treated at work, they may in turn mistreat members of their families. But, adults who experience the value of positive learning at work are likely to transmit that value to their children. How people are treated at work affects their ideas about what qualities are important in adulthood and thus influences child-rearing patterns (Hoffman, 1986). Work affects family life, and the quality of family life is the most potent form of education and training.

Gordon (1974) described theories about family poverty and underemployment and how the political and economic system tends to perpetuate social class position. Other writers (Gottfredson, 1986; Hunter, 1986) have pointed to the relationship between general cognitive ability and employment. General cognitive ability has proven to be a strong predictor of occupational level, productivity, and job performance. Flynn (1987), however, has noted that tests of cognitive ability probably don't really measure intelligence since the increased IQ scores over the past 30 years are not associated with great advances in scientific discovery nor any other evidence of a cultural renaissance. The number of patents granted in the period of the growth in cognitive ability has actually diminished. The IQ tests probably measure formal school-like abstract problem-solving ability rather than innate intelligence.

There are advantages in viewing intelligence as a changeable entity because those who believe that effort enhances their ability will be more persistent in the face of failure, and that very persistence will more than compensate the person for an initially modest level of general cognitive ability. Besides, those who don't have high general cognitive ability often find a way to use what skills they do have. Jobs are molded to some extent to conform to the abilities of incumbents. Job changes respond to the nature of the available employees and vice versa. Changing skill demands are softened by the need to shape jobs around the available talents possessed by the average worker.

Independent of their influence on children's cognitive ability, families can have a strong impact on the school-to-employment transition by helping their children find good jobs.

Most jobs are obtained through acquaintances or casual personal contacts (Granovetter, 1974). Families that have extensive social networks and contacts, and that provide support and inside information about desirable jobs, can play an important role in their children's success in job placement. Unfortunately, most working class parents have limited social networks and need job search assistance.

Basic Skills

Business leaders often say they need workers with better basic skills, complain that high school graduates lack acceptable skill levels, and seek applicants for their best jobs from higher education. One reason for the current emphasis on completing a college education is its expected contribution to high levels of basic skills. A review of the research on basic skills by the U.S. Department of Education and U.S. Department of Labor (*The Bottom Line*, 1988) identified workplace literacy problems and recommended that state education agencies, local school districts, colleges, universities, employment and training agencies, libraries, community-based literacy groups, and other organizations all take action to improve workers' basic skills. The U.S. Office of Education Research and Improvement (OERI) summarized research about teaching and learning that can be used to improve basic skills and to help youth make a successful school-to-work transition (*What Works*, 1987). Most of their suggestions aim at getting students to spend more time on learning tasks, for example, increasing homework assignments.

Barton and Kirsch (1990) reviewed the research on workplace literacy and employment readiness for OERI. They also conducted a survey of some 40,000 households to inquire about educational experiences, exposure to the labor market, and reading activities, and they administered reading exercises to respondents. They concluded that for the total population "illiteracy" is not a major problem, and most workers can perform routine literacy tasks but do not perform very well on more complex tasks. But entry-level workers coming directly from the high schools and dropouts had a lower level of literacy than the general population. They also cite other studies showing that poor attitudes toward work on the part of recent high school graduates kept many employers from hiring them. Employers want conscientious workers who work well with others, can communicate, and are ready to work. They want schools to teach employability skills, including good attendance, punctuality, and positive work attitudes.

In another policy report, Barton (1990) notes that the inability of high school graduates to apply basic skills learned in school to the workplace is due to the differences between the literacy skills that are acquired in the classroom and those needed at the workplace. His suggested solution is to strengthen the linkages between school and the workplace and to integrate academic and vocational education.

Employer Needs

The Department of Labor's Secretary's Commission on Achieving Necessary Skills (SCANS) (1990) interviewed employers and workers to find out what skills high school graduates need to enter the work force. They found that teamwork, reasoning, ability to apply knowledge, a passion to learn, and the ability to use a computer and allocate resources, were considered as important as basic skills.

The American Society for Training and Development (ASTD) and the U.S. Department of Labor conducted a three-year study of the skills employers consider most essential (Carnevale, Gainer, & Meltzer, 1990). The authors group the important skills into seven categories that include learning to learn, basic skills, communication, adaptability, developmental skills, group effectiveness, and influencing skills. These skills are prescribed for all workers, including nonsupervisory employees. The authors recommend training programs to develop these skills in employees.

Ascher (1988) also found that employers want it all. But, for entry-level jobs, employers were less interested in high school grades or job competencies of high school graduates. For such jobs they were more concerned with social skills and good work habits (e.g., ability to present themselves well, enthusiasm, cooperativeness, discipline, responsibility, flexibility, and willingness to learn).

Changing Skill Requirements

Rising employer expectations of high school graduates are generally attributed to changes in the labor market. The Hudson Institute published a popular report called *Workforce 2000* (Johnston & Packer, 1987) that projected a small net growth in a workforce dominated by female, black, Hispanic, immigrant, and heretofore neglected special-needs populations. The report also forecast increasing skill requirements of entry-level workers. Thus, as jobs have become more complex and are demanding more, applicants are providing less. These two changes have placed the quality of education on the corporate policy agenda and have encouraged major American businesses to become involved in strengthening the connection between education and work. Executive officers now seek to help their companies by helping schools improve the school-to-employment experience of youth.

The question of whether America's present and future jobs demand more, or less, of employees is a matter for debate. Both parties in this debate often see the labor market as a single unilateral entity, not as a changing complex whose segments have different skill requirements that vary by industry, occupation, location, time, and available labor supply.

Berg (1970) and Freeman (1975) presented early evidence of the negative effects of overeducation and inflation of educational credentialing in the U.S. Carnoy and Levin (1985) and Levin and Rumberger (1987) have emphasized the de-skilling effects of modern technology, which substitutes sophisticated programs for the skills of workers. (Consider how the optical scanner and computer released the sales clerk from using arithmetic skills.) Although high-technology occupations are increasing at a rapid rate, the absolute number of such jobs is very small. The largest growth in absolute number of jobs is in low-level service jobs, such as those of sales clerk, waiter, nurse's aide, and custodian. The rate of growth of computer service technicians is much higher than that for auto mechanics, but the absolute increase in the number of jobs for auto mechanics will be much larger than for computer technicians—around six times as large. There were still more hand bookkeepers in the U.S. in 1980 than all workers in the computer-related occupations combined.

Radical critics of the reformers, who demand ever higher levels of schooling for entry-level workers, say that the demand for longer periods of schooling under the pretext of preparing a skilled labor force is merely serving to keep people out of an already overcrowded labor market. When those people graduate with high expectations for meaningful employment, the jobs available to them will actually demand less understanding, authority, and responsibility than they need for personal fulfillment. The problem is not the failure of education so much as the inability of the economy to generate enough good jobs. The surplus of graduates with degrees reduces the value of those degrees for everyone except those who do not have them.

Other authors project increasing numbers of jobs that will require more postsecondary education and training (Cetron, 1984; Silvestri & Lukasiewicz, 1987, 1989; Cyert & Mowery, 1989; *Wall Street Journal Reports*, 1990; Cetron & Gayle, 1991). Spenner (1985) reviewed the literature on the upgrading and downgrading of occupations and concluded that there will be aggregate stability in skill requirements. Some jobs experience rapid upgrading while others are downgraded. Some people have responded to the overeducation/underemployment concerns of those who take the de-skilling position by noting that workers retain the same relative place in the job queue regardless of absolute increases in credentials and skills of all workers in the queue. Changes in amount of training required of all workers doesn't alter the relative advantage of individuals.

Bailey (1991) notes that the big weakness in the skill levels of U.S. workers is in middle- and lower-level occupations, not in professional and high-tech occupations. But he also points out that employers need to make better use of the skills that workers already have. Many of the apparent skill and training problems faced by employers result from employers' human management policies rather than from deficiencies in the educational preparation of the workforce. Blaming our schools for the poor management and failure of our fiscal, monetary, and trade and industrial policies will not solve those problems.

School-To-Employment Experience in Other Countries

If we are to achieve a high-skill society, we must provide more jobs that reward those who have achieved competencies in high school. Bishop (1989) attributes apathy in American high schools to the lack of connection between how much students learn in school and their future success in the labor market. The labor market does not reward their effort and achievement in high school. This is in sharp contrast to other industrialized countries, such as Germany and Japan, for example, which reward students for their high school achievement and have a carefully supervised structure for helping students make the transition from school to work. Of course those countries also subsidize growth industries and protect manufacturing jobs. They encourage long-term investment over short-term speculation and promote participative management systems which make better use of the existing talents and skills of their entry-level workers.

The U.S. General Accounting Office (GAO) (1990) examined four countries—England, Germany, Japan, and Sweden—and compared their methods of preparing noncollege youth for employment with those in the U.S. The other countries invest more in noncollege education and training, give more assistance to youth in the transition from school to work, and expect more in the way of national competency standards than does the U.S. The GAO report recommended earlier intervention and more school-employer linkages, particularly for apprenticeship-type programs.

Nothdurft (1989) describes the German "dual" apprenticeship system, which begins at age 16. Students must pass a test to be admitted to the program. Once admitted, they spend three or more years in the program, attending classes one to two days a week, where they learn job-related academic principles and theory, and three to four days a week on the job, where they learn how to do the work. They get paid for working, but there is no employment guarantee built into the system. When they complete the program requirements, which are set by national standards, they enter the labor market as journeymen. The dual system of vocational education applies to almost 70 percent of all school leavers and prepares the major core of the labor force. About 40 percent of university students also finish an apprenticeship prior to their studies.

The dual system in Germany has some problems of equity and rigidity. For example, there is a mismatch between apprenticeship opportunities and actual job openings. Small firms account for 40 percent of dual system apprenticeship positions, yet they comprise only 17 percent of the labor force. Furthermore, the largest firms, which have the best training facilities, tend to select only the best students (those from the Gymnasium and Realschule) and leave the graduates from the lower status Hauptschule to find less desirable apprenticeships with smaller firms (e.g., bakeries). Furthermore, a graduate who wishes to change vocations must go back and complete another three-year apprenticeship.

Hamilton (1990) examined the possible utility of applying the German apprenticeship system in the U.S. He proposed that we begin with exploratory apprenticeships that would expose young people, by means of community service and mentoring programs, to a variety of occupations. Then students would move to a school-based apprenticeship, such as a school-based enterprise, that would expose them to vocational activities in the school. Finally, students would engage in formal work-based apprenticeships for a specific occupation. This latter phase would be a 2 + 2 system, beginning during the junior year of high school and extending through two years of a community or technical college. Precautions would have to be taken in this system to avoid the dual tracking of students into separate work-bound vs. college-bound categories which might close off more opportunities than it opens for members of the lower work-bound track.

Rosenbaum and Takehiko (1989) describe the high-school-to-work transition in Japan. Most Japanese companies hire their employees directly from high school with little or no previous job experience or training, but they use employment selection tests and accept recommendations of school personnel in selecting their new employees. Although the vocational schools have lower status than the academic high schools, they still have a good reputation for the employability of their graduates. Schools compete with each other to maintain their share of job contracts, and employers compete with each other to maintain their share of capable job applicants from the schools with which they have contracts. Schools seek dependable future demand for their graduates, and employers seek a dependable future supply of graduate applicants. These relationships are governed by institutional agreements or contracts that provide specified numbers of job guarantees for each school, allowing schools to nominate students on the basis of grades. The Japanese system delegates much of the screening for jobs to schools, which provides a strong incentive for high school achievement and maintains the authority of school personnel. Like the German system, the Japanese system also has its problems and may not be very transferrable to the more diverse and individualistic culture in the U.S.

Effects of School-to-Employment Experience

The current emphasis on providing school-supervised work experience for youth has raised a question about the effects of the part-time jobs that most young people engage in while attending school. Steinberg (Freiberg, 1991) cited U.S. Department of Education surveys that showed that half of all sophomores, two-thirds of all juniors, and nearly three-fourths of all seniors hold jobs during the school year. The average high school senior works more than 20 hours weekly, in addition to a 30-hour school week. In contrast, Steinberg noted that only 5 percent of Japanese and 20 percent of European students work during the school year.

The research findings on the effects of part-time employment are mixed. Greenberger and Steinberg (1986) and Steinberg and Dornbusch (Freiberg, 1991) present data emphasizing the potential risks of employment during the school year. Those risks increase with increasing time commitment to a job. Excessive time on the job was found to have detrimental effects, not only on school achievement, but also in creating cynical attitudes toward work itself. Mortimer, Finch, Shanahan, and Ryu (Freiberg, 1991) found that most part-time work for teenagers is in low-level repetitive tasks that involve little interdependence with other workers. The prime motivation for such work is to earn money so the students can buy things. But they found no adverse effects on the students. They concluded that work experience could be beneficial if it was perceived as providing useful skills and if the work was restricted in intensity and well-integrated with schoolwork. Conrad and Hedin (1982) found that students reported that they had become more responsible as a result of their work on community service projects. The effects of employment depend on the quality and amount, not on whether a student works.

MacArthur (1989) obtained data from 400 public high school juniors (200 working and 200 not working during the fall of 1988). She found that the working students had significantly lower mean GPAs and lower attitude and study habit scores than the nonworking students. In these correlational studies, one always questions whether the results are due to the employment or to differential self-selection of students. Bachman, Bare, and Frankie (Freiberg, 1991) found that seniors who worked long hours reported no more physical symptoms than their classmates, but that work intensity was positively correlated with delinquent behavior and drug and alcohol use. They said the evidence was too mixed for them to conclude that working long hours in the last year of high school is the cause of the negative outcomes.

Charner and Fraser (1988) also reviewed the research on the effect of students working. They concluded that the effect of working on grades is unclear. There seems to be a curvilinear relationship between hours worked and grades, with 20 hours being the point where a negative effect emerges. Working appeared to have little effect on educational plans but is positively associated with employment and income after high school completion, at least in the short run. Working during high school appears to promote desirable work habits. Charner and Fraser also found that relationships with parents and siblings were generally not affected by working. They concluded that the findings regarding the effect of working on delinquent behavior are inconclusive and contradictory.

Barton (1989) summarized the research on the effect of student work on school performance from data collected in the National Assessment of Educational Progress. The key findings were that there was little or no difference, on average, in performance among students who did not work and those who worked up to 20 hours per week. For students working longer hours, performance was slightly lower. Students who worked more than 20 hours were more likely to be enrolled in the vocational track, less likely to have taken advanced courses in math and science, and more likely to expect to work after high school rather than attend four-year colleges.

Some studies have found that the effect of school-to-employment experience depends on the quality of supervision of the work experience and the integration of the work experience with the school curriculum. Silberman (1974) collected data from a thousand students in grades 9-14 from 50 work education programs and from 700 similar students who held non-school-supervised part-time jobs but were not participating in any work education programs. The school-supervised students were significantly more satisfied with their jobs than the non-school-supervised part-time workers. Group atmosphere, availability of adult role models, meaningfulness of work roles, and availability of feedback accounted for much of the variation in job satisfaction among the two groups of student workers.

Moore (1986) described a qualitative study showing how workers learn their jobs through internships. Stern, McMillion, Hopkins, and Stone (1990), using survey methods, found that students in school-supervised work experience programs report more favorable job characteristics than students in non-school-supervised work experience. The school-supervised students had more contact with adults; were more likely to use academic skills on their jobs; had a greater variety of work tasks; found their work more motivating, meaningful, and satisfying; and reported a closer relationship between their work and studies. These results were similar to previous findings by Stone (1980), who evaluated the learning that occurred in a student-operated school store, and by Stern (1984), who evaluated a school-based enterprise in which students operated two restaurants. Students said their jobs helped prepare them for future employment, were more interesting than part-time jobs outside of school, and gave them an opportunity to work together as a team. Stone and Hopkins (1990) reviewed the literature on high school work experience and concluded that the outcomes depend on the type of work students perform. Some studies report positive outcomes such as increased punctuality, dependability, and motivation, while others report that work has undesirable effects. When it is low-level work that does not use basic academic skills, the results are not as desirable as when the work is provided in more challenging school-based programs.

The critical factor determining the outcome of part-time work appears to be the level of cooperation between schools and employers necessary to assure the educational value of the effort. Partnerships between local schools and employers are attempting to strengthen the connection between school and work environments. The U.S. Department of Education's Office of Vocational and Adult Education published a report, *Combining School and Work* (1991), that describes two ways of achieving that objective: (1) including field-based experiences such as apprenticeships, cooperative education, and school-based enterprises, and (2) integrating academic and vocational courses by means of 2+2 tech-prep programs and vocational academies. The two options (structured work experience and integrated curricula), however, are expected to be achieved without resorting to separate curricular tracking of students. The report describes a variety of exemplary business-school partnerships throughout the country.

Work-Experience Programs

There is a sizable literature describing successful applications and evaluations of the above work-experience and curricular integration programs. Some examples from that literature follow.

The Indiana PLUS program (Walters, 1991) successfully engaged high school seniors to conduct field research on job requirements and prepare TV broadcast presentations of their findings for middle-school children. The Commonwealth Fund sponsored a successful summer career exploration program for youth at Hunter College. Wentling (1990) evaluated tech-prep programs at five sites in Indiana, and all were doing well. The Southern Regional Education Board (1985) has developed a set of 10 standards for successfully incorporating basic skills in vocational education programs.

Wall and Luther (1988) describe innovative examples of successful school-based enterprises. For example, a New York high school has a greenhouse, built by students, with annual plant sales of $1,000. In Iowa, high school students are operating a small jobs subcontracting service. Students in Alaska plan an herbal export business. High school students in Georgia operate a child development center and a swine-breeding farm that sells feeder pigs. In North Carolina, high school students run a delicatessen with a monthly payroll of $7,000. Students in Indiana have two businesses: a pedigree hog enterprise and a truck and tractor salvage business. A South Dakota high school has altered its curriculum to provide marketing opportunities for students in several classes. Lake and Williamson (1986) describe four school-based enterprise projects to improve the employability of aboriginal students in Australia.

The Mott Foundation (1982) sponsored school-based development corporations in five Arkansas towns in which students worked on their own newspaper, a roller skating rink, a day care center, a temporary employment service, a photo lab, a movie theater, and a public beach. Bloomfield (1989) evaluated a school-business partnership which included career guidance, tutoring, work experience, and adult mentoring. Participants are targeted during their junior year in high school and matched with a mentor for periodic meetings. Ninety-five percent of the disadvantaged youth in the program graduated from high school, and 65 percent attended college. Pfeiffer (1985) describes a program in which senior high students are employed part time as registered apprentices by local employers in New Jersey and continue as full-time apprentices once they have graduated, yielding a smooth transition from part-time to full-time apprenticeship employment, a link between cooperative education and apprenticeship.

Crim and Odom (1987) described a program involving four technology-oriented magnet high schools in Atlanta, Georgia, supported by private firms and area universities. The firms are involved in curriculum design and internship opportunities. Blake (1986) examined Project MAIN (Mobile Assistants in Nutrition); a 12-month demonstration project; a collaborative effort of an urban university; a high school; and a senior services agency, which employed students aged 14 to 19 to research, plan, and operate a grocery delivery and escort service for elderly and disabled citizens. Knopke (1986) described a program where students from five rural high schools in Alabama assessed water quality, health care, and quality of life in their communities and recommended solutions at a public forum.

Conclusion

Young people are too isolated from the adult world to see the connection between school and work. We must involve youths in programs that give them a chance to feel needed and that help them to achieve adulthood. For example, community service activities, exploratory work experiences, school-based enterprises, and apprenticeships in respected occupations, all offer genuine responsibility from which young people can learn the essential skills and attitudes that employers and communities need.

References

Alsalam, N., & Nevzer, S. (1989). *Employer training of work-bound youth.* (Background Paper No. 43). Department of Labor, Washington, DC: Commission on Workforce Quality and Labor Market Efficiency.

Ascher, C. (1988). *High school graduates in entry level jobs: What do employers want?* (ERIC/CUE Digest Number 40). New York: ERIC Clearinghouse on Urban Education.

Bachman, J., O'Malley, P., & Johnston, J. (1978). *Youth in transition.* Ann Arbor, MI: University of Michigan.

Bailey, T. (1991, March). Jobs of the future and the education they will require: Evidence from occupational forecasts. *Educational Researcher.*

Barton, P. E. (1989). *Earning and learning: The academic achievement of high-school juniors with jobs.* (Report No: 17-WL-01). Princeton, NJ: Educational Testing Service.

Barton, P. E. From school to work. (1990). Princeton, NJ: Policy Information Center, Educational Testing Service.

Barton, P. E., & Kirsch, I.S. (1990). *Workplace competencies: The need to improve literacy and employment readiness.* Washington, DC: Office of Educational Research and Improvement, U.S. Department of Education.

Berg, I. (1970). *Education and jobs: The great training robbery.* Praeger.

Bishop, J. H. (1989, February). Why the apathy in American high schools. *Educational Researcher, 18* (1), 6-10.

Blake, G. F. (1986). Project MAIN: Community collaboration benefits senior citizens. *Children Today, 15* (4), 31-34.

Bloomfield, W. (1989). *Career beginnings: Helping disadvantaged youth achieve their potential.* Bloomington, IN: Phi Delta Kappa Educational Foundation.

The bottom line: Basic skills in the workplace. (1988). Washington, DC: U.S. Department of Labor & U.S. Department of Education.

Carnevale, A. P., Gainer, L. J., & Meltzer, A. S. (1990). *Workplace basics: The skills employers want.* Washington, DC: The American Society for Training and Development & U.S. Department of Labor, Employment & Training Administration.

Carnoy, M., & Levin, H. (1985). *Schooling and work in the democratic state.* Stanford, CA: Stanford University Press.

Cetron, M. (1984). *Jobs of the future.* McGraw Hill.

Cetron, M., & Gayle, M. (1991). *Educational renaissance.* New York: St. Martins Press.

Charner, I., & Fraser, B. S. (1988). *Youth and work: What we know, what we don't know, what we need to know.* Washington, DC: William T. Grant Foundation, Commission on Work, Family and Citizenship.

Combining school and work: Options in high schools and two-year colleges. (1991). Washington, DC: U.S. Department of Education, Office of Vocational and Adult Education.

Commission on Work, Family and Citizenship. (1988). *The Forgotten half: Non-college youth in America.* Washington, DC: The William T. Grant Foundation.

The Commonwealth Fund, NY. (1984). *Career explorations: The program and management report.* Public/Private Ventures, Philadelphia, PA.

Conrad, D., & Hedin, D. (1982). The impact of experiential education on adolescent development. *Child and Youth Services,* 57-76

Crim, A. A. & Odom, B. D. (1987, April). Preparing students for technology: The Atlanta experiment. *Curriculum Review, 26* (4), 21-23.

Cyert, R.M., & Mowery, D.C. (1989, May) Technology, employment and U.S. competitiveness. *Scientific American, 1* (5), 333-354.

Doeringer, P., & Piore, M. (1975). Unemployment and the dual labor market. *Public Interest, 38,* 67-69.

Elliott, D. S., Huizinga, D., & Menard, S. (1989). *Multiple problem youth: Delinquency, substance use and mental health problems.* New York: Springer-Verlag.

Flynn, J. (1987). Massive IQ gains in 14 nations: What IQ tests really measure. *Psychological Bulletin, 101*(2), 171-191.

Freeman, R. (1976). *The overeducated American.* Academic Press.

Freiberg, P. (1991, June). Teens' long work hours detrimental, study says. *American Psychological Association Monitor.*

Gil, D. (1991). Children and work: Rights to become creative and productive. *School Psychology Review, 20* (3), 389-400.

Gordon, D. (1974). *Theories of poverty and underemployment.* D.C. Heath.

Gottfredson, L. S. Societal consequences of the G-factor in employment. (1986, December). *Journal of Vocational Behavior 29* (3): 337-410.

Granovetter, M. *Getting a job: A study of contacts and careers.* Harvard University Press, 1974.

Greenberger, E., & Steinberg, L. (1986). *When teenagers work: The psychological and social costs of adolescent employment.* New York: Basic Books.

Hamilton, S. F. (1990). *Apprenticeship for adulthood: Preparing youth for the future.* New York: Free Press

Hoffman, L. (1986). Work, family, and the child. In M. Pallak & R. Perloff (Eds.), *Psychology and work: Productivity, change, and employment.* Master Lectures. American Psychological Association.

Hunter, J. E. (1986, December). Cognitive ability, cognitive aptitudes, job knowledge, and job performance. *Journal of Vocational Behavior 29,* 340-362.

Johnston, W., & Packer, A. (1987). *Workforce 2000: Work and workers for the 21st century.* Indianapolis, IN: Hudson Institute.

Karasek, R., & Theorell, T. (1989). *Healthy work: Job stress, productivity, and the reconstruction of working life.* Basic Books.

Knopke, H. F. (1986). *Assessing the quality of life in rural Alabama: Results of high school students' community investigation.* Tuscaloosa: Alabama University College of Community Health Sciences, West Alabama Planning and Development Council.

Lake, J., & Williamson, J. (1986, April). A case study of a community-based transition education project. Paper presented at Annual Meeting of the American Educational Research Association, San Francisco, CA.

Lande, J., Scarr, S., & Gunzenhauser, N. (Eds.) (1989). *Caring for children: Challenge to America.* Hillsdale, NJ: Erlbaum.

Levin, H. M., & Rumberger, R. W. (1987). Educational requirements for new technologies. *Educational Policy, 1* (3), 333-354

McClelland, K. (1990, April). Cumulative disadvantage among the highly ambitious. *Sociology of Education, 63* (2), 102-121.

McPartland, J. M. (1986). *The school's role in the transition from education to work: Current conditions and future prospects.* (Report No. 362). Baltimore, MD: Johns Hopkins University, Center for Social Organization of Schools.

Moore, D. T. (1986, September). Learning at work: Case studies in nonschool education. *Anthropology and Education Quarterly 17,* (3), 166-184.

Mott Foundation. (1982). *Year one: An evaluation of school-based development corporations in five rural Arkansas towns.* Little Rock: Arkansas Community Education Development Association.

MacArthur, S. S., et al. (1989, November). Employment among high school juniors. Paper presented at Annual Meeting of the Mid-South Educational Research Association, Little Rock, AR.

Murphy, K., & Welch, F. (1989, May). Wage premiums for college graduates: Recent growth and possible explanations. *Educational Researcher, 18* (4).

National Commission on Excellence in Education. (1983). *A nation at risk: The imperative for educational reform.* Washington, DC: U.S. Government Printing Office.

National Commission on Secondary Vocational Education. (1984). *The unfinished agenda.* Columbus, OH: National Center for Research in Vocational Education, Ohio State University.

Nothdurft, W. E. (1989). *Scholworks: Reinventing public schools to create the workforce of the future, innovations in education and job training from Sweden, West Germany, France, Great Britain and Philadelphia, Pennsylvania.* The German Marshall Fund of the United States.

Panel on Youth. (1973). *Youth: Transition to adulthood.* University of Chicago.

Patrick, D. C. *The value of human capital formation: The perspective of rural minority students.* (1988). Washington, DC: Cooperative State Research Service, Department of Agriculture.

Pfeiffer, E. W. (1985, December) School to work linkage: The apprenticeship connection. Paper presented at the Meeting of the American Vocational Association, Atlanta, GA.

Reich, R. (1991). *The work of nations.* Knopf.

Rosenbaum, J. E., & Takehiko, K. (1989, May). From high school to work: Market and institutional mechanisms in Japan. *American Journal of Sociology, 94* (6), 1334-1365.

Saginaw Public Schools. (1989). Follow-up study of

1988 graduates. Department of Evaluation Services, Saginaw, MI.

The Secretary's Commission on Achieving Necessary Skills. (1990, September). *Identifying the skills required by work.* Pelavin.

Silberman, H. F. (1974). Job satisfaction among students in work education programs. *Journal of Vocational Behavior, 5*, 261-268.

Silvestri, G. T., & Lukasiewicz, J. M. (1987, September) A look at occupational employment trends to the year 2000. *Monthly Labor Review.*

Silvestri, G. T., & Lukasiewicz, J. M., (1989, November). Projections of occupational employment, 1988-2000. *Monthly Labor Review, 112* (11).

Southern Regional Education Board. (1985). *Ten recommendations for improving secondary vocational education.* Atlanta, GA: Author.

Spenner, K. (1985, Summer). Upgrading and downgrading of occupations. *Review of Educational Research, 55* (2), 125-154.

Stern, D. (1984). School-based enterprise and the quality of work experience: A study of high school students. *Youth & Society 15* (4), 401-427.

Stern, D., McMillion, M., Hopkins, C., & Stone, J. R., III. (1990). Work experience for students in high school and college. *Youth and Society 21* (3): 355-389.

Stone, J.R., III. (1980). The evolution of a school business enterprise. *VocEd 55* (2), 47.

Stone, J.R., III, & Hopkins, C. (1990). *Working teens: The influence of school intervention.* Reston, VA: Marketing Education Association.

Stone, J.R., III, Stern, D., Hopkins, C., & McMillion, M. (1990). Adolescents' perceptions of their work: School-supervised and nonschool-supervised. *Journal of Vocational Education Research 15* (2).

Stone, J.R., III, Stern, D., Hopkins, C., & McMillion, M. (1991, May). Learning from school based work experience programs. *Beacon,* American Vocational Education Research Association, *25* (2). Springfield, IL: Sangamon State University.

U.S. General Accounting Office. *Training strategies: Preparing noncollege youth for employment in the U.S. and foreign countries* (GAO/HRD-90-88). Washington, DC: Author.

Wall, M., & Luther, V. (1988). *Schools as entrepreneurs: Helping small towns survive.* Lincoln, NE: Heartland Center for Leadership Development.

Wall Street Journal Reports. (1990, February 9). Education: The knowledge gap. Dow Jones & Co.

Walters, L. S. (1991, July 29) Indiana schools pave the path to jobs. *The Christian Science Monitor.*

Wentling, T. L. (1990). *Technology preparation pilot test. School year 1989-1990 evaluation report.* Indianapolis: Indiana State Department of Education.

Willis, P. (1977). *Learning to labor.* Columbia Press.

What works: Research about teaching and learning. (1987). U.S. Department of Education, Office of Educational Research and Improvement.

Zajonc, R. (1986). The decline and rise of scholastic aptitude scores: A prediction derived from the confluence model. *American Psychologist, 41* (8), 862-867.

7

Experiences
of High School Graduates
in Finding Employment

David W. Stevens

Twenty-five years ago, the distinguished participants in a Princeton University symposium recommended nine priorities in studying the transition from school to work (Harbison, 1968). Included among them were: (1) pathways and obstacles in the transition, (2) employer practices in hiring and training youths who do not become college enrollees, (3) the costs and benefits of different types of education for these youths, and (4) the effects of wage levels on their employment opportunities.

This chapter describes what today's researchers have concluded about each of these topics. Two notable themes emerge: (1) few of the available research findings are likely to be accepted without challenge, and (2) if the 1968 symposium participants reconvened today, the same priorities for future research would probably be reaffirmed.

Pathways and Obstacles

A recent comprehensive study (Haggstrom, Blaschke, and Shavelson, 1991; also see U.S. Department of Labor, 1992) identifies three phases in what is referred to as the sorting-out process for American youth: (1) before high school graduation, (2) immediately following graduation, and (3) roughly the period covering the next five years.

The pregraduation phase is important because a substantial number of high school

students work (Yasuda, 1991). Thus, the transition from school to work begins for many students while they are still in high school. Both benefits and costs that arise from this shared activity pattern have been identified. The work experience itself affects other decisions—such as whether to persist to high school graduation, and, if so, whether to continue on to college. Student employment is often viewed as harmful because it reduces the quantity and quality of time spent in traditional academic pursuits and student activities. Critics also bemoan the limited exposure most students have to a high-expectation work setting. They argue that poor work habits are formed early, and then have long-term consequences.

The immediate postgraduation phase reveals student choices among the traditional pathways to employment—select universities and four-year colleges, public community colleges, private career schools, the military, and the search for full-time work. Literally hundreds of combinations of these pathways have been documented (*The Wall Street Journal*, 1990).

The distribution of former students among these postgraduation options is affected by both structural and cyclical events. For example, the 1990-91 recession wiped out a substantial number of job opportunities for newly emerging high school graduates in the United States. Simultaneously, declining state and local government revenues led to rising tuition levels at public four-year and community colleges. Recent high school graduates were therefore offered an unattractive choice— seek admission to an increasingly costly postsecondary program or search for work in a deteriorating market for new hires. Ironically, many of those who chose to continue their education were also forced to seek work to pay the higher fees, thereby further limiting the job opportunities that remained for other recent high school graduates. At the same time, the combination of more applications for admission and budget crises led some schools to adopt more selective admission standards. So, some students who were already devoting more time to earning enough money to be able to enroll in a postsecondary program encountered higher academic expectations as well. The frequency of these occurrences would have been even higher if the 1990-91 recession had taken place at a time when the number of 18-year-olds was not declining nationwide.

These cyclical dynamics coincided with two structural events that also affected the recent graduates' phase two decisions: the end of the Cold War, and Congress's debate of reauthorization of The Higher Education Act. The looming downsizing of the armed forces in the United States is expected to quickly reduce the size, and alter the probable demographic composition, of one traditional pipeline from high school to adult career opportunity: military service. Similarly, the student loan provisions that ultimately emerge in the reauthorization of The Higher Education Act will have important effects on students' need to work while in school. These changes will have predictable effects on the decision to pursue postsecondary studies, the timing of initial enrollment, the intensity and duration of enrollment, and the likelihood of satisfactory completion.

Phase three of this sorting-out process is what many critics lament as the "milling-around period" (Grubb, 1989; Osterman, 1980), which is frequently alleged to limit the nation's international competitiveness. Some of these critics point with envy to the more prevalent patterns of early educational tracking, coupled with readily identifiable career paths, found in other industrialized countries. The evidence (Doeringer, 1991; Osterman, 1988) shows that many young workers in the United States combine education and work in varied patterns, which lengthens the time it takes for completers to finish and increases the percentage of enrollees who never receive a degree. In addition, many of those who do not enroll in postsecondary programs exhibit frequent movement from job to job, often without apparent improvement of circumstances. Evidence is accumulating that this pattern increasingly extends at least into the young student workers' late twenties.

The message from this research literature is clear: The ways in which youths in the United States combine work, education, and other pursuits is very different from those typically found in competing nations. Indeed, the sorting-out process is so varied that it has been difficult for researchers to record reliable evidence of stability in this sorting. One important source of this difficulty has been the poor quality of information that has been available to investigate school-to-work transition issues.

Measurement Problems

The intent of this chapter is to broaden public understanding of what economists and human resource experts have concluded about high school graduates' transition from school to work. A necessary preliminary in pursuing this goal is to warn readers that all of the authors whose research is referenced here are extremely critical of the quality of data that was necessarily relied upon in their investigations. Three particularly important examples of this data quality problem are introduced in this section: the definitions of high school graduate, employer skill requirement, and employee training.

Two major sources of information about the employment and earnings of high school graduates have been the U.S. Census Bureau's monthly current population survey and its decennial census of population. Prior to 1988, the Current Population Survey did not distinguish between exam-certified equivalency and actual high school graduation (Cameron and Heckman, 1991). The General Educational Development test administered by the American Council on Education is the most familiar exam certification option. The 1990 census is the first census of population that distinguishes exam certification from high school graduation. This is important because Cameron and Heckman conclude that exam-certified high school equivalents exhibit the same earnings, job tenure, and unemployment patterns as high school dropouts. The only payoff to exam certification they find is the access this provides to postsecondary admission. Even then, the average earning level of the exam equivalents is below that of actual high school graduates who pursued the same postsecondary programs. This is a controversial and important issue. Many public and private remediation programs encourage, and even require, exam certification.

The difficulty of defining what is meant by high school graduation is increasing with the spread of weighted grading practices in the nation's high schools. This two-tier approach is intended to encourage students to enroll in more challenging courses by offering them an opportunity to earn more grade points in such classes. However, an unintended side-effect of this practice is expected to be that school administrators may now be less concerned about social promotion practices that had been dwindling in response to complaints that such permissiveness was stigmatizing all graduates from affected schools. In the absence of a two-tier grading scheme, it is alleged to be difficult to send a clear signal of student achievement to employers and admissions officers. With a two-tier grading system high achievers will be rewarded by enhanced candidacy for coveted spots in selective postsecondary programs, unless the practice becomes so pervasive that the new exclusivity quickly dissipates, while those who succeed only in less challenging courses will be further stigmatized. This appears to present a particularly pernicious threat to students with special needs, if the necessary resources are not forthcoming to permit them to succeed in upper-tier courses.

It is costly to collect more precise information about students' competency attainment. This cost may be hard to justify if the resulting precision is subsequently ignored by those whose decisions are being targeted: employers and admissions officers. There is substantial evidence that U.S. employers have not sought detailed and reliable information about high school graduates' specific competency achievements (Bishop, 1991 and 1992). Bishop concludes that recorded competence in mathematical reasoning, science, and language arts has had no effect on high school graduates' wage rates for up to eight years following graduation. This raises a crucial public policy question: Will the recent surge of interest in authentic assessment techniques translate into greater enthusiasm in the employer community for using the results of these assessments in hiring decisions? Bishop is skeptical because there is little reliable evidence of a causal link between measures of student performance using the emerging assessment techniques and differences in subsequent job performance. In the absence of such evidence, there is no obvious reason for employers to adopt the new measures.

This daunting conclusion offers a natural transition to the second of the three examples of measurement problems that are encountered in studying school-to-work transition: What is meant by *employer skill requirement*? A lively debate continues about whether the U.S. economy is currently exhibiting net de-skilling or rising skill requirements (Bishop, 1991; Bishop and Carter, 1991; Cappelli, 1991). Unfortunately, given the importance of the policy implications that might be drawn from either conclusion, the data that are available to investigate this issue are atrocious.

At the outset of any consideration of the skill requirements topic, it is essential to distinguish between two fundamentally different sources of change in employers' skill requirements. One source of change is the shifting importance of particular occupations in the overall composition of employment. A second source of change is the redefinition of the skills that are required to perform particular occupations. Even the causal forces that produce such redefinitions are difficult to document. Cappelli concludes, for example, that most of the observed changes in skill requirements in the manufacturing sector of the U.S. economy can probably be traced to changes in personnel management practices, which in turn reflect the continuing decline of organized labor's influence over job definition and control. Many of the changes in the clerical sector have followed the spread of technological innovations.

Some readers are familiar with the recommendations of the Secretary of Labor's Commission on Achieving Necessary Skills, follow the deliberations of the National Advisory Commission on Work-Based Learning, keep informed about progress in carrying out America 2000's National Education Goals, and are aware that the Advisory Panel on Revision of the Dictionary of Occupational Titles has released an interim report. They are urged to be cautious in accepting a particular definition of what is meant by employer skill requirement. At a minimum, it is important to recognize that skill requirements respond in many ways to intervening forces. For instance, requirements escalate during a recession when the pool of available candidates expands, and they are often lowered during prosperous times when it is more difficult to attract or retain employees. This warning is of particular importance when the skill requirements faced by recent high school graduates are being investigated.

A third measurement problem that is encountered by those who study school-to-work transition issues, and that merits discussion in this section, arises in the documentation of work-site training. Abundant evidence shows that number of years of education is a reliable predictor of the amount of work-site training a person will subsequently receive (Tan, Chapman, Peterson, and Booth, 1991), although the size and reliability of such estimates are affected by former students' demographic attributes and other forces. Unfortunately, there is no consensus about the causal reasons for this association. Furthermore, available data that purport to measure work-site training are seriously deficient (Bishop, 1991). Bishop concludes that interpretation of the term "training" is respondent specific and depends on the particular context in which the term is used. Most of what is known about the pervasiveness of work-site training comes from survey sources of information, which typically focus on so-called formal training. The blossoming array of work-site training techniques

and settings heightens the confusion that respondents express in trying to provide accurate information.

The three examples of measurement weakness that have been described in this section—the definitions of high school graduate, employer skill requirements, and work-site training—offer compelling evidence that there is ample opportunity to improve the quality of data to inform the public policy debate about what is "broke" in the nation's school-to-work transition and how to fix it.

There is another urgent need to advance the knowledge base in this dialogue—to educate the public about what Doeringer describes as "turbulence" in the American workplace (Doeringer, 1991). There has been so much hyperbole about Workforce 2000, which focuses on the alleged trends in the demographic mix of the workforce, that dramatic changes in the workplace itself are often overlooked. The next section provides a brief glimpse of some of the fundamental changes that have occurred in the workplace in recent years. It would be futile to attempt to understand the available evidence about recent high school graduates' job-finding success without this understanding.

Employer Hiring and Training Practices in the United States

The workplace issue of the 1990s in the United States is incumbent employee insecurity. Interim evidence from ongoing research programs (Barley, 1991; Doeringer, 1991) documents the decay of employment security. However, what is of more immediate interest here is the understanding that is emerging of new patterns of employer-employee interaction.

A pivotal issue, particularly with respect to recent high school graduates, is how to establish commitment in the workplace (Ghemawat, 1991; Osterman 1988; Ouchi, 1984). Reciprocity—the golden rule—lies at the core of this matter. Consider four different types of management-employee relationship. The most familiar type for most readers is the traditional industrial relations model that features precisely defined job classifications that were frequently codified in collective bargaining agreements. This model applies most commonly to large manufacturing firms, and its relevance for today's high school graduates is fading.

A second type of management-employee relationship defines a quid pro quo between employer and employee. In this case, employees agree to accept repeated reassignment among particular jobs within a company. In return, a company offers a guarantee of employment for a specified interval. The so-called lifetime employment contract has also receded from recent high school graduates' grasp in the United States. (Its pervasiveness in other countries has never been as sweeping as many people apparently believe.)

A third type of employer-employee relationship is termed employment-at-will. Here, there is a clear understanding that neither party has any commitment to the other. Until recently, this type of relationship was typically seen in small business personnel practices. However, today it has become more common in large business settings as well. Critics point out that the short-term management flexibility and cost-cutting benefits of this approach will be paid for in the future when the productivity consequences of training deficiencies and low employee morale become more apparent. The growing prevalence of so-called contingent worker arrangements (e.g., outsourcing, hiring of contract employees, and reliance on temporary employees) is one highly visible manifestation of this trend.

A fourth type of management-employee relationship has begun to appear in larger firms in the United States. Employees are told that they will be given extended job rights. What this means in typical practice is that employees are assured that the training they receive is general enough that they will be employable somewhere, even if the company itself cannot guarantee job security. Cynics charge that in many cases this will turn out to be an empty promise that cost the employer nothing. Enthusiasts counter that this approach exemplifies what has long been sought in the United States—a demonstration of corporate responsibility for employees' well-being that is not totally driven by a particular company's profit motive. Regardless, today's high school

graduates will be affected by this emerging business practice.

Together, these models of management-employee relationships in the United States should alert readers to the complex and dynamic nature of the personnel practices that future high school graduates will encounter. The diversity and instability that is revealed must be reflected in strategic decisions about how the education community—public and private, secondary and postsecondary—should respond to these events. One example must suffice here. Barley's path-breaking research program is documenting a fundamental change in traditional superior-subordinate legitimacy within some work units (Barley, 1991). Historically, executives and supervisors usually knew how to perform the work of their subordinates, which gave them legitimacy in monitoring the behavior of their employee. Increasingly, Barley finds, technicians have become so specialized—in other words, the occupational mix has become so fragmented—that managers can no longer step in to perform the jobs of those they supervise. One consequence of this is an evolving empowerment of an entire strata of workers, many of whom are high school graduates who have not subsequently received baccalaureate degrees. This is just one illustration of changes in the pathways between school and work.

A final observation about current activities that will affect future high school graduates focuses on spreading advocacy for broader youth apprenticeship opportunities in the United States (Lerman and Pouncy, 1990; Nothdurft, 1990; Sheets, 1991). The Office of Work-Based Learning in the Employment and Training Administration of the U.S. Department of Labor is a focal point of this advocacy, which involves a large number of affiliated organizations. The core issue is skill standards and how to instill them in today's youth in the United States. Ironically, many of those in already apprenticed occupations oppose the adoption of the term *apprenticeship* to describe a broad range of techniques for instilling and documenting skill competency. Similarly, many members of the vocational-technical education community express skepticism about the motives of the advocates of this broadening, while offering case-examples of such certification already being provided through traditional vocational-technical education auspices. Regardless of how this movement evolves, future high school graduates will have more opportunities to acquire immediately applicable skill competencies.

An immediate and critically important conclusion from this brief review of current research findings is that educational organization, administration, and policy programs must aggressively pursue ways to become and remain aware of the implications these dynamics have for their own curricula and research agendas.

Up to this point, attention has been limited to the dynamic nature of the workplace settings that high school graduates have encountered in the recent past and are certain to face in the near future. This review of what recent research has revealed has been accompanied by repeated warnings that the data that have been available to investigate these issues are far from satisfactory for the intended applications. The next section steps back to examine what can be said about the actual employment and earnings of high school graduates in the United States.

The Employment and Earnings of High School Graduates

It is difficult to keep up with the most recent research on this topic (Bishop, 1992; Blackburn, Bloom, and Freeman, 1991; Kosters, 1991). Blackburn, Bloom, and Freeman conclude from a comparison of 1980 and 1989 current population survey data that the economic well-being of less educated adults declined relative to that of their more educated counterparts. The emphasis here is on the phrase "declined relative to." Education mattered in the 1980s—it created a widening gap between more- and less-educated workers. However, the fortunes of members of particular demographic groups were affected by different forces. Individuals' economic well-being depends on many factors in addition to education: where they live; what, if any, industry attachment they have established; what occupation-specific competencies they have developed; whether they are a union member;

whether they have dependents, are dependent themselves, share in another person's earnings, enjoy non-wage benefit coverage, or have access to non-earnings sources of income; and, unfortunately, whether they are a man or woman, white or of color, young or old, or physically or mentality challenged. In other words, it is dangerous to generalize about the employment and earnings of high school graduates per se. For instance, Blackburn, Bloom, and Freeman found that the growing earnings advantage enjoyed by more-educated full-time workers was most pronounced for whites. At the same time, less-educated blacks appear to have suffered more of their relative loss of economic well-being from a declining employment rate compared to their more-educated counterparts. These differences highlight an important issue regarding high school graduates' employment opportunities and incentives. There are three components in any recorded annual earnings figure: (1) full-time versus part-time employment; (2) year-round versus seasonal employment; and (3) the dollar amount received for each time-unit that is worked. More-educated white workers appear to have benefited more from component (3) during the 1980s, while more-educated blacks benefited more from (1) and (2).

When data for combined race-gender groupings are examined, these three authors found that less-educated white women and men suffered losses in the real purchasing power of full-time annual earnings between 1979 and 1988, with women incurring a smaller deterioration; that more-educated white women and men enjoyed a modest increase in economic well-being, with women realizing a greater improvement than men; that young (ages 25-34) black male high school graduates and college graduates both suffered losses in economic well-being relative to their high school dropout counterparts; and that black women who were high school graduates only also suffered a relative deterioration of position when compared to their high school dropout counterparts. Again, the reasons given for these disparate patterns are complex, and they involve geographic location, industry affiliation, occupational attachment, and union membership, among other factors.

Blackburn, Bloom, and Freeman also provide a thorough treatment of the responsiveness of postsecondary enrollment patterns to changes in occupation-specific earnings trends and the cost of attending school. The authors conclude that there is substantial evidence that high school graduates are very sensitive to changes in each of these determinants of their expected net reward from pursuing postsecondary studies in general, and a particular major once enrolled.

The Blackburn, Bloom, and Freeman conclusions provide one more reason why advice givers must remain alert to recent and expected changes in the flow of high school graduates into the immediate post-graduation decision phase, and to changes in the level and mix of employment opportunities that await those who decide to seek immediate employment. A high school graduate's decisions regarding whether to enroll in a postsecondary program, as well as whether to seek work, are interdependent and affected by demographic factors.

This is an appropriate place to introduce what is described as "a curious hypothesis about supply" (Rosen, 1991), which illustrates how difficult it is to distill reliable evidence of causal ties between educational attainment and subsequent earnings. Rosen speculates that Bishop's finding that there is no apparent short-term labor market reward awaiting high school students who take more challenging courses might be explained by the fact that more-able students who are enrolled in postsecondary programs temporarily hold the same types of jobs as those held by their less-able high school classmates who did not subsequently enroll in a postsecondary program. A test of this hypothesis would require controlling for ability in statistical analyses of the relationship between earnings and previous educational competency attainment. There is certainly no danger of depleting the inventory of interesting and important questions about how high school graduates fare in the workplace (Taubman, 1991).

Research on the employment and earnings outcomes of vocational-technical education programs has been particularly active in the past year (Grubb, 1991; Meyer, 1991).

Grubb investigated the sub-baccalaureate postsecondary program topic, examining the relative rewards for young men and women who graduate from high school and then complete postsecondary certificate or associate degree programs, or enter but do not complete a four-year degree program. Consistent with what has been said up to this point, Grubb concludes that it is difficult to generalize. Women appear at first to receive a differential return from receiving a business or technical certificate relative to their high school graduate classmates who did not continue on to a postsecondary program. Both male and female students appear at first to have benefited from completion of a vocational associate degree program, and women also realized a return from academic associate degree completion. However, in a more sophisticated analysis that took subsequent employment and training into account, these independent advantages over their high-school-graduate-only counterparts, who exhibit similar employment and training profiles, disappeared! Grubb concludes from this that the sub-baccalaureate certificates and degrees are serving as one pathway to gain access to subsequent packages of employment and training, while other high school graduates have followed a different route to the same end. Again, the data that support this conclusion leave much to be desired, as Grubb acknowledges. However, the reported findings reinforce the point that there are multiple pathways, and obstacles, that face high school graduates in the school-to-work transition.

Meyer reports evidence of a serious underutilization of competencies learned in high school vocational-technical education programs, at least in the early years of former students' subsequent work histories. His recommendation for more refined research of this type is particularly compelling because of the nature of the policy options that follow from this conclusion. If this finding is upheld in future research, then either more attention needs to be given to improving the quality of match between student competencies and employer skill requirements, or the high school curriculum needs to be revised to de-emphasize the development of occupation-specific competencies. Ironically, the current frenzy of activity that is being devoted to each of these modifications will increase the difficulty of ultimately deciding which, if either, makes a difference in how high school graduates fare in the workplace.

The quality of research that has investigated race-gender differences in access to employer-provided training is high (Berlin and Sum, 1988; Chiswick, 1988; Lynch, 1988). Chiswick focuses on differences in the original motivation for international migration to the United States by particular immigrant populations. He concludes, for example, that Mexican migration is most accurately described as being motivated by economic considerations, while Cuban migration since 1959 has been largely motivated by political factors, and Puerto Rican migration patterns exhibit a recurring to-and-fro regularity. This alerts us to the need to incorporate international considerations into investigations of the sorting-out process of high school graduates in the United States, since a rising percentage of these graduates are first- and second-generation immigrants from other nations. Cultural, language, and goal differences will introduce new complexities into future research designs.

Berlin and Sum demonstrate the interdependency of household poverty and students' competency attainment in school. The evidence is compelling that students who live in poor households are more likely to perform less well than their more advantaged classmates on standardized tests. This, in turn, sets into motion well known cycles of intergenerational dependency. More recently, as most of the states have introduced statewide performance measurement and performance standards systems, expected responses are appearing in how schools treat low-achievers. A common response to special needs students is to exclude them from the measurement process. While there are legitimate reasons for considering this approach, such as concerns about untoward effects on the students' self-esteem, there are equally compelling reasons to guard against further exclusion and stigmatization of these students. Because employability is a common student goal, it is very important that the necessary resources be made available to assure that special needs students, too, meet the employer community's skill requirements. Insulating these students from competitive standards and pressure is a self-serving excuse, not a favor. The timing to make the necessary commitment at the state and local level is ideal. Budgets have been pared to unprecedented levels, at least in terms of recent memory, which means that as prosperity returns and tax revenues rise again there will be new opportunities to allocate additional resources to this deserving population.

Lynch documents how young women who enter employment following high school graduation continue to be denied access to the most attractive on-the-job training opportunities, which is the dominant pathway to future promotion, earnings improvement, and career opportunity and security. As any walk through a production facility indicates, this is not a matter of never gaining access, but rather a matter of relative opportunity at the outset combined with treatment during the early stages following hiring. It is particularly important for young women who are still in high school to have access to accurate information about current management-employee practices, so they can make informed decisions about their postsecondary years.

The focus of the previous paragraphs has been on the traditional study of education-earnings and education-subsequent training relationships. This narrow perspective must be balanced by an explicit recognition of the many nonmarket impacts that high school graduation may have on the graduates themselves and on the nation (Haveman and Wolfe, 1984). These authors catalog 20 "channels of impact" of schooling, including direct enhancement of a student's own productivity as just one of the 20 impacts. Among the other impacts listed are development of do-it-yourself competencies; intra-family impacts, including exposure to spousal candidates and what some economists refer to as child quality; health consciousness; consumer choice effectiveness; crime reduction; technological creativity; charitable giving; and social cohesion.

So far, this chapter has addressed pathways and obstacles, measurement problems, employer hiring and training practices, and employment and earnings outcomes. In the next section, a highly contentious topic is discussed: the impact of minimum wage laws on high school graduates' employment opportunity.

Minimum Wage Laws and Employment Opportunity for Youths

Although controversial, the dominant view has long been that an increase in the minimum wage level reduces young people's employment opportunities by "pricing them out of the market." What this generally means is that the higher wage is not offset by an expected increase in employee productivity. The higher cost cannot be justified, which results in employees being fired or not hired in the first place. Minimum wage levels have typically risen during prosperous (i.e., inflationary) periods, which has often meant that the increased wage level coincided with continued growth in the employment of affected workers. This has introduced substantial confusion into the debate among often self-interested parties who either advocated or opposed minimum wage legislation.

Federal minimum wage legislation that took effect in 1990 provided for payment of a sub-minimum wage to teenage workers for up to six months (Katz and Krueger, 1990). Since 1961, the Federal Fair Labor Standards Act has permitted payment of a sub-minimum wage to full-time students. In a limited case study of the impact of the new law, Katz and Krueger found very little use being made of the new opportunity to pay a lower wage. They speculate that this may be attributable to factors such as the importance of maintaining stability of wage levels within a company's personnel mix, horizontal equity considerations, and effort considerations—what is often called the psychological effort contract.

Similar findings are reported from a study of a recent increase in California's state-imposed minimum wage level (Card, 1990). Card found that the teenage employment-population ratio increased in California after the minimum wage law went into effect. Teenagers' labor force participation increased and teenage unemployment fell slightly. Card concludes that these trends cannot be explained by other obvious changes in labor market conditions, so he concludes that they represent an anomaly that cannot be explained within the traditional framework.

A more recent paper offers a possible explanation for what Katz and Krueger, and Card, observed (Rebitzer and Taylor, 1991). These authors claim that the reported findings are not counter-intuitive if the incumbent teenage workers are seen as being enticed by the new higher wage level to engage in less shirking of expected employee responsibilities. This behavioral response is not suggested to arise from loyalty or reciprocity, but rather from simple self-interest—the loss that would result from being fired for poor performance is now higher. More responsible employees do not require as much supervision, which permits affected employers to reduce management costs. This, in turn, frees up resources to hire additional teenage workers. Together, these three recent papers demonstrate that what many have traditionally accepted as a transparent open-and-shut case of cause and effect may be far from obvious. Stay tuned.

Conclusions

This chapter has reviewed the economist's perspective on what is known about high school graduates' experiences in finding jobs. Dynamic workforce and workplace conditions combine with new theories and new data sources to offer continuous challenges to previously held views about the pathways and obstacles that high school graduates encounter in making the transition from school to work.

While diversity of opportunity and outcome have been highlighted throughout the chapter, and caution has repeatedly been urged in acting on often tenuous evidence of cause-and-effect, there is reason for optimism. Exciting research programs are underway. New data sources are becoming available. Data processing costs continue to fall. Together, these promise to further the relentless advance of knowledge about high school graduates decisions and their consequences. The only question is whether these factors are adequate to keep up with the pace of institutional change.

References

Barley, S. R. (1991). *The new crafts: On the technization of the workforce and the occupationalization of firms.* Philadelphia: National Center on the Educational Quality of the Workforce, University of Pennsylvania.

Berlin, G., & Sum, A. (1988). *Toward a more perfect union: Basic skills, poor families, and our economic future.* New York: The Ford Foundation.

Bishop, J. (1991). *A program of research on the role of employer training in ameliorating skill shortages and enhancing productivity and competitiveness.* Philadelphia: National Center on the Educational Quality of the Workforce, University of Pennsylvania.

Bishop, J. (1992). Workforce preparedness (Working Paper 92-04). Philadelphia: National Center on the Educational Quality of the Workforce, University of Pennsylvania.

Bishop, J., & Carter, S. (1991, Fall). The worsening shortage of college graduate workers. *Educational Evaluation and Policy Analysis.*

Blackburn, M. L., Bloom, D. E., & Freeman, R. B. (1991). Changes in earnings differentials in the 1980s: Concordance, convergence, causes, and consequences (Working Paper No. 3901). Cambridge, MA: National Bureau of Economic Research.

Cameron, S. V., & Heckman, J. J. (1991). The nonequivalence of high school equivalents (Working Paper No. 3804). Cambridge, MA: National Bureau of Economic Research.

Cappelli, P. (1991). *Are skill requirements rising? Evidence from production and clerical jobs.* Philadelphia: National Center on the Educational Quality of the Workforce, University of Pennsylvania.

Card, D. (1990). Minimum wages and the teenage labor market: A case study of California, 1987-89. *Proceedings of the 1990 Annual Meeting of the Industrial Relations Research Association* (pp. 234-242).

Chiswick, B. R. (1988, November). Hispanic men: divergent paths in the U.S. labor market. *Monthly Labor Review, 111* (11), 32-34.

Doeringer, P. B. (Ed.). (1991). *Turbulence in the American workplace.* New York: Oxford University Press.

Ghemawat, P. (1991). *Commitment: The dynamic of strategy.* New York: The Free Press.

Grubb, W. N. (1989). *Access, achievement, completion, and "milling around" in postsecondary vocational education.* Berkeley, CA: MPR Associates.

Grubb, W. N. (1992). Postsecondary vocational education and the sub-baccalaureate labor market: New evidence on economic returns. *Economics of Education Review, 11*(3), 225-248.

Haggstrom, G. W., Blaschke, T. J., & Shavelson, R. J. (1991). *After high school, then what? A look at the postsecondary sorting-out process for American youth.* Santa Monica, CA: Rand.

Harbison, F. H. (ed.). (1968). *The transition from school to work.* Princeton, NJ: Industrial Relations Section, Princeton University.

Haveman, R. H., & Wolfe, B. L. (1984, Summer). Schooling and economic well-being: The role of nonmarket effects. *The Journal of Human Resources, 19* (3), 377-407.

Katz, L. F., & Krueger, A. B. (1990). The effect of the new minimum wage law on a low-wage labor market. *Proceedings of the 1990 Annual Meeting of the Industrial Relations Research Association.* (pp. 254-265).

Kosters, M. H. (Ed.) (1991). *Workers and their wages: Changing patterns in the United States.* Washington, DC: American Enterprise Institute Press.

Lerman, R. I., & Pouncy, H. (1990, Fall). The compelling case for youth apprenticeships. *The Public Interest, 101,* 62-77.

Lynch, L. (1988). Race and gender differences in private-sector training for young workers. *Proceedings of the 1988 Annual Meeting of the Industrial Relations Research Association.* (pp. 557-565).

Meyer, R. H. (1991). The efficiency of specific occupational training. (Chapter 3 of an unpublished manuscript). Madison, WI: Economics Department, University of Wisconsin-Madison.

Nothdurft, W. E. (1990). *Youth apprenticeship, American style: A strategy for expanding school and career opportunities.* Somerville, MA: Jobs for the Future, Inc.

Osterman, P. (1980). *Getting started: The youth labor market.* Cambridge, MA: MIT Press.

Osterman, P. (1988). *Employment futures: Reorganization, dislocation, and public policy.* New York: Oxford University Press.

Ouchi, W. (1984). *The M-form society.* Reading, MA: Addison-Wesley Publishing Company.

Rebitzer, J. B., & Taylor, L. J. (1991). The consequences of minimum wage laws: Some new theoretical ideas (Working Paper No. 3877). Cambridge, MA: National Bureau of Economic Research.

Rosen, S. (1991). A curious hypothesis about supply. In M. H. Kosters (Ed.), *Workers and their wages: Changing patterns in the United States.* Washington, DC: American Enterprise Institute Press.

Sheets, R. G. (1991). *Building a world-class front-line workforce: The need for occupational skill standards in state workforce preparation programs.* Philadelphia: National Center on the Educational Quality of the Workforce, University of Pennsylvania.

Some young people take the great circle route. (November 29, 1990). *The Wall Street Journal,* p. B-1.

Tan, H., Chapman, B., Peterson, C., & Booth, A. (1991). *Youth training in the United States, Britain, and Australia.* Santa Monica, CA: Rand.

Taubman, P. (1991). *Report of the Conference on the Rate of Return on Education.* Philadelphia: National Center on the Educational Quality of the Workforce, University of Pennsylvania.

U.S. Department of Labor. (1992). Dilemmas in youth employment programming: Findings from the Youth Research and Technical Assistance Project (Research and Evaluation Report Series 92-C). Two volumes. Washington, DC: Employment and Training Division.

Yasuda, K. E., Sr. (1991). *The school-to-work transition: Third report.* Concord, NH: New Hampshire Department of Employment Security.

8

The Effects
of Part-Time Work Experience
on High School Students*

Bassem N. Kablaoui and Albert J. Pautler, Jr.

The incidence of youth employment while still in high school has increased steadily, particularly over the last decade. The Office of the President's *Employment and Training Report* (1982) states that, in 1982, 44 percent of males and 41 percent of females aged 16 to 17 years participated in the labor force while still attending high school. More recently, the *Earning and Learning Report,* conducted by the National Assessment of Educational Progress [NAEP] (1989), found in its *National Report Card* that 54 percent of eleventh-grade students were employed at least part-time, and early returns of this report for 1988 indicated that 66 percent of high school seniors were working while still in school. This increasing trend of student employment is of growing concern for educators and lay people alike, as reflected in recent headlines of major newspapers such as *USA Today, The Wall Street Journal, The Christian Science Monitor,* and *The Buffalo News*: "Students' Jobs Cut School Activities," "Learning in the Market Place," and "Should Kids Work Flipping Burgers?"

Ironically, this trend of increasing student employment comes at a time when the nation is seeking ways to raise the educational standards of its system (Bennett, 1988; National Commission on Excellence in Education Report, 1983). This situation has forced educators, parents, and researchers to warn that holding a job while still in school could adversely affect students' academic and personal life, by distracting them from school-related activities and possibly causing them to misplace priorities or exhibit delinquent behavior. Studies on this subject often produce conflicting findings, however, and for this reason the related literature will be reviewed as part of this chapter.

For this review, over 1,700 items were found in ERIC and other sources under the subjects of: "academic achievement," "student employment," "high school employment," "part-time employment," "work experience," and "student achievement." Of this list, approximately 50 microfiche records, 200 journal articles, 5 dissertations, and 20 books were consulted. Of these, 30 microfiches, 10 articles, 2 dissertations, and 3 books directly addressed the relationship between employment and academic achievement for students in grades 9 through 12 in the last 10 years.

How Many Students Work?

The American phenomenon of high school students embracing both learning and earning has been increasing steadily in the last 30 years

*Permission to use The Effects of Part-Time Work Experience on High School Students by Bassem N. Kablaoui and Albert J. Pautler granted by Human Services Press. The work first appeared in the Journal of Career Development, Vol. 17, No. 3, Spring 1991.

(Table 1). This is partly in response to the rather widely held view that American students are inadequately prepared for employment, advocating improving the transition from school to the working environment (Ford Foundation, 1983; National Commission on the Reform of Secondary Education, 1973; Carnegie Council on Policy Studies in Higher Education, 1980; National Commission on Youth, 1980; National Panel on High School and Adolescent Education, 1976; President's Science Advisory Committee, 1974). These studies argued for increasing the exposure of students to the world of work through a variety of programs, on the assumption that work contributes to the development of attitudes and knowledge that are important to success in the adult labor market, and that it facilitates the transition to adulthood.

A listing of the exact figures on the percentage of students in various categories who work during high school is not possible here be-cause of the asymmetries in data collection between studies. However, the trends across the data from 1953 to 1986, adapted from the *Earning and Learning Report* (1989), which were computed from the *Handbook of Labor Statistics*, show that such employment has been increasing since 1953 and has become commonplace for many students (however, note the decrease among males in 1986 in Table 1).

Several recent surveys suggest that the percentage of student employment is actually underestimated by the figures in Table 1 (Lewin-Epstein, 1981). These surveys obtained their information via questionnaires given to the students themselves, rather than to employers or parents (Greenberger and Steinberg, 1986).

As indicated in Table 2, which combines information taken from studies undertaken in the 1980s and in various regions of the country, the percentage of high school students

Table 1—Percentage of 16- and 17-Year-Old Students Working: 1953-1986

Year	Male	Female
1953	27	17
1960	30	20
1970	32	28
1980	35	34
1986	32	35

This table was adapted from Table 17 of the *Earning and Learning Report* 1989. These data for 1953-1986 were computed from the *Handbook of Labor Statistics,* U.S. Bureau of Labor Statistics.

Table 2—Percentage of Students Employed

Study	Year	Location	Grade	Sample Size	Employed
Greenberger	1980	California	10th-11th	531	40
Lewin-Epstein	1981	National	10th & 12th	58270	26.5
Berryman	1982	Georgia	9th-12th	1277	34.3
Lewis	1983	National	10th & 12th	2857	52
Gottfredson	1984	17 cities	9th-12th	2000	70
Green & Jacquess	1984	Oklahoma	11th	477	58
McNeil	1984	Wisconsin	11th & 12th	1577	60
Meyer	1985	Wash. St.	10th-12th	2787	33.3
Gordan	1985	National	12th	2800	75

who were employed ranged from 26.5 percent (Lewin-Epstein, 1981) to 75 percent (Gordon, 1985). The former study surveyed secondary students in 14 urban and suburban Georgia high schools, and the latter was based on data from the 1979 *National Longitudinal Survey of Youth Labor Market Experience*. From the information in these two tables, one can safely conclude that employment is indeed commonplace among high school students and appears to be an integral component of adolescent life across the nation.

Frequency of Employment by Gender

The analysis of the labor market of in-school students revealed that the proportion of female students' participation in the work force has increased more than males'. For example, the number of employed 16-year-old students increased between 1940 to 1970 six-fold among males but eleven-fold for females (Greenberger & Steinberg, 1980; NAEP, 1989).

However, throughout the 1980s, which is the period on which the majority of the relevant studies focused, the actual numbers of male and female students employed may have differed by only a few percentage points, although there are many discrepancies in this regard in the literature. For example, as illustrated in Table 3, females were often found to be more frequently employed than males (Berryman & Schneider, 1982; NAEP, 1989; Schill, McGartin, & Meyer, 1985), the numbers varying from 42.5 to 54 percent for female students and from 46.0 to 57.5 for males. In contrast, other studies found that males were employed significantly more often than fe-

males (Gade & Peterson, 1980; Greenberger & Steinberg, 1980; McNeil, 1984). In averaging the findings of the above studies one finds that approximately 50.2 percent of female students worked during high school, while the figure is 49.8 percent for males. Note that these values are very similar to those obtained in the study by Jaquess (1984).

However, it is important to note that the results found in the report *High School and Beyond* (Lewin-Epstein, 1981) stand in great contrast to those mentioned above. This study encompassed a nationwide sample of approximately 60,000 high school sophomores and seniors. The investigators found that 75 percent of 16- to 17-year-old males and 68 percent of females were participating in the labor force. In contrast, another study, generated by the Bureau of Labor Statistics (Office of the President, 1982) for the same year, found that 44 percent of female students and 41 percent of males were employed.

Discrepancies in the data may be attributed to students self-reporting employment, some of which may well be "off the books" and not included in the Bureau of Labor Statistics. Further, it is possible that the conflicts in the values for student employment by gender occurred because some data contained divergent trends among different ethnic groups. The next section addresses that issue.

Employment Examined by Race

Student employment appears to be common across many ethnic groups. However, every study revealed that white students are more likely to participate in the labor force than Hispanics and blacks; indeed, the percentage

Table 3—Percentage of Students Employed by Gender

Author	Females	Males
Lewin-Epstein	32	43
Greenberger & Steinberg	42.5	57.5
Berryman & Schneider	52.9	47.1
Schill, McCartin & Meyer	54	46
Gade & Peterson	48.4	51.6
Barton (NEAP)	53	47
McNeil	51.2	48.8
Green & Jacquess	49.7	50.3
Average	50.24	49.76

of white students who work is roughly twice that of Hispanics and blacks (Borus, 1983; D'Amico, 1984; Gottfredson, 1984; Lewin-Epstein, 1981).

Black and Hispanic males apparently had more difficulty obtaining employment than white males, blacks being employed at the lowest rate (Borus, 1983). Hispanic males were employed relatively more often. These trends were also observed for females, whites again having the highest employment rate. However, Hispanic females experienced the lowest labor force participation rate, as found in the 1979 study of the *National Longitudinal Survey of Youth Labor Market Experience* (Borus, 1983). Nevertheless, it is likely that these values are not truly representative, in that the majority of the studies discussed here took place in small, white-dominated school districts.

The Contribution of Socioeconomic Status

Large numbers of students at all income and educational levels are involved in the work experience. However, Lewin-Epstein (1981) suggested that middle-income youths are more likely to participate in the workforce than are upper- or lower-income students. This finding is supported by that of Lewis, Gardner, and Seita (1983), whose data indicated that 60 percent of low-income students were employed compared with 73 percent of middle-income youths. *The Youth Employment: Its Relationship to Academic and Family Variables* study (Schill et al., 1985) concurred with these reports, finding that working students were more likely to be from higher-income families and have a parent who is employed in a higher-status occupation. Interestingly, both Lewis and col-

leagues (1983) and Gade and Peterson (1980) further found that the rate of participation in the workforce for females increased with socioeconomic status.

What Types of Jobs Are Students Taking?

Employed high school students were found to work in a wide variety of occupations. By far, the majority of these jobs required only low skill levels, such as in-service, labor, sales, or clerical positions (Berryman & Schneider, 1982; Borman, 1986; Jaquess, 1984; Lewis et al., 1983; Meyer, 1987). Perrone and colleagues, in their study entitled *Secondary School Students and Employment* (1981), surveyed 2,055 junior and senior high school students from four schools in the Grand Forks and Fargo, North Dakota, public school systems. They found that 41.4 percent of the employed students worked in food service, 17.8 percent in sales, 9.9 percent in supermarkets, and 6 percent in clerical positions; these findings are similar to those of other studies listed in Table 4.

As revealed here, more than 50 percent of high school students were employed in food service and retail sales (Berryman & Schneider, 1982; Greenberger & Steinberg, 1986; Jaquess, 1984; McNeil, 1984; Meyer, 1987; Perrone et al., 1981).

Interestingly, employment patterns with regard to job type differ between males and females, following traditional value systems. Female students held primarily sales, clerical, and health-related positions, whereas males had a tendency to dominate food service, labor, repair, and custodial jobs (Perrone et al., 1981; Borus, 1983; McNeil, 1984).

Table 4—Job Occupation of High School Students

Study	Food	Retail	Clerical	Farm	Labor	Skill	SupMkt	Custodial
McNeil	41	18	6.6	4	9.6	4.1		
Greenberger	33	13	9	4	15	6		
Perrone	41.4	17.8	6				9.9	8.6
Berryman	30	10						
Jaquess	30	36	19					
Meyer	49.9	8.8	8					

The Number of Hours Worked by Students

In general, the majority of studies found that employment during high school adversely affected academic achievement when the numbers of hours worked exceeded 20 (Steinberg, Greenberger, Gorduque, & Ruggiero, 1982; Wirtz, Rohbeck, Charner, & Fraser, 1987; see also Berryman & Schneider, 1982; Greenberger & Steinberg, 1981, 1986). In an effort to correct this problem, a number of states are attempting to enact laws which somewhat restrict the amount of time that students can legally work. For example, the Tennessee Senate passed a bill which prohibits high school students from working after 10 P.M. (Ruthman, 1989), and the Minnesota House of Representatives has passed a similar measure barring them from working past 11 P.M. Furthermore, in May 1989, Governor Cuomo of New York acknowledged that work experience can be valuable, and that America's youth are an important labor pool (Lawrence, 1989). However, he added that "it would be very short-sighted for New York to have any child labor policies that limit our young peoples' educational achievement." He also proposed a plan to limit, to 28 hours per week, the number of hours that 16- to 17-year-old students could work.

If high school employment is indeed one cause of lower academic achievement, one would expect a correlation between the number of hours worked and the decrease in student performance. In order to assess whether this relationship exists, it is first necessary to examine the number of hours typically worked by high school students. (See Table 5 below.)

According to the survey, *High School and Beyond* (Lewin-Epstein, 1981), the average number of hours worked by sophomore females and males were 10.5 and 14.8 per week, respectively. Comparable figures for senior females and males were 17.8 and 21.1, respectively. Steinberg and colleagues' study, performed in Orange County, California, found that the average number of hours worked were between 20 and 24 (Steinberg et al., 1982). Using cross-sectional data, they found that employment depressed school grades for tenth and eleventh graders, who worked, respectively, more than 14 and 19 hours per week.

Because several researchers found that more than 15 or 20 hours of work per week was the point at which working adversely affected academic achievement, the data from Table 5 were broken down in Table 6 to show the percentage of students who worked more than 15 and 20 hours per week. These numbers ranged from 26 percent (Lewin-Epstein, 1981) to 89 percent (Jaquess, 1984). On the average, males worked more hours than females (Lewin-Epstein, 1981; NAEP, 1989; Perrone et al., 1981), and white males worked fewer hours than blacks. Hispanics worked the most (Borus, 1983; NAEP, 1989).

Relatively few studies examined the question of the typical hourly salary for high school students. Perrone and colleagues' study (1981), conducted in North Dakota, revealed that 73 percent of those working were making less than $3.00 per hour. McNeil (1984) found

Percentage of Students Who Work a Given Number of Hours Per Week

Hours Worked/Week/Study	Hours Worked/Week					
	11-15	16-20	21-25	26-30	31-35	36+
McNeil	22%	26%	15%	7%	0	0
Perrone	18%	33%	30%	7%	0	0
Berryman	58%	0	0	0	40%	2%
Barton	9%	12%	8%	7%	3%	0
Jacquess	0	21%	27%	26%	15%	0
Squires	0	20%	12%	7%	0	12%
Lewin-Epstein	33%	20%	0	0	0	6%

that 65.5 percent of her sample made be-tween $3.00 and $3.50 per hour, with 6 per-cent earning more than $4.50 per hour. In general, males were paid more than females (Lewin-Epstein, 1981; Lewis et al., 1983; McNeil, 1984; Perrone et al., 1981; Shapiro, 1983).

Motivations for Working During High School

Some have suggested that possible benefits of working during high school are the building of character and the learning of budgeting and handling money (Cole, 1980). It is also likely that some of the students are in dire financial need and work to help support a family. Several studies examined the question of why students work, with the hope of understanding why this trend is on the rise, and the results of these studies are examined below.

The major reasons for employment among high school students were found to be, in the order of decreasing priority: (1) to make money for pleasurable pastimes (Berryman & Schneider, 1981; Borus, 1983; McNeil, 1984; Perrone et al., 1981; Wirtz et al., 1987), (2) to support a family (Berryman & Schneider 1982; Perrone et al., 1981; Wirtz et al., 1987), (3) to learn skills (Wirtz et al., 1987), (4) for something to do with extra time (Perrone et al., 1981), and (5) to save for college (Perrone et al., 1981). It was interesting that the great majority of the students said that their earned money was spent on leisure activities, such as dates, cars, luxury items, and so forth (Berryman & Schneider, 1982; McNeil, 1984; Perrone et al., 1981; Wirtz et al., 1987). Mary Bicouvatien (Lawrence, 1989, p. 9), national Teacher of the Year in 1989, asked her students to put a

priority on their schoolwork. "They are very busy people," she said. "What I find deplorable many times is they work school into the business schedule rather than fit business into the school schedule."

The Effects of Student Employment

In the last few years, numerous researchers have attempted to assess the costs and benefits of student employment. Some investigated the possible adverse effects of student employment, while others looked at the positive features, especially with regard to the transition from school to the work environment. Still others dealt with factors related to academic achievement among employed high school students. These findings are summarized in Table 7.

One rather consistent finding emerged regarding an often negative relationship between a student's grade point average and employment. In a study of four schools in Orange County, California, entitled "High School Students in the Labor Force: Some Costs and Benefits of Schooling and Learning" (Steinberg et al., 1982), it was found that tenth graders who worked more than 15 hours per week and eleventh graders working more than 20 hours per week had significantly lower grades than students who worked fewer hours (see also Greenberger & Steinberg, 1981; Schill et al., 1985; Squires, 1983; Wirtz et al., 1987). Moreover, Mortimer and Finch (1986) showed that boys who worked during the tenth, eleventh, and twelfth grades tended to also have lower grades as ninth graders—that is, before they started working more hours. However, a longitudinal study failed to confirm this effect of employment on academic achievement (Steinberg,

Table 6—Percentage of Students Who Work More than 15 and 20 Hours Per Week

Study	15+	20+
McNeil	48%	22%
Perrone	67%	37%
Berryman	0	42%
Barton (NAEP)	30%	18%
Jacquess	89%	68%
Squires	51%	31%

Greenberger, Gorduque, Ruggiero & Vaux, 1982).

Some other studies of the relationship between student work and school performance showed that employment generally had no adverse effects on school performance. D'Amico (1984), for example, examined data from the National Longitudinal Survey of the Labor Market Experience of Youth, funded by the U.S. Department of Labor. Five thousand high school students were selected from a national sample of 12,000 youths in 1979. D'Amico investi-gated the employment records of these students while they were in school, from 1979 to 1982, and summarized his conclusions as follows:

> Most importantly, whatever constraints high school employment puts on school involvement, no adverse effects for either work intensity variable emerged in the class rank equations for any race/sex group. Working students simply do not appear to have impaired academic achievement in these data. (D'Amico, 1984, p. 159)

Table 7—Negative and Positive Effects of Student Employment

Negative Effects	Study
Lower grades	Greenberger et al., Wirtz et al., Squires, Mortimer and Finch
Less time devoted to homework and extracurricular activities	Greenberger et al., Jacquess, D'Amico, McNeil, Perrone, Lewin-Epstein, and Hotchkiss
Increased rate of dropping out	D'Amico and Shapiro
Increased delinquent behavior (such as smoking, drinking, and stealing)	Greenberger et al., D'Amico, Berryman and Schneider, Lewis et al., Perrone et al., and McNeil
Weakened ties with family and friends	Greenberger et al.
Cynical attitudes developed toward work	Greenberger et al., Hotchkiss
Academic conflicts created with teachers	Perrone et al., and McNeil

Positive Effects	Study
Increased punctuality, dependability, and personal responsibility	Greenberger et al., Perrone, and Hotchkiss
Increased earning power	Gottfredson, Meyer and Wise
Gain practical knowledge about the business world	Greenberger et al., Hotchkiss
Developed social skills	Greenberger et al.
Improved grades, school attendance, and participation in school-related activities	Farkas et al., and Gottfredson
Lowered unemployment rate after graduation	Lewis et al., D'Amico, Meyer and Wise, after Lewin-Epstein, and Stephenson
Found better jobs after graduation	D'Amico, Meyer and Wise, Lewin-Epstein, and Stephenson

In addition, Schill and colleagues (1985) found in their study "Youth Employment: Its Relationship to Academic and Family Variables" that for relatively few hours worked per week there were no obvious adverse effects. This sample constituted 4,587 students from the state of Washington, representing 31 schools. They observed that students who worked fewer than 20 hours per week had the highest grade point averages; even higher than those who did not work at all. However, students who worked more than 20 hours per week displayed the lowest grade point average (Berryman and Schneider, 1982; Gottfredson, 1984; Green and Jaquess, 1987; Lewin-Epstein, 1981; Schill et al., 1985).

In the study entitled "High School Work Experience and Its Effects," Lewis, Gardner, and Seita (1983), analyzed the data from *High School and Beyond* of the national longitudinal surveys. They found that work experience had either no effect or a minimal effect on grade point averages for males, while the results for females were mixed. Finally, other studies have failed to find any adverse impact between hours worked and academic achievement (Gade & Peterson, 1980; Hotchkiss, 1986; Lewis et al., 1983).

Effects on School-Related Activities

Researchers interested in student employment investigated other variables to determine the general impact of working on other facets of students' lives, to see if it affected the general state of well-being of the adolescent individuals. In general, this research suggested that student employment had both positive and negative consequences. (See Table 7.) For example, the research found that when students are employed, and particularly when they work long hours, there is less time devoted to homework and extracurricular activities (D'Amico, 1984; Green & Jaquess, 1987; Greenberger and Steinberg, 1980; Hotchkiss, 1986; Lewin-Epstein, 1981; McNeil, 1984; NAEP, 1989; Perrone et al., 1981). However, other studies showed that employment does not affect participation in school-related activities. Indeed, these studies said that employment actually encouraged such participation (Gade and Peterson, 1980; Gottfredson, 1984).

However, it is important to note that very extensive work involvement of white male sophomores and white female juniors is associated with an increase in the rate of dropping out (D'Amico, 1984).

The Effect of Employment on Social Behavior

A major argument of the proponents of student employment is that it promotes responsibility, builds character, and instills high occupational aspirations. On this positive side, the research generally concluded that students who take part-time jobs experience a number of benefits, including increased punctuality, dependability, and personal responsibility (Greenberger, 1983; Hotchkiss, 1986; Perrone et al., 1981; Steinberg et al., 1981, 1982). These attributes apparently are advantageous in the post-school period, in that high school graduates who worked during school experienced a much lower unemployment rate and found better jobs than those that did not work (D'Amico, 1983; Lewin-Epstein, 1981; Lewis et al., 1983; Meyer & Wise, 1980, 1982; Stephenson, 1980), increased their earning power (Gottfredson, 1984; Meyer & Wise, 1982), and gained practical knowledge about the business world (Greenberger & Steinberg, 1982; Hotchkiss, 1986; Steinberg et al., 1981). They also tended to view their employment positively (Berryman & Schneider, 1982; Borus, 1983; Green & Jaquess, 1987), and developed some form of social skills and meaningful relationships with other older adults (Greenberger and Steinberg, 1980).

Opponents of student employment claim that working distracts students from their educational goals and increases the tendency toward delinquent behavior (Greenberger and Steinberg, 1980). Other negative aspects presumably stem from students being prematurely pushed into the responsibility of adult roles, sometimes being used by employers (Cole, 1981). They also had a tendency to have more school problems such as skipping classes, being tardy, and delaying completion of their assignments (D'Amico, 1984; Greenberger & Steinberg, 1980; Hotchkiss, 1986; Lewis et al., 1983; Lewin-Epstein, 1981; McNeil, 1984; Perrone et al., 1981). Further, there was a correlation between student employment and delinquent behavior, such as smoking, drinking, stealing, and giving away goods (Berryman & Schneider, 1982; D'Amico, 1984; Greenberger, 1980; Greenberger & Steinberg, 1980; Lewis et al., 1983; McNeil, 1984; Perrone et al., 1981). In addition, they had less time available for homework and extracurricular activities (D'Amico, 1984; Steinberg et al., 1982), reduced time spent with family and weakened ties with friends (Greenberger & Steinberg, 1980, 1986), and developed cynical attitudes toward work (Greenberger and Steinberg, 1980; Hotchkiss, 1986). Further, students who worked had little opportunity for learning and advancement while on the job (Greenberger, Steinberg, & Ruggiero, 1983; Lewin-Epstein, 1981), had little opportunity to cooperate with others on joint tasks (Greenberger, 1983), and had little contact with adults and minimum training (Greenberger 1980; Hotchkiss, 1986; Lewin-Epstein, 1981). Perhaps most important, conflicts often arose between teachers' academic priorities and students' choices to work, which resulted in the "cycle of lowering expectations" of teachers: the phenomenon of teachers lowering their classroom standards to accommodate the students who cannot achieve their goals in the available time (McNeil, 1984; Perrone et al., 1981). Finally, student employment has increased the dropout rate (D'Amico, 1984).

Summary

The findings of the empirical studies on the subject of high school student employment suggest that this phenomenon is increasing and is becoming a way of life for many American students. The effects of such employment appear to be mixed. Employment among high school students has been cited as having negative effects on the general attitudes of students and on their social environment. Some examples of these effects are decreased student participation in school-related activities, academic performance, and grades, as well as increased delinquent behavior, dropout rate, and friction with teachers (McNeil, 1984; Schill et al., 1985). However, there are several positive aspects as well. It decreased post-school joblessness; increased earning power, dependability, and responsibility; developed social skills; and increased knowledge about the business world (Greenberger et al., 1982; Stephenson, 1980). Interestingly, there were a number of exceptions to many of the above findings. For instance, sometimes student employment was found to improve grades, school attendance, and participation in school-related activities and homework (Farkas, Smith & Stromsdorfer, 1983; Gottfredson, 1985).

References

American Federation of Teachers. (1989). *Focus on education*. Interview with David T. Kearns, Chairman and CEO of Xerox Corporation. PBS Program, aired February 19.

Bad report card for the nation's schools. (1989, February). *The Buffalo News*, 5.

Bennett, W. (1988). Text of report, American education: Making it work. *Chronicle of Higher Education*, 34, 29-41.

Berryman, C., & Schneider, D. O. (1982). *Part-time employment of in-school youth: An assessment of costs and benefits*. (ERIC Document Reproduction Service No. ED 224 766)

Bohrmidt, G., and Khake, D. (1982). *Statistics for social data analysis*. Chicago: F. E. Peacock Publishers.

Borman, M. K., & Reisman, J. (1986). *Becoming a worker*. Norwood, NJ.

Borus, E. M. (1983). *Tomorrow's workers*. Boston: Lexington Books.

Bureau of Labor Statistics. (1981). *Youth unemployment: An international perspective*. Raymond J. Bonovan, U. S. Department of Labor Bulletin No. 2098. Washington, DC: Author.

Carnegie Commission on Policy Studies in Higher Education (1980). *Giving youth a better chance*. San Francisco: Jossey-Bass.

Cole, S. (1980). Working kids on working. New York: Morrow.

Cowen, C. R. (1989, February 23). Improving math, science teaching. *The Christian Science Monitor*, p. 7.

D'Amico, R. (1983). The nature and consequences of high school employment. In Borus (Ed.), *Pathways to the future, 1*, Columbus, Ohio Center for Human Resources Research.

D'Amico, R. (1984). Does employment during high school impair academic progress? *Sociology of Education*, 57, 152-164.

Farkas, C., Smith, O., & Stromsdorfer, E. W. (1983). The youth entitlement demonstration: Subsidized employment with a schooling requirement. *Journal of Human Resources*, 18, 557-573.

Ford Foundation. (1983). *Not working: Unskilled youth*

and displaced adults. New York: Author.

Ford Foundation. (1989). *The common good: Social welfare and the American future.* New York: Author.

Gade, E., & Peterson, L. (1980). A comparison of working and non-working high school students on school performance, socioeconomic status, and self-esteem. *Vocational Guidance Quarterly, 29,* 65-69.

Golden, C., & Reynolds, B. (1988, August 10). Price of illiteracy. *USA Today,* p. 9.

Gordon, R. (1985). *Part-time work experience of high school seniors: Education and employment.* Columbus, Ohio: National Center for Research in Vocational Education. (Eric Document Reproduction Service No. ED 262 254).

Gottfredson, D. C. (1984). *Youth employment, crime and schooling: A longitudinal study of a national sample* (Report No. 325). Baltimore, MD: Johns Hopkins University, Center for Social Organization of Schools.

Green, C., & Jaquess, N. (1987). The effect of part-time employment on academic achievement. *Journal of Educational Research 6,* 325-329.

Greenberger, E. (1980). A researcher in the policy area. *American Psychologist, 38,* 104-111.

Greenberger, E. (1983). Children, families, and work. In N. D. Reppucci, A. Lois, E. Weilhorn, & J. Monahan. *Mental Health, Law, and Children.* (pp. 103-122). Beverly Hills, CA: Sage.

Greenberger, E., & Steinberg, L. D. (1980). *Part-time employment of in-school youth: An assessment of costs and benefits.* Washington, DC: National Institute of Education. (Eric Document Reproduction Service No. ED 227 334)

Greenberger, E., & Steinberg, L. D. (1981). *Part-time employment of in-school youth: An assessment of costs and benefits.* Final Report. Irvine, CA: University of California.

Greenberger, E., & Steinberg, L. D. (1986). *When teenagers work.* New York: Basic Books.

Greenberger, E., Steinberg, L. D., & Ruggiero, M. (1983). A job is a job is a job . . . or is it? *Work and Occupation, 9,* 79-86.

Hayes, J. (1988a, April 26). Blunt Bennett rates USA's schools. *USA Today,* p. 11a.

Hayes, J. (1988b, April 26). Despite progress we are still at risk. *USA Today,* 11a.

Hotchkiss, L. (1986). *Effects of work-time on school activities and career expectations.* National Center for Research in Vocational Education. (ERIC Reproduction Document Service No. ED 229 654)

Jaquess, N. S. (1984). *The influence of part-time study habits and attitudes on academic performance of high school juniors.* Unpublished doctoral dissertation, University of Oklahoma.

Johnson, C. (1980). Schools and work: Do they ever mix? *Today's Education,* 50-52.

Kenneth, B. In C. E. Finn (1987). Education that

works: Make the school compete. *Harvard Review,* 127.

Lawrence, J. (1989, July). For teens, holding down jobs brings drawbacks and benefits. *The Buffalo News,* p. 9.

Lewin-Epstein, N. (1981). *Employment and attitudes toward working among high school youth.* Chicago: National Opinion Research Center (Eric Document Reproduction Service No. ED 208 183)

Lewis, M. V., Gardner, A. J., & Seita, P. (1983). High school work experiences and its effects. In I. Charner & B. S. Fraser, *Youth and Work.* Washington, DC: The William T. Grant Foundation Commission on Work, Family and Citizenship, 1987.

Maddox, P. (1989, January 5). Giving students something to build on. *The Christian Science Monitor,* p. 18.

McNeil, L. M. (1984). *Lowering expectations: The impact of student employment on classroom knowledge.* Madison, WI: Wisconsin Center for Educational Research. (ERIC Document Reproduction Service No. 242 941)

Melinda, B., & Tessa, N. (1988). A nation at risk. *Newsweek,* pp. 70-76.

Meyer, A. K. (1985). *Part-time employment of high school youth: Differences in status and monetary reward based on school characteristics.* Chicago, IL: American Educational Research Association. (ERIC Document Reproduction Service No. 253 662)

Meyer, A. K. (1987, December). The work commitment of adolescents: Progressive attachment to the work force. *Career Development Quarterly, 36,* 140-147.

Meyer, R. H., & Wise, D. E. (1980). *The youth employment problem: Its dimensions, causes, and consequences in youth knowledge* (Report No. 2.9). Washington, DC: U.S. Government Printing Office.

Meyer, R. M., & Wise, D. A. (1982). High school preparations and early labor force experience. In R. B. Freeman (Ed.), *The youth labor market problems: Its nature, causes and consequences.* Chicago, IL: University of Chicago Press.

Mortimer, T. J., & Finch, D. M. The effects of part-time work on adolescent self-concept and achievement. In K. Borman & J. Reisman (Eds.), *Becoming a worker* (1986). Norwood, NJ: Ablex.

National Assessment of Educational Progress. Educational Testing Service. (1988). *The science report card: Elements of risk and recovery.* Princeton, NJ: Author.

National Assessment of Educational Progress. Educational Testing Service. (1989). (Paul E. Barton). *Earning and learning* (Report No. 17-WL-01). Princeton, NJ: Author.

National Commission on Excellence in Education. (1983). *A nation at risk: The implications for educational reform.* Washington, DC: U.S. Government Printing Office.

National Commission on the Reform of Secondary

Education. (1973). *The reform of secondary education*. New York: McGraw-Hill.

National Commission on Youth. (1980). *The transition of youth to adulthood: A bridge too long*. Boulder, CO: Author.

National Panel on High School and Adolescent Education. (1976). *The education of adolescents*. Washington, DC: U.S. Government Printing Office.

Office of the President. (1982). *Employment and training report of the president*. Washington, DC: U.S. Government Printing Office.

Ordvensky, P. (1989, February 18). Kids learned basics, but not their use. *USA Today*, p 9.

Perrone, V., Landry, R., Ahler, J., Traugh, C., Hill, R., Dahl, I., Larson, J., Williams, J., King, L. (1981). *Secondary school students and employment*. Grand Forks, ND: North Dakota University, Bureau of Educational Research and Service. (Eric Document Reproduction Service No. ED 212 774)

President's Science Advisory Commitee. (1974). Youth: Transition to adulthood. Chicago: University of Chicago Press.

Razik, T., Thompson, A., Abdel Galil, N., Wu, Y., Zabranskey, M., & Abbott, P. (1989). *Evaluation of curriculum: The case of Oman*. Oman.

Ruthman, R. (1989, April). Jobs link with academic harm disputed. *Education Week*, 4.

Schill, J. W., McCartin, R., and Meyer, K. (1985). Youth employment: Its relationship to academic and family variables. *Journal of Vocational Behavior, 26*, 155-163.

Shanker, A. (1988, April 22). Where we stand. *The Christian Science Monitor*, p. 12.

Shapiro, D. (1983). Working youth. In F. M. Borus, *Tomorrow's workers* (pp. 23-58). Boston: Lexington Books.

Squires, G. W., Jr. (1983). *Part-time employment as a predictor of grade point average for secondary school students in an urban school district*. Unpublished doctoral dissertation, University of Florida.

Stephenson, S. (1980). In-school labor force status and post-high school wage rates of young men. *Applied Economics, 13*, 134.

Steinberg, L. D., Greenberger, E. Gorduque, L., & Ruggiero, M. (1982). High school students in the labor force: Some costs and benefits to schooling and learning. *Educational Evaluation and Policy Analysis, 4*, 363-372.

Steinberg, L. D., Greenberger, E. Gorduque, L., Ruggiero, M., & Vaux, A. (1982). The effects of early work experience on adolescent development. *Developmental Psychology, 18*, 385-395.

Steinberg, L. D., Greenberger, E., Vaux, A., and Reggiero, M. (1981). Effects of early work experience on adolescent occupational socialization. *Youth and Society, 12*, 403-422.

The William T. Grant Foundation Commission on Work, Family and Citizenship. (1988). *The forgotten half: Non-college youth in America*. Washington, DC: Author.

Wirtz, W. P., Rohbeck, A. C., Charner, I., & Fraser, S. B. (1987). *Intense employment while in high school: Are teachers, guidance counselors, and parents misguiding academically oriented adolescents?* Washington, DC: George Washington University. Graduate Institute for Policy Education and Research.

9

Non-College-Bound Urban Minority Youth: Issues of Transition

Douglas R. Cochrane, P. Rudy Mattai, and Barbara Huddleston-Mattai

Introduction

One of the goals of our educational system is, or should be, to make every adult a productive, respected member of society. This goal is becoming more critical as international competition forces us to train, and train well, all members of society, minorities and women included, regardless of socioeconomic status. This raises the hope that for the first time in decades our social agenda is becoming aligned with our economic self-interest, providing a much brighter prospect for success. Our specific concern is with the transition from school to work or career that is experienced by urban economically disadvantaged minority students who are not college bound. The transition for this population represents an uneven struggle against skill, language, and socialization constraints of their poor urban background; physical isolation from the workplace; isolation from information; changing economic structures; cultural preferences; and discrimination.

Children of Promise

It is very easy to blame the victim; it is also fallacious and futile. It is not uncommon to see stereotyping of minority students because of their reputedly high dropout rates, yet Rumberger (in Wehlage et al., 1989) found that when socioeconomic status was held equal, African-American youths were somewhat less likely to drop out than Caucasian youths. In actuality,

the total number of Caucasians dropping out was significantly higher than the combined minorities dropout population. The difficulty for minority students lies not with the students themselves, but with the conditions that inhibit their full acceptance into American society.

We have no doubt that given an appropriate environment and the surety of a valued place in society, which includes being able to earn an income sufficient to support a family and live with pride, these youths would aspire to work productively and would succeed. To that end, we need to start seeing these youths in a positive light, not merely as students at risk. During the 1992 FIPSE Program RICE (Fund for the Improvement of Postsecondary Education, Responsive Inner City Education) for majority and minority inner-city teachers held at the State University College of New York at Buffalo, one majority pre-K teacher noted that the "kids were great." However, many central city schools are currently unable to actualize the potential these children represent. It is clear that one thing needed is a marked shift in attitude. If our society can learn to embrace these students as *children of promise*, we will have gone a long way toward actualizing that reality.

At-Risk

The social science and educational literature on non-college-bound at-risk youth has focused on poor urban minority youth, partly because of the recent marked rise in their numbers and partly because of the increasing severity of the conditions that put them at-risk for failure. *At-risk*, for our purposes, is defined as having a reduced likelihood of making a successful transition to work. Dropping out of school is included in our at-risk status as it significantly decreases one's chances of making an effective transition to work. Given that we are addressing youth from minority populations (with minority status an educational risk factor in itself), all with any factor related to perceived educational failure—being poor or from a single-parent family, having poorly educated parents, or language deficits—are educationally at risk. They are therefore less likely to have acquired the basic skills and attitudes that will sustain them in the workplace and are included in our at-risk status.

We are most interested in identifying the schools and communities which have a high proportion of at-risk students. Wehlage, Rutter, Smith, Lesko, and Fernandez (1989) found dropouts to be diverse, not stereotypical, and Fine (1991) found dropouts to have a better self-image and stronger sense of personal control than those who stayed to complete school. Fine also felt that dropouts were making consumer-oriented decisions that rejected their educational choices. Unfortunately, as Fine noted, there was no one there to tell them of the long-term costs of limited education, costs which they later discovered only after repeated failure in the job market. These findings indicted the school system. As has been pointed out by the W. T. Grant Foundation and others, some schools have been making positive changes. More important, schools are not solely responsible. Responsibility lies with the whole socioeconomic structure: the family, business, community, and educational systems, which we ultimately need to understand and address.

The Truly Disadvantaged

The conditions contributing to at-risk status are particularly severe in poor urban communities in which minorities are greatly overrepresented. Within the population described as disadvantaged either because of poverty or poor academic performance (Carl D. Perkins

Vocational Education Act, 1984, Public Law 98-524) is a subset of poor urban minority youth, called the *truly disadvantaged*. This subset closely correlates to Julius Wilson's "truly disadvantaged underclass" (1987). Wilson found that very few non-Hispanic whites, poor or not, live in central city areas of extreme poverty (i.e., where more than 40 percent of residents are poor). Definitions for the truly disadvantaged are so diverse that the size of this subset ranges from 5 percent to 50 percent of the central city poor minority population. Factors and characteristics cross boundaries, confusing the identity of targeted populations and jeopardizing the success of programs for central city minorities.

The Simply Disadvantaged

Minorities in the central city who are marginal, who work sometimes, and/or support families on minimum wages, but who do not live in as densely poor and violent neighborhoods as the truly disadvantaged, are called the disadvantaged or, by some, the fringe. A clear definition for this group is not available.

Although poverty is a major component and the best single indicator of being at-risk, minority status, single-parent family status (most prevalent in minority populations), language deficiency, and dwelling in a city form combinations that increase the severity of at-risk status. A statewide study of dropout rates in Colorado school districts (Brennan & Anderson, 1990) found that poor, urban districts with high minority populations had the highest dropout rates. While Denver does not have the dense minority populations that make up the "truly disadvantaged" populations of other cities, the identification of economically disadvantaged urban areas with high dropout rates involves the simply economically disadvantaged urban ghettos as sources of at-risk populations.

Wilson (1978) and the W. T. Grant Foundation Commission on Family and Youth (1988) identified ghetto conditions of urban minority youths, which include inner-city *social isolation*. Social isolation severely limits these youths from access to the institutions and people needed to move out of the ghetto or to improve the conditions that put them at risk. This lack of access enhances structural constraints, which further exacerbates problems of unemployment, underemployment, poverty, single-parent families, and so forth. While this defines minority youths in dense poverty populations (more than 30 percent poverty), it is not clear where the boundaries lie between the fringe and the truly disadvantaged. The Task Force on Minorities and the Work Force (1990) addresses two disadvantaged minority populations, the fringe and the truly disadvantaged.

Funds and Programs

Funds and programs directed to the truly disadvantaged may not take into consideration the depths of their need. As a result, they provide inadequate funding and further create images of the intractability of situations for this population. Not knowing who the truly disadvantaged are, because of inconsistent and/or deficient definitions, adds greatly to this difficulty. The Task Force on Minorities and the Work Force (1990), for example, suggests that the fringe makes use of funds directed to the truly disadvantaged because the fringe are less handicapped and better prepared to take advantage of these programs.

The fringe is not clearly defined or is said to have less need, and/or it is a group whose nebulous nature makes it politically expedient to ignore. Under many definitions, this body of youth would most likely make up the majority of average central city students. At this time, they are not college bound and are very susceptible to the urban-minority-transition-to-work syndrome addressed here. Hammersley (1992), in her article on schools in Buffalo, noted that while elementary schools fund talented minorities through magnet schools, and a percentage of the educationally and economically disadvantaged populations receive some remedial support in elementary schools, the middle group—the largest population, which is comprised of average students—is left with few resources. The lack of resources for the non-college-bound in high schools is well documented by the W. T. Grant Foundation. Funding problems assume greater proportions in urban high schools with large minority populations. As in elementary schools, all of the resources continue to go to the upper and lower percentiles, but the large body of average students—most of whom are not college bound in these general academic high schools—are not supported and do not receive resources to assist them in effectively transitioning to work.

The W. T. Grant Foundation, the Business-Higher Education Forum, the National Center on Education and the Economy, and others who inform national policy have helped focus attention and some resources on disadvantaged populations. In addition, pressure has increased to direct students to college. For everyone—and particularly for minorities—this is important because of the social mobility achieved after completing four years of college. Most students in general education schools in central city settings are enrolled in academic courses, even though only a third of the minority population will go on to college (Bloomfeld, 1987). Many minority students are in college-bound programs, yet have no clear sense of the reality of that possibility. Career and guidance counselors and such resources as grants and other financial aid are available mainly for those who will go on to postsecondary schooling. Furthermore, only 50 percent of minorities going on to college will attend their second year of college. As a result of the attention and resources being spent on the upper or lower extremes of the minority central city student population, average minority central city youths, most likely largely defined as the fringe, lack the resources, direction, or support they need to succeed.

Demographics and International Competition

The declining birth rate of the majority white population, the graying of the workforce, and the increasing minority populations indicate that the white population will not be able to fill the demand for labor, so there will be opportunities for previously unemployed urban minorities. International competition now demands more highly trained workers. In combination with the demand for urban minorities, this further increases the need to better prepare and transition urban, minority, non-college bound youth to careers. A countervailing force is the current influx of immigrants into the workforce and the increasing participation of women in the work force. These trends will continue to place competitive pressures for low-skill job openings on minorities.

Physical Urban Location

Gender, Cultural Mores and Norms, and Peer Pressure

LeCompte and Dworkin (1992) acknowledge that dropping out, a major impediment to a successful transition to work, is no longer limited to economically disadvantaged, poorly motivated, minority students. Nevertheless, they are quick to point out several pupil-related and macrosystem factors associated with at-risk students. We are interested in the principal effects of physical urban location on those factors that tend to push students out of or pull them away from school.

Gender is one largely overlooked factor in the urban area, although it has tremendous consequences for success in school. There is a plethora of research data (Coleman, 1961; Eder & Parker, 1987; Fine & Zane, 1989) which show that being female is a barrier to academic success. Low-income minority urban females have an especially hard time, because the mores and norms of their communities place a greater value on the academic success of males than of females. Schools appear to be oblivious to these "folkways," so they treat these female students as though gender was of no account. Furthermore, because the educational system tends to be undergirded by an ideological base that is largely influenced by Anglo, middle-class cultural capital, even when the low-income urban minority female succeeds academically, she has further problems. This system of socialization puts an unrealistic role strain on urban minority males because their female peers now perceive them as having to deliver in the same way as the Anglo male. The net effect is that many low-income urban minority females see academic success as limiting their chances for fulfilling, romantic relationships with minority males.

This problem is part of a larger dilemma in which a great degree of peer pressure is exerted on students to opt out of school. Furlong (1980), Stinchcombe (1964), and Willis (1977) document clearly the refusal of minority students to do well academically apparently because they believe there is little if any correlation between academic success and career opportunities. LeComte and Dworkin's (1992) notion of the *culture of cutting* is relevant here: To gain acceptance by the "in crowd" of one's peers, one must demonstrate a deliberate decision to reject school and merely "hang out." Fordham and Ogbu (1986) and Willis (1977) detail the way in which academic success by some students is viewed by others in the black community. Those students who excel are seen as having capitulated to the culture of the dominant ideological group in society (Anglo, middle-class) and, therefore, deserving of being ostracized from black society.

These factors, together with factors that pull urban minority students out of school—like the high incidence of drugs, sexually transmitted diseases, and violence—contribute significantly to the case that lower-income urban minority youths are particularly at-risk for a poor transition to work. If these students do not drop out, these attitudes will surely diminish their interest in acquiring the basic skills they need for transition.

Inner-City Employment

The late 1970s and 1980s have seen significant structural economic changes in the United States. International competitive pressures (for example, automobiles built better and at lower cost in Japan) have dealt severe blows to the city. First, there is the well publicized loss of many industrial jobs because of poor quality and high cost. Most of these jobs were low-skill or entry-level jobs requiring little education. Second, competitive pressures have moved many other manufacturing facilities to foreign sites, particularly Mexico, where cheap low-skill labor can at least address the high cost of American labor. Accompanying these two more widely advertised changes is the move to the suburbs of many manufacturing jobs. Table 1 shows the most current census figures available, which clearly display that shift. One can only surmise that this move shadows the migration from the cities, first, of

Table 1—Manufacturing Jobs, USA 1970 & 1980
Central City vs Urban Fringe

	Central City	Urban Fringe	Difference
1970	5,949,624	5,852,015	+97,609
1980	5,714,168	7,585,848	-1,871,680
Change	-235,456	+1,733,833	

Source: United States Bureau of the Census. *Census of the Population.* Washington, DC: Government Printing Office, 1970, 1980.

the white middle class, and, in the past decade or so, of the minority middle class.

Counterbalancing the loss of many low-skill jobs in cities is the new dominance of service industries. In cities, this has meant the increase of high skill service jobs. The rise of information service industries in this country in the last decade or so has created jobs in the cities that are now largely mismatched with the skills of most minority city residents. High-skill service jobs, which include those of banker, lawyer, stock broker, and so forth, and low-skill, low-wage, retail food service jobs have replaced some low-skill, high-wage jobs lost in the industrial exodus during the same period. This has not helped economically disadvantaged urban minorities with employment. While there are some jobs available in the cities for those with a high school or vocational education, these are limited particularly to the public sector, hospitals, and retail food service.

Suburban Employment

Table 1 shows the migration of jobs to the urban fringe. More entry-level or low-skill service and industrial jobs have moved to the suburbs. Suburban industrial parks and shopping malls are where the non-college-bound youth should find many of their first employment opportunities.

Physical Access

Another consequence of the migration of industries to the suburbs is that for economically disadvantaged urban youth isolation from the job site is an issue. Access to jobs becomes an issue of transportation and time. Census data for 1980 shows that approximately 88 percent of white urban fringe workers over age 16 own vehicles compared to approximately 66 percent of black central city workers over age 16. Furthermore, only 10 percent of white central city workers use public transportation compared to 33 percent of the central city African-American workers. Thus, central city poor minorities depend significantly more on public transportation than do their more affluent counterparts. It is a safe assumption, given the low minimum wages and high poverty levels of youth, that minority youths will rely even more on public transportation than older minorities in the central city.

The 1980 census also shows that approximately 10 percent of white urban or city fringe workers spent more than 45 minutes getting to work compared with 20 percent of central city African-Americans. Similar differences were found in other measures of time to work. For example, half as many central city African-Americans as central city or urban fringe whites lived less than 10 minutes from work. Similarities in time to work for both central city and urban fringe whites support the notion that there is a better-educated, wealthier central city population that works in the high-skilled service industries of the cities—a population that is mainly white. They also suggest some time costs that arise from using public transportation.

From personal experiences and anecdotal accounts (as recounted by impecunious doctoral candidates or recent graduates), it is clear that around the country public transportation is available in some but not all suburbs. For example, Amherst, New York, a middle class suburb of Buffalo, has restricted public access, due, it is thought, to a fear of rising crime. This limited access exists despite the considerable expansion of SUNY at Buffalo to the Amherst campus and the ensuing call for expanded subway and bus service.

Access to the Amherst campus is available for students and city residents who have no other means of transportation via a shuttle bus from the city (Main Street) campus. Approximately six to eight buses per hour leave the Main Street campus, most of them full. In the evening however, both public and University transportation service is less frequent. A trip home after the library closes at 9:00 or 9:30 P.M. can take up to three hours, compared with 45 minutes to an hour earlier in the day.

City-based service to the suburbs, where it exists, is often inadequate or inconvenient, given limited evening, weekend, and holiday service. This translates into many hours of waiting and can add to the cost of needed services like child care, or it can limit one's ability to hold more than one job. McGreary (Lynn & McGreary, 1990) reviewed numerous transportation studies and concluded that federally financed freeway systems, radial transit systems, and federal operating subsidies have provided transportation benefits to the suburbs and to highly skilled suburbanites, have expanded suburban bus service at the cost of city bus service, and have encouraged the poor to remain in the central cities. Federally subsidized, fixed-rail systems, while designed partially to benefit the poor, have mainly aided the suburban highly skilled worker. McGreary also noted both the reduced "work trips" within the cities and between the cities and the suburbs and the reduction in bus schedules in the central cities. Obviously, this limits access to the suburbs and within the cities and particularly affects the poor who mainly use the bus. These transportation patterns make it more difficult for poor central city residents to acquire and maintain what are often minimum-wage jobs.

In Philadelphia, Ihlanfeldt and Sjoquist (in Lynn & McGreary, 1990) were able to identify 16- to 19-year-old school leavers and 20- to 24-year-olds who lived at home, by race and in terms of city vs. fringe dwelling. Controlling for distance to work, the racial gap in employment was reduced by 30 percent (in Lynn & McGreary, 1990). Even Jencks and Mayer (in Lynn & McGreary, 1990), who were conten-

tious, and to use their own word "parsimonious," in acknowledging the implications of studies by Kasarda (1989), Ellwood (1986), Leonard (1986), and Ihlanfeldt and Sjoquist (in Lynn & McGreary, 1990), agreed with Ihlanfeldt and Sjoquist's findings that poor central city minority youth are negatively affected by limited access to jobs.

Job-Related Information

Information about available suburban jobs is also not readily accessible to urban youth. Job information often comes through informal local notices. These include local job postings like those found on the doors of businesses, small-circulation local shopping guides, community papers, or penny savers. Another very common and successful route to a job is through friends or family who pass on job openings they learn of at work or through their network of friends and family. Employers like to hire "known" quantities, and the recommendations of family or friends can go a long way. Urban minority youth are often isolated from people who might recommend them, and because of their cultural differences lack other "known" qualities that employers prefer. Reisner and Balasubramaniam (1989) cite numerous studies confirming that disadvantaged youths lack personal employment contacts, and that these contacts are of value in acquiring work. They note that employers prefer the informal network approach to filling positions because of their belief that it is less expensive and provides more and better job seekers who will be more productive and stay longer. Blacks tend to find public sector jobs, which provide them with fewer contacts and connections, and less information regarding possible future work than do the private sector jobs most often found in the suburbs.

Swinton and Morse (1983) in a review of the most often cited factors negatively and increasingly affecting employment for minority youths included access to job information. A report on minority youth unemployment by the Los Angeles County Commission on Human Relations (1985) included in its major recommendations a polling of students that would allow them to identify the information systems students used to look for work. In this study, an occupational and vocational director of a local school district included access to information as an important issue. There was a lack of adequate guidance counseling and it was argued that 80 percent of the students were in college programs but only 20 percent would go to college, and that those who were qualified would be actively recruited and provided scholarships and other financial aid. Yet, school counselors were geared for the college bound, not the non-college bound.

Discrimination

Discrimination also plays a part in both the efficacy of acquiring work in the suburbs and in actually acquiring a job. Urban minority youth can doubt their ability to get a job in the suburbs because of their lack of fit or their fear of racial discrimination. They can also be excluded from a job because of their appearance, attitudes, race, or ethnicity.

Interpersonal Skills, Work Habits, and Attitudes

Poor interpersonal skills, work habits, and attitudes are a barrier to employment. Poor urban dwellers often develop attitudes that are not well accepted in the mainstream of American employment. Swinton and Morse (1983) note the poor expectations and attitudes of blacks compared with those of white youths. Feichtner & FMW Associates (1989) included deficits in all three as reasons for unemployment or underemployment. Deutschman (1992) discusses the poor discipline and dedication toward work developing in suburban youths as well. Part of the cause is thought to be parents who are both working and who do not come home to convene the kids around the dining room table to talk of work, but instead, arrive home exhausted and go to bed early. This seems related to the problems of limited parental involvement sometimes associated with inner-city minority academic failure.

Reisner and Balasubramaniam (1989) discussed a wealth of research which confirms employers' preferences not to hire disadvantaged youth because of seeing them as poor risks whose attitudes toward the company and other employees need to be improved, whose basic work habits, such as follow-through and dependability, need to be developed, and whose basic communication and academic skills are as limited as their ambition and motivation.

Discriminating Employment Decisions

A study by Cross, Kenney, Mell, and Zimmerman (1990) of disparate hiring practices in two cities found a 31 percent differential in hiring of Hispanics as compared with matched Anglos applying to the same jobs. They noted that discrimination may be an important factor in the employment gap between Hispanics and Anglos and suggested paying more attention to this problem for all minorities. Equal Opportunity Program (EOP) measures in this country have been and continue to be based on the presence of documented discrimination in the workforce.

The Los Angeles County report on minority urban youth unemployment (1985), mentioned earlier, included interviews with African-American and Hispanic students who described their personal experiences of discrimination in hiring practices and on the job. These included being asked what race they were over the phone and appearing for a job interview and being told the job was taken, only to find later that a white person subsequently applying for the job was hired. One African-American youth, a high school graduate with several years of related experience, was told she did not qualify for a job when she went in person, but was hired later for the same job when an employment agency got involved, which demonstrates a reluctance to discriminate with a third party present. Other testimonies included the awareness that many minorities who are qualified are not hired for lack of experience. This is seen as an excuse used to get around minority hiring is when a seasoned and qualified minority is not hired for lack of experience.

A Hispanic youth was told over a period of three years, starting when he was 15, that he was too young for a particular job. White youths working for the company where he had applied told him they were 16, a year younger than he was when he last applied for a job. An African-American student was given an application and told to return soon by a personnel manager, only to be told the next day by a second person that no job would be available for two to three months.

On-the-job discrimination included racial slurs, differential wage scales for minorities and whites, discriminatory scheduling and few promotions of minorities to supervisory positions. Students felt that members of minorities were often let go before there was a need to promote them. Several youths described sexual harassment or sexual expectations related to being hired or promoted.

Access, Discrimination, and Efficacy

An oral history describing American suburbs by African-American professionals included accounts of overly active police forces keeping potential urban criminal elements (read "African-American males") in line. The recent movie *Grand Canyon* showed an African-American youth who had moved from an inner-city community chased and arrested for running through his new, better neighborhood. *Boyz 'N the Hood*, another popular movie, showed the effect of recent negative racial perceptions of many police on an African-American policeperson. The black policeperson was verbally and physically abusive of African-American youth as he harassed them in their own neighborhood. The events in Los Angeles around the Rodney King beating and trials, in the same year as the release of these two movies, validate the prevalence and impact of racially motivated police activity.

These actions and events can discourage minorities from freely moving around in a community, which can affect their seeking out or interviewing for a job or maintaining an employed presence in the town. A likely side effect of racial/ethnic discrimination is that it could take very little actual police harassment for a suburb to acquire a reputation for being unfriendly to minorities. As a result, minorities, particularly minority youth, could easily judge a community as hostile and feel uncomfortable or have little faith in being able to find work.

Cultural Differences in Suburbs and Cities

In some communities, there may also be cultural differences between Hispanic and Af-

rican-American populations involved in migration to the suburbs due to differences in social and family structures. Bearing in mind the vast differences in Hispanic origins, in some cities there are tight Hispanic communities that view their neighborhoods as home and resist moving to the suburbs. (This may be due in part to the more recent emigration of a community's residents from similar regions in their country of origin.) This creates a strong loyalty to a neighborhood, which includes applying social pressure to maintain the community.

One large northeastern city with a predominantly Puerto Rican Hispanic population provides a good example. Several Puerto Rican professionals in this community described encounters with community acquaintances who had heard that they planned to move out of the community. One successful professional woman had made a commitment to the neighborhood for 10 years, but indicated that she now wanted to move to the suburbs. A male professional from the same community moved to the outer fringe of the community to buy property for himself, but maintains his presence.

Within this same community, there appears to be good support of Hispanic businesses by Hispanics. This includes restaurants, small specialty food stores, and street mechanics, as well as larger companies that hire Hispanic youth and cater to Hispanics. Various news releases verify the growing Hispanic business organizations geared specifically to Hispanics. This includes Hispanic marketing and advertising companies that have specialized in targeting Hispanic populations since the early to mid-1980s. DeFreitas (1991) describes the Miami Cuban refugee community as the latest "ethnic enclave." A group of immigrant-Cuban-owned businesses has been fostered by and in turn revitalized the Miami Cuban community, hiring new entrants and training those who want one day to start their own businesses. It is thought that in Miami one-fifth of all commercial banks and one-third of all construction companies are owned by Cubans.

African-American families and social units have been split up by migration to the north.

There appear to be weaker community ties. While there is some movement of middle class Hispanics to the suburbs, there seem to be fewer community ties to the city for skilled middle class African-Americans, who have followed the middle class white exodus to the suburbs, often creating their own suburbs.

The black community is noted for its lack of cohesive business/entrepreneurial presence. Struggles with Asian entrepreneurs in poor urban centers of several cities have brought national attention to the ill will of some inner-city African-Americans to Asian entrepreneurial success in their neighborhoods. Green and Pryde (1990), using 1980 census data, found African-Americans to be half as likely as Asians or Hispanics and a third as likely as whites to be self-employed. They also noted Bates and Fusfeld's (1984) ground-breaking work on the economic structure of the urban ghetto, which described the historical limitations of black entrepreneurship; issues of access related to credit, education, and training; and discriminatory attitudes that restrict roles of minorities in society. In spite of poor participation in self-employment, Green and Pryde (1990) quote Stevens' study (1984) which found little difference between the success rates of African-American businesses and other businesses, thus concluding that capital formation, and not high business failure, was the major problem. In other words, raising the money to start and develop a business was the major impediment to African-American business formation.

Most businesses are started with personal financing. The average white per capita wealth was 3.2 times that of the African-American per capita wealth, and the household wealth differentiation was 2.8. The difference between the per capita wealth and household wealth reflects the larger size of African-American households compared to white households. African-Americans are also the least likely to ask their family for financial support in starting a business. This underscores a profound need to assist black businesses.

Green and Pryde (1990) make a strong case throughout their book for the need of African-Americans to become involved in businesses and the need for the country to support their efforts. The experience and influence of owning a business provides skills and insights that are greatly needed now in this society—particularly within the central cities. Minority businesses are also seen as providing a valuable development tool for minority populations and the poor inner cities.

Language

Language differences are a problem for both urban Hispanics and African-Americans. Many Hispanics who are immigrants or second- or third-generation Americans often have families who speak Spanish at home. As a result, students from these families can have English-as-a-second-language problems in school that later restrict them. African-Americans have in some cases developed their own language variation called Black English vernacular (BEV), which means they also learn school English as a second language.

Valdivieso (in Keshner & Connolly, 1991) describes the controversy over the impact of language problems for Hispanic students. The importance of the language difficulties of Spanish-speaking youths is diffused by some of the problems that develop early in the school life of these students. Language problems often hold Hispanic youths up a grade or two in school. As a result, they are more advanced physically and emotionally than their classmates and behind their age peers a class or two. Twenty-five percent of Hispanics enter high school over age. Being over age at entrance and/or being held back a grade or two, in combination with having poor grades and the attractiveness of work, often results in students dropping out. The root cause of this problem is English language comprehension, but confusion over the other complications described above cloud the issue. As a result of the ensuing lack of inclusive language policies that might address the problems, schools avoid the language development problems of their students.

Houston in Keshner and Connolly (1991) addresses BEV as a possible barrier to learning. Some African-American students use nonstandard prepositions and conjunctions. For these children, this is not a mistake but is how they have learned and understand English. The usage of BEV or Black English or any number of other dialects used by African-Americans can make a negative impression during job interviews or on the job with employers and fellow employees. This may may affect the view of an employee's ability to communicate effectively within the company and with customers. Language differences then, can present negative images that could cost a job offer or advancement.

Traditional Career and Training Options

School and Vocational Placement

Schools have no programs linking students to work. As noted in the introduction, resources go to college bound programs or to a limited number of students at risk of dropping out. Very few resources are available to the average central city youth. Career guidance is also designed for the college bound, and in central city schools counselors' load is so heavy that they have little time per student. Nationwide, only about 30 percent of all minority students go on to college (Bloomfeld, 1989), which means that minorities are underrepresented in college bound or college populations. With an average of 70 percent of minorities not going to college or dropping out before graduating, it can be too easy to track minorities into useless programs that do not help improve their transitioning to either work or postsecondary education.

A vocational option would seem appropriate for some, though tracking becomes an issue (Neubert & Leak, 1990), and particularly as a result of behaviors associated with truly disadvantaged and at-risk minority students in middle school (Reisner & Balasubramaniam, 1989). Nationally, the job placement rate for vocational programs is only 35 percent. Perhaps more important, recent work force trends demanding new skills are changing prerequisites that include postsecondary vocational education programs for entry-level jobs. Minorities and the economically disadvantaged had the lowest completion rates in these postsecondary programs (National Assessment of Vocational Assessment [NAVE], 1989). Reisner and Balasubramaniam (1989) suggest that disadvantaged students need assistance in job locating beyond that which is available in most vocational programs.

Also, schools with the largest percentages of disadvantaged students provide 40 percent fewer vocational options and half as many upper-level vocational courses as schools with the fewest disadvantaged students (NAVE, 1989). These inner-city students also take the most limited range of vocational courses and are at risk of being tracked into isolated prevocational curriculums. None of these approaches provides minority youth with skills that will make them employable at the end of their school tenure.

Vocational technology programs can be strong in some cities. Interviews with a former administrator in a large Northeastern city found this blue collar city to be more supportive of vocational programs than suburban counterparts, but that the programs were strongly union oriented and expensive to keep current. As a result, the programs were still largely oriented toward industrial skills and because of current economic restructuring, little work is available from the industrial track. Only a student who was one of the very best and brightest might get a union job, and for those who were not the options were limited. Their options included work in low-paid scab shops with no benefits and no access to the union system that would allow them to acquire the master-level skills needed to advance in the trade.

The vocational programs were reasonably integrated in this city by dropping exams that at the time disqualified virtually all minorities. However, here as elsewhere, there were not enough spots open for those interested. There was also little direct employment connection to industry. There were some school apprenticeship experiences, but there are not many such opportunities. Minorities can be discouraged from vocational programs because of parents' fear of tracking. These programs were designed largely to prepare students for union work. Some notable exceptions included limited places in computer and technology training programs whose graduates go into high-skill, low-wage jobs in banks, and so forth.

Unions

Initially, unions were white family systems. Because of government pressures tied to contract requirements they were forced to become integrated to some extent. Anti-union sentiment has grown in the last two decades with the result that unions now have significantly less clout than they did just after World War II. Entry through apprentice programs allows workers to enter at the laborer level. Most apprenticeship programs are in just a few occupations, mainly the construction trades. Despite efforts to "overcome and prevent discrimination," apprenticeship program enrollment primarily involves white males who are "in their mid-20s" and "clear about their career paths," with less than 5 percent of graduating high school seniors and only 1 to 2 percent of those three years out of school enrolled in apprenticeship programs (Carnavale & Johnston, 1989).

As previously noted in discussing access to the suburbs, transportation can be a problem for urban minorities, particularly for youth. When the union shop calls with a job, a union member has to go regardless of where this job is. Those who don't or can't go find their names at the bottom of the list. Union shops and apprenticeship programs allow trainees to get a start in a trade, at the bottom, as a laborer. Mandated quotas assure minorities they will be accepted on the job site, but they do not assure them that their employers will provide the necessary training or the exposure and opportunity to move up the union ladder to master craftsman status.

Buffalo recently heard a court case in which an African-American is claiming that because he is from a minority group, he was not given adequate electricity-related training during his apprenticeship, which ultimately denied him the ability needed to become a master electrician. New York City has several unions in court at present for allegedly inappropriate racial and ethnic hiring practices. General Motors was recently put under a 10-year monitored affirmative action hiring program because of a no contest plea in an affirmative action case. GM was required to hire and maintain a closely monitored percentage of minorities regardless of the size of local

minority populations. This year, a grant will be used in Buffalo to help examine an existing local database of women and minorities who entered apprentices programs over the last several years. These former apprentices will be contacted to evaluate how many have remained in the union system, how many have moved up grade levels in the system, if they have gone on to other careers, and, if so, why.

In New York state in 1991-1992, African-Americans held approximately 12.4 percent of the available apprenticeship programs and Hispanics held 8.6 percent. Dropout rates were approximately 17.6 percent for blacks and 13.7 percent for Hispanics. The vast majority of minorities were in the construction trades (New York State Department of Labor, 1992).

Job Training Partnership Act

The current national Job Training Partnership Act (JTPA) criteria for eligibility for youth training programs are related to economic disadvantage. A new national emphasis on dropouts will change the populations being served. The needs of dropouts must be addressed, though this is a good example of the average urban minority non-college-bound youth's potential for finding access to available programs restricted.

Local JTPA programs are monitored by Private Industry Councils (PICs) who have some discretion as to whom to serve, and to some extent how to serve them. For the city of Buffalo, the local PIC chooses approximately 70 percent minority youth representation for their training program. At the program's beginning, 40 percent of the youth served will be dropouts, rising to 50 percent the following year.

Those who walk in the door of an agency providing career and training services are the ones who are motivated to do something. Colleen Cummings, a senior planner for the Buffalo and Erie County Private Industry Council talked of the many disenfranchised youth who find no validity in their life for training or careers. Lack of work or access to only minimum-wage jobs adds to a sense of alienation from the system which leaves many youths unwilling to consider a positive future outcome from training or career development. With available funding, JTPAs can help an estimated 59 percent of the disadvantaged population they are designed to assist. The PIC in Buffalo chooses to serve those who have at least one more at-risk factor than the basic economic prerequisite. Third-party vendors provide the actual service. In Buffalo, the primary third-party vendor is the Carlton Community Center, which provides services for 500 youths per year in JTPA programs. The center, to reach the youths it targets, conducts outreach programs in the Buffalo high schools; it has 2,300 to 2,500 youths who walk in its door, many of whom will not be served. There are also JTPA programs designed for dropout prevention in the high schools whose clients are non-college-bound.

The Armed Forces

The role of the armed forces as a traditional alternative for training and work for minorities has been seriously diminished. The changing political and economic structure is limiting the military as an option for all as national defense spending is going through radical readjustments as a result of the disintegration of the former Soviet Union and Eastern Bloc, which ended the cold war. Bases and personnel are being cut back dramatically (Lawton, 1992).

For many central city minorities with educational deficits, this is having a profound effect. The armed forces are no longer the "dynamic force for racial integration and upward mobility" that they were just a few years ago (Newhouse News Service, 1992). Reduction in recruiting has raised standards for entry to a point where only those with a high school degree will be admitted into the armed forces. Some branches, like the Marines, will not accept a GED as a substitute.

All new recruits must take a military screening test, which is not unlike any other academic skills tests. One needs a 30 out of 100 to be accepted into the armed forces, although this may vary between different branches of the forces and with regard to changes in short-term recruitment quotas. According to interviews with two armed forces recruiters, unless you score 50 or more on this test you will get limited or no training or opportunity to ac-

quire additional skills while enlisted. Those scoring between 30 and 50 are usually given menial jobs during their enlistment (dishwasher, janitor, grounds keeper, etc.). This quickly tracks many urban minorities to low level labor slots with no training options. The situation is further compounded by stiff internal competition for continued service appointments which are based on continued testing and improved test performance. Many African-Americans will be allowed just one enlistment period with little or no advancement. This is a severe blow for the thousands of poorly prepared African-Americans who previously found refuge and training and social place in what had been our most prominent color-blind employer.

Cultural Differences and Military Service

The armed forces recognize African-Americans as a distinct racial group, but identify white Hispanics as white. Recruitment is quota driven and is often very specific in terms of the high school, program background, sex, race, and grade point average of new recruits. There are quotas for African-Americans who are officer material. Political pressure has resulted in increased African-American officer quotas because of current underrepresentation. To meet quotas, African-American youths can score approximately 100 points lower on combined SAT scores and be accepted into the officer training programs. Interviews with armed forces recruiters suggest that this unfortunately leads to reverse discrimination tensions within the service.

The Costs

Welfare amounting to $8.6 billion provides basic benefits to more than 3 million eligible families. It costs $20,000 per year to keep a person in jail; $2,400 for one person to repeat a grade; $3,000 for prenatal care of an unemployed single mother; an average of $12,000 for postnatal care of an underweight newborn; and $7,300 for welfare, food stamps, and heating assistance for a mother of two unable to afford to work because of child care costs (Business Higher Education Forum, 1990). There are also astronomical amounts of lost taxes on unearned or underearned wages, as well as costs to the community through expansion of police forces and the judicial system. Public expenditures on appropriate solutions can be justified by measurable reductions in these costs.

Stephens and Repa (1992) find that a disproportionate number of prison inmates have no high school diploma. Conditions of unemployment and underemployment fuel violence in the streets, contribute to poor health care, and add innumerable pressures that can lead to an early death, a significant concern for African-American males in the central city. The difference in life expectancy between the average white and the average black in 1987 was 6.2 years, a gap that has been growing. The ineffective and poor transition from school to work for central city minorities, whether as dropouts or non-college-bound high school graduates, is a root cause of the social dilemmas of this population, the cities, and the country. These problems contribute to major losses of financial resources directed at a condition that is becoming more urgent. Effective solutions need public support. Will we respond while we can?

Recommendations

Perhaps the most basic recommendation, with the fewest apparent costs would be to adopt Pautlers' suggestion of a school handoff for each student. A handoff would be a signature from a postsecondary educational institution, a training program, or employer of some kind, representing at least several months to a year commitment on the part of all parties to a continued educational or career/employment process. The school would remain responsible and provide further education, training and or career guidance/counseling and placement as needed or appropriate. This deceptively simple expectation places the school in a much more accountable role with every student.

To better inform schools and other parties involved in a structural resolution of this problem, a local assessment should be done of schools, students, parents, the business community, jobs, colleges/universities, community groups, and agencies. It is becoming common knowledge—and was evident to us in collecting information through local experts and literature reviews—that we can no longer generalize to all cities that which is a fact in one. Addressing the needs of non-college-bound urban minority youth is a complex problem with many variables, including regional and city differences in economic factors, business resources, differing characteristics of racial and ethnic populations, differing qualities of race relations, and variations in specific localized issues. An assessment can inform and help develop a collaborative spirit and commitment from the groups mentioned above that can serve as the start of a coalition resolved to solving these problems. A commitment to the schools providing training and businesses guaranteeing jobs for graduates have been outcomes of joint business/school/community collaborations.

To play a proactive and preventative role, schools—particularly those responsible for educating central city minorities—need to provide all students with good exposure to many lifestyle, career, and work environments. This should not wait until the middle grades but should be part of a hands-on elementary school program. Deutschman (1992) researched the British program KAPOW (Kids and the Power of Work), sponsored by food conglomerate Grand Metropolitan, a growing multimillion dollar elementary school program involving 88 schools. It is aimed at developing pro-work attitudes and habits, exposing youths to occupations early on, and encouraging team work.

A preventative approach to eliminating tracking would include assuring that the maintenance of basic academic skills, even in vocational technical programs, would be mandatory. Youths should be able to switch to academic programs as late as grades 10 or 11, which would keep their postsecondary educational options open. Career development, life planning, creative problem solving, and self-efficacy enhancing programs should be mandated and incorporated into the curriculum for all youths in central city schools. Community people providing mentoring roles and minority youths donating needed community service will help develop attitudes of interest and responsibility within the community.

References

Bates, T., & Fusfeld, D. R. (1984). *The political economy of the urban ghetto.* Carbondale, IL: Southern Illinois University Press.

Bloomfield, W. M. (1989). *Career beginnings: Helping disadvantaged youth achieve their potential.* Bloomington, IN: Phi Delta Kappa Educational Foundation. (ERIC Document Reproduction Service No. ED 316 618)

Bossone, R. M., & Polishook, I. H. (1986). *School to work transition: Proceedings of the Conference of the University/Urban Schools National Task Force.* New York: City University of New York, Graduate School and University Center. (ERIC Document Reproduction Service No. ED 266 200)

Brennan, T., & Anderson, F. (1990). *A longitudinal study of factors producing high school dropout among handicapped students.* Final report. Washington, DC: Institutional Development and Economic Affairs Service, Inc., Nederland, Co., & Special Education Programs. (ERIC Document Reproduction Service No. ED 334 762)

Carnevale, A. P., & Johnston, J. W. (1989). *Training America: Strategies for the nation.* Alexandria, VA: American Society for Training and Development. Rochester, NY: National Center on Education and Economy.

Coleman, J. S. (1961). *The adolescent society.* Glencoe, IL: Free Press.

Commission on the Skills of the American Work Force. (1990). *America's choice: High skills or low wages.* Rochester, NY: National Center on Education and the Economy.

Cross, H., Kenney, G., Mell, J., & Zimmerman, W. (1990). *Employer hiring practices. Differential treatment of Hispanic and Anglo job seekers.* Washington, DC: Urban Institute Press.

DeFreitas, G. (1991). *Inequality at work. Hispanics in the U.S. labor force.* New York & Oxford: Oxford University Press.

Deutschman, A. (1992, August 10). Why kids should learn about work. *Fortune, 126*(3), pp. 86-89.

Eder, D., & Parker, S. (1987). The cultural production of reproduction of gender: The effect of extracurricular activities on peer-group culture. *Sociology of Education, 60,* pp. 200-213.

Feichtner, S. W., & FMW Associates. (1989). *School-to-work transition for at-risk youth* (Information Series No. 339). Columbus, OH: ERIC Clearinghouse and Vocational Education Center on Education and Training for Employment. (ERIC Document Reproduction Service No. ED 335 425)

Fine, M. (1991). *Framing Dropouts.* Albany, NY: State University of New York Press.

Fine, M., & Zane, N. (1989). Bein' wrapped too tight: Why low-income women drop out of high school. In L. Weis, E. Farrar, & H. G. Petrie, *Dropouts from school: Issues, dilemmas, and solutions.* Albany, NY: State University of New York Press.

Fordham, S., & Ogbu, J. U. (1986). Black students' school success: Coping with the "burden" of "acting white." *Urban Review, 18,* 176-206.

Furlong, M. (1980). Black girls in a London comprehensive. In LeCompte & Dworkin, *Giving up on school.* Newbury Park, CA: Corwin Press.

Green, S., & Pryde, P. (1990). *Black entrepreneurship in America.* New Brunswick & London: Transaction Publishers.

Hammersley, M. (1992, September 18). School board asks for budget of 9.2 million. *Buffalo Evening News,* B1, p2.

Kershner, K. M., & Connolly, J. A. (1991). *At-risk students and school restructuring.* Washington, DC: Office of Educational Research and Improvement. (ERIC Document Reproduction Service No. ED 335 425)

Lawton, M. (1992, June 10). Downsizing military curtails job options for some graduates. *Education Week,* pp. 8-9.

LeCompte, M. D., & Dworkin, A. G. (1991). *Giving up on school. Student dropouts and teacher burnouts.* Newbury Park, CA: Corwin Press.

Leonard, J. S. (1986). *Space, time and unemployment: Los Angeles 1980.* Unpublished paper.

Lynn, L. E., Jr., & McGreary, G. H. (1990). Inner-city poverty in the United States. Washington, DC: National Academy Press.

Los Angeles County Commission on Human Relations. (1985). *Minority youth unemployment: Barriers to success in the labor market. Report on a public hearing.* Los Angles: Author.

Neubert, D. A., & Leak, L. E. (1990). Serving urban youth with special needs in vocational education: Issues and strategies for change. *TAASP Bulletin, 2,* (2)1-3. (ERIC Document Reproduction Service No. ED 326 695)

Newhouse News Service. (1992, May 16). Opportunities in military disappearing for blacks. *The Union Tribune,* p. A18.

New York State Department of Labor. (1991, December; 1992, June). *AP-1 status of participants in New York state apprenticeship programs by selected target groups.*

New York State Department of Labor. (1991, December; 1992, June). *AP-2 distribution of apprentices by major industry group and selected target groups.*

Reisner, E. R., & Balasubramaniam, M. *School to work transition services for disadvantaged youth enrolled in vocational education.* Washington, DC: Policy Studies Association. (ERIC Document Reproduction Service No. ED 315 539)

Stephens, R. T., & Repa, J. T. (1992, January). Dropping out and its ultimate consequence. A study of dropouts in prison. *Urban Education, 26*(4), 401-422.

Stinchcombe, A. L. (1964). *Rebellion in a high school.* Chicago: Quadrangle.

Swinton, D. H., & Morse, L. C. (1983). *The source of minority youth employment problems.* New York: Andrew W. Mellon Foundation. (ERIC Document Reproduction Service No. ED 254 573)

Task Force on Minorities and the Work Force. (1990). *Three realities: Minority life in the United States.* Washington, DC: Business-Higher Education Forum & American Council on Education.

United States Bureau of the Census. (1970; 1980). *Census of the population.* Washington, DC: Government Printing Office.

W. T. Grant Foundation Commission on Work, Family, and Citizenship. (1988). *The forgotten half: Non college bound youth in America.* Washington, DC: Author.

Wehlage, G. G., Rutter, R. A., Smith, G. A., Lesko, N., & Fernandez, R. R. (1989). *Reducing the risk: Schools as communities of support.* London, New York, Philadelphia: Falmer Press.

Willis, P. (1977). *Learning to labor: How working class kids get working class jobs.* Lexington, MA: D. C. Heath.

Wilson, W. J. (1978). *The declining significance of race.* Chicago: University of Chicago Press.

Wilson, W. J. (1987). *The truly disadvantaged.* Chicago: University of Chicago Press.

Part III:

Program Analysis and Reviews

10

Improving the School-to-Employment Transition with Lessons from Abroad*

Gerald D. Cheek and Clifton P. Campbell

One of the new fads in vocational education is the movement to implement *transition-from-school-to-work programs*. This movement was spawned by recent federal legislation, school dropout problems, high youth unemployment, unrelated employment of vocational program graduates, national studies that questioned the effectiveness of vocational education, fear of a shortage of skilled workers, increased international competition, and a host of other perceived deficiencies in our socioeconomic and education systems.

Our impoverished, misdirected, and antiquated educational system continues to release vast numbers of unprepared graduates who must fend for themselves in finding and keeping a job. However, without addressing all the problems and changing the educational system, the fad is to focus attention on the transition from school to work.

An effective transition from school to work does not begin suddenly after students have completed their vocational programs. It starts very early and continues throughout the life of every child. The tragedy in today's schools comes from the perceptions that (a) education is separate from life experiences and (b) work should occur only when education has been completed. This elitist point of view is both undemocratic and unrealistic.

Our education system has ignored the right of every citizen to obtain an education for the purpose of experiencing life and preparing for what comes next. Without preparation that produces marketable skills, the educational system makes it difficult for a person to enter an occupation of his or her choice. Elitists value book learning and have disdain for on-the-job learning. To them, ideas are more important than experiences. Content to be taught is that which the liberally educated and leisure classes consider important, not that which is practical.

Easily duped policymakers have deprived students of both the right and privilege of preparing for work by diminishing its importance and allocating resources disproportionately in favor of liberal education and education for those with special needs. In addition, the image of vocational education has declined until it is viewed, by many, as suitable only for those with special needs, troublemakers, and those not earmarked for college. Given these and other unfavorable conditions, what should be done to assist students in the transition from school to work? Will simple and separate programs be effective in assisting students with this transition? Hardly! Don't be fooled

*Authors' Note

This chapter was based on information collected through (a) a review of the literature; (b) personal communications; (c) study visits to Germany, Sweden, Switzerland, and the United Kingdom; and (d) interviews with government, school, and industrial officials.

into thinking that lessons on how to write resumes and participate in job interviews will solve the problems facing graduates in today's marketplace.

Before suggestions are made for designing transition programs, a definition of *transition* is needed. A transition connotes a change, movement, development, or evolution from one stage to another. It involves placing students in their next learning arena. Designing an effective transition program won't be easy and it will take time. However, in the long run, the effort will pay off. The following suggestions are intended to help students with the school-to-work transition.

A transition-from-school-to-work program should not be separate from existing offerings—it should be part of an integral, natural, and continuous process. The outcomes of an effective school-to-work transition program include (a) well-prepared graduates, (b) public awareness of what the school has to offer, and (c) relevant workplace training experiences offered by businesses and industry. In addition, transition programs should include the following provisions:

1. Students go through career development stages, including occupational awareness, exploratory experiences, assistance with planning, and job preparation.
2. Students are carefully selected for programs that meet their employment objectives and provide the requirements for their success.
3. Students participate in quality vocational programs that provide the identified essential elements of their chosen occupation, along with experiences in realistic settings.
4. Schools and employers cooperate to provide alternate learning experiences in appropriate settings.
5. Schools provide students with vocational guidance and job-search assistance. They conduct follow-up studies to keep in touch with labor demands and program effectiveness.
6. Students are expected (and required) to obtain a strong academic preparation that enables them to progress in their

occupation or to continue with post-secondary education.

Defining Program Priorities and Goals

Not all programs under the vocational umbrella prepare students for job entry. Several have different priorities and goals. For example, some offer general education designed to provide universal life skills. Others are exploratory, providing experiences that enable students to make logical and reasonable choices about the direction their education will take. The secondary articulated "tech-prep" programs are designed to better prepare students to enter and complete postsecondary technical programs. Other programs are intended to prepare students in the "basics," allowing them to better utilize other educational programs. Since these programs do not directly prepare students for work, the transition from school to work is logically delayed. The point is that every program should be designed to properly advance students to the next stage. Evaluations of program effectiveness should be based on how well students progress or make the transition to the following phase.

Vocational programs have borne the brunt of mainstreaming, and many teachers are having difficulty preparing students with special needs for the world of work. In general, special needs students are misplaced in a phase of vocational education where they have extreme difficulty or cannot attain program goals. Developing transition programs will not solve the problem of placing students in jobs when they are not capable of doing the required work. Students with special needs should be placed in programs where they can succeed and progress to occupations suited to their abilities.

Recent federal legislation provides a road map to disaster. Secondary vocational education has been misdirected to serve the role of trying to solve social problems. Funds are set aside to serve those with special needs, eliminate sex stereotyping, provide AIDS awareness and prevention, reduce the dropout rate, teach the basics, and the like. Instead of focusing on economic issues, the availability of federal funding has lured administrators away from vocational education's real purpose, that of *preparing youth for gainful and productive employment*. It would be refreshing for legislators to remind us that a job is the best solution for solving social problems. In any case, we must not forget that providing well-trained graduates is the first and most important step in accomplishing an effective transition.

Implementing Career Education

A comprehensive transition program does more than help graduates get their first job. It involves students in career (a) awareness, (b) exploration, (c) decision making and planning, and (d) preparation. Each of these four phases builds on the ones before it. Skipping or eliminating even one limits the effectiveness of programs designed to meet the objectives of the following phases. If all phases are not available, teachers must expend considerable time and effort merely to catch up. Simply stated, it is difficult to prepare students for work if they have not:

1. Been exposed to career possibilities and occupational requirements.
2. Become comfortable with their personal abilities and interests.
3. Decided to enter an occupation.
4. Made plans for the education and training needed to enter a career.
5. Been motivated to achieve all that is necessary to become a successful worker.

These experiences are viewed by many as being appropriate only after students have completed high school. However, they cannot be logically separated from the complete transition process. The career education concept was meant for all students, whether college- or work-bound. Since the four phases of career education are not generally available in all schools, many students are ill prepared to enter work or postsecondary education. They often flounder as nonmajors in college or are ignored by employers until they have "matured enough to hire." Massive resources are squandered on students who don't know why they are in college. The resources of the United States are great but limited, and they should not go to waste on programs that do not benefit the recipient or society.

A model career education program has existed in the St. Louis School System since the early 1970s. It encompasses all grades and provides services to over 50,000 students. Every teacher acts as a guidance counselor, and each year teachers are aided by more than 1,400 active private sector representatives who help inform students about the world of work. The program has gained well-deserved national and international recognition for its accomplishments. However, many transition-to-work programs ignore the lessons that can be learned from this and other successful programs.

Developing Linkages With The Private Sector

No matter what strategy a school-to-work process uses, employers must be convinced that graduates are prepared for the job. Moreover, vocational educators alone should not decide what to offer or establish performance standards. They should be advised and assisted by incumbent workers, supervisors, and employers. This and other involvement will help convince employers that program graduates are well trained prior to hiring and able to perform once on the job. Since successful transition from school to work requires employers' cooperation, they must be included in the planning and implementation of such programs. Vocational education is too important to be left solely in the hands of educators. Critically important expertise about jobs resides within the business and industrial community. Cooperative partnerships provide the only assurance that vocational programs will remain accountable to students and to employers.

Given the complexities of changing technologies, remaining current with new practices, declining school budgets, reduced time for training, and the like, schools alone cannot prepare youngsters for work. Consequently, approaches other than total in-school training must be adopted. The private sector remains, as always, a quality provider of vocational education.

Joint-Venture Partnerships

Partnerships between vocational education programs and the private sector are essential to maximize learning opportunities.

Such partnerships must receive continuous input from both parties to remain relevant and up to date. Since business and industry employ the graduates of vocational programs, they must provide input into the nature and quality of the training provided.

In the past, advisory committees have been used to form linkages between vocational programs and the private sector. However, educators often misused and exploited this relationship. Committees typically served reactive roles, responding only to problems identified by teachers and administrators. A joint-venture partnership offers a solution to this state of affairs. It creates a long-term commitment between vocational education and employers, in which both contribute to the educational process and draw some benefit from it.

Traditionally, society has observed events that mark significant life changes with a ceremony and public announcement. This is true of marriage, graduation, baptism, death, and other important occasions. The signing of a joint-venture partnership agreement is such an event. Its ceremony should be held in a public setting, such as a school board meeting, with all parties present. The ceremony indicates that major changes are about to occur. School officials should arrange for media coverage to maximize the impact of this public relations opportunity. Private sector partners benefit from an improved public image. Once a public commitment is made, those involved try harder to make the partnership work.

The Hamilton County School System in Tennessee provides an excellent example of a school system that has implemented the concepts of *working partnerships*. In this community, the public is well informed and involved in vocational education. Under a joint-venture partnership agreement, vocational programs are linked with businesses that have made a commitment to providing quality learning experiences. As a result, program improvements are made and employers hire "their" graduates, not just graduates.

Real-Life Work Experiences

Schools' efforts to keep pace with the complexities of today's labor market appear to be futile. Some of the problems facing vocational educators are (a) remaining current with new technologies, (b) providing realistic work experiences in an actual or simulated environment, (c) having sufficient uninterrupted time for training, and (d) keeping in touch with employers, supervisors, and incumbent workers on current workforce requirements. The only apparent solution to this dilemma is to *expand the learning environment to work sites.* Today, business and industry provide the only realistic environment in which youngsters can learn occupational skills. Schools do not have the resources or the will to provide all the experiences necessary to properly prepare students for work. Any attempt to implement a school-to-work transition program without required work experience will be ineffective.

Cooperative education programs have traditionally had better placement rates than other secondary vocational programs. This is partially because teachers and students are involved with employers. Supervisors become instructors on the job and have opportunities to evaluate the student as a potential employee before a position is offered. They have an investment in the educational process and most want a return on this investment.

In the past, work experience has been provided to students in a variety of forms. Some of the most successful have been:

- **Apprenticeships**—These training programs usually serve learners who have completed their full-time school. Apprentices are indentured by a contract between employers, union, and the local joint apprenticeship training committee. They function as full-time workers with normal working conditions, for a specified period of time, under the supervision of skilled workers (journeymen). They receive part-time related instruction in school for a few hours per week.

- **Cooperative Education**—After students have the necessary initial preparation in a vocational program, they are placed in training stations with cooperating businesses or industries that provide the necessary supervised occupational experiences. While in the cooperative education program, students continue to take general education courses and courses in related theory at school. A coordinator develops a training plan and works with the employer to ensure that the student receives the training and experience specified in the plan.

- **Internships**–Generally, internships go to advanced students who need experience putting into practice what they have learned in a vocational program. Teachers arrange for employers to hire students during the summer or after school. Employers agree to provide a variety of experiences, most of which the school could not provide. Students and employers prepare weekly reports on work performed and evaluate the experience.
- **Shadowing**–In this learning situation, an advanced vocational student is assigned to observe worker(s) performing their duties. Students receive specific instructions on what observations to make and what to include in required written reports. Workers receive training on how to conduct themselves with the students and on their role in the learning experience. Often, workers being observed explain in detail how, when, and why they perform certain tasks. While students do not get hands-on experience, they do have a chance to see first-hand the application of principles and theories learned in school.

Because schools are having difficulty providing the quality and quantity of graduates needed, employers and trade unions ought to be involved in the educational process. Not only will this improve the quality of the graduates, but the public will be more informed about their training, and their public image will be enhanced as well. Vocational education can once again become a contributor to the economic development of our nation.

Several innovations can improve the quality of vocational training and help students make the transition from school to work. The Secretary of Labor has publicly supported an apprenticeship program for American youth, patterned after the German apprenticeship system. In the German system, youngsters can begin their apprenticeships at age 16, after completing compulsory full-time schooling. Roughly 85 percent of all German youth who end their general schooling go into vocational training. Most get their postcompulsory education through the apprenticeship system. Apprenticeships are offered in 380 different trades or professions within the fields of agriculture, industry, mining, construction, and commerce.

Apprentices attend a part-time school called the *berufsschule*. This school provides compulsory in-school training required during the term specified in the apprenticeship. About 40 percent of the curriculum is devoted to general subjects, such as German, social studies, economics, and religion. Sixty percent of the curriculum is composed of technical subjects related to the apprentices' profession. Apprentices usually attend the *berufsschule* one or two days per week. In-company training and work experience are provided by employers. Because two places–school and company–cooperate in providing complete training, the term *dual system* is used. In Germany, employers, workers, unions, industrial and trade organizations, schools, the government, parents, and community agencies are all committed to the dual system. The transition from school to work is not a problem, since in effect students go from work to work. In Germany, university graduates are the most at-risk population for unemployment.

Recently, many Americans have become interested in testing models to determine the value of implementing elements of the German dual system in the United States. Some examples of activities that show this level of interest include:

- The University of Tennessee and the Tennessee Valley Authority conducted a major research study and published a book on their findings titled *Workforce Development in the Federal Republic of Germany*.
- The U.S. Department of Labor plans to create a youth apprenticeship system.
- Senator Sam Nunn of Georgia and Representative Dick Gephardt of Missouri plan to implement an Institute of Youth Apprenticeship.

- Governor Tommy Thompson signed legislation establishing a statewide apprenticeship system for youth in Wisconsin.
- Arkansas passed a law that will establish several model apprenticeship programs.
- Oregon is presently establishing standards for training which may provide for youth apprenticeships.
- The city of Boston has implemented a model four-year apprenticeship program for training workers in allied health occupations.
- Tennessee, Georgia, and Arkansas plan to take policymakers to Germany to investigate the dual system.

Success Stories Abroad

In addition to the information provided on apprentice training in Germany, the remainder of this chapter details exemplary vocational education and training (VET) approaches in three other European countries (Sweden, Switzerland, and the United Kingdom). The examples described show how VET programs in these countries successfully provide youth with a natural and progressive transition from school to work. The imaginative and effective practices delineated will, we hope, provide initiatives for making the transition as seamless as possible for American youth.

While there are cultural, historic, economic, political, and other differences between the U.S.A., Sweden, Switzerland, and the United Kingdom, the underlying causes of youth unemployment, school dropout, and other related problems are fundamentally the same. What differs are the approaches to solving the problems. "Lessons" learned from the European success stories described here could be incorporated into a transition model for American young people.

Borrowing good practices from formal and nonformal VET approaches that have been tested over time and proven solid makes more sense than haphazardly experimenting. This does not mean, however, that vocational education in the U.S. should blindly adopt the practices of other countries. No answers exist that can be transferred without forethought and adaptation.

The Swedish Approach

The formal education system in Sweden includes a compulsory nine-year *grundskola* for 7- to 16-year-olds and an upper integrated secondary school for 16- to 19-year-olds. The curriculum is regulated by the National Board of Education, with some flexibility at the local education level.

Grundskola. Students at the grundskola are introduced to the world of work through:

1. Individual and group vocational counseling sessions.
2. Experience with their parents at their places of employment.
3. Group visits to local workplaces.
4. Work experience in the school, such as answering the telephone, operating duplication machines, serving lunch, and shelving books in the library.
5. Work experience in nearby public institutions, such as kindergartens, post offices, and senior citizen centers.

In eighth grade, students have three one-week workplace experiences. For a week each, they are assigned to a workplace associated with: (a) manufacturing and technology; (b) commerce, communications, services, agriculture, or forestry; and (c) clerical or administrative work or nursing. Vocational orientation counselors combine student choices in such a way that boys become acquainted with a predominantly female occupation, and girls with one that is predominantly male. In their final year at the compulsory grundskola, each student participates in a minimum two-week work experience. To the extent possible, preferences for a particular workplace or experience are facilitated.

More than 80 percent of compulsory grundskola completers apply for the upper integrated secondary school. Those who choose to leave school (compulsory schooling ends at age 16) remain the responsibility of local education authorities, who are required to stay in touch with them and offer counseling up to age 18. Many school leavers find employment; others enroll in short outreach courses which concentrate on life skills and a basic orientation to work. Youth centers have been established as guidance and contact centers to cope with the problems of preparing school leavers for employment. There is a pattern, however, for some young people to take a break from school for a year or two to gain work experience or travel abroad. Not even all those who are accepted by the upper integrated secondary school start immediately (Turner & Rawlings, 1982).

Upper integrated secondary school. Prior to the establishment of the upper integrated secondary school in 1971, those who continued their education beyond the compulsory nine years selected one of three different types of schools. To eliminate this historic division, the new upper integrated secondary school combined the: (a) gymnasium, with its academic tradition; (b) vocational school, with its trade courses; and (c) professional school, which prepared students in commerce and some professions.

There is a common core curriculum in upper integrated secondary schools consisting of Swedish, civics, and career guidance. Most schools also include mathematics and English. In addition, there are 23 courses from which to choose, 18 of which are two-year vocational courses. Not every school offers all 18 vocational courses since this would not be cost effective and could lead to unemployed graduates in some regions. A number of the vocational courses provide for different specializations as the learning period progresses. For example, in Wood Technology, students can specialize in carpentry, boat building, or pattern making.

Specialized courses are also offered, for vocations which do not require large numbers of skilled workers. These are available only when there are employment opportunities. They vary in length from three weeks to three years. Examples include bus driver (three-week course), medical attendant (23-week course), foundry worker (one-year course), machine operator (two-year course), and furrier (three-year course).

The upper integrated secondary school offers **higher specialized courses** as well. Examples include computer servicing, industrial electronics, industrial electricity, machine assembly, saw mill technician, and tool-making technology. These one-year "capstone" courses are taken after completing an appropriate two-year vocational course. Enrollment is regulated to avoid training more specialists than the labor market can absorb (Turner & Rawlings, 1982).

Overall, the trend has been for increasing numbers of students to select a two-year vocational course. This is because such courses lead to good jobs. Course selection decisions are made by students and their parents in consultation with ninth-grade teachers at the grundskola. Preferences are accommodated to the extent possible, but the number of places in each course is controlled nationally so that output does not exceed labor market needs. Consequently, when demand exceeds available places, preference is given to applicants on the basis of achievement in the grundskola and relevant work experience. Some applicants who are not admitted to the course of their choice take jobs and gain work experience which helps in future admissions decisions. Others accept their second or even third choice (Turner & Rawlings, 1982).

The three-year scheme. Vocational orientation and exploratory experiences at workplaces seemed adequate at the grundskola. However, many felt that there was insufficient work experience in the upper integrated secondary school. It became a serious criticism that these schools were out of touch with employers and the world of work and were, therefore, not adequately preparing students for jobs.

Consequently, a scheme was introduced during the 1988-89 academic year to extend vocational courses from two to three years to facilitate a compulsory workplace component. This workplace component adds a variety of educational and social benefits as a result of the students' involvement in productive work on the job. In grades 10 and 11, at least 10 percent of a student's time is spent at a workplace. This is increased to 60 percent, equivalent to three days per week, in grade 12 (Nothdurft, 1989). In addition to the day-release approach, a block release is possible.

The National Board of Education decides which part of each vocational course is to be completed at the workplace. This decision is made after consulting representatives of educational mandators and vocational committees. Different parts of a course are completed wherever the best results can be attained. The workplace portion is conducted under the direction of supervisors made available by the enterprise. A grant is provided by the state to cover the cost of these supervisors (Swedish Ministry of Education and Cultural Affairs, 1988).

Under this scheme, and in accordance with school regulations and labor laws, no employer-employee relationship exists during the workplace component. Students, however, receive insurance coverage comparable to that of employees. Schools have the responsibility and authority to arrange for necessary training and refer students to a workplace. They are also fully responsible for instruction, even during time students spend in the workplace. Students are not paid a wage, but they do receive the study grant available to all upper integrated secondary school participants. They may also qualify for loans and travel or accommodation supplements (Holmes, 1983). The training experience complies with the school calendar and students observe school holidays, as opposed to employee days off. Workplace activities, on the other hand, comply with the daily hours of the enterprise rather than the school.

Enterprises participating in the scheme receive government grants toward the cost of new equipment. This is an important part of the scheme, since a successful strategy for the renewal of vocational training requires investments in up-to-date equipment. The inclusion of workplace training calls for student experiences to be on modern production processes and equipment. Otherwise, closer contacts between schools and the workplace and alternation between periods of in-school and on-the-job learning would be less effective.

Summing up. Among the best known achievements of Sweden is the quality of its formal education system. Education is free, including books and lunch. Study grants, loans, and travel or accommodation supplements are available. All this is based on the principle that an individual's right to education is guaranteed and no one need forego it for financial reasons. By United States standards, the low school dropout and youth unemployment fig-

ures are remarkable. The key to this is an education with an explicit vocational orientation.

The Swedish education system has moved away from academic tracks and is closely related to the labor market and economic structure of the country. Sweden has a national work force policy which is an essential part of economic planning. While the allocation of students to courses reflects the expected needs of the economy, the broad-based curriculum within each course enables students to "fine tune" their choice of vocational specialization in response to labor market changes.

For the Swedes, work is what responsible people do, for themselves and for the country, and education is the means by which they learn to do it more effectively and efficiently. The seriousness of Swedish students and the dignity accorded vocational training are praiseworthy.

The Swiss Approach

In Switzerland, compulsory schooling ends when students complete ninth grade, usually at age 15. The vast majority (over 75 percent) of the graduates choose a vocational career at this point. Most of the others continue in academic programs; 17 percent attend grammar schools to prepare for university admission exams, and 7 percent enroll in continued general education schools and teacher training programs. There are a few school leavers (less than 1 percent) and they generally find employment or take a break before entering an apprenticeship (Berger, 1988).

Vocational guidance. Both schools and cantonal (state government) agencies provide vocational guidance and counseling services. From an early age, students are guided in selecting an occupation in which they can develop. While undergoing compulsory education they receive classroom instruction on careers, career orientation classes, and pre-apprenticeship classes. In addition to the schools, community-based professional information centers offer career information and advisory services. These centers provide details on opportunities appropriate to an individual's aptitudes and aspirations. As a result of these combined efforts, students have ample opportunities to learn about numerous vocations before making a career choice (Benglen, 1989).

Vocational apprenticeship schools. Among the options for initial vocational training in Switzerland is a totally school-based apprenticeship. This four-year formal education program is selected by 9 percent of those who complete compulsory education. Students follow apprenticeship regulations for training and work experience, but practical training and experience are provided in a school workshop, rather than on the job with an employer. The school operates an enterprise and apprentices produce quality products, which are sold at competitive prices. Some products are designed and manufactured as training aids for math, chemistry, physics, electronics, and numerical control machining; even furniture and machine tools are produced. The sale of manufactured items provides an important source of funding, generating up to one-third of a school's budget.

Apprentices who successfully complete the school requirements and pass the final apprenticeship examination are awarded the same certificate as apprentices who go through the dual system. However, a larger percentage of the graduates of full-time vocational apprenticeship schools gain admission into applied engineering programs at polytechnical colleges. It is reported that in Bern 95 percent of the graduates are admitted.

Dual system of apprenticeship. Most apprenticeships are conducted under the dual system rather than in a full-time vocational apprenticeship school. The dual system couples employer-sponsored training in an enterprise with compulsory classes at a government-sponsored vocational school.

Apprenticeships start at age 15, after the compulsory nine years of schooling. However, as a result of the high standards set by vocational schools and the competition for selection at the most desirable enterprises, some vocations are all but reserved for applicants who complete additional formal education before beginning an apprenticeship.

An apprenticeship contract sets the training period, from two to four years depending on the vocation. It is drawn up in conformance with the Swiss Code of Obligations and signed by the employer, the trainee, and the trainee's parents. Before training begins, the contract is presented to the responsible cantonal authority for approval. Authorization is granted only when the enterprise's vocational tutor or *meister* (instructor) possesses the professional capabilities and personal qualities required and if the contract conforms to the legal provisions in force. If the trainee abandons the apprenticeship after a trial period, penalties can be imposed on the trainee or the trainee's parents (Dickey, 1981).

Dual system apprenticeships are conducted in three different enterprise settings:

- State or private workshops (special training workshops), where apprentice training is separated from production (Steiner, 1983).
- Small businesses, where a *meister* (master) electrician, plumber, or baker, for example, has, in addition to other employees, one or two apprentices (Steiner, 1983).
- Large enterprises, where many apprentices are trained by *meisters* in their vocation. In the French-speaking cantons, there is a tendency toward the use of special training workshops.

Regardless of the enterprise setting, the regulations for training and work experience in a vocation must be followed. Those who fail to adhere to regulations are subject to fines and penalties. Naturally, demand for apprenticeships concentrates on those enterprises which offer the highest quality training and most favorable working conditions. Nevertheless, the training efforts of the least desirable enterprises must also conform to regulations.

Apprentices attend compulsory classes at a vocational school. Here they study both theoretical and occupation-specific subjects. The scope of the training, subjects taught, and number of lessons are determined for each vocation and apply throughout the country. However, the cantons are responsible for organizing this tuition-free training. As a result, they either operate these schools themselves, or authorize the local communes, enterprises, or professional associations to do so.

Three-fifths of the school curriculum is

directly connected to the apprentice's specialization. The remainder focuses on language(s), literature, commercial law, correspondence, business, civics, and economics (Dickey, 1981). Instruction is based on the program contained in the apprenticeship regulations.

Each week, apprentices receive at least one full day off, with pay, to attend a vocational school. Those who are qualified and so motivated are permitted an additional half day to take optional complementary courses. In addition, apprentices who achieve high standards of performance in both vocational school and enterprise training have the opportunity to take courses at an advanced vocational college for a maximum of two days per week. The law requires that absence from the enterprise not exceed two full days per week (Benglen, 1989).

Vocational training conducted within an enterprise was criticized because it was limited by being directly coupled to the work in which the enterprise was involved at any one time. In response to this criticism, introductory courses were established by professional associations to ensure that all apprentices attain the required level of competence and experience. These annual courses, of one to several weeks duration, are arranged under the guidance of the Division for Vocational Training. They are conducted outside the enterprise, usually in a vocational school, and methodically address pre-work needs as well as basic and up-to-date work techniques. The federal government and the cantons subsidize these introductory courses (Benglen, 1989).

After completing the training period, all apprentices take a final examination. The two-part exam covers theoretical knowledge learned at the vocational school, as well as the practical skills acquired within the enterprise. Scores on both parts are considered in calculating the final result. Practical test scores count for approximately two-thirds of the total.

All the partners concerned with vocational training participate in establishing final exam regulations. Theoretical and practical examinations take place over three or four days, depending on the vocation. After a six-month waiting period, either part can be repeated, if the first attempt was unsuccessful.

Those who pass the final exam are awarded the Federal Certificate of Competence (journeyman's certificate), a nationally recognized vocational qualification. This certificate protects the reputation of the vocation and certifies those who hold it as qualified for employment. In many instances, it is a prerequisite to advanced training (Benglen, 1989).

Summing up. Initial vocational training is acquired through: (a) a school-based apprenticeship, which offers both practical training and theoretical instruction, or (b) an apprenticeship in a public or private enterprise coupled with part-time attendance at a vocational school. The majority of young people serve their apprenticeship under the latter dual system approach.

During the full duration of the apprenticeship (which varies from two to four years, depending on the vocation), trainees attend a vocational school for one to two days per week. Here they are taught theoretical and occupation-specific subjects. The scope of the training is determined for each vocation, and instruction is based on the program contained in the apprenticeship regulations.

Apprenticeships are designed so that, through their completion, apprentices acquire good work habits, a concern for craftsmanship, cooperative attitudes, and a readiness to accept responsibility. As skilled workers, they are competent and fully prepared to meet all the demands of a skilled job. Most of the training is provided in an enterprise. Because it is closely related to production, costs are reasonable. Some enterprises, however, offer high-cost training separate from production. They consider this an investment in the competency of Switzerland's workforce and, therefore, an investment in their long-term prosperity. Learning environments range from the regular workplace, to specially designed workshops, to the classroom. In addition, there are inter-company training workshops which relieve small and medium-sized enterprises of much of the training burden. Regulations specify the content of practical training for each vocation. Approximately 300 sets of vocational regulations are in force.

Once the apprenticeship is completed, trainees must take a final examination. This exam tests both the knowledge gained at the vocational school and the skills acquired within the enterprise. Those who pass the exam are awarded the Federal Certificate of Competence. With this credential, journeymen can work throughout Switzerland or proceed to advanced training.

The British Youth Training Scheme

In the United Kingdom, compulsory schooling ends at age 16. About 75 percent of 16-year-olds, more than 450,000 each year, choose to leave school. The other 25 percent remain in school until age 18, to prepare for university admission. School leavers have three principal choices in preparing for a working career: (a) seek admission to a technical college, (b) join the Youth Training Scheme, or (c) find a job with an employer who offers company-funded traineeships.

The traditional route, for those students deciding to pursue a formal vocational education and training (VET) program, is enrollment in a technical college. These students work toward certification examinations administered by bodies such as The City and Guilds of London Institute (Barnes, 1988).

To reduce school-to-work transition problems for those who leave school at age 16, the British government introduced the Youth Training Scheme. It is a nationally integrated program of education, training, and work experience. Originally launched in 1983 as a one-year program, it was extended in 1986 to provide two years of guaranteed training for all 16-year-old school leavers. This training guarantee applies to unemployed as well as employed young people. By 1988, more than half of all school leavers had joined the Youth Training Scheme; hence, it has become a major force in the transition from school to work (Peck, 1990).

By providing a broad-scope, nonformal (outside the formal education system) VET, the scheme enables trainees to earn vocational certification relating to competency in the workplace or credit toward that qualification. The City and Guilds of London Institute developed a systematic certification approach which articulates the nonformal VET route, from a Certificate in Pre-Vocational Education to management levels (City and Guilds of London Institute, 1986). In addition to a broad-scope VET, the scheme provides: (a) career information and guidance, as well as counseling throughout the program; (b) opportunities for personal development; (c) instruction in basic skills, when needed; and (d) guided work experience (Elliott, 1984).

The government intended that the scheme be employer-led and employer-based. However, some programs are based at colleges of further education, training workshops, or community projects (European Centre for the Development of Vocational Training, 1986).

Nevertheless, a central feature of the scheme is that all programs are work based. The majority are based with employers who provide both on-the-job training and work experience. In addition to this on-the-job learning experience, at least 20 weeks of the two-year training period are spent off the job, in classrooms and workshops, with studies which reinforce and support the work-based experience. Normally, the first year provides for 13 weeks of off-the-job education and training, alternating with 39 weeks of on-the-job learning. During the second year, the relationship is 7 off the job to 45 on the job (Evans, et al., 1989).

A stated objective of the scheme is that it provide four outcomes:

1. Competence in a job and/or a range of occupational skills.
2. Competence in broad-based occupationally transferable core skills.
3. The ability to transfer skills and knowledge to new situations.
4. Personal effectiveness, including planning, problem solving, and interpersonal skills (Evans et al., 1989).

The intent of these outcomes is to facilitate employability and subsequent effectiveness at work. It is hoped that trainees will become versatile, adaptable, and highly motivated employees.

The credibility of the scheme depends largely on the quality of the work-based learning experience. In an effort to ensure high quality training, programs are organized and delivered by a network of managing agents.

These agents come from a range of organizations, including (a) a single large employer, (b) a consortia of small companies, (c) chambers of commerce or trade, (d) statutory and volunteer industry training organizations, (e) group training associations, or (f) a consortia of both employer and education/training organizations (European Centre for the Development of Vocational Training, 1986). Managing agents may or may not provide the training, but they retain responsibility for its quality and for trainee progress. While trainees are on the job, program coordinators visit to see how they are doing, to provide counseling, and to ensure that they are not being exploited as cheap labor.

All Youth Training Schemes operate within a nationally agreed and funded framework. Unemployed trainees receive a stipend and a travel allowance. The stipend is marginally more than they would receive from unemployment benefits which are available to school leavers even if they have never held a job (Dale, 1988). In addition to the government stipend, some companies also provide trainees with a monetary enhancement.

Despite the scope and scale of the Youth Training Scheme, some employers prefer to operate outside of it, offering their own company-funded initial training for young people. Others operate the scheme for nonemployed trainees alongside their employee traineeships. In some cases, the Youth Training Scheme is used as a funding mechanism to enable a few additional school leavers to join an existing company-funded program. The mixed approach of funding by companies and the government has the advantage of assuring that training resources are used to their fullest (Evans, et al., 1989).

Final Thoughts

Helping students make the transition from school to employment is both a challenge and an opportunity. The transition should be *a structured process, not an event.* The process can be successful only with cooperation between schools and employers. Ideally, young people will pass from school to employment, not only with the initial skills, knowledge, and experience required, but also with a forward-looking plan for their continuing further education and training.

References

Barnes, J. A. (1988, April). The United Kingdom's education and training revolution. *Vocational Education Journal*, pp. 39-45.

Benglen, D. S. (Ed.). (1989). *Vocational training in Switzerland.* Zurich, Switzerland: Swiss Association for Vocational Guidance.

Berger, U. (Ed.). (1988). *Statistical data on Switzerland.* Berne, Switzerland: Swiss Federal Statistical Office.

City and Guilds of London Institute. (1986). *A brief guide to City and Guilds.* London, England: Author.

Dale, R. (1988, February 2). U.K. youth training plan: Hope but no panacea. *International Herald Tribune,* p. 13.

Dickey, K. N. (1981). *Switzerland: A study of the educational system of Switzerland and a guide to the academic placement of students from Switzerland in educational institutions of the United States.* Washington, DC: American Association of Collegiate Registrars and Admissions Officers.

Elliott, J. (1984). *The organization of productive work in secondary technical and vocational education in the United Kingdom* (Unesco Publication No. ED-84/WS/49). Paris, France: United Nations Educational Scientific and Cultural Organization.

European Centre for the Development of Vocational Training. (1986). *Regional development and vocational training—Analysis and promotion of coordination between development and vocational training* (Catalog No. HX-45-85-090-EN-C). Luxembourg, Belgium: Author.

Evans, K., Dovaston, V., Holland, D., Brown, A., Fisher, J., & Haffenden, l. (1989). *The in-company trainer of young people in the United Kingdom* (Catalog No. HX-56-89-304-EN-C). Luxembourg, Belgium: European Centre for the Development of Vocational Training.

Holmes, B. (Ed.). (1983). *International handbook of education systems* (Vol. 1). Chichester, England: John Wiley & Sons.

Nothdurft, W. E. (1989). Innovations in education and job training from Sweden, West Germany, France, Great Britain and Philadelphia, Pennsylvania. Unpublished manuscript, The German Marshall Fund of the United States, Washington, DC.

Peck, J. (1990). The youth training scheme: Regional policy in reverse. *Policy and Politics, 18* (2), 135-143.

Steiner, G. (1983). Current problems in vocational education in Switzerland: Report on a national research program (Occasional Paper No. 93). Columbus, OH: National Center for Research in Vocational Education. (ERIC Document Reproduction Service No. ED 239 108)

Swedish Ministry of Education and Cultural Affairs.

(1988). *A new scheme of upper secondary vocational education.* Stockholm, Sweden: Author.

Turner, C., & Rawlings, P. (1982). Vocational education and training in Sweden (Comparative Papers in Further Education No. 9). Blagdon, England: Further Education Staff College. (ERIC Document Reproduction Service No. ED 240 247)

11

Transition Experiences of High School Students Planning to Attend College

Ursula B. Cargill

The quest for education is a continuous cycle, yet our educational system is designed with specific ends in mind. Grade levels determine the educational curriculum a student will receive, yet each grade level functions independently of others. Third-grade teachers communicate with each other with the same degree of infrequency as we see in communication between high schools and colleges. The compounded result is that students enter higher grade levels with differing abilities and differing educational experiences. Although these differences in students can result from several variables, curriculum articulation will be examined as a mechanism to facilitate a reduction in miseducation due to miscommunication between high schools and higher education.

As a system, the educational process should provide each student with similar, though not identical, skills when they complete a specific grade. In the ideal educational system, students entering third grade would have similar educational experiences, and students leaving high schools and entering colleges would also have similar skills and educational experiences. On examination of the skills of freshmen in higher education, there is a wide disparity in the socio-academic preparation of students. Students with the desire to attend college may be given the opportunity of admission; however, students labeled "at-risk" drop out of higher education at alarming rates. For

example, Tinto (1987) found that during the past 100 years, approximately 55 percent, or about half of all students who entered college, never completed a degree within the traditional four- to five-year time period. Tinto held that nearly 50 percent of students who enter higher education never complete the program in which they first enroll.

For many high school students, a college education is seen as the key to a successful future. However, Inger and Larsen (1990) found that 50 percent of high school seniors who had planned in 1972 to complete college had completed college by 1979. They also found that 11 percent of students who planned to complete college had not started by 1979. The acquisition of a college education helps high school graduates build a foundation for the future. Successful college matriculation, culminating in graduation, may provide students with the socio-academic background necessary for contributing to and participating in society. Through successful college matriculation, students are enabled to enter a saturated labor market and be differentiated from other employment seekers who do not hold college credentials. In addition, social experiences acquired during college eventually carry over to interaction with the broader society. For example, Bowles and Gintis (1976) found that education has been an active attempt to instill ideological conformity. The authors also posited that social relationships formed in college paralleled relationships in the economy and workplace.

Transition to college is a significant step in the education process of many high school graduates. Examining the experiences of these high school students would facilitate an understanding of the role high schools play in preparing students for college. Students entering the higher education system are faced with an educational frame of reference acquired through high schools. As a result, some of the limitations and experiences of these students determine their success in academe. For example, Fine (1991) found that young people who start their lives at the greatest risk of class, racial, ethnic, or gender exploitation attend the most traumatized schools and receive the most impoverished education. These students, according to Fine, are most likely to drop out of high school.

However, some students from impoverished environments do complete their high school experience and present themselves to colleges for further education. This type of academic training from impoverished high schools affects the probability of success in college. Retention patterns for college freshmen suggest that students enter higher education with diverse backgrounds and differing ability/tenacity to persevere through the college experience. Ultimately, almost half of students who enroll will eventually withdraw from higher education before program completion. An examination of the transition experiences of these students may illustrate that the socio-academic experiences they have in high school play a role in the educational processes of students during college. Consequently, examining the high school environment may contribute to an understanding that the high school experience has a role in students' transition from high school to college. I will examine the preparation that students receive during high school, as I believe socio-academic preparation in high schools is essential in determining the success of students in college.

What Is Transition to College?

Colleges recruit students who seem capable of completing their academic require-ments. College recruitment personnel review the potential of incoming students to participate in the institution's academic and social demands. Yet, again, almost half of students fail to complete college and ultimately withdraw. This withdrawal confounds the issue of transition to college. Is a successful transition from high school to college characterized by college entrance/admittance, matriculation, or graduation? For measurement purposes, successful transition can be identified by admittance/acceptance into college. High schools can possibly track students into their first year of college matriculation, which makes it easier to determine the percentage of students who have gone to college.

High schools provide more than a transition point from which students enter college. Transition is a process through which students enter college having learned the skills they need for active participation in higher education. The acquisition of skills places the responsibility of educating students, or socio-academically preparing them, within high schools. Education is a holistic process. Success in education does not end when a student leaves high school. High school provides an environment that can enable students to simulate the activities of college. The alignment of the high school environment to the college environment may ease the transition from high school to college by facilitating the transfer of training from one environment to another (English, 1987).

High schools prepare students for life experiences by providing planned educational experiences in a regulated environment. English (1987) posited that schools provide a preparation period for life in the real world. However, students graduate from high schools without the skills necessary for active participation in college. The first year of college may serve as remediation for the unprepared student rather than as a period of intellectual exploration. The congruency between the high school experience and real life at college predetermines the success of transition to college. This congruency suggests that a cooperative relationship should exist between high schools and colleges, as more and more of our students are opting for the college choice. The high school curriculum plays a role in the academic preparation of the student who decides to enter college. Study skills and classroom assignments provide the college-bound student with an opportunity to acquire academic skills. Curriculum alignment between high school and college should consider students' needs and abilities for attending college. A high school curriculum aligned with higher education would simulate college life inside and outside the classroom.

High Schools and Socio-Academic Preparation for College

High schools provide a transition point for thousands of students every year. As one group of young adults moves into the nation's workplace, another group moves into college, and still another moves into unemployment or idleness. The shift into one of these categories can be influenced by a variety of factors. One is the high school environment itself. One of the charges of high schools is to prepare students for broader society—college, work, or even unemployment. The extent of this preparation is proportionally related to the experiences of the individual student. High schools offer the last institutional opportunity for society to shape the behavior of students. The behavior modification function of high schools provide what Nyberg and Egan (1981) would call "socialization."

Socialization in schools is evident in the controls found within the organizational structure. Controls are empowered in the high school educational systems by state regulations and mandates (New York State Education Law). Schools administer state-mandated tests that "measure" student achievement. In addition, the organizational ethos or culture facilitates a degree of control over the socio-academic preparation of students by indirectly stimulating an environment conducive to learning. At the same time, contractual regulations shape the relationships of school personnel among themselves and with students. Employment contracts determine such factors as class size, time on task, and after-school meetings with faculty and students. When these factors are synthesized, we have an educational organization that is created for the pur-

pose of "educating" students. However, the activities of the organization are impediments to the college preparation of high school students. For example, an educational system established to enrich the learning experiences of students by providing standardized tests to measure competency may actually create a system that fosters mediocrity. Schools are established without objectives related to all students attaining subject mastery. As a result, system-wide objectives provide an official legitimation of low standards in our public education system.

Schools prepare students to enter the broader society. The effectiveness of this preparation may depend on the ethos or culture of the school. One of the fundamentals of establishing an effective school calls for providing a safe and orderly environment. Although there is some dispute over the extent of the relationship between an effective school and student achievement, Wilson (1989) would posit that creating an environment that is secure and fair is a necessary prerequisite for learning. Hence, disciplinary regulations permit schools to control the deviant behavior of students.

The college preparatory training provided by high schools depends on several characteristics similar to qualities found in any effective school. College preparatory training can best be described using a method of causal pluralism that considers multiple causes to explain college preparation rather than isolated variables in the transition process. Training reflects an institutional commitment to student education and student willingness to work and to learn. For example, schools can effectively provide academic training for the college-bound student when the school has a strong principal and when teachers have high expectations of student achievement, emphasize learning basic skills, maintain order and discipline, evaluate students regularly, devote large amounts of time to study, and articulate the high school curriculum with higher education. Schools administer state-mandated or district-approved curricula with an objective of a minimum number of students passing state-approved exams. Schools administer these bureaucratically endorsed standardized tests and have significant numbers of students passing. Yet, students enter a higher education system that has an attrition rate of almost 50 percent.

The most significant issue becomes whether there is socio-academic preparation of college-bound students to ease their transition into higher education. Primary academic preparation of high school students comes in the classroom. Primary and secondary socialization of students occurs both inside and outside the classroom. Within the classroom, students learn to respect the formal authority of the teacher. Students may believe that teachers are omniscient and the students themselves but "empty barrels" to be filled with knowledge supplied by the teacher. Students are socialized into conforming to rules, maintaining order, and respecting authority. They learn to assimilate and "fit in" rather than to question. Classroom demands also provide students with a catalyst for acquiring study skills. Students participate in socializing activities both inside and outside high schools. Here, high schools are seen as an implement of society, employed to impose rules of behavior on students.

The alignment of the high school socio-academic activities to the collegiate experience eases the transition from high school to college. However, a lack of congruency between the precollege experience and college may create a more difficult transition. Difficulty arises when there is an impediment to the transfer of training that students acquired during high school. First-year college then may either serve as remediation to teach incoming students or as a filtering-out process for the unprepared student. Colleges may shift the responsibility of student preparation to the student, the family, or the high schools. However, as I posit that formal education is a holistic experience, high schools and colleges should each bear some responsibility for the matriculation of students entering college.

Curriculum articulation between high schools and colleges would create educational continuity for the college-bound student. Articulation becomes a process of coordinating policies and procedures among institutions of the educational system to ease the transition of students from one sector to another. Curriculum articulation would integrate collegiate requirements into the high school experience, and thereby create a similarity or alignment between the high school and the college curriculum. A 1991 report of the Government Accounting Office indicated that only 25 percent of students leaving high schools now go on to complete college. Statistics like this suggests a need to facilitate continuity in the education process whereby more students who opt for postsecondary education actually complete their prescribed course of study. Curriculum articulation coordinated with curriculum alignment between high schools and colleges would create a similarity between these two educational systems thereby facilitating an ease in transition from high schools to college. For example, alignment could be fostered by similarities in freedom/autonomy of high school students, opportunities for decision making in socio-academic activities, and time management. These three elements provide some of the everyday activities of college students that could be simulated in the high schools.

Socio-academic preparation may not be the sole reason for successful transition to college. Some students persevere with the transition to college without socio-academic preparation. However, by highlighting it, I believe we can reduce the number of students who drop out due to lack of preparation. For example, Astin (1975) conducted a longitudinal comparison study of students who planned to earn a bachelor's degree but eventually failed to do so. These students who entered academe intending to complete a program and failed to do so can be identified as "dropping out for the wrong reason." Astin found that in 1968, 535,656, or 40.4 percent, of the sample population planned to obtain a bachelor's degree. On reexamination of this group in 1972, 45.4 percent actually held the degree.

Stakeholders of College Preparation of High School Students

When considering the socio-academic preparation of high school students for college life, one of the most significant variables to consider is the stakeholder in the transition process. Stakeholders are individuals, groups, or organizations who have a vested interest in the transition of high school students to college. I have identified seven stakeholders in the high-school-to-college-transition process: colleges, administrators, financial planners, parents, individual students, teachers, and school guidance counselors.

Colleges as Stakeholders

A college education is a considerable financial investment for both students and higher education. For example, a college obtains financial resources from its enrolled student population through tuition and fees, and from alumni contributions. The average in-state student tuition and fees expenses for students at the State University of New York at Buffalo rose by more than 100 percent from 1979 to 1990. Tuition and fees for the 1979-1980 academic year were $900, and for the academic year 1989-1990 they were $2,983 (Central Staff Office of Institutional Research, 1990). Alumni contributions totaled almost $5 billion for private institutions and about $2.5 billion for public colleges and universities (Sowell, 1989). In addition, the federal government contributes to the financial resources of higher education in the form of grants, student financial aid, and enrollment-based full-time equivalents (FTEs).

The college's stake in the transition of students is evident in the cost of recruitment and admission of new students. For example, colleges face a declining population pool and higher costs resulting from competing with other colleges for students. Competition for students has led to colleges having a greater sensitivity to the collegiate environment. This includes an awareness of recruitment strategies of other institutions, population trends of potential students, and the economic costs of obtaining a college education. Since the 1960s, the population pool of college-aged students has declined, while the cost of a college education has risen. For example, the number of high school graduates declined after a peak in 1976-1977 when 3.2 million students received diplomas. The more than 100 percent increase in tuition and fees between 1970 and 1990 was reported by the New York state education department as necessary to offset the costs of operation in the wake of declining federal funds. I believe the cost to academe for participation in the transitional experiences of high school students is minimal when compared to costs associated with remediating students who are socially and academically unprepared for college-level requirements.

High School Principals as Stakeholders

High school academic achievement level is one admissions criterion for acceptance into college. Academic performance as measured by student achievement has been found to be an outcome of effective schools. One of the factors identified as prevalent in effective schools is strong administrative leadership. Principals are stakeholders in the transition of high school students to college because they play a role in the academic preparation of students for college.

As stakeholders in the transition experiences of high school students, principals can foster a positive ethos, or school culture. For example, the National Association of Secondary School Principals (1990) found student satisfaction to be a mediating variable that influenced student achievement. The association found that student satisfaction was influenced by student-teacher interactions. Effective schools, as measured by promotion of student outcomes, had a strong principal and a functioning administrative team. Student achievement, though not directly an outcome of a positive ethos, was a reflection of the educational experiences of students during their high school tenure. Performance evaluation criteria of high school principals suggest that student outcome is a terminal process. For example, evaluations are based on student outcomes up to but not exceeding high school graduation. Evaluations of high schools should consider the successful transition of students from high school to college. As a holistic process, education does not end when college-bound students enter college. Academic preparation is a reflection of the experiences of the student prior to college admission and the active participation of the student while in college. High school principals can provide strong administrative leadership while considering the needs of the college-bound student to be socially and academically prepared for a successful transition from high school to college.

Financial Planners as Stakeholders

President Bush (1988) identified financial need as a consideration in planning for college. He said that access to college should not be denied due to financial need. According to the president, financial planning for a college education should take place using money from parents, with student aid and wages earned during college, and with loans to be paid after graduation. Financial planning for college would also suggest a knowledge of the resource base provided by the federal government as well as scholarships provided by the private sector. These several sources of college financial aid illuminate the role financial planners play in students' transition.

The cost of financing college has been steadily rising. The affordability of a college education has created an obstacle for high school students planning to attend college. Financial need is more significant when considering that more students from disadvantaged families opt for the college choice. To offset the rising costs of a college education, families are turning to private financial institutions for support. Financial institutions that have committed to providing loans to students have a vested interest in the successful transition of these high school students to college. Loan default can be a considerable expense for financial institutions and indeed for the federal government. Socio-academic preparation of high school students for college may not reduce the actual expense of a college education. However, the preparation may minimize the attrition of college students, thereby providing a financial return on investment of a college education. The financial return may be found in the vocational transition after college.

Parents as Stakeholders

Parental involvement has been identified as important in the schooling of children (VanScriver, 1990). However, the philosophical belief that parental involvement is necessary for the promotion of student success in school has not been translated into actual school-initiated strategies for parental involvement. The federal government has taken a proactive strategy to involve parents in the schools. For example, the Chapter 1 program as described by D'Angelo and Adler (1990) provides a stimulus for schools to assess the effectiveness of their parental involvement programs. The authors posit that one of the outcomes of successful parental involvement strategies is better communication with families that schools may have identified as hard to reach. For example, in Buffalo, New York, the Chapter 1 Parent Resource Center invites parents to visit and review the resource materials or take part in workshops. Parents at this center can borrow computers after they receive training in computer use. Loans of computers can extend to eight weeks.

Scholars on student retention in higher education have identified family background as a factor in the persistence of students. For example, Astin (1971) identified parental education and income level as related to student "dropout proneness." Hence, by examining parents as stakeholders in the transition of students to college, the research suggests that students from disadvantaged families are more prone to drop out. Here we may have a cycle of attrition because the parents involved may be educationally disadvantaged.

By examining socio-academic preparation as a holistic process, the educational organizations should realize that parents can "only lead where they can go." In other words, it may be difficult or impossible for parents who have dropped out of school to be the critical variable in socio-academic preparation of students when the parents are also "at risk." Schools (both high school and college) should realize that parents want their children to accomplish more than they did. However, if parents are educationally disadvantaged, then the school may either need a strategy to increase quality parental involvement or need to develop school-based programs to improve socio-academic preparation for the college-bound student. By establishing parental involvement as the basis for improving student achievement, the educational system releases itself from the responsibility of education.

Schools were established by law and entrusted by parents with the responsibility of educating students.

Students as Stakeholders

The public school system provides an institutional mechanism whereby education is distributed with equality and equity. This statement suggests that education is open to all students without a bias or preference for one group over another. As much as I may want to believe in the equality of opportunity in education, I have come to realize that it is a myth because public education is segregated and inequitable. In 1954, the United States Supreme Court in Brown v. Board of Education held that segregation in the public schools was inherently unequal and charged the states to desegregate the public schools "with all deliberate speed." How far have we come since Brown? Upon further examination of the educational system, there is an inherent inequity, a bias, against the urban poor. Kozol (1991) presented a descriptive portrait of the educational experiences of poor and homeless children. He found that with the current way the public schools are funded, the rich receive a richer quality of education than the poor. Kozol held that public schools are mostly segregated and less equal when compared to the educational system of 1954.

Students who come from impoverished school environments may have difficulty in the transition to college. One of the characteristics of the impoverished school environment, as described by Fine (1991), is the silencing of students' voices so that they do not fully develop cognitively, and thereby are limited in the academic training they need to succeed in higher education. In addition, teacher labeling and grouping of students as fast or slow learners may perpetuate the class structure of the larger society (Rist, 1970). Rist and Fine imply that students inadvertently begin to behave in the manner expected of them by their teachers and their peers. Hence, through self-fulfilling prophecies, students may have a low self-esteem, which can carry over into their higher education experience or even throughout their lives. Students may ultimately succumb to the class for which they have been prepared and

withdraw from social and academic educational experiences.

Students have the greatest stake in the transition to college, as it is their future the education system is developing. The socio-academic future of students is entrusted in an educational system that has been designed with standardized curriculum delivery mechanisms to a diversified student body. Standardization in schools and diversity of students makes it difficult to deliver one curriculum to all students. An individualized or student-focused curriculum would abate the problems of standardization by entrusting a greater degree of autonomy to the teacher. The role teachers play in transition experiences will be examined further as teachers provide the linkage between the educational system and students.

Teachers as Stakeholders

Teachers have direct contact with students because of the nature of classroom structure. As stakeholders, teachers are in a position to foster the academic and social bonding of students. For example, Wehlage, Rotter, Smith, Lesko, and Fernandez (1989) posited that in a positive teacher culture, educators accept personal accountability for the success of each student. This personal accountability is a great responsibility for teachers, but as members of a system entrusted with educating our youth, teachers should be empowered to *teach* the college-bound student. Teacher attitude and expectations may subsequently influence the achievement and learning outcomes of students (Kaufman & Lewis, 1968). Although I do not embrace the notion of cultural deprivation cited by Kaufman and Lewis, the authors' report was significant in highlighting the importance of school environment, and what is now known as school ethos, on the success of the disadvantaged/at-risk student.

The at-risk student who enters post-secondary institutions from an academically effective high school are few and far between. Academically effective schools that provide academic training for the at-risk student are the exception rather than the norm. Armed with this realization, higher education should be cognizant that students are a product of both their natural ability and their academic/social environment.

School Guidance Counselors as Stakeholders

Counseling has been identified as the most significant experience in the transition of college-bound high school students. Just as a lighthouse helps ships navigate through unknown seas, a school guidance counselor provides direction for the college bound. Counselors navigate students through the waters of higher education by helping students to learn about opportunities that are available. According to Morris, Dillenbeck, and Merritt (1964) the school counselor helps students to learn about opportunities outside of high school. The knowledge of these opportunities may lead to students making plans and decisions about their future.

From a historical perspective, guidance counseling originated with an orientation to vocational guidance. Guidance in education may have commenced in 1908 in Boston, when Frank Parsons began a vocational guidance placement program for out-of-school youth. Guidance was primarily applied to the efforts of high schools to find job opportunities for their students (Kelley, 1955). Guidance counseling has come to be characterized by the National Vocational Guidance Association (1942) as a process through which individuals are assisted in choosing, entering, and progressing in an occupation. This definition suggests that guidance counseling is not a terminal process, but the impact of guidance counseling may continue after the high school experience.

By providing information to the college-bound student, school counselors function as a liaison between the student and higher education. A counselor who has command of the data base describing colleges and universities may provide broad-based guidance to the college-bound student. However, in light of the dynamic nature of the higher education environment, it becomes difficult for any one school or any school counselor to have command of the repository of educational information. Processing *and* use of the data base on higher education is necessary to guide the college-

bound student. Kerr (1963) found evidence that out of 39 NDEA-reimbursed counselors, 40 percent gave misinformation on NDEA loans. According to Kerr, students also reported having been given erroneous information by counselors regarding post-high school educational requirements and opportunities. For the college-bound student, accurate information is important in making decisions pertaining to college.

The information received from counselors should be current, valid, and applicable. For example, some colleges change tuition, curricula, or entrance requirements annually. A counselor with command of the data base on colleges may be aware of this new information and counsel students using current information. Although recency does not mean accuracy, most information on counseling the college bound will not be accurate unless the information is recent. There has been a proliferation in the number of colleges and universities. For example, in 1984-1985, there were 3,331 colleges, universities, and branch campuses in the United States as compared with approximately 2,400 such institutions in 1968. The data base on the numbers of institutions of higher education is constantly evolving. By having command of the data on academe, counselors can provide the information that may lead to a match between the student's plans for the future and the specializations available in higher education.

The role of guidance of the college-bound student is not exclusive to informational guidance. Guidance includes a concern for the whole student, as in counseling the student on the discovery of self. This traditional personal-social role of counselors suggests that attention should be given to all students in the school. The guidance of students in the discovery of self may be apparent in the consultation between the student and guidance counselors in the selection of a course of study. For example, counselors may assist students in the selection of curricula relevant to the future plans of the students. These future plans may be based on the results of standardized skills tests. Added to the counseling of all students in the discovery of self are the administrative demands placed on guidance counselors with simultaneous reductions in school budgets and resources. Paradoxically, the enthusiasm of students to receive counseling for college from within the high school may overwhelm the guidance office. However, some students seeking college counseling beyond the resources of the high school may consult independent/private counselors for help in making the final selection of a college.

The guidance counselor is a practitioner who significantly influences the future paths of millions of graduating high school students. Schools are served well by providing school counselors with the resources necessary to help students navigate the world beyond high school. Guidance counseling transcends the entire high school experience as it is not limited to individual grade levels or subject matter. The impact of guidance accompanies students well beyond high school. The ability of guidance to positively shape students is paramount in the socio-academic preparation of students for college.

Holism in Transition to College

"The whole is greater than the sum of its parts." Statements like this reflect the fact that systems, including educational systems, are made of several parts that function together to create a limited whole. The efficiency of the educational system cannot be fully examined by highlighting one of its parts. Maximum explanation of the system can be achieved by examining the system itself. I believe the transition experiences of students planning to attend college should be viewed from a holistic perspective. Holism in examination of the experiences of high school students should begin with collaboration among the stakeholders in the transition process.

Holism suggests an active participation of stakeholders that should facilitate a socio-academic preparation of the college-bound student. Schools as extensions of the community should provide an environment where stakeholders have the opportunity or freedom to become involved in the transition experiences of college-bound students. A healthy organizational culture would provide the impetus for participation in open and direct communication between stakeholders.

True preparation for college is facilitated by the similarity of the environment of high school and college. Similarity may be found in socio-academic thrusts, demands on the student, and curriculum requirements. Students from environments dissimilar to those found in higher education should learn of the differences before entering college. Information on the differences should be provided to college-bound students by any and all stakeholders to minimize any negative experiences caused by misinformation. Transition is a process that extends beyond the high school. Successful college transition is more than entrance into college. Successful transition emanates from the opportunity of students to actively participate in the social and academic experiences of college.

High school is the last educational institutional opportunity for society to affect student transition to college. Hence, schools should be geared toward the preparation of students for the demands of college. Examination of the transition experiences is the point of departure in gaining insights into the progression of students after high school. Follow-up of actual student accomplishments would facilitate a comparison between planned and realized objectives after high school.

References

Astin, A. (1971). *Predicting academic performance in college*. New York: The Free Press.

Astin, A. (1975). *Preventing students from dropping out*. San Francisco: Jossey-Bass.

Bowles, S., & Gintis, H. (1976). *Schooling in capitalist America*. New York: Basic Books.

Bush, G. (1988). The Bush strategy for excellence in education. *Phi Delta Kappan, 70*, 112-118.

Central Staff Office of Institutional Research. (1990). *Trends in enrollment and degrees granted*. New York: State University of New York.

D'Angelo, D., & Adler, C. (1990). Chapter 1: A catalyst for improving parental involvement. *Phi Delta Kappan, 72*, 350-350.

English, F. (1987). *Curriculum management for schools, colleges, business*. Springfield: Charles C. Thomas.

Fine, M. (1991). *Framing dropouts*. Albany: State University of New York Press.

Inger, M., & Larsen, E. (1990). The decision to start college: Factoring in uncertainty. *National Center on Education and Employment, 11*, 1-2.

Kaufman, J., & Lewis, M. (1968). *The potential of vocational education*. University Park: Pennsylvania

State University, Institute for Research on Human Resources.

Kelley, J. (1955). *Guidance and curriculum*. Englewood Cliffs, NJ: Prentice-Hall.

Kerr, W. (1963). High school counselors and college information. *Journal of College Student Personnel, 5*, 45-48.

Kozol, J. (1991). *Savage inequalities: Children in America's schools*. New York: Crown Publishers.

Morris, C., Dillenbeck, D., & Merritt, R. (1964). Introduction. In *From high school to college: Readings for counselors*, pp. v-vi. New York: College Entrance Examination Board.

National Association of Secondary School Principals. (1990). Second volume of principalship study released in San Diego. *NewsLeader, 37* (7), 2-3.

National Vocational Guidance Association. (1942). Committee on Purpose and Functions Report. *Occupations, 20*, 289-291.

Nyberg, D., & Egan, K. (1981). *The erosion of education: Socialization and the schools*. New York: Teachers College Press.

Rist, R. (1970). Student social class and teacher expectations: The self-fulfilling prophecy in ghetto education. *Harvard Educational Review*. (Paper based on research aided by a grant from the United States Office of Education, Grant No. 6-2771).

Sowell, T. (1989). The economics of academia. *Conservative Digest, 15*, 14-15.

Tinto, V. (1987). *Leaving college: Rethinking the causes and cures of student attrition*. Chicago: University of Chicago Press.

VanScriver, J. (1990). Teacher dismissal. *Phi Delta Kappan, 72*, 318-319.

Wilson, J. (1989). *Bureaucracy: What governments do and why they do it*. New York: Basic Books.

Wehlage, G., Rotter, R., Smith, G., Lesko, N., & Fernandez, R. (1989). *Reducing the risk: Schools as communities of support*. New York: Palmer Press.

12

Transition Programming for Individuals from Special Populations

Michelle Sarkees-Wircenski and Jerry L. Wircenski

In September 1988, the first high school graduating class of the next century entered the first grade. They will be the workers, parents, taxpayers, citizens, and leaders of the twenty-first century. They have a great challenge ahead of them as they face the reality of new technology, participative management, sophisticated statistical quality controls, and other changes in the workplace (Carnevale, Gainer, & Meltzer, 1988).

About 50 percent of youth in this country do not go on to college, and only about 20 percent of all American youth get a four-year college degree. By age 19, only 81 percent of all students complete high school. Even so, our schools provide few bridges linking school to employment. Typically, U.S. youth work during their school years, but without a formal link between jobs and school, work is likely to be more of a means to a paycheck than to a career. Also, schools do not make students aware of the implications of the work experience for future education and employment (General Accounting Office, 1991).

A review of the data also indicates that

- Young adults aged 18 to 23 with deficiencies in basic academic skills are 5.4 times more likely to be receiving public assistance and 5 times more likely to be at poverty level in income (William T. Grant Foundation, 1988).
- Approximately 300,000 youths with dis-

abilities leave high school each year, and the majority of them are faced with unemployment and underemployment (Human Services Research Institute, 1985).

- Sixty-seven percent of all Americans with disabilities aged 16 to 64 do not work. Of the 33 percent who do work, 75 percent work only part time (Apolloni, Feichtner & West, 1991).
- The unemployment rates for 16- to 21-year-olds are 2 to 2.5 times the overall population's unemployment rate, and minority youth unemployment is anywhere from 2 to 4 times that for white youth. In addition, there is a large but undetermined number of "discouraged workers", especially among minority youth, who do not show up in labor statistics because they have quit the labor market (Leroy, 1983).
- In June 1988, the unemployment rate of black youth ages 16 to 19 was 34 percent compared with 14 percent for white youth of the same age (Markey, 1988).

O'Neil (1992) reports that more than half of the juniors and seniors in our schools hold part-time jobs. However, these jobs generally bear little resemblance to their school work or career path. Specialized vocational training, cooperative education, and other school-based programs serve only about 25 percent of America's youth.

In examining the recommendations of the Commission on the Skills of the American Workforce, Magaziner and Clinton (1992) report that more than 20 percent of our students drop out of high school, with a dropout rate of about 50 percent in many of our inner cities. These dropouts comprise more than a third of our front-line labor force. Failing to prepare these workers jeopardizes our national productivity.

Youth with special needs comprise a large portion of our nation's total enrollment in the public school sector. Phelps (1986) defines this population to include those individuals who because of a disability, different cultural or linguistic background, or educational or economic disadvantage will require special programs or services to successfully pursue education, training, and employment.

According to the Carl D. Perkins Vocational and Applied Technology Education Act of 1990 (P.L. 101-392) the term *special populations* is defined as including individuals with handicaps (disabilities), educationally and economically disadvantaged individuals (including foster children), individuals who have limited English proficiency, individuals who participate in programs designed to eliminate sex bias, and individuals in correctional institutions.

Feichtner (1989) states that the purpose of addressing a transition from school to work is to provide individuals with experiences that will assist them in developing the skills and attitudes needed to secure and keep employment, to secure and maintain an adult lifestyle, and to develop positive interpersonal relationships. This process is ongoing and should focus on the characteristics, needs, and options of the individual. It results in the development of realistic long-term appropriate programs and services to meet those goals.

Rationale for Transition Programming for Individuals from Special Populations

Feichtner (1989) identifies several barriers in the current school-to-work transition process for individuals from special populations. These barriers include

- Lack of a systematic process for delivering transition services.
- Lack of career development programs.
- Lack of coordination between agencies, which often causes service duplication and gaps.
- Low level of parent participation in transition activities.
- Shortage of adult service providers, particularly in rural areas.
- The absence of a management system to collect and interpret the vast amount of information that is necessary to make appropriate transition decisions and to evaluate learner outcomes and associated service costs.

Making a successful transition from school to postschool opportunities is difficult for individuals from special populations. Reisner and Balasubramaniam (1989) have analyzed the circumstances that make transition into the labor market difficult for these individuals. Problems that confront them include (1) lack of information about jobs and careers, (2) too few role models in good jobs, (3) lack of skills and attitudes needed in the workplace, (4) inadequate access to high-quality vocational education programs, (5) negative perceptions and attitudes of potential employers, and (6) poor labor market conditions for youth.

America faces a chronic youth employment problem and, without higher education or specific vocational and technical skills necessary to succeed in today's labor market, these youth are finding it increasingly difficult to find and maintain full-time employment with salaries adequate to support a family (Lacy, Johnson & Heffernan, 1989).

Transition-Related Legislation

Over the past two decades, legislation has been passed to assure transition programming for individuals from special populations. An overview of the key pieces of legislation is provided as follows:

- **Rehabilitation Act of 1973** (P.L. 93-112)-Described as "the Bill of Rights for the handicapped," this act prohibits discrimination in programs that receive federal funds. Section 503 encourages employers to use local educational agencies to train persons with disabilities to develop their vocational skills. Section 504 prohibits discrimination on the basis of handicap in any private or public program or activity receiving federal financial assistance.

- **Job Training Partnership Act of 1982** (P.L. 97-330)–This act promotes programs that prepare youth and unskilled adults for employment and trains those individuals who have special needs in relationship to vocational preparation programs. Services provided through this act include career development, remedial education, classroom instruction, vocational counseling, temporary work experience, on-the-job training, job upgrading and retraining, job search assistance, and job placement.
- **Americans with Disabilities Act of 1990** (P.L. 100-336)–This act extends to individuals with disabilities civil rights similar to those previously available on the basis of race, color, sex, national origin, and religion under the Civil Rights Act of 1964. Employers may not discriminate against qualified individuals with disabilities in areas related to the selection, testing, hiring, and promotion of employees.

  State and local governments are also under the mandate that disallows discrimination against individuals with disabilities. All government facilities, services, and communications must be accessible consistent with the requirements of Section 504 of the Rehabilitation Act of 1973. Reasonable accommodations must be made for employees with a disability. Places of public accommodation (restaurants, theaters, schools, hotels, etc.) may not discriminate against individuals with disabilities. All new buildings must be made accessible and existing buildings must remove barriers if doing so is "readily achievable." Finally, any common carrier that offers telephone services to the public must make accommodations for persons with disabilities.
- **Individuals with Disabilities Education Act** (P.L. 101-476)–The Education of the Handicapped Act Amendments of

1990 changed the title of the earlier law to the Individuals with Disabilities Education Act (IDEA). This act defines transition services as "a coordinated set of activities for a student, designed within an outcome-oriented process, which promotes movement from school to postschool activities including postsecondary education, vocational training, integrated employment (including supported employment), continuing and adult education, adult services, independent living or community participation. . . . [T]his coordinated set of activities shall be based upon the individual student's needs, taking into account the student's preferences and interests, and shall include instruction, community experiences, the development of employment and other postschool adult living objectives, and when appropriate, acquisition of daily living skills and functional vocational evaluation." In addition to formally defining and outlining transition services for individuals with disabilities in special education programs, this legislation also mandates that a statement of a student's needed transition services be developed in the Individual Education Program (IEP) for students beginning no later than age 16 and annually thereafter. Interagency responsibilities for linkages related to providing transition services for these individuals must also be placed in the IEP.

- **Carl D. Perkins Vocational and Applied Technology Act of 1990** (P.L. 101-392)–This act defines special populations and provides several assurances to them. Programs receiving funding under this legislation must provide information regarding available vocational education opportunities to students who are members of special populations and their parents before the ninth grade. Students with disabilities entering vocational education programs must be assisted in fulfilling the transitional service requirements of the Individuals with Disabilities Act. The special needs of students must be assessed with respect to their successful completion of the vocational program in the most integrated setting possible. Supplementary services must be provided to special populations including curriculum modification, equipment adaptation, classroom modification, supportive personnel, and instructional aids. Guidance, counseling, and career development activities must be conducted by professionally trained counselors and teachers. Finally, counseling and instructional services must be designed and provided to facilitate the student's transition from school to postschool employment and career opportunities.

Transition Program Components for Individuals from Special Populations

The job of developing, implementing, and evaluating transition programs and services for individuals from special populations should be a shared responsibility. Before the components of a sound transition program are discussed it is essential that a transition team be developed to review the elements of transition programming in the local district. Someone at the local level must assume the leadership role in convening the transition team and ensuring that the transition plan is developed and implemented according to the needs of the student.

Transition team members should examine the approach, the definition, and the philosophy that guides the support services that are an integral part of any transition effort.

Members of a transition team could include
- Secondary and postsecondary administrators.
- Students from special populations.
- Parents and family members.
- Guidance counselors.
- Resource specialists.
- Instructors (vocational education, special education, academic education).
- Special needs coordinators/transition specialists.
- Community and government agency representatives.
- Business and industry personnel.

- Employment and training representatives.
- Adult service providers.
- Representatives from institutions of higher education.

There are a variety of options that individuals from special populations can select from in planning their transition from school. These options include, but are not limited to
- Postsecondary training/continuing education.
- Competitive employment.
- Apprenticeship programs.
- Job Training Partnership Act (JTPA) training programs.
- On-the-job training.
- Service in the military.
- Self-employment.
- Supported employment (job coach model, work crew model).
- Rehabilitation facilities/agencies.

Reisner and Balasubramaniam (1989) identified a variety of transition services for individuals from special populations. They are
- Activities to familiarize students with possible barriers (career exploration).
- Training in personal behaviors important in obtaining and retaining a job.
- Knowledge about how to look for a job (employability skills).
- Training in skills needed to manage one's personal affairs, including personal decision making, personal finances, public transportation, health care, and raising children (life skills).
- Activities to improve reading and mathematics competencies (basic skills).
- Supervised experience in the workplace, either paid or unpaid (work experience).
- Services that are not directly related to obtaining or holding a job but that make it possible to participate in training-related activities, including counseling, child care, and transportation (support services).
- Assistance in identifying available jobs and in applying for them (placement assistance).
- Assistance in dealing with problems that occur after starting a job (follow-up assistance).

Based on the research that has been conducted on the development and implementation of transition services for individuals from special populations, there are 10 important components that are crucial in any transition program efforts.

Career Development

The first component in a successful transition program for individuals from special populations is *career development*. Career development is a lifelong process and should begin at as early an age as possible and continue through the lifetime of an individual. Career development is usually delivered in phases. The first phase is commonly referred to as career awareness. Career awareness activities should be provided during the primary years. Activities at this level assist individuals from special populations in developing and acquiring an awareness of self, identification with workers, respect for people and the work they do, and the concept of work as a valued institution.

The *career orientation* stage follows career awareness. It is usually provided during the intermediate years. Through participation in career orientation opportunities, individuals are assisted in developing and acquiring the knowledge in a wide variety of occupational fields.

The third phase, *career exploration*, allows individuals to sample and explore career areas. For example, rotation programs can be established where students explore a variety of vocational classes for a short period of time. In-school, unpaid work experiences can be developed (e.g., office, cafeteria, horticulture/grounds maintenance, clinic). Opportunities to observe and learn about a variety of occupations and work sites can be provided through field trips, class visitations by workers, job shadowing, and videotape instruction. Classroom simulations and projects relating to specific jobs can also be set up. Formulation of tentative career goals should also occur during this phase.

The fourth stage is referred to as the *career preparation* stage. The career preparation stage should begin once a decision has been made concerning a potential career path. Career guidance services accompany the specific skills training of this phase. These services should include information such as filling out applications, developing a resume, locating employment, interviewing for a job, career ladder opportunities, and postsecondary options.

Vocational Assessment

Vocational assessment is the second component of a successful transition program for individuals from special populations. Vocational assessment is a process that is conducted over a period of time by a multidisciplinary team to provide educators with information about a person's individual characteristics, interests, abilities, and special needs. Individuals from special populations desperately need to receive objective information about their strengths and limitations because in many cases they have a difficult time formulating an objective image of themselves in relationship to the world of work.

Some of the information obtained through the process of vocational assessment includes functional academic skills, vocational interests, vocational aptitudes, auditory and visual discrimination, manipulation, coordination and dexterity skills, fine and gross motor skills, strength and stamina, eye-hand coordination, ability to work with others, ability to work unsupervised, ability to work under pressure, and work tolerance and endurance.

A variety of tools can be used during the vocational assessment process. Tool selection will depend on the individuals to be assessed and on the resources available in the district. Some commonly used vocational assessment tools are paper and pencil interest and aptitude tests, teacher-developed performance samples, achievement tests, direct observation checklists, manual dexterity tests, entry-level skills inventories for specific vocational programs, and student interviews.

This information should be summarized in a student profile format and used in (1) determining vocational potential (strengths and limitations), (2) determining realistic career goals and objectives, (3) identifying appropriate vocational program/training site placements that will help students meet their goals and objectives, (4) identifying appropriate instructional goals and objectives, (5) utilizing appropriate instructional methods and curriculum adaptations, and (6) providing relevant support services.

There are a number of important benefits from the vocational assessment process for individuals from special populations. Results should help to establish an understanding of the relationship between educational experiences and future vocational opportunities, and the acquisition of skills for making wise educational and vocational choices, and help to provide an increased understanding of personal values, interest, skills, and deficits as they relate to the workforce.

Functional Curriculum

A functional curriculum is a third component of a successful transition program for individuals from special populations. A functional curriculum is one in which learners develop functional skills in the setting appropriate for acquiring specific skills. Curriculum content prepares the individual for adult living.

Students receive age-appropriate instruction to help them perform competencies necessary in the various environments or domains that they will encounter in the future—education, work, domestic and community life, and recreation and leisure. Real-life situations are used in teaching functional curriculum whenever possible.

West, Bliss, and Kearns (1989) identify the following basic components of a functional curriculum:

- Communication skills
- Generalizable skills
- Functional academic skills
- Community access/mobility/transportation skills
- Employability skills
- Social skills
- Independent living skills
- Leisure/recreation skills
- Health and grooming skills
- Vocational competencies

Providing a functional curriculum to individuals from special populations is crucial in order for them to successfully make the transition from school to employment and the community. Functional curriculum objectives and instructional delivery are individualized according to the learner's age and specific needs. A wide variety of resources should be used in delivering this instruction.

Generalizable Skills

The fourth component of a successful transition program for individuals from special populations is the inclusion of generalizable skills. Generalizable skills are those that are basic to, necessary for success in, and transferable across vocational programs and occupations. Research indicates that 115 generalizable skills are clustered into the following four areas (Greenan, 1986):

Mathematics Skills
- Whole numbers
- Fractions
- Percentages
- Mixed operations
- Measurement and calculation
- Estimation

Communication Skills
- Words and meanings
- Reading
- Writing
- Speaking

Interpersonal Relations Skills
- Work
- Instructional and supervisory conversations
- Conversations

Reasoning Skills
- Verbal reasoning
- Problem solving
- Planning
- Listening

Generalizable skills are critical assets that give the student and worker greater flexibility and potential for success in a number of areas including (1) completing a vocational training program, (2) making the transition from school to employment, (3) successfully entering the labor market, (4) changing jobs, (5) transferring skills from one program or job to another, (6) pursuing further education or retraining, and (7) achieving career advancement.

Specific Skills Training

A successful transition program for individuals from special populations must include a fifth component: specific skills training. There are a variety of options that can be selected to teach specific vocational skills to individuals from special populations. These options include public secondary and postsecondary vocational education programs, cooperative education, internships, apprenticeships, state and local youth corps/job corps, Job Training Partnership Act (JTPA) programs, community-based organization programs, rehabilitation programs, and supported employment programs. Individuals should be placed in training programs that are appropriate for their interests, abilities, and special needs. The information collected during the vocational assessment process is crucial in making this decision.

One option that is frequently used to provide specific skills training to individuals from special populations is enrollment in vocational education programs. Vocational instructors are not expected to lower program standards for students from special populations. If these students are to be employable in the competitive labor market, they must meet the same competency and employability levels as any other applicant. For students from special populations to succeed in vocational programs, curriculum modification may have to occur. Curriculum modification is the tailoring of all vocational program experiences and activities to meet the unique needs of the individual student. The changes made are not in the basic objectives of the vocational program nor in the standards established for its completion but in the elements of the teaching-learning process (Sarkees & Scott, 1985).

Curriculum modification strategies include (1) an open-entry/open-exit process for vocational programs, (2) extended time arrangements in the vocational program, (3) schedule modifications, (4) single-skill training as opposed to expecting the student to master all program competencies, (5) modification of facilities and equipment, (6) instructional materials modification, (7) provision of necessary support services, (8) identification and use of appropriate teaching techniques, and (9) use of appropriate evaluation methods.

The supported employment approach is an alternative between competitive employment and sheltered employment for individuals with moderate to severe disabilities. Supported employment programs offer individuals (1) pay for their work, (2) work in an integrated setting, and (3) ongoing support services. Supported employment provides assistance in areas of job development, on-the-job training, family counseling and support, and follow-up assistance (Berkell & Brown, 1989). Supported employment programs offer services needed to develop appropriate interpersonal and job-related skills, as well as transportation to and from the work setting, until entry-level skills are mastered.

In many supported employment programs, trained job coaches accompany disabled individuals to their jobs on the first day. These coaches learn how to perform the job and teach the disabled individual all of the specific job tasks and general work habits that are required for job retention. Job coaches work continuously with the individual and provide one-to-one assistance until the job is mastered. The job coach gradually fades from the work site and the support role is turned over to a co-worker or supervisor on the job.

Parental Involvement

Parental involvement is the sixth component of a successful transition program for individuals from special populations. Involvement of parents should be an integral part of the transition planning and implementation process. Parents probably know a student better than anyone and they often have very valid questions and concerns that should be addressed when developing a transition plan. The influence of parents in career decision making has been researched and widely documented. Parent input can help in identifying transition goals, assessing student potential, identifying student interests, deciding on an appropriate placement for the development of specific skills, identifying necessary support services, and evaluating student progress. Parents and family members can provide motivation and encouragement, in addition to reinforcing specific training objectives at home. In addition, problems or concerns that may occur in the home can be reported by parents so that implementation of the transition plan can be as smooth as possible.

Responsibilities that parents should assume during development of transition programs include (1) checking to make certain that specific skills training and support services are part of their child's IEP, (2) insisting that a transition plan that specifies employment training and job placement be designed three to five years before their child's graduation from high school, (3) working with their child at home to promote appropriate behavior, grooming, functional skills, and attitudes, (4) keeping track of their child's progress during employment training, and (5) learning about the services of agencies and adult service providers in the community, as well as their eligibility requirements.

Some districts are establishing parent resource centers that serve as information clearinghouses, counseling centers, and support centers for parents who need assistance. These centers can provide career exploration activities such as mentoring, job shadowing, and individual counseling for individuals from special populations. The parent resource centers often post job opportunities and help students and parents in applying for and securing posted jobs (Sarkees, 1989).

Individual Transition Plans

A successful transition program for individuals from special populations should include the seventh component: the development of individual transition plans (ITP). The individual transition plan will not easily occur for individuals from special populations unless a formal transition planning process is developed. This includes creating an actual transition planning form. The form should focus on the process of transition, including the services the student will need to make the transition to the world of work or other appropriate postschool options. It should specify who might be in the best position to provide these services (Sitlington, 1986).

A systematic method of planning for transition must be developed to ensure that individuals from special populations receive, to the maximum extent possible, appropriate transition services. The local educational agency, along with community representatives, parents, and other agencies, should combine efforts to

- Identify the elements of a transition program currently in place in the district.
- Identify the voids in a transition program that must be addressed to put an effective program into place for all individuals from special populations.
- Coordinate the various agencies and institutions in the state and local area that are involved in the transition process.
- Develop a plan to enhance existing transition elements and fill voids that exist.
- Develop an evaluation system to insure that the transition process is comprehensive and fits the needs of all the students (West, Gritzmacher, Johnson, Boyer-Stephens & Dunafon, 1985).

The Individuals with Disabilities Education Act of 1990 mandates that a statement of needed transition services be made a component part of the individualized education programs (IEPs) of students with disabilities, beginning at age 16 and each year thereafter, and to the extent appropriate, in the IEPs of students with disabilities age 14 or younger (Section 602 (a)(19)). This IEP component must also include, where appropriate, a statement of interagency responsibility if a state or local agency other than the public agency responsible for the student's education is responsible for providing or paying for needed transition services. Finally, where a participating agency has failed to provide agreed on transition services, the local school district must convene a meeting of the participants on the IEP team to identify alternative strategies to meet the transition objectives in the student's IEP.

While the IEP focuses on academic achievement and related behavioral skills, the mandated transition services portion of the IEP includes goals and objectives related to vocational and personal development in areas such as vocational competence, job-seeking and retention skills, personal and social skills, recreation and leisure skills, and community and independent living skills.

Support Services

Providing good support services is the eighth component of successful transition program for individuals from special populations. Support services include planning, developing, implementing, and evaluating transition programs for individuals from special populations. It requires time and effort from many individuals. The success of these learners depends to a great degree on a cooperative relationship established among professionals. Individuals who may be called on to plan, implement, and/or evaluate necessary support services include administrators, vocational education instructors, special education instructors, special needs coordinators, transition specialists, academic instructors, interpreters, note takers, readers, social work services personnel, psychologists, guidance counselors, medical personnel, bilingual teachers, basic skills instructors, orientation and mobility specialists, and speech therapists.

Examples of support services that may be needed by individuals from special populations include, but are not limited to, diagnostic/prescriptive services, reader and interpreter services, career development activities, curriculum modification, academic support services, counseling, medical assistance, prevocational training, program planning, psychological assistance, therapy (speech, occupational, physical), transportation, child care, financial assistance, vocational assessment, vocational placement, work adjustment, and postemployment assistance.

Interagency Coordination

The ninth component of a successful transition program for individuals from special populations is good interagency coordination. Interagency coordination is a process by which two or more agencies join together to increase their effectiveness in providing services. Interagency cooperation will be most effective if the focus remains on the needs of individuals from special populations and the services available to them. Graham (1992) states that although there is no single model of successful coordination among agencies that can be replicated at every local level, there are a number of benefits for school districts, parents, students, and agencies when interagency cooperation occurs. These benefits include (1) reduction of services that are duplicated and overlapping, (2) covering gaps and oversights for necessary services that are not currently available,

(3) minimizing conflicts, and (4) giving smaller agencies a voice.

Before coordination can take place, members of the interagency team must understand the role, function, and operating procedures of the other agencies involved. Once the adult role services have been determined for individuals from special populations, the agencies and organizations involved in cooperative planning to provide these services must be identified. This can be done by developing a list of all local and state agencies and adult service providers and the services each makes available to individuals from special populations. The list should be made available to agency personnel, parents, students, and educators.

Placement and Follow-up

The tenth, and last, component of a transition program for individuals from special populations is successful placement and follow-up. In addition to being one of the most difficult adjustments any individual must make, the transition from school to work is also one of the most critical. This transition can be especially difficult for individuals from special populations because of real or imagined employment barriers. Once these individuals have found a job they may require follow-up assistance. This assistance may be conducted by a vocational instructor, placement counselor, social service worker, or rehabilitation services counselor. School districts often administer follow-up of all students two and five years after they leave school.

An important part of the placement process involves gathering descriptive and evaluative information on each individual and organizing it into a student profile format. This format can include vocational assessment information, a competency profile from the training program that the individual has been enrolled in, and a career portfolio including job-seeking tools such as a resume and a list of references.

Surveys, telephone interviews, and personal interviews are often used to gather follow-up data. Questions concerning employment status, salary level, job satisfaction, duties, and chances for promotion are usually asked. It is also important to determine whether the transition programming provided for the student was sufficient. Suggestions as to improving the transition process can be sought in an attempt to better meet the needs of future students. Individuals who are unemployed when contacted for the interview can be directed toward programs or agencies that can assist them in further developing their vocational skills or in finding a job.

Summary

About 50 percent of youth in this country do not go on to college, and only about 20 percent of all American youth get a four-year college degree. Only 81 percent of all students complete high school. Young adults aged 18 to 23 with deficiencies in basic academic skills are 5.4 times more likely to receive public assistance and five times more likely to have a poverty-level income. Approximately 300,000 youths with disabilities leave high school each year. Sixty-seven percent of all Americans with disabilities aged 16 to 64 do not work. Of the 33 percent who do work, 75 percent work only part time. The unemployment rates for 16- to 21-year-olds are 2 to 2.5 times the overall population's unemployment rate, and minority youth unemployment is anywhere from 2 to 4 times that of white youth. There is a large but undetermined number of "discouraged workers", who do not show up in labor statistics because they have quit the labor market. The unemployment rate of black youth ages 16 to 19 is 34 percent compared with 14 percent for white youth of the same age. Yet, specialized vocational training, cooperative education, and other school-based programs serve only about 25 percent of America's youth.

To assist individuals from special populations in the transition process, transition programming must include 10 necessary components: career development, vocational assessment, a functional curriculum, generalizable skills, specific skills training, parental involvement, an individualized transition plan, support services, interagency cooperation, and placement and follow-up.

References

Apolloni, T., Feichtner, S., & West, L. (1991). Learners and workers in the year 2001. *The Journal for Vocational Special Needs Education, 14*(1), 5-10.

Berkell, D., & Brown, J. (1989). *Transition from school to work for persons with disabilities*. New York: Longman.

Carnevale, A., Gainer, L., & Meltzer, A. (1988). *Workplace basics: The skills employers want*. Alexandria, VA: American Society for Training and Development.

Feichtner, S. (1989). School-to-work transition for at-risk youth. Columbus, OH: ERIC Clearinghouse on Adult, Career and Vocational Education, The Center on Education and Training for Employment.

Government Accounting Office. (August, 1991). *Transition from school to work–Linking education and worksite training*. Washington, DC: Author.

Graham, J. (1992). Transition through interagency coordination. *Missouri Lincletter, 14*(3), 1-3.

Greenan, J. (1986). Curriculum and assessment in generalizable skills instruction. *The Journal for Vocational Special Needs Education, 9*(1), 3-10.

Human Services Institute. (1985). Summary of data on handicapped children and youth. Washington, DC: U.S. Department of Education.

Lacy, G., Johnson, C., & Heffernan, D. (1989). Tackling the youth unemployment problem. Washington, DC: Children's Defense Fund, Adolescent Pregnancy Prevention Clearinghouse.

Leroy, C. (1983). Youth employment in the labor market in the 1980's. *Urban Review, 15*(2), 119-29.

Magaziner, I., & Clinton, H. (1992). Will America choose high skills or low wages. *Educational Leadership, 49* (6), 10-14 .

Markey, J. (1988). The labor market problems of today's dropouts. *Monthly Labor Review, 111*(6), 36-43 .

O'Neil, J. (1992). Preparing for the changing workplace. *Educational Leadership, 49* (6), 6-9.

Phelps, L. A. (April 21, 1986). Transitional programming for special needs youth. Paper presented at the 1985-86 Distinguished Lecture Series on Employment-Related Education and Training for Special Populations. Long Beach, CA: California State University.

Reisner, E., & Balasubramaniam, M. (1989). School-to-work transition services for disadvantaged youth enrolled in vocational education. Washington, DC: U.S. Department of Education.

Sarkees, M. (1989). Developing effective assistance programs for parents of at-risk students. *The Journal for Vocational Special Needs Education, 11*(2), 17-22.

Sarkees, M., & Scott, J. (1985). *Vocational special needs*. Homewood, IL: American Technical Publishers.

Sitlington, P. (1986). *Transition, special needs and vocational education*. Columbus, OH: The ERIC Clearinghouse on Adult, Career and Vocational Education, The Ohio State University.

West, L., Bliss, S., & Kearns, D. (1989). Functional curriculum for transition: A resource guide. Columbia, MO: University of Missouri-Columbia.

West, L., Gritzmacher, H., Johnson, J., Boyer-Stephens,

A., & Dunafon, D. (1985). Missouri transition guide. Columbia, MO: University of Missouri-Columbia, Department of Special Education & Department of Practical Arts and Vocational-Technical Education.

William T. Grant Foundation Commission on Work, Family and Citizenship. (1988). *The forgotten half: Non-college youth in America.* Washington, DC: Author.

13

Firm Size:
The Overlooked Variable
in School-to-Employment Transition

Kenneth Gray

Conceptually, promoting the transition of graduates from school to work would seem a rather clear-cut process. Educational programs should equip graduates with the skills and personal attributes required by employers. Armed with these skills, graduates should gain employment successfully, with only minimal assistance. Considering this, one must ask: What is the problem?

As documented in earlier chapters, the transition process is less than optimal in the U.S. While the causes of inefficiencies are numerous, primary among them is a general confusion among educators about the exact skills and attributes that will help in finding a job. One reason for this confusion lies in a failure to realize that the skills and attributes required or preferred by employers vary both among different types of industries and among firms of different sizes within a particular industry. The labor force requirements of small firms often differ significantly from those of large firms. Unfortunately, while the workforce requirements of large firms receive the greatest attention, small firms employ most young workers. Thus, those who seek to promote improvement in the school-to-work transition process are urged in this chapter to "think small."

Employability Skills

To have a framework for discussion of differences in skills preferred by large and small firms, employability skills must be examined. What do firms, large and small, look for when making hiring decisions? The typical and most simplistic answer is "basic skills." In reality, however, the criteria used by employers are considerably more complex, and thus the definition of "basic" is more involved.

A review of the many and varied studies of employability skills suggests that employers seek four levels or types of basic skills. The first is a set of behavioral attributes, such as following directions and punctuality, that are requirements for all employment. The second level is a set of basic academic skills, such as reading and math competencies. As the technical nature of the work increases, the level of competence in technical academic basics also increases. Emerging blue-collar technical occupations, for example, are said to require sound understanding of relevant science principles, as well as reading and computational skills. The third level of basic skills is an emerging set of behavioral skills sometimes referred to as "workplace literacy" skills or "hands off" skills. These skills include the ability to work effectively in groups and the ability to teach oneself new tasks on the job. The fourth level includes basic traditional occupational skills specific to a particular occupation; the efficient and safe use of tools and materials is one example.

This final set of occupational skills is often overlooked and frequently misunderstood. As will be explained, this confusion stems partly from the importance attributed to these skills by employers of different sizes.

Firms: Large and Small

For purposes of discussion and research, firms typically are divided into four groups according to the number of people employed by them. The smallest firms are those that employ 19 workers or less; the largest employ 500 or more. In between these two groups are two additional categories—small, which employ 20-99 employees; and large, which employ 100-499.

One myth that should be dispelled at the outset equates the small firm with a fast-food outlet that pays minimum wages and offers only limited opportunity for advancement. Small firms are in fact found in all industrial sectors. A majority of printing firms, construction firms, and wholesaling firms are, by our definition, in the smallest or small firms categories. Small firms are noted for being on the cutting edge of the adoption of new technology and for their ability to bring new products to market quickly. Thus, many of the smallest firms are found in the fastest growing technological areas of the economy.

It is important to note that small firms are the major source of "new" jobs. It is estimated that the smallest firms create up to 88 percent of new jobs, particularly in poor economic times. While the average salary in small firms is less than that found in large ones, the average salary in small firms is nonetheless considerably above minimum wage. Most important, small firms are also the major employer of young workers.

Small Firms
and Young Workers

According to the U.S. Department of Labor, the work force is fairly evenly divided among the four firm-size groups. However, an examination of the average age of workers in each firm-size group reveals a different picture. Older workers are more apt to work in the large or largest firms. Young workers tend to work in the small or smallest firms. An analysis of the National Longitudinal Study, New Youth Cohort (NLS-Y) data found, for example, that 65 percent of young workers (average age 25) worked in the small or smallest firms; 40 percent worked in the smallest firms.

The educational level of young workers is also related to the size of the firm that will likely employ them. In general, the less education young workers have, the more likely they will work in the smallest firms. High school dropouts are more likely to be employed in the smallest firms, while college graduates are more likely to be employed in the largest firms.

Gender differences in the firm-size distribution of workers have diminished in recent years. The majority of both young men and young women in the NLS-Y study were employed in the smallest or small firms.

To summarize, small, not large, firms should be the main focus of school-to-employment transition efforts for young workers. The majority of young men and women are employed in firms containing 99 or fewer employees. This distinction is important in light of the significant differences in large and small firms' requirements or preferences for new workers.

Worker Skills Required
by Large and Small Firms

The differences in the entry-level skills required by large and small firms are notable. Large firms need entry-level employees who are trainable, while small firms need entry-level workers who are trained. Large firms are more likely than small ones to be involved in linear mass production or service delivery. In these manufacturing modes, workers perform very specific functions that are often unique to the firm and relatively stable over time. Unlike small firms, large firms can afford to absorb the cost of on-the-job training for tasks. Thus, when large employers stress level-one behavioral skills and level-two basic academic skills they do so because they can afford and prefer to provide the level-four skills training. Thus, for large firms, new employees should have the ability to benefit from training quickly, an end that is enhanced by good basic academic skills. The needs of small firms are quite different.

Small firms are less likely to be involved in linear manufacturing operations and more likely to use modular techniques, in which workers perform a variety of tasks until the product or unit is finished. Small firms are also less able than large ones to absorb the lost time from on-the-job training. Thus, compared to large firms, small firms prefer and hire first-job applicants who have not only level-one, -two, and -three skills but also level-four basic relevant vocational skills. Beginning workers in small firms are one-half as likely as new workers in large firms to receive any formal on-the-job training during their first three months of employment. Consider too that 65 percent of new workers in small firms indicated that they learned vocational skills in public or private vocational schools or in the military before employment. Small firms generally consider occupational preparation the responsibility of the employee—only 21 percent of small firms reported reimbursing employees for outside training costs.

Preparing Clients for Transition to Employment in Small Firms

It has been argued that since the majority of young workers are employed in the smallest or small firms, efforts to assist in the transition from school to employment should focus on the preferences of small, not large, businesses. What are the preferences of small firms when hiring new employees? Obviously, their exact hiring preferences will vary according to the nature of work performed and the professional level of those hired. The following discussion focuses on small firms' hiring practices for blue-collar technical workers such as machinists, electronic technicians, and building construction workers.

Level one—conducive behavior. All jobs require a common basic set of behavior that does not vary by either industry group or firm size. Reporting to work on time is just as important in a large aerodynamics plant as it is in a small wholesaling firm; failure to do so will result ultimately in termination regardless of firm size. As another example, a recent study of electronics firms of various sizes found that the ability to follow directions was the most important skill required by all employers studied.

It stands to reason, however, that as the size of a firm decreases, the importance of other individual behavior, such as interpersonal skills, becomes more critical. The likelihood, for example, of employees dealing directly with customers increases as the size of the firm decreases. In the smallest firms, everyone picks up the phone at some time or deals directly with clients. Likewise, as the size of the firm decreases, group dynamics come to resemble a team or big family. As small business owners know well, efficiency often depends more on cooperation and teamwork, than on employee skills. Thus, small firms can be expected to be more concerned with how a new employee will fit into the group.

Level two—basic academic skills. Employers of all sizes in all industry groups prefer employees who are literate over those who are not. It is not uncommon, for example, for employers to first screen out applicants who do not have the ability to complete a job application correctly, regardless of whether the ability to write is necessary for the job. As mentioned previously, large firms consider basic academic skills to be necessary to complete the training they provide. There is some evidence, however, that situations that require employees to actually use these academic basic skills outside of the training setting occur more often in small firms than in large.

In large firms that use linear production methods, blue-collar technicians are infrequently required to read involved instructions, perform mathematical calculations, or write. Most of this type of work is done by middle managers, supervisors, and foremen. On the other hand, a small firm typically has few if any middle managers, supervisors, or foremen. Conversely, workers in small firms, particularly in firms that change product lines frequently, must be able to read for comprehension, sometimes perform complex math, complete written documentation of work completed, and communicate directly with clients.

Level three—workplace literacy skills. Numerous studies have been completed recently that were designed to identify the new skills required in the emerging technical workplace. The American Association of Training and Development, for example, has compiled such a list after extensive research sponsored by the U.S. Department of Labor. Central to these studies is the assumption that the future workplace will require individuals who on the one hand can learn a new task and develop solutions independently, and on the other hand can function effectively in a work group. This perception is based on the assumption of widespread replacement of linear production with modular techniques that will require worker groups to perform complete assemblies. At present, this type of production is most often found in small firms. Thus, workplace literacy skills ultimately may be equally important to firms of all sizes; at this point, they are probably more critical to small firms.

Level four—relevant occupational skills. To the large firm, basic skills typically mean academic competencies. Studies of small firms reveal, however, that the definition of basic skills is more expansive. When a small firm indicates requiring basic skills for entry-level workers, they mean both academic and relevant basic occupational skills. In the study of electronics firms mentioned earlier, the most important skill required for entry-level blue collar technicians by small electronics manufacturers was relevant occupational skills.

Small firms need individuals who can be productive immediately. In most industry groups, this means an individual who has basic occupational skills. In the machine tool field, these skills include knowledge of speeds, feeds, and numeric machine control; in electronics firms, the ability to read electronic schematics and use test equipment; and in construction firms, they include the ability to read blue prints, identify various building materials, and use electrical/pneumatic construction tools safely and effectively. These skills are required, not preferred, by small firms—individuals who do not have them are not hired.

In summary, the level of competence required by small firms is typically higher than that of large firms. In small firms, interpersonal skills conducive to co-worker harmony are critical. Employees are much more likely to actually have to read for comprehension, perform mathematical calculations, and correspond using the written word. Small-firm employees are also more likely to be expected to learn or solve problems independently. Most important, small firms need workers who have had training in relevant occupational skills. Job seekers with these skills have the advantages in finding better jobs in small firms.

Even with these skills, however, finding job opportunities in small firms can be a challenge. Job openings in small firms are like deer in the wild—they may be numerous, but they are still hard to find.

The Small Firm Job Market: A Job Placement Challenge

As many newly minted college graduates discover, credentials (in our example, level-one through level-four job skills) do not automatically translate into employment. Reliable mechanisms that match qualified job seekers with relevant employers simply do not exist. For this reason, any effective school-to-work transition program must include a strong job placement assistance service. The nature of the job market for small firms makes job placement efforts quite a challenge.

The common model of a job market is reflected in many job-seeking training efforts. It consists of personnel managers placing ads in newspapers, visiting campuses, reviewing resumes and job applications, conducting formal interviews, and making hiring decisions based on careful analysis of objective facts. This perception of the job market is accurate but, again, only for large firms, not for small firms where most opportunities for young workers exist. While the term "formal" may apply to the hiring process in large firms, "informal" more accurately describes the small firm hiring process.

In small firms, particularly those with less than 50 employees, the hiring process differs dramatically from that in large firms. Small firms do not have personnel offices. In small firms, the hiring is done by owners, foremen, and office managers. These "part-time" personnel officers do not have the time to read extensive credentials, typically do not request resumes, and may not even have a formal job application. It is a challenge just to find small firms that are seeking employees.

The Informal Job Market

Small firms do not run want ads in the papers unless they are desperate, because they do not have the time to respond to large numbers of applications. Instead, they rely mostly on the informal word-of-mouth job market. It has been long understood that knowing someone in a firm helps in getting work. While some see this as a form of nepotism and possible job discrimination, it really reflects the limited resources small firms have to devote to finding new employees; a small firm that is seeking employees first asks current employees the classic question, "Do you know anyone who . . . ?" Thus, those seeking to promote transition to small firms must access this informal job market. This means much leg work and personal contact with small firms.

While this job market is informal, it is not closed or impervious. Small firms are just as interested as large firms in hiring the best and welcome help in finding them. In fact, small firms have the most to gain from an organized school-to-work transition process.

The Importance to Small Firms of Improving the School-to-Work Transition

The beneficiaries of an improved school-to-work transition are not just graduates. While large firms with highly developed personnel departments, higher wage scales, and preferences for older workers may be somewhat impervious to an inefficient school-to-work transition system, small firms are not. Small firms and the nation have as much to gain by improving the system as do graduates.

Many economists argue that small firms play a more important role in economic development than large firms. Small firms often bring new products to the market or experiment with high-risk innovations. Small firms are particularly effective at bringing products to the market quickly, a critical element in international competition. As mentioned earlier, small firms are responsible for the creation of most new jobs in the economy. Thus, the old saying that what is good for business is good for the country seems somewhat valid for small firms. One item that would help small firms is a more reliable mechanism for obtaining adequately trained employees, particularly if it attracts those presently underrepresented in the workforce, as will be discussed next.

Small Firms and Underrepresented Groups

Considerable attention is now devoted to the need to improve the school-to-work transition of groups currently underrepresented in the labor force such as minorities, the handicapped, and the poor in both urban and rural areas. The report *Workforce 2000* notes that this issue is not simply a matter of social justice, but an economic imperative. According to the *Workforce 2000* analysis, a lack of traditional white male workers to fill jobs will lead to serious labor shortages, unless other groups become more active in the labor force. Keeping in mind that small firms traditionally employ beginning workers, particularly noncollege graduates, small firms may be the ones to experience this shortage. Small firms in some regions are already experiencing shortages. Thus, small businesses may have the greatest stake in improving the transition of underrepresented groups into the labor force. It is important to note the existence of some evidence that small firms are having difficulty recruiting minority workers.

Research I have conducted has shown that while a majority of all young workers are in small firms, a higher percentage of whites than African-Americans or Hispanics work in the smallest firms. While the reason for a disproportionate percentage of whites in the smallest firms is not certain, the situation predicts a great challenge for small firms, because in the future they may only avoid labor shortages by hiring minorities, the handicapped, and the poor.

An improved school-to-work transition system could greatly assist better connections among the underrepresented groups in the labor force and small firms. Small firms rely on the informal job market. Underrepresented groups in the labor force are the least likely to have the contacts necessary to get into this "inside information" job market. Thus, a school-to-work transition system that cracks this job market is critical to the participation of minorities, the handicapped, and the poor—and to avoiding labor shortages for small firms.

Think Small

America may have the worst school-to-work transition system among developed nations, according to the National Center on Education and the Economy. Improving this state of affairs is a national priority. Those who take on this enormous task are cautioned to "think small." The process of preparing graduates for employment in small firms, not large, is "where it's at."

References

Carnevale, A., & Schulz, E. (1988, November). Technical training in America: How much and who gets it. *Training and Development Journal, 42* (11), 18-32.

Gray, K. (1991, January). Thinking small. *Vocational Education Journal.*

Gray, K., & Wang, D. (1989). An analysis of the firm size variable in youth employment. *Journal of Education Research, 14* (4), 35-49.

Hudson Institute. (1987). *Workforce 2000: Work and workers for the 21st century.* Indianapolis, IN: Author.

National Center on Education and the Economy. (1990). *America's choice: High skills or low wages.* Rochester, NY: Commission on the Skills of the American Workforce.

Thomas, D. (1991). Entry-level skill requirements for blue-collar technicians in electronics firms of various sizes. Unpublished doctoral dissertation, The Pennsylvania State University, University Park.

14

The At-Risk Student and Vocational Education

Robert R. Hanson and Lawrence M. DeRidder

Introduction

The really at-risk students in America's high schools are the forgotten half who do not intend to go to college (William T. Grant Foundation, 1988). Our schools continue to be in the throes of the "excellence" movement, focusing on the abstract and college-oriented curriculum and giving other types of skill development limited attention.

Despite considerable evidence to the contrary, most teachers still think that retention, or holding students back, is useful in helping students achieve previously determined levels of basic skills. The impact of failure on self-esteem and the consequent being over-aged in subsequent years is related to a student eventually dropping out. At the same time, comparably performing students who are allowed to "pass" to the next grade do surprisingly well (Mantzicopoulos & Morrison, 1992).

Tracking presents a problem, too. For despite considerable evidence that tracking, or ability grouping, is both nonproductive and unfair, most schools still use this approach, which is primarily based on socioeconomic background and/or minority status. The resulting curricular dilution for presumed low-ability students limits learning as well as teacher expectation of learner performance (DeRidder, 1989; Slavin, 1987).

Many students reach high school having had alienating and frustrating school-related experiences, which limits their motivation, their vision of possible careers, and their feelings of personal adequacy. In high school, this group typically has access only to activities such as athletics and/or choral groups and it is rarely involved in other activities, with the exception of those students who take part in the many club activities sponsored by the vocationally oriented curricula. Social and interpersonal skill development is critical but typically left to chance in most high schools.

By high school, many students have not developed the level of basic skills employers demand. High schools do not offer instruction in reading, computation, oral and written communication, and listening skills for this group. They lack instruction that approximates real life experience and practice.

The non-college-bound students, like others, seek independence and security but lack both direction and confidence. Because this group gets considerably less career assistance, less attention, and less praise and recognition than their college-bound counterparts, they are typically not adequately prepared to exit into immediate and gainful employment. Our economy currently requires technological competence; those with less education must scramble for unsteady, low-paying, and, frequently, only part-time jobs. In addition, they need help in application and interview skills and in moving from school to jobs related to their chosen careers. Possibilities include increasingly involving business and industry in school activities and providing more instruction in out-of-school real-life settings that reflect local practices.

Since today's students are tomorrow's workers—and all of them should be enabled and empowered to enter society competently—each student must have access to an adequate learning base that emphasizes problem solving and interpersonal skill development. Since the challenging economic period we are in demands high skill development and lifelong learning, our noncollege (at-risk) students must receive equity in time, attention, energy, and meaningful learning experiences.

An alarming—yet not surprising—report on job preparation cited the almost fanatical interest Americans now have for competitors from their country in the world Olympics. Millions of dollars are spent by companies that support TV coverage of events that most U.S. television viewers watch in a mesmerized fashion (Kolberg & Smith, 1992).

In striking contrast, the media completely disregarded the first U.S. champion ever to earn gold at the International Youth Skill Olympics (IYSO). To date, the U.S. has competed in nine IYSO competitions. Not only were we slow to join in, but we placed last in our first five Olympiads. By 1985, we reached a high point when we placed eleventh out of the 18 countries competing. Robert Pope reached a milestone in 1991 for the U.S. by earning a gold medal for demonstrating his skill in the electric welding competition. Only one U.S. newspaper carried the story of Pope's unprecedented victory, his hometown newspaper in St. Petersburg, Florida. The priorities of Americans and/or media concerning the mastery of job skills vs. athletic skills is apparent. As stated by Kolberg and Smith (1992, p. C5), in America "athletic skills are more important than job skills; athletes are more important than frontline workers. The United States may be the only industrialized country with such attitudes—an important reason why the nation's productivity rates and standard of living are not growing as fast as those of other countries."

"To meet the challenge of building a world-class workforce, we need to know how voca-

tional-technical education in the United States compares with that of other nations" (Warnat, 1991, p. 23). Some very basic differences exist between the United States and the other industrialized nations. One major difference is that our competitors have national work policies. Countries we compete with monitor and upgrade skills of their workforces on a continuous basis. Korea, which has won seven team titles in the IYSO, provides a monetary reward system for its country's competitors that is funded by a payroll tax (Kolberg and Smith, 1992).

The focus of our public education is clearly on preparing our youth to advance to a college program. Our productivity has grown less than that of competing nations for the last 20 years. The opportunity for youngsters to select and receive up-to-date blue-collar training should concern all of us. We must reverse the image that educators, counselors, and some parents have of blue-collar training as being of lesser grade or importance or we will continue in our downward economic spiral. Blair (1992, p. 3) emphasized that "[a]s a society, we must reaffirm our belief in the economic importance and inherent dignity of all kinds of work."

In 1988, the William T. Grant Foundation coined the term "the forgotten half" to describe students who do not attend college. The Commission on the Skills of the American Workforce (1990) concluded that in America "our whole system conspires to produce minimal educational effort or achievement among our students who are not college bound," (p. 43) and recommended that the imbalance in resources and attention our education system devoted to college-bound and non-college-bound students needs to be corrected and is long overdue.

According to Warnat (1991, p. 23), the U.S. General Accounting Office studied the United States and four competitor nations—England, West Germany, Japan, and Sweden—and reported that our competitors

- Expect students to do well in school, while the U.S. accepts as a given that some of our youngsters will not keep pace.
- Have competency-based national training standards, while the U.S. merely certifies program completion.
- Invest major sums of money in programs

for students preparing for work, while we spend half as much on these individuals as those destined for college.

- Provide substantially better guidance than do we for students who have prepared for work and are in transition toward a job.

In 1989, Britain introduced a new national curriculum that includes the study of technology, along with math and science, beginning in the primary school. Atkin (1990, p. 19) stated that technology "is a type of thought and action seldom fostered in schools, yet it may have more to do with economic well-being than the subjects that currently dominate the curriculum."

In 1990, 30 professors from the Department of Technological and Adult Education at The University of Tennessee and leaders in the Department of Education and Skills Development at the Tennessee Valley Authority in Knoxville, Tennessee, were selected for a study tour. They visited German schools, businesses, and industry to learn more about that country's approach to vocational preparation for employment. Initially, the tour group was divided into six teams that focused on particular areas of interest. Each team researched the available literature about German vocational-technical education and then wrote a preliminary chapter to a book to be published after the trip to Germany verified or refuted the research findings. The chapters were rewritten on the basis of their data and observations. The unique differences between the German and American approaches might well be incorporated into our educational plan for preparing a workforce ready to compete in the world economy.

Germany's Three Tracks for Primary Students

In Germany, schools place a major responsibility on the fourth-grade teacher and the student's parents, who together decide on one of three options for the student: the *Hauptschule* (main school), the *Realschule*, or the *Gymnasium*. Graduates of the Hauptschule are likely to go directly to work or to enter a vocational training program. Because the children of immigrants dominate this program, the popularity of this choice has declined over the recent past. The Realschule (intermediate school) provides a variety of elective academic and vocational choices and is more demanding. A vocational program is commonly selected by students. The number of students in the Realschule has doubled over the last 25 years. Students who obtain a "leaving" certificate from the Realschule find that its market value to the employer is increased; the opportunity for apprenticeships and further training are the most significant outcomes. The last choice, the Gymnasium, is the most academically oriented program. It concludes at age 19 with the *Abitur* examination in the areas of physics, mathematics, English, and economics. The Abitur qualifies the holder to attend any university (Raggatt, 1988).

The Hauptschule, the most practically oriented program, recently added the *Arbeitslehre*, an orientation to and preparation for work. The curricula of the Arbeitslehre includes introductory economics coupled with career guidance. Some laboratory experiences are also common to this offering (Raggatt, 1988).

The age of 15 or 16 is a time of transition for approximately 70 percent of the students who have finished at the Hauptschule or the Realschule. They now enter full-time vocational schools or an apprenticeship that will last from two to three and one-half years. The poor performers, approximately 10 percent, have limited vocational opportunities. Some will enter the unskilled job market, with little hope of rising out of it, and others will be enrolled in the *Berufsgrundbildungsjahr* (BGJ). This Berufsschule provides one year of basic vocational training. Students may choose among the 13 occupational fields offered in this school. One form of BGJ is entirely school based, while the more successful plan links the school, through agreements, with various companies that provide a training site for the student.

The Dual System

The most fortunate students who enter vocational education and training are the 85 percent of the school "leavers" who have prepared themselves to take advantage of the dual system. This is truly the best of the German vocational education preparation programs.

The term *dual system*, commonly used since the 1960s, has four components:

1. A strong connection exists between the company and the vocational school.
2. The company shares costs and is responsible for in-company training, the training materials required, and the pay that is earned by the apprentice. Costs associated with the school itself are the responsibility of the state (Lander).
3. The Vocational Training Act regulates the in-company training and the Lander regulates the vocational education of the school (Berufsschule).
4. The individual student serves in two roles, as trainee (Lehrling) and student (Berufsschuler) (Raggatt, 1988).

The apprenticeship is entered into as a formal agreement among trainee, parents, and the firm that provides the hands-on portion of the training. There are 490 occupations from which trainees may select their trade; however 20 to 30 occupational areas receive the majority of the candidates. The training program must be settled on before the apprenticeship can begin. The minimum information required in the formal apprenticeship agreement includes: the type of factual and chronological organization, objectives of training for the job for which the apprentice is being trained; the beginning and ending dates of the training program; the training measures for evaluating progress; the regular daily working hours; the duration of trial period, payment and rate of wages, and length of holidays; and the conditions under which a training contract can be terminated (Dyer, 1977).

Sixty percent of the school-based portion of the apprenticeship is the development and application of the skills needed by a skilled craftsman. The remaining 40 percent emphasizes politics, language, and social affairs (Dyer, 1977).

Of the students in Germany who have qualified for the university by passing the Abitur, an increasing number opt to enter the dual system. The popularity of the dual system has also made it difficult for some students to gain acceptance into the program of their choice at the time they are ready to enter. Also, some who do not have high enough qualifica-tions for one of the more popular apprentice-ships may have to wait and/or to improve their skills. Others may choose a different occupa-tion in which there is room for another entry. Each of these factors has the effect of raising the average age of individuals who are begin-ning their apprenticeship training program (Raggatt, 1988).

Furthermore, as more students seek the higher (Realschule) level of education, the students who have completed their studies in the Hauptschule have greater difficulty in ob-taining the more favorable apprenticeships. This has limited their choices to the manual forms of occupation with lower-level manage-ment and technical careers increasingly being reserved for the graduates of the two upper tiers of education (Raggatt, 1988).

Verifying Quality

The procedure for determining the effec-tiveness of the apprenticeship is set forth in the training regulations at the time the training plan for the trainee is initiated. The agreement outlines the content and sequence and calls for a written and oral examination. The agree-ment also recognizes that there will be a prac-tical assessment of work skills performed un-der supervision for technical trades or a dem-onstration of abilities in a social interactive setting for commercial apprentices. Training contracts are registered with the authorities who have jurisdiction over each trade area. The chambers of agriculture, commerce, crafts, industry, and the professions, which are self-governing, have responsibility for insuring that the quality of training is satisfactory and that the apprentice has scored high enough on the exam to be passed into the trade for which he or she has prepared. Training advisors who are employed by the various chambers monitor the training and offer advice to trainees and to companies that are involved in providing the experience. Trainees keep records of their progress, and at mid-term a formative exami-nation is administered to let each of the entities involved determine the adequacy of training to date. Results that reveal poor performance may lead to discussions about remedial help, a change in the training plan, transfer to another company, or extending the training to include another site. Complaints by either party are also generally handled by the training advisor. Should there be need to accelerate or lengthen the training period, the advisor will handle these matters as well (Raggatt, 1988).

The record or log that must be kept by the apprentice is reviewed by the individual responsible for the trainee at regular intervals. The log provides the background information for counseling concerning skill development, work behavior, and relationships with fellow workers. The written record is an important link to the attainment of future goals and opportunities and it is required by the examination board for review of qualifications, responsibilities, self-esteem, and increases in pay for the selected occupation (Raggatt, 1988).

That the apprenticeship training in German industry is working rather well is evident. Results indicate that 80 percent of all apprentices in this sector remain with the industry in which they received their training (Raggatt, 1988).

The individual who serves as trainer of apprentices is highly qualified to work with apprentices. The company or business that looks to engage in providing a site for such training cannot do so without having a previously qualified trainer in its hire who has

- Completed an apprenticeship and all tests in the trade of the incoming apprentice.
- Experience in the particular trade.
- Reached 24 years of age.
- Passed a test of technical and pedagogical competence.
- Become a master (meister) craftsman (Raggatt, 1988).

The German vocational education training act of 1969 was enacted to tighten regulations and to increase uniformity in on-the-job training. Prior to the law, control of training was very lax and anyone in business or industry could participate. Today, the field has been narrowed considerably with only 16 percent of all firms qualifying as training sites. Because of limited availability, demand for these apprenticeships is very high and the selection criteria, consequently, has increased. Those applicants who have been initially unsuccessful and have then selected an occupation for which they have less interest or talent often

drop out of their training program, or, after a considerable wait, they may be pushed into an unskilled job (Raggatt, 1988).

Comparing the U.S. and Other Countries

Hamilton (1990, p. 116) contrasts German and U.S. vocational schools as follows: "The critical difference between German Berufsschulen and U.S. vocational high schools is the one noted by Georg Kerschensteiner. Berufsschulen are designed to supplement apprenticeships; U.S. vocational high schools were developed to replace apprenticeship." While most would agree that the vocational high school experience has had a positive effect on some youngsters, it has not been nearly as productive as the dual system in providing the nurturing relationship that develops between the trainee, meister, and employer. The program that most closely approximates the alliance generated by apprenticeship in the U.S. is cooperative education. However, the cooperative education program has a much shorter duration and does not generally provide the wide variety of occupational choices afforded by the dual system (Hamilton, 1990).

The ingredient most lacking from the vocational high school program in the U.S. is more extensive job experience directly related to the student's chosen occupation. Through the delicate mix of providing challenging academic course work together with developing practical skills, the Germans have found the means for equipping their most capable youths with valuable job skills through the dual system. The near-phenomenal success of apprenticeship training in Germany has caught the attention of Americans associated with vocational training who are wondering why it cannot be made to work as well in the U.S. The school reform movement in America is beginning to recognize that success rests on a much closer relationship between school and work (Grant, 1991).

A major difference exists between the stated goals of public education in Germany and Sweden and those in the U.S. Practical job training is a proudly selected and seriously planned outcome for most young people in these two countries. The U.S. public school focus is unmistakenly biased toward preparation for college. Further, Sweden has a nationally mandated 6- to 10-week work experience program for all students. This program, which must be accomplished before the student's sixteenth birthday, may include observation or working for a company without pay. The dual system has the support of the German employment agency, school, employment agency counselors, and the labor unions that help identify sites for apprentices in the over 400 apprenticeable fields.

The U.S. Commission on the Skills of the American Workforce prepared a report, based on the feelings of American employers, that suggests that 90 percent of the respondents believed that a high school diploma only signifies that the individual has occupied a seat in school. The diploma makes no statement regarding knowledge learned or skills developed (Grant, 1991). Ray Marshall, a former U.S. Secretary of Labor, stated: "Because we have failed to force a relationship between how well a student does in school and what kind of job he or she can get, we have turned our high schools into little more than 'holding tanks' for non-college-bound students" (Grant, 1991, p. 37).

Impact of Part-Time Work Experiences

A large number of recent research studies have examined the impacts of part-time work experiences on students in the United States. The effects of such employment appear to depend on the amount of work and on the appropriateness of the work setting for the student.

Extensive work involvement (beyond 20 hours per week) decreased the amount of time for study, interfered with social and school-related activities, resulted in lower grade-point averages, and increased dropping out (Bachman, 1986; D'Amico, 1984; Lillydahl, 1990; Steel, 1991; Wirtz, Rohrbeck, Charner, & Fraser, 1988). Bachman (1986) also concluded that work intensity may increase cigarette and drug abuse and delinquent behavior. These behaviors are likely to have resulted from the increased influence of working peers or from the work environment. On the other hand, 20 hours or less of work experience had no significant negative impact on grades in school (D'Amico, 1984; Green & Jaquess, 1987; Wirtz, et al., 1988; Yang, Lester, & Gatto, 1989).

A number of research studies also examined the usefulness of the work experience to the students involved. McNelly (1990a) found that the experience helped students to manage their time and money, to make more realistic career decisions, and to understand what employers want from employees. Work experience, however, did not necessarily provide each student with the prevocational skills that others may have experienced. Bachman (1986) found that seniors in this study saw little or no connection between their present work and their long-range aspirations. On the other hand, when the work and school experiences were related, using a cooperative work setting, McNelly (1990b) concluded that the student's school achievement was enhanced.

For the work experience to be least interfering and most positive, the identified studies recommended that work time be limited to the 20 hours or less per week. In addition, students need help with locating work and job settings related to their current career choices, and they need supervision from parents and the school. Students should also be assisted to identify the transferrable skills that had been developed as a result of the work experience (Barton, 1989; McNelly, 1990a; Steinberg & Dornbusch, 1990).

The largest segment of America's workforce is students who go directly to work following dropping out or graduating from high school. Consequently, considerable attention has been focused on identifying the skills that employers actually seek. Employers are demanding skills quite different from what most schools emphasize (i.e., grades). The employees that employers prefer have previous work experience and positive interpersonal and social skills and habits. In addition, employees must be competent in the basic skills of reading; computation; oral, written, and listening communication; and problem solving. They must be enthusiastic, responsible, flexible, cooperative, and willing to learn, and they must have some understanding of the social and economic workaday world (Ascher, 1988; Barton & Kirsch, 1990; Baxter & Young, 1982; Committee on Science, Engineering and Public Policy, 1984; Junge, Daniels, & Karmos, 1984). In a recent study of Tennessee employers, McNelly, Petty, Thomas and Mann (1991) reported that the attributes most needed for entry-level employment, beyond those already listed, are dependability, a good attendance record, commitment to quality, and pride in work.

Conclusion

Because what a student learns in the first few years in school sets the stage for future school progress, the most flexible, tolerant, and capable teachers must be provided. Preferably, as recent research continues to suggest, students must be able to progress at their own developmental level based on whatever skills or limitations the home and/or neighborhood has provided. An ungraded approach that permits individual as well as group learning activities is recommended for the first few years, in a setting where expectation and consequent teacher/parent approval is related to student readiness and ability. Although grouping is useful for some learning activities, the grouping should be for short-term experiences, with regrouping occurring as students respond differentially. Retention practices must be reexamined and largely eliminated—and not based on academic achievement alone or on the perceived requirements of the next grade.

More cooperation must be sought from business, industry, and the community in general to provide the real life experiences required for our youth to succeed economically. Educators must seek the help of those who are currently employed. To more nearly reflect and approximate the job market, a useful method would be to create early-on linkages with individuals who can be coerced or convinced that they have a stake in America's success in our global economic recovery.

The techniques developed in Germany suggest that we solicit and gain the commitments from business and industry to plug a gigantic hole in America's education system. The challenge is great, but it could be worth the time, energy, and expense to restructure

the skill preparation of the largest segment of our public school population, our forgotten half. The Germans have helped their young people to focus on career choice at a much earlier educational stage. In the U.S., we have postponed career decision making. This has caused many to have delayed so long as to have had no focus whatever or to have lost interest because of the general nature of the high school curriculum.

The beginnings of a solution suggest that we first recognize that there is a problem. College preparation is a worthy goal for some but not for a majority of our youth. Not enough attention and monetary support has gone to those who will pursue other worthy career objectives.

Opportunities to reintroduce career education, as it was conceived during the 1970s, could provide a positive additional school goal of helping students to make tentative career choices. The tentative decisions made by youngsters can be further refined through their teachers' increased emphasis on connecting basic skills in reading, writing, speaking, and teamwork to job-related examples in the community.

With the multiplicity of career choices they have, students need as much knowledge about themselves as possible. Experiences that allow them to sample tasks representative of various occupations could provide a sense of their potential success in a wide variety of jobs. Hands-on sampling of a variety of job skills should be required for all students. The more exploration a student experiences, the better his or her chances of uncovering a viable option.

As students begin to solidify possible choices to match their interests, abilities, aptitudes, and aspirations, they should have access to options through teachers and counselors who have secured community support through purposeful contacts. Students should make firsthand visits to appropriate work sites. Shadowing workers can help further enhance or refute their preconceived notions about a particular job.

The typical recommendations suggest that our high schools should incorporate the following changes:

- Encourage all students to gain some

work experience prior to graduation and to get involved in some school-sponsored activity.

- Emphasize information-processing skills and higher levels of basic skills.
- Provide instruction that simulates real-life experiences.
- Help students acquire job application and interview skills.

In addition, to prepare students adequately for work, employers, school boards, school administrators, high school teachers, parents, and other community members must cooperate in both the career and critical skill development that prospective workers need.

While we may find useful suggestions for our vocational programs, the dual system does include some trouble spots. These include numerous government regulations, vocational choices made at too early an age, and no assurance that students will be hired into the trade for which they have trained. But regardless of these shortcomings, apprentices learn to be on time, get along with fellow workers, and solve work-related problems. They also develop positive self-esteem (Grant, 1991).

To review the increasing number of dropouts in the U.S. is to recognize that school does not satisfactorily meet the needs or expectations of a large group of potential learners.

The number of existing vocational programs could be expanded so that training opportunities are made more attractive to students. The work-study programs now available could be used to provide meaningful learning experience (Grant, 1991). By encouraging students with a work-study option, more are likely to stay in school longer and to continue the lifelong need for additional education/training.

Today, better linkages are being created between high schools and community colleges. The program involved, termed *tech prep*, requires more rigorous academic and vocational preparation than was previously available. Similar to the advanced placement concept used for college-bound students, tech prep's two-plus-two design has students transferring upgraded and revised vocational education courses from high school to community colleges. In Richmond, Virginia, where tech

prep has been introduced, "the annual dropout rate has declined from 7.2 percent to 4.8 percent" (The Commission on the Skills of the American Workforce, 1990, p. 177).

The Commission on the Skills of the American Workforce recommends that "[a] comprehensive system of technical and professional certificates and associate's degrees should be created for the majority of our students and adult workers who do not pursue a baccalaureate degree" (1990, p. 130). It lists four elements for such a program:

1. Establish performance-based assessment standards equal to those of other advanced industrialized countries.
2. Create courses that are available in high school that could lead to technical and professional certificates and associate's degrees that are accredited by state boards of higher and vocational education.
3. Encourage employers to provide part-time work and training as a part of the certification or degree program with incentives for those who excel.
4. Provide state and federal financing sufficient to gain four years of additional education beyond the certificate at some later date in their adult lives (Commission on the Skills of the American Workforce, 1990).

As Blair (1992, p. 3) points out, "If we are to compete in the world economy, we must guarantee all our young people, our future workforce, access to a wide range of education and training opportunities beyond high school."

References

Ascher, C. (1988). High school graduates in entry level jobs: What do employers want? *ERIC Clearinghouse on Urban Education*, 1-4.

Atkin, J. M. (1990, September 26). Teach science for science's sake; For global competitiveness, try technology. *Education Week*, Sept. 26, X(4), 19.

Bachman, J. G. (1986). Correlates of employment among high school seniors. *Institute for Social Research, 20*, 1-121.

Barton, P. E. (1989). *Earning and learning: The academic achievement of high-school juniors with jobs* (pp. 1-21). Princeton, NJ: National Assessment of Educational Progress.

Barton, P. E., & Kirsch, I.S. (1990). *Workplace competencies: The need to improve literacy and employment* readiness (pp. 1-44). Washington, DC: U.S. Government Printing Office.

Baxter, M. B., & Young, J. L. (1982). What do employers expect from high school graduates. *NASSP Bulletin, 66* (458), 93-96.

Blair, S. J. (1992, April). Achieving work force competitiveness: A challenge for every American. *Chronicle Guidance Publications,* CGP reprint, pp. 1-3.

Commission on the Skills of the American Workforce. (1990). *America's choice: high skills or low wages!* (pp. 43, 130-133, 152-155). Rochester, NY: National Center on Education and the Economy.

Committee on Science, Engineering and Public Policy. (1984). *High schools and the changing workplace* (pp. 1-68). Washington, DC: National Academy Press.

D'Amico, R. (1984). Does employment during high school impair academic progress? *Sociology of Education, 57* (3), 152-164.

DeRidder, L. M. (1989). Integrating equity into the schools. In *Career development: Preparing for the 21st century* (pp. 23-38). Ann Arbor, MI: ERIC Counseling and Personnel Services.

Dyer, N. (1977). Vocational education and training in the Federal Republic of Germany. *Industrial and Commercial Training, 9* (2), 63-66.

Grant, C. L. (1991). How Europeans link school and work. *Tennessee Teacher, 58* (8), 33-34, 36-37.

Green, G., & Jaquess, S. N. (1987). The effect of part-time employment on academic achievement. *Journal of Educational Research, 80* (6), 325-329.

Hamilton, S. F. (1990). *Apprenticeship for adulthood: Preparing youth for the future* (pp. 107-116). New York: Free Press.

Junge, D. A., Daniels, M. H., & Karmos, J. S. (1984). Personnel managers' perceptions of requisite basic skills. *Vocational Guidance Quarterly, 33* (2), 138-146.

Kolberg, W., & Smith, F. (1992, February 23). Our unsung Olympic hero. *Washington Post,* p. C5.

Lillydahl, J. H. (1990). Academic achievement and part-time employment of high school students. *Journal of Economic Education, 41* (3), 307-316.

Mantzicopoulos, P., & Morrison, D. (1992). Kindergarten retention: Academic and behavioral outcomes through the end of second grade. *American Educational Research Journal, 29* (1), 182-198.

McNelly, D. E. (1990a). Does working part-time enhance secondary education? Paper presented at the American Vocational Association Convention, Cincinnati, Ohio.

McNelly, D. E. (1990b). Enhancement of secondary education for cooperative and non-cooperative students through part-time employment. Paper presented at the American Vocational Association Convention, Cincinnati, Ohio.

McNelly, D. E., Petty, G. C., Thomas, C. D., & Mann, E. C. (1991). *Tennessee vocational needs assessment: Employers.* Knoxville: University of Tennessee.

Raggatt, P. (1988). Quality control in the dual system of West Germany. *Oxford Review of Education, 14* (2), 164-178.

Slavin, R. E. (1987). Ability grouping and student achievement in elementary schools: A best evidence synthesis. *Review of Educational Research, 57,* 293-336.

Smart, K. F. (1975). Vocational education in the Federal Republic of Germany: Current trends and problems. *Comparative Education, 11* (2), 156-163.

Steel, L. (1991). Early work experience among white and nonwhite youths. *Youth and Society, 22* (4), 419-447.

Steinberg, L. D., & Dornbusch, S. M. (1990). *Negative correlates of part-time employment during adolescence: Replication and elaboration* (pp. 1-48). Madison: National Center on Effective Secondary Schools.

Warnat, W. I. (1991). Preparing a world class work force. *Vocational Education Journal, 66* (5), 22-25.

William T. Grant Foundation (1988). *Youth of America's Future.* Final report. Washington, DC: Author.

Wirtz, P. W., Rohrbeck, C., Charner, I., & Fraser, B.S. (1988). Employment of adolescents while in high school. *Journal of Adolescent Research, 3* (1), 97-105.

Yang, B., Lester, D., & Gatto, J. (1989). Working students and their course performance. *Psychological Reports, 64* (1), 218.

15

Special Problems for Rural and Urban Youth in Transition

Lynda L. West and Lisa B. Penkowsky

Introduction

The movement to foster transition from school to work presents unique challenges to today's educators. Students with special needs who are in the transition process face a variety of problems and barriers, regardless of whether they reside in urban or rural settings. The success of transition for youths with special needs depends largely on how educators respond to the challenges of today's increasingly complex settings. Just one of the changes facing us is the shifting demographics of American schools and their effect on further diversification of students' needs.

Berlin and Sum (1988) believe that the new demographics of the youth population add a new urgency and a new dimension to education. Recognizing that we must make immediate changes in America's educational public policy, their formula for educational reform includes

- Focusing reform efforts on all children, but paying special attention to students with special needs who require improved basic skills and higher-order thinking skills
- Recognizing the intergenerational causes of low basic skills and offering a continuum of services for both parents and children
- Addressing the phenomenon of summer learning loss
- Developing standards that make local institutions accountable, while allowing local officials to exercise necessary autonomy
- Smoothing the transition from school to work for high school graduates who are not college bound
- Improving the quality and availability of the nation's second-chance job-training and community college programs. These goals focus on the surrounding issues and importance of the transition movement. Yet American public policy on transition is still insufficient.

According to Barton (1991), roughly half of the nation's high school graduates enter a hostile employment environment for applicants without experience, training, or postsecondary education. Typically, non-college-bound students receive very little help in making the transition from school to work. The results of this neglect are economic hardship, reduced productivity for industry and an appalling waste of human potential. Barton identifies several obstacles facing today's students, which include that

- High school counselors spend a disproportionate amount of time counseling the college bound compared with what they spend on students who want to go directly to work.
- Budget cuts in the 1980s eliminated federally funded job-counseling services.

- Traditional academic skills are often insufficient or do not transfer into the workplace.
- Students going directly to work have no way to demonstrate their employment potential while in school.
- Large firms offering career paths to well-paid jobs no longer hire new high school graduates.

Until America develops a comprehensive transition policy, Barton believes transition programs should

- Integrate academic skills and vocational education.
- Encourage local school systems to work with employers to promote collaborative education.
- Provide students with access to community-based occupational counseling and employment assistance services.

These key transition program features apply equally to urban and rural education. While both settings have unique aspects and differences, educators can take advantage of some of the same features as they decide which strategies to implement. This chapter will address strategies, the planning process, and the special problems urban and rural youths face in transition.

Urban Issues in Transition

There are abundant options, services, and opportunities available for students making the transition from school to work in urban centers. At first glance, educators may think that successful transition in urban centers is a much easier task than it is in rural communities. After all, the available network in urban centers is much larger than the rural programs offer, and transportation is rarely a problem. However, secondary educators concerned with transition for young adults with special needs face a long list of barriers as they try to help the students. Sometimes the barriers outweigh the conveniences of urban living.

Piccigallo (1989) identifies the following major problems facing all urban youth today:

- Poverty
- Dislocated families
- High rate of teen pregnancies
- Poor job prospects
- Physical state of school buildings
- Inadequate school funding
- Overcrowded classrooms
- Neighborhoods ravaged by crime, drugs, parent absenteeism, and so forth

In isolation, these problems do not prohibit transition, but their existence severely impedes the transition process. Identifying and isolating problems such as the ones cited by Piccigallo is one strategy for moving toward overcoming the overriding problems found in urban settings.

Outside perceptions of schools also hamper educators' efforts to implement transition programs. Among the most frustrating problems facing urban youths is public school bureaucracy. Carlson (1989) explains that parents, students, and community leaders distrust what they perceive as the insulated public school bureaucracy. They believe that schools are repressive institutions and are not really committed to helping students "get ahead." Also, Carlson pointed out that the worsening fiscal crisis facing schools today threatens their capacity to respond effectively to problems. Furthermore, at the root of the urban school crisis lies the everyday struggle for teachers to maintain a sense of order and purpose with resistant, angry, and cynical students who are not willing participants in the school process. These interactive components of the urban education system have had a great impact on the school-to-work transition process of many urban youth. The focus of educators and students alike is often and understandably diverted under such circumstances.

Rural Issues in Transition

Urban educators often envy the individualized approach to transition that rural educators can often provide for their students. Many urban educators would like to have the rural school's more personalized approach to the transition process, which allows educators to get to know their students better. Furthermore, rural teachers often know most employers in the community personally and have more immediate access to available services. However, for every advantage of a rural setting a drawback exists.

Slow changes in attitudes, particularly

towards individuals with disabilities or special needs, may be a major problem in rural areas. Parents may act more protective of their children due to increased isolation, and there will most likely be a shortage of employment opportunities and inadequate adult services in these communities. Despite the existence of these barriers, Halper and Taymans (1990) note a benefit in that rural areas are also rich in valuable attributes ranging from people who share common dialects and similar everyday experiences to cooperative attitudes toward community schools.

What problems face students in transition in rural areas? Helge (1983) identifies the major problems facing students with disabilities in rural areas:

- Funding inadequacies
- Difficulty recruiting and retaining qualified staff
- Transportation inadequacies
- Unavailable services for low-incidence populations
- Need for staff development
- Resistance to change in community
- Need for support services
- Negative attitudes toward students with disabilities
- Long distances between schools and services
- Difficulties involving parents
- Isolation
- Cultural differences
- Climate-related problems and marginal roads
- Problems serving transient populations
- Inadequate post-high-school services
- Inadequate facilities
- Foster care inadequacies
- Interagency collaboration

This list presents a broad synthesis of social, psychological, and cultural factors that may affect transition service delivery in rural school districts and communities. Several of the factors are dilemmas indigenous only to rural settings, while others are problems confronting educators everywhere.

Strategies for Success

Ten strategies provide educators in both urban and rural settings with a framework for building a strong transitional program and continuing successful transition planning. These strategies for success are based on the premise that, while our legislation consists of mere fragments of public policy, Americans have begun to understand that reaching the goals of transition will improve the quality of life for students with special needs. This premise extends to the ever more urgent idea that educators must continue to help this population contribute to society and halt the present loss of human resources. Until American policymakers more fully recognize these goals, the following strategies will aid educators in using available resources to build strong transition services in both urban and rural settings:

1. **Self-advocacy/self-determination**– One of the cornerstones of successful transition is developing students' ability to take control of their futures. Students must be trained in self-advocacy and/or self-determination. Students who are self-advocates learn to better understand their legal rights, goals, and responsibilities, and they feel confident expressing their knowledge throughout all phases of their transition.

2. **Mentoring and tutoring**–(a) An educator becomes a mentor by taking a "one-on-one" interest and developing a personal relationship with a student. A mentor addresses many needs in his or her relationship with the student, including working to build self-esteem; offering career exploration, counseling, advising; and serving as a role model and as an adult with experience in daily living. For example, the mentor would meet at least once a week for 30 minutes to discuss the students' skills development or concerns. The mentor could expand the student's experience by providing an educational experience once every 6 to 8 weeks outside the traditional school environment. (b) A peer can develop a tutoring relationship with a student with special needs by offering assistance and academic support, and by accepting and encouraging the student to feel more a part of hisor her own age group. Both mentoring and tutoring give the student individual attention, personalized feedback, and the opportunity to improve interpersonal skills. Development of these skills is a significant component of transition.

3. **Functional curriculum**–Transition educators must carefully examine their program's curriculum. Increased concern about test scores, literacy rates, and basic skills acquisition finds educators questioning the appropriateness and usefulness of curricula taught in public schools today. From a transition perspective, functional curriculum generally refers to the teaching of social skills, employability skills, academic skills integrated into vocational education, and other survival skills necessary for independent living.

4. **Career exploration and job shadowing**–Effective transition requires exploration of the labor market for students to find a realistic and available place for themselves in the job market. Students who are informed about various occupational options can contribute to the systematic planning of their vocational training and job placement. Success of the placement is much greater if it is based on the interests and strengths of the student. Job shadowing is one method that gives students a chance to explore the details of potential occupations through a one-on-one experience with an adult working in the field.

5. **Vocational training**–Specific occupational training provides students with critical entry-level skills. Meeting immediate employer needs through school training is an elemental component of transition. The training takes place in the community, classroom, laboratory, or various secondary and postsecondary settings.

6. **Parent involvement and training**–Transition requires the assistance and support of various individuals in the home, school, and community. The better informed the transition team members are in transition options and services, the more successful the transition process becomes. Planners of quality transition programs provide parent outreach services, organize training sessions, and share information necessary for parents to help facilitate the transition process for their young adults. Parents become effective advocates for their children when they are supplied with legislative information about adult service providers.

7. **Partnership**–Developing teamwork and collaborative arrangements is necessary if the transition team is to achieve successful transition. Effectual transition requires team members to assemble a variety of services and ask for the assistance of outside agencies to contribute to training and skill acquisition efforts. Agencies, employers, adult service systems, parents, and educators all become partners in the transition process.

8. **Interagency agreement**–The interagency agreement is a written document outlining and guaranteeing cooperation and shared resources among vocational rehabilitation, vocational education, and special education. The agreement is designed to break down barriers and facilitate collaboration among professionals in different facets of the transition process.

9. **Job placement/follow-up**–The importance of educators' familiarity with the needs of the labor market cannot be understated. Educators must vigilantly monitor their community to identify potential placement options and effectively match students to employers. After making job-matches, follow-up contacts are critical for determining the success of the placement for all involved.

10. **Staff development and training**–Professionals involved in the transition process are frequently unaware of the adult service system and other support services outside of the educational system. Professionals engaged in transition planning must develop their own skills and improve their knowledge base of available services. Generally, educators foster this development through professional affiliations, conferences, workshops, graduate classes, professional journals, and so forth.

These strategies for success ask transition planners to tackle many different areas of the transition process. The job is not an easy one, but working on these strategies is essential for improving transition training. Continued innovation will help students become contributing members of American society.

Coordinating a Transition Program

Developing a comprehensive approach to the delivery of transition services requires careful organization and planning. This is both a complex and necessary component of the process. No one individual can take responsibility for all the various services needed for transition, but one individual should be identified as the transition coordinator for the district (rural) or the school (urban). The transition coordinator facilitates the overall planning of transition programs and services that together form the transition process.

States and local educational agencies have found that the transition process requires a "team" approach. States and districts have designed variations of teams, referred to as task forces, advisory committees, interagency councils, and so forth. The transition team coordinates activities of various services and assistance from transition-related agency representatives. The transition team is generally made up of the following representatives:

- Parents/guardians
- Business and industry leaders
- Private industry council members
- Language experts from minority communities
- School administrators
- School-based pupil service staff
- Employment services administrators
- Case managers
- Private, nonprofit organizations officials
- Special education advocates
- Teachers
- Students

These representatives meet regularly with the transition coordinator, who acts as the team facilitator. The agenda for each meeting focuses on issues needing clarification, revision, or action by the team. The better informed the team is about all the options and services, the more effective and creative it can be in assisting students in the transition process. Some goals of the transition team might include

- Conducting a needs assessment to determine transition services needed.
- Selecting referral procedures.
- Identifying financial responsibilities.
- Exchanging information about services.
- Identifying potential job sites.
- Selecting functional assessment procedures.
- Planning staff orientation on transition services.
- Revising the interagency agreement.

Creativity and flexibility are important characteristics for transition team members. Transition is not a precise or traditional process. The procedure requires individuals to look beyond convention and to envision what should happen for the good of students' futures. Goals should be realistic and immediate, but the team should also be capable of developing far-reaching innovations and possibilities for improving transition services.

Transition programs should offer a continuum of services beginning in elementary grades and continuing through postsecondary settings. Successful transition cannot just happen at the last minute in the student's senior year. Instead, the step-by-step process builds on the student's individual experiences and strengths both within school and in the community. Examples of transition services at various levels include the following activities:

Elementary
- Career awareness
- Community visitations
- Independent living skills instruction
- Social skills instruction

Middle School
- Career exploration (e.g., job sampling)
- Vocational assessment
- Vocational readiness instruction
- Speech therapy
- Counseling

Secondary
- Vocational assessment
- Vocational training
- Transportation training in the community
- Employability skills training (e.g., job interview)
- Applied academics

Postsecondary
- Vocational training
- Child care support
- Community living
- Supported work
- Follow-up

Effective transition planning is future oriented and outcome based. Students with special needs require a lifetime of preparation to make successful transitions from the insulated school network to the outside world of work. Furthermore, incorporating related activities into students' school experiences will help them achieve independent living once they leave the school setting.

Steps to Program Planning

Various intangible factors scattered throughout transition programs contribute to program success in both rural and urban settings. These success factors make a difference to students, the school, and the community, and are critical if not always immediately evident and essential steps in the planning process. What are these invisible factors that make such a significant difference? Gruskin (1987) calls them "best bets" for keeping students in school and helping them to achieve. They include

1. **Implementing early intervention**– Encouraging students to develop competence and confidence in their learning ability is an excellent way to instill an immediate desire to learn while also preparing students for a lifetime of learning.

2. **Creating a positive school climate**– Effective schools possess strong leaders who stress academic achievement, help teachers maintain an orderly and structured environment, and instill positive values and self-confidence in their students.

3. **Setting high expectations**–Research repeatedly shows that educators who maintain realistically high standards of attendance, academic performance, and behavior standards are rewarded by having students work to reach these expectations. However, support must be available for maintaining these levels of attainment.

4. **Selecting and developing strong teachers**–Teachers exert tremendous influence on students' education and attitudes toward school. It is important that we select and train teachers to be sensitive to the needs of students.

5. **Providing a broad range of instructional programs**–Responding to and accommodating students with diverse needs calls for providing as many optional transition services as possible.

6. **Initiating collaborative efforts**–

Schools, communities, and families will far more likely succeed in retaining students in school if they work together in meaningful partnerships, promoting a comprehensive approach to meeting students' varied needs.

Smith (1991) identifies six steps in successful program planning for dropout prevention programs. These steps are equally as applicable and adaptable for transition programs. Smith's steps are adapted for transition planning as follows:

1. **Identify student population to be transitioned.** A single approach to all at-risk students will not succeed as well as separating segments of the population according to their specific needs. Differentiating among students by generating a list of students who require immediate transition services and another list of students with future needs is one approach. Needs can be identified by either formal assessment or by an individual teacher's observations and perceptions.

2. **Form a collaborative team.** Successful program planning requires motivated and committed individuals working together toward the common goal of helping at-risk students succeed at and complete their education. This group of individuals must be able to organize and implement transition support services, as well as include a wide variety of representatives who would share their clear vision of what the team wants to accomplish through collaboration.

3. **Identify program vision and goals.** Creating an appropriate program vision depends on the needs of the target population and how the ideas and individual expertise of team members reflects the vision of the team as a unit. This vision includes developing a mission statement guiding the function, roles, and responsibilities of transition team members.

4. **Conduct research on programs that have demonstrated success.** The process of creating new educational ventures includes incorporating re-

searchers' findings of successful approaches with at-risk students. Identifying proven transition activities and services makes adaptation and modification easier than beginning the process anew. Building on past knowledge permits educational innovation to improve on existing practices.

5. **Develop an implementation strategy, including identification of potential supporters and sources of funding.** An essential part of planning is cultivating the help of potentially supportive individuals and businesses. Community interest and participation provides the broad base of support needed for successful educational programming. Identify networks of individuals, employers, and agency representatives who can play an instrumental role in changing the status quo and who will support new or expanded services.

6. **Evaluate program effectiveness.** Dealing with the immediate and pressing problems of at-risk youth sometimes impedes educators in keeping systematic measurements and records of the impact of their programming efforts. However, educators should not rely on anecdotal information as a way to report program effectiveness. Systematically collected data provides an infinitely more convincing tool for showing student progress.

These steps to successful transition program planning offer basic guidelines for both urban and rural districts struggling with the special problems facing youth and educators. Developing strong transition programs requires an overall commitment to student success from all involved.

Cuban (1989) identifies certain features of successful schools and classrooms which, he believes, can most effectively deal with urban problems: (1) small school or program size encourages personalized relationships and instruction between old and young; (2) a trained and committed staff works together to educate at-risk students; (3) program flexibility includes risk-taking approaches, team teaching, and innovations in time and scheduling; and (4) classroom communities build extended families and self-esteem in at-risk students. Although Cuban is writing about urban education, these strategies also work with transition approaches.

Finally, because transition programs are generally not yet well defined or well organized, educators may have difficulty incorporating planning procedures. In some districts, transition is only another part of the IEP. Now that it is required by legislation, transition is in danger of becoming just another mandate that must be attended to as a federal requirement. Unfortunately, transition is still not viewed as a public policy nor as involving a commitment to quality programming. Consequently, special problems in urban and rural settings may not be viewed with the urgency or importance with which they should.

Evaluating Program Effectiveness

Transition programs will remain troubled unless educators determine evaluation criteria and standards by which schools measure program effectiveness. There are a number of issues to consider in evaluating success or failure in either urban or rural districts. The questions guiding districts in measuring program effectiveness include the following:

1. Is there a clearly defined purpose, mission, vision, or philosophy of the transition program?
2. Are goals and/or objectives guiding transition activities and services?
3. Is there a transition coordinator who facilitates transition team meetings? Are there regularly scheduled meetings?
4. Has there been a community needs assessment or labor market analysis identifying potential employers and job placement sites?
5. Have the transition activities or transition services been well publicized to students, teachers, parents, and the community?
6. Are educators aware of the interagency agreement? Is the agreement used?
7. What are the placement rates for students in transition program?
8. Are there careful follow-up procedures in place?

9. Are students aware of vocational training options available to them?
10. Are school board members and district administrators aware of the transition program? Does the program have a budget?

These questions are only the "beginning" set of issues that require investigation. As transition evolves into a national agenda, the issues will undoubtedly multiply as well. Program evaluation continues to be a complex process of various activities designed to provide educators with the most current and pertinent information on which to base future program decisions (West, 1991). Professionals in special education, vocational education, vocational rehabilitation, employment, and training must focus on transition programming to integrate their various areas of expertise. Clearly, transition is an interdisciplinary concern and commitment for all special needs professionals. To evaluate program effectiveness, it is necessary to examine measures and standards across disciplines and from a variety of perspectives.

Summary

Educators across the country face an increasingly diverse student population with complex and urgent needs. We must educate and prepare today's young adults for an increasingly complicated and technologically advanced world with rapidly dwindling school and community resources. Educators working with individuals with special needs—such as those who make the transition from school to work in rural and urban settings—are even more challenged by the additional barriers found in those settings. By concentrating on strategies for success and finding ways to reach goals through collaborative efforts, and by developing comprehensive coordination of services, educators can bring positive change to students' lives at a time when our country greatly needs its citizens to contribute to economic recovery. The ultimate goals of transition programming are still evolving, so the process remains open to innovation through creative planning. We do know that the most effective approach calls for linking innovation with successful practices and proven strategies of previous transition efforts. By identifying the unique qualities of their particular settings, educators in rural and urban settings can take the best practices and incorporate their characteristics into the established principles of current beliefs in transition planning.

References

Barton, P. E. (1991). The school-to-work transition. *Issues in Science and Technology, 7* (3).

Berlin, G., & Sum, A. (1988). *Toward a more perfect union: Basic skills, poor families, and our economic future.* New York: Ford Foundation

Carlson, D. L. (1989). Managing the urban school crisis: Recent trends in curricular reform. *Journal of Education, 171* (3).

Gruskin, S. J., Campbell, M. A., & Paulu, N. (1987). *Dealing with dropouts: The urban superintendent's call to action.* Washington, DC: Office of Research and Improvement.

Halper, A., & Taymans, J. (1990). *The rural transition training manual and parent handbook for transition.* Washington, DC: George Washington University, Department of Teacher Preparation and Special Education.

Helge, D. (1983). *Images: Issues and trends in rural special education.* Bellingham, WA: American Council on Special Education.

Piccigallo, P. (1989, January). Renovating urban schools is fundamental to improving them. *Phi Delta Kappan,* 402-406.

Smith, G. A. (1991). Program planning for at-risk students. In L. L. West (Ed.), *Effective strategies for dropout prevention of at-risk youth.* Gaithersburg, MD: Aspen Publishers, Inc.

West, L. L. (1991). Evaluating transition programs. In K. H. Jones (Ed.), *Career education for transition: Curriculum implementation.* Athens, GA: University of Georgia, Department of Vocational Education.

16

Apprenticeship Training from a Provincial Perspective: Alberta*

Clarence H. Preitz

Introduction

Alberta is one of Canada's 10 provinces. Its southern border, the 49th parallel, is coterminous with the northern border of Montana to the 60th parallel, the southern border of the Northwest Territories, a distance of 756 miles. There are four biophysical regions within the province, which has a land area of 248,800 square miles, making it slightly smaller than Texas.

Alberta has approximately 2.4 million people, a mixture of native people and other ethnic and racial groups from every continent of the world. These people live in cities, towns, and villages, with the majority residing in eight large cities scattered throughout the province.

Alberta's population is classified as 77.3 percent urban, 14 percent rural nonfarm, and 8 percent farm. The major industries of the province are (1) agriculture, (2) extractive, and (3) service. One of the major subsets of the service industry is tourism and hospitality. Alberta is Canada's leading producer of crude petroleum, natural gas, and coal.

*Author's Note

The author wishes to acknowledge the contributions of A. A. Day, Associate Director, Curriculum, Alberta Education, and Pieter Rietveld, Senior Program Design Officer, Apprenticeship and Industry Training Division, Alberta Career Development and Employment. They read the manuscript and made recommendations that added reliability.

Provincial Apprenticeship Legislation

Apprenticeship as an approach to training skilled workers has existed in some form since the days of antiquity. This form of training had been a neglected field in Canada until just prior to Canada's entry into World War I when both the Canadian Pacific and the Canadian National Railways found that they were unable to fulfill their needs for skilled workers. Around 1914, the Canadian National Railway introduced an industrial apprenticeship program in 11 trades specific to the railway to meet its needs for skilled workers. As a member of the allied forces during World War II, Canadian authorities, through the country's industries, helped to supply war materiel. As a result of that effort, national manpower authorities soon discovered that the nation was tragically short of skilled tradespeople and had to use stopgap measures to meet its requirements. Near the height of the war in 1942, the Canadian government enacted permissive legislation, the Vocational Training Coordination Act, that provided federal funds on a matching basis to the provinces to undertake apprenticeship training as a public responsibility. As a result of the federal act, Alberta was among a number of provinces that legislated an apprenticeship act. Royal assent was given this provincial act in 1944 to promote an organized system of apprenticeship. With the infusion of federal dollars, the province's new apprenticeship program became operational in early 1945. The act provided the structure of Alberta's apprenticeship program, which remains essentially unchanged.

The Apprenticeship Act was shaped by the Tradesmen Qualification Act 1936, which was passed in recognition of a need to establish standards of proficiency for the trades, and The Welding Act of 1941, which put in place a structure for administering the provisions of the Tradesmen Qualification Act, as they applied to the welding trade. The Apprenticeship Act of 1944 combined these two acts and made provision for the registration and training of apprentices. As a result of this act, an industry advisory system was put into place that consisted of local and provincial advisory committees for each trade. These committees reported to the Provincial Apprenticeship Board. The board consisted of representatives from industry who were appointed by the Lieutenant Governor in Council (Cabinet). This committee and organizational structure for the apprenticeship system was integrated into the Manpower Development Act of 1976, which amalgamated and updated previous provincial apprenticeship legislation. Under this legislation, a non-civil servant was appointed chairman of the Apprenticeship and Trade Certification Board. Membership on the board was expanded to provide for a wider representation of employers and employees, as well as two representatives of the general public. The Apprenticeship and Industry Training Act of 1991 maintained the committee and organizational structure of previous legislation and also established the Alberta Apprenticeship and Industry Training Board. It grants the Minister of Career Development and Employment the right by regulation to designate an occupation for certification.

The apprenticeship program falls under provincial jurisdiction with the province responsible for program structure, program delivery, regulation, administration, and certification requirements. Apprenticeship in Alberta is viewed as a four-way partnership among industry (which employs journeymen), the apprentice, and the two levels of government, provincial and federal. Because of industry's

heavy involvement in the program, it is considered to be "industry driven." Program funding is provided by industry, indirect costs to the apprentice, and the provincial and federal governments both of whom are involved in funding aspects of the apprenticeship program.

Alberta's apprenticeship program is designed by legislation and regulation to satisfy three conditions. First, to provide for adequate supervision and instruction of the apprentice before certification as a journeyman. Second, to offer both general and trade-specific training, thus preparing each person as a citizen and as a skilled worker. Third, to prepare the individual with the skills, knowledge, and attitudes to enter the labor force with specific preparation in a skilled trade.

Defining Apprenticeship

The primary emphasis of apprenticeship in Alberta is workplace training. Apprenticeship is essentially an educational process that has two major components: on-the-job training (the practical component) and technical training (the theoretical component). It is a system in which the apprentice earns while learning. On-the-job training, which accounts for more than 80 percent of the apprentice's time, is done on the work site under the direct supervision of a qualified journeyman. Work site training is supplemented by technical training classes provided by personnel of one of the nonuniversity postsecondary institutions that are administered by Alberta Advanced Education. Technical training is delivered on a regionalized basis at any of three institutes of technology or at one of the seven public colleges that provide this type of training for certain trades. There are a number of recognized private vocational schools in the province that have been granted the privilege of offering both phases of training. Private vocational school or industries that offer an apprenticeship program must follow the prescribed curriculum for the trade developed by the Apprenticeship and Industry Training Division in consultation with industry.

The basic time requirement for technical training is 240 hours of instruction per period of apprenticeship. (A period is the equivalent of one year of training.) Regardless of where it is presented, classroom instruction is given by a certified journeyman for the trade being taught. In many instances, these instructors have a Bachelor of Education degree and are certificated teachers with Alberta Education. This component of training can vary from 3 to 12 weeks for each period of training depending on the trade. The school portion of related instruction is a major component of the total training and its importance in developing skilled and efficient journeymen cannot be over emphasized.

Both the components—on-the-job training and technical training—ensure competency in a skill trade, which is a trade with established standards that promote quality work and skill excellence among those in the trade as well as protect the safety of the public. To achieve this goal, personnel of Apprenticeship and Industry Training work collaboratively with industrial leaders of designated trades, through the committee structure, to set training and certification standards that promote a well-organized and well-orchestrated apprenticeship training system.

A distinguishing feature of apprenticeship is the existence of the contractual relationship in which the employer and the apprentice sign an agreement that specifies the terms of the apprenticeship. If the apprentice is a minor, the contract (indenture) must be signed by a parent or guardian. Once both parties sign the contract it is registered with the Apprenticeship and Industry Training Division. The contract of apprenticeship formally indentures the apprentice to the employer for a fixed period of time. Under terms of the contract, the indentured apprentice agrees to

- Observe the established hours of work.
- Show due regard for the tools and goods of the employer.
- Follow safe work practices.
- Take responsibility to make the necessary financial arrangements for attending technical training.
- Regularly attend the technical training courses prescribed by the Apprenticeship and Industry Training Division.
- Complete any additional training not specified in the contract of apprenticeship but related to the trade that may be

referred by the employer or the local apprenticeship committee.
- Purchase all required textbooks and supplies.
- Ensure that the record book is reviewed with the *direct supervisor* of the apprentice and kept up to date.

The contract provides for the apprentice's employment on a reasonably continuous basis for the length of the apprenticeship. In addition, the contract gives the apprentice a feeling of stability and purpose and emphasizes the importance of the apprenticeship program.

The employer as signatory to the contract is bound by it to

- Provide adequate training for the apprentice in all branches of the trade insofar as facilities and the character of the work permit.
- Provide supervision by journeymen tradespeople in accordance with the published trade regulations.
- Keep the apprentice employed as long as work is available, pay wages to the apprentice at a rate not less than is prescribed in the trade regulations (usually an increasing percentage, according to year of apprenticeship, of the firm's pay rate).
- Encourage and allow the apprentice to attend the technical training courses regularly prescribed by the Apprenticeship and Industry Training Division.
- Monitor and record in the apprentice's record book the progress of the apprentice during each period of training.

Once the contract is registered with the Apprenticeship and Industry Training Division, the executive director issues the apprentice an identification card and a record book. The record book is kept by the apprentice and monitored by the immediate supervisor, who logs trade-specific activities and the amount of time the apprentice devotes to them. The employer also provides in the record book an evaluation of the apprentice's progress through the various periods of training.

Apprenticeship training represents a long-term commitment by all those involved—the employer, the apprentice, the provincial and federal governments. Regulation rigidly determines and controls the period of apprenticeship, hours and conditions of work, and wages. At the expiration of the indentureship, the apprentice becomes a journeyman.

Apprenticeship in the province is not commonly used as an entry-level program to the skilled trades. Most apprentices become indentured after trying work in a number of occupations before entry into the program. The average age of an apprentice in Alberta in 1990 was 27 years.

Industry Involvement

Industrial goodwill is the philosophical foundation of the apprenticeship system, which in Alberta is considered to be "industry driven." The cooperation of both labor and management is assumed to be essential for the success of any program that involves both. Industry has found that apprenticeship on-the-job experience acquired under the direct supervision of a qualified journeyman offers one of the best ways to train young people to become skilled workers.

As a major partner in apprenticeship, industry must provide leadership. Employers, primarily in the private sector, are well aware of their training responsibilities. They include: providing the apprentice with on-the-job training with diversified work experience; adequate supervision and assistance that allows the apprentice to learn the work in the most efficient way; paying the apprentice a wage (always lower than the wage of a journeyman); giving the apprentice release time to attend technical training classes; and serving with employees on provincial apprenticeship advisory committees. Apprenticeship in Alberta receives direction from an extensive legislatively established advisory network that consists of employers and tradesmen who may serve on the Alberta Apprenticeship and Industry Training Board, provincial apprenticeship committees, or local apprenticeship committees. The committee structure strengthens the role and involvement of industry in the operation of the apprenticeship training program.

The primary functions of the board are to advise the Minister of Career Development and Employment on all matters pertaining to apprenticeship training and certification; to

react to all matters pertaining to apprenticeship training referred to the board by the minister; to appoint members to local and provincial apprenticeship committees; to monitor the activities of provincial apprenticeship committees; and to develop policies for recognizing other training programs considered equivalent to training offered under the Apprenticeship and Industry Training Act. The authority of the board is subject to the minister's approval and relates primarily to trade or occupation specific issues.

Through the committee structure, recommendations are made to the Alberta Apprenticeship and Industry Training Board concerning the policies that guide the apprenticeship program. To assist in making policy decisions, the board draws on the expertise found in the 52 provincial apprenticeship committees, one for each designated trade. Membership of a provincial apprenticeship committee includes representatives of all local apprenticeship committee members and consists of employers and employees who are engaged in the work of the trade—a total of approximately 900 members for all areas of the province. Provincial apprenticeship committees advise the board regarding trade designation, regulations, and development and content of training programs, including examinations and course outlines. All of this ensures that the province and the nation have the skilled manpower needed to compete in the world marketplace.

The foundation of the committee structure for apprenticeship is the local apprenticeship committee, which comprises employers and employees from a designated trade within the province. Approximately 900 committee members provide an advisory function to the system by recommending to the board tradespeople to serve as members of a provincial apprenticeship committee; monitoring apprenticeship training in the area; and, subject to regulations, resolving disagreements between employer and employee for matters arising from the Apprenticeship and Industry Training Act.

The Apprentice

The word *apprentice* is derived from the French *apprendre*—"to learn". Thus, an apprentice is one who is learning a trade. An apprentice is considered to be a learner as well as a worker. As a learner, an apprentice works under the supervision of a certificated journeyman to gain familiarity with the principles, skills, tools, and materials of a trade. As an employee, an apprentice is paid an hourly wage which increases progressively as the apprentice gains experience in the trade and enters the next period of training. Wages can range from 45 percent of the current journeyman's rate of pay and increase to 90 percent, depending on the trade and the period of apprenticeship. Apprentices are obligated by their contract to perform the job to the best of their ability. It is anticipated that mistakes will be made by the apprentices as they learn.

An applicant who wants to register in an apprenticeship program must meet certain minimum standards of training which have been established under regulation and legislation. To be less restrictive, there is no minimum or official maximum age limit set for admission of an apprentice. The applicant must have the educational qualifications required for the trade, normally graduation from high school.

Applicants who do not meet prescribed educational requirements must write an entrance examination. Those who have an unsuccessful experience with the examination may enroll as an apprentice, though they must upgrade in their area of weakness before attending the first period of technical training. Only in trades where a compulsory entrance examination is required (for instance, the electrical trades) must a person who fails an examination rewrite the exam.

A major criterion for becoming a registered apprentice is to find employment with an employer who is a journeyman or employs journeymen in the trade. Without an employer, the applicant cannot enter the program.

Apprentices must attend technical training, which may vary from 3 to 12 weeks, depending on the trade. Apprentices must attend school in each period of apprenticeship. Formal schooling is available in 47 of the 52 designated apprenticeable trades. While attending technical training classes, apprentices are not assessed any tuition fees but they must purchase their books and supplies.

Normally, when an apprentice is to attend school for technical training, the employer officially "lays off" the apprentice. Income support for the apprentice is provided through payments under the Unemployment Insurance Act. These payments follow the 60 percent ruling. One of the major weaknesses of this system is the allowance payment procedure, which can be financially disruptive and injure the apprentice's morale. In most instances, these benefits are not received until the apprentice has returned to the work site to begin the next period of on-the-job training. To alleviate this problem, the system used to issue these benefits must be streamlined so that the benefits are paid to the apprentice at the end of the first week of schooling.

At the end of each technical training class, apprentices must write an examination prepared by personnel of the Apprenticeship and Industry Training Division in collaboration with members of the provincial apprenticeship committee for the trade concerned. The passing mark for the examination is 65 percent. Apprentices who fail this examination are granted the privilege of writing a supplemental examination. Should the apprentice fail the supplemental examination, he or she must repeat the course.

For an apprentice to progress from one period of apprenticeship to another and receive an increase in wages the apprentice must:

- Pass the apprentice exam for the period of training concerned.
- Receive an acceptable mark in the technical training course.
- Secure the required number of hours of work experience.
- Receive a satisfactory report from the employer.

With these conditions met, personnel of the Apprenticeship and Industry Training Division send a progress report to both the apprentice and the employer.

The Provincial Government

In Alberta, the provincial government administers the apprenticeship system and programs through the Apprenticeship and

Industry Training Division within the Department of Career Development and Employment. This is accomplished with the cooperation of Alberta Advanced Education, the agency responsible for postsecondary institutions, and the federal government, through Employment and Immigration Canada.

The Apprenticeship and Industry Training Division has complete operational control of apprentice training. Central office personnel of the division are responsible for registering the apprentice; developing training programs and tests under the guidance of the appropriate provincial apprenticeship committee; maintaining records of apprentice progress; placing and scheduling classroom space and assigning apprentices for their technical training; and negotiating with Alberta Advanced Education to broker training seats for Employment and Immigration Canada. The "brokerage" arrangement is between the two provincial agencies and the federal government, and does not involve the institutions that conduct these courses. Technical training comes primarily through the technical institutes and the public colleges that are located in various regions of the province, making this type of training regionalized.

The division is under the leadership of an appointed executive director who must carry out the purpose of the Apprenticeship and Industry Training Act. With the exception of support staff which oversees the administration and supervision of the apprenticeship system, most personnel of the division are skilled tradesmen who themselves trained as apprentices. Field consultants work out of 13 career development centers operated by the Department of Career Development and Employment. As a formal duty, the field consultants monitor the progress of the apprentice to ensure that both the employer and apprentice meet program requirements. These individuals maintain the division's primary contact with industry by keeping ready access for both parties either through office visits by staff or visits to the job site. Other major activities of a field consultant include school liaison and committee work. Consultants stand in a unique position to assume an active placement role because they become aware of openings that

may exist for new apprentices through their job site visits. Consultants are certified journeymen who have been recruited from industry to provide this function, which helps to add to the creditability of the system.

One of the major responsibilities of the executive director is to serve as a member of the Canadian Council of Directors of Apprenticeship, a coalition comprising the directors of apprenticeship from across Canada and a representative from Employment and Immigration Canada. This council establishes national standards for apprenticeship through the Interprovincial Standards Program or Red Seal Program. More on this program appears later in this chapter.

Federal Government's Participating Role in Apprenticeship

As one of the four partners involved in apprenticeship training, the federal government mainly plays a financial support role having little to say in substantive matters as they relate to apprenticeship, which is considered a provincial responsibility. Under the National Training Agreement negotiated with the province, the federal government contributes to the course costs for technical training as well as associated administrative costs. The agreement details the amount of money the federal government will spend on the purchase of seats in the provincial training institutions. Note the difference between the Apprenticeship and Industry Training Act and the National Training Agreement. The former is a provincially enacted piece of legislation that provides a structure to the system; the latter is an agreement between the two levels of government on the funding arrangements for formal trade training.

The main channel of communication between the federal government and the Apprenticeship and Industry Training Division is the Winnipeg regional office, Employment and Immigration Canada. This office approves the unemployment insurance payments that go to individual apprentices who attend technical training. It also negotiates with the division for the purchase of training seats under the provisions of the Employment and Immigration

Canada/Alberta Training Plan Agreement. Training seats are purchased annually at a per diem rate based on projected use. This rate varies annually, depending on the number of seats used. No apprentice can be placed in technical training for which a seat had not previously been purchased. Once a training seat has been purchased it becomes the responsibility of the Apprenticeship and Industry Training Division to fill that seat.

A representative from the national office of Employment and Immigration Canada serves on the Canadian Council of Directors of Apprenticeship as a full voting member to help the council achieve the objectives of the Interprovincial Standards Program.

The Interprovincial Standards Program

The Interprovincial Standards Program (the Red Seal Program) was brought into effect to increase the mobility of skilled tradesmen across jurisdictions in the country and to promote high national standards in occupational training, examinations, and certification. The program was first discussed among apprenticeship-oriented officials from both levels of government at meetings held in Ottawa in 1954, but it did not become operational until 1958. Motor mechanic, in 1959, was the first trade in the province to receive designation under this national program.

For a trade to be designated for a Interprovincial Standard the following criteria must be met:
- A minimum of six participating provinces must agree that a particular trade should have a national standard;
- A detailed occupational analysis of the trade is done by the Occupational and Career Information Branch, Employment and Immigration Canada, and occupational analyses are validated by all participating jurisdictions. Non-participating jurisdictions also have the opportunity to validate these analyses; and
- A Red Seal examination for the trade is prepared by participating members and all examination items are validated by industry.

Occupational analyses are developed by Employment and Immigration Canada under the Interprovincial Standards Program coordinating Committee—now the Canada Council of Directors of Apprenticeship—following these objectives:
- To identify the tasks performed by a journeyman in a particular trade.
- To obtain interprovincial and territorial acknowledgment that the tasks stated in the analysis apply to journeymen in every province and territory.
- To develop an instrument for use in the preparation of interprovincial standards examinations (Interprovincial Red Seal) and in the preparation of curricula for instruction leading to journeyman qualification.
- To facilitate the mobility, in Canada, of journeymen holding certificates with the interprovincial seal, which is recognized by all provinces and territories.
- To supply government, employers, unions, training institutions, and members of the labor force with an exhaustive list of tasks in a particular occupation that they can readily assess and use in such operations as job information and placement, assessment of training needs, and occupational inquiries.

The Red Seal Program is administered by the Canadian Council of Directors of Apprenticeship. The federal government's financial contribution to this program helps to pay for administrative support, occupational analysis, and the printing and distribution of examinations. Alberta has been a strong supporter of the Interprovincial Standards Program and continues to offer support through its developmental work on interprovincial examinations and participation in the continuous development and revision of the Standards Program's National Occupational Analysis Series. When an examination is being developed or revised for a trade, each province involved with that trade must unanimously accept the examination. Interprovincial examinations are revised every two or three years. Of the 52 designated trades in Alberta, 23 are recognized as Red Seal trades; nationally, 29 trades are designated under the Red Seal program.

In Alberta, the Red Seal examination is

administered at the time that the apprentice writes the qualification examination for journeyman status. Provincially certified journeymen have the privilege to challenge the Interprovincial examination. Those who successfully attain a passmark of 70 percent on an approved interprovincial examination have a numbered Red Seal affixed to their journeyman certificate and wallet card. Among completing apprentices in Alberta, up to 90 percent continually qualify for the Red Seal. The Red Seal permits journeymen to practice their trade in any province or territory that participates in the program for that trade. This program gives journeymen increased mobility to work in participating provinces without having to re-qualify by examination. This means that certified tradesmen can move freely between the provinces and territories in response to changing economic cycles that help to dictate employment supply and demand.

Cost of Apprenticeship Training

The four partners involved in apprenticeship in some measure contribute to the cost of training. Although federal and provincial expenditures for the program are readily available and documented, the costs incurred by the employer and the apprentice are not recorded and are difficult to determine. Through legislative enactments, both the federal and the provincial governments can participate in the training of apprentices. Legislation has produced a succession of Canada-Alberta training agreements which have resulted in intragovernmental cost-sharing arrangements for apprenticeship.

Public funding supports only the technical training component of the program. Under the Canada-Alberta Agreement on Training, 4 percent of all apprenticeship allocations are directed toward the administration of the program. The federal government also incurs additional costs in the administration of payments for unemployment insurance and training allowances, as well as for regional office functions related to apprenticeship. Costs to the federal government in 1990-91 were approximately 16 percent of the total costs.

In terms of costs, the province supports

administration of the system and maintaining the technical training infrastructure that is the primary cost component of the system. Technical training is a collaborative effort between the Apprenticeship and Industry Training Division and Alberta Advanced Education and is delivered through a network of private and public institutes and colleges located throughout the province. The administration of apprentice registrations, scheduling for technical training, and certification are also responsibilities of the province. In 1990-91, these costs represented approximately 11 percent of the total costs for the program.

Most training costs are paid by industry. Employers find it difficult to provide an accurate accounting of these costs because of the number of phantom costs involved. The real costs incurred by employers involved in apprenticeship training are based on the following factors:

- Lost productivity of journeymen during job site supervision and instruction.
- Where applicable, the wages and benefits of apprentices while attending technical training and/or the costs of replacement workers during that period of time.
- Waste and breakage in excess of that of a journeyman.
- Company classroom instruction including instructors or supervisors.
- The differential between the wage of the apprentices and the proportionate productivity of a journeyman.
- Additional hiring or other administrative costs associated with apprentices.

The employers' contribution to training costs for 1990-91 was nearly two-thirds of these costs, 64 percent.

Apprentices, the fourth partner in apprenticeship, are also confronted with real and assumed cost, some of which cannot be documented. Among the real costs of apprenticeship to the apprentice these include:

- Reduced wages and benefits while attending technical training.
- Tools and special clothing.
- Texts and supplies.
- Travel and accommodation costs in excess of reimbursements.

- Other miscellaneous costs not provided for by governments.

Of the total system cost for 1990-91 the apprentice contribution was approximately 9 percent.

Military Occupations Credit

Through the cooperation and the collaborative efforts of the provincial directors of apprenticeship and personnel of the Canadian armed forces, the Military/Civilian Training Accreditation Committee (M/CTAC) was formed in Ottawa in November 1974. The committee's major goal was to have service personnel receive equivalent civilian trade certification from an apprenticeship agency while performing a trade in the Canadian forces. This committee functions to present to the directors of apprenticeship those military trades that it believes can be recognized for civilian certification.

In the Canadian Forces *Manual of Occupations*, all occupations of the Canadian Armed Forces are placed in 1 of 10 groups. Ninety-nine of the service trades listed are considered apprenticeable by provincial certifying agencies.

In Alberta, the Apprenticeship and Industry Training Division recognizes these nine service trades as apprenticeable: cook, electrical technician, instrument electrical technician, gas fitter, machinist, plumber, radio technician, structures technician, and refrigeration and maintenance technician.

The requirements for a military tradesman to receive journeyman status varies among the provinces and territories. In Alberta, service tradesmen who wish to be certified must follow these procedures for eligibility to take the journeyman certification examination following separation:

- Provide proof of acceptable work experience in the designated trade.
- Provide proof of formal training in the designated trade while in the service.
- Provide the amount of time actively employed in the designated trade.

On separation, the service tradesman must be employed by an employer who is a journeyman or employs a journeymen, and he or she must sign an apprenticeship contract.

Acceptance of service personnel for involvement in a designated trade has the advantages after discharge of enhancing the individual's employment opportunities, shortening the term of apprenticeship, and providing an alternate source of registered skilled tradesmen to meet the manpower requirements of the nation.

Registrations/Cancellation

One of the major administrative responsibilities of apprenticeship personnel is apprentice registration. As one entrance requirement, the would-be apprentice must find an employer who is a journeymen or who employs journeymen in the designated trade. The employer must agree to sign the contract of apprenticeship, a three-party binding contract.

At the end of 1990, of the 22,574 registered apprentices, 13,391 were enrolled for technical training. The number of new apprentices in that year was 8,043, an increase of 460, or approximately 6 percent, over the previous year. The number of registered apprentices will fluctuate with the economic cycles of the province.

Apprentices who withdraw from training before completing their apprenticeship program cancel their contract with the Apprenticeship and Industry Training Division, where it is recorded as a cancellation. By the end of 1990, 3,228 apprentices had cancelled their contracts. This resulted in an 11 percent rate of cancellation for that year. (Cancellation rate is the ratio of cancelled contracts during the year to the total of registered apprentices at the beginning of the year, plus new apprentices in that year.) The cancellation of a contract of apprenticeship should not be considered an "apprenticeship dropout," because no hard data are available that distinguish between those who left the trade and those who moved to a related apprenticeship program either in the province or in another jurisdiction.

Among the reasons an apprentice may withdraw from the program are (1) low income level as compared with journeymen, (2) reduction of income while attending technical training and administrative delays in receiving unemployment insurance, (3) costs of tools in some trades that the apprentice must purchase, (4) loss of interest in the trade, (5) inadequate educational preparation, and (6) cyclical downturns of the economy, which cause employers to release apprentices from their contracts, making apprentices ineligible to attend technical training classes.

Designation of a Trade

For a trade to be designated for certification, a demonstrated need for a formal apprenticeship training program must exist, including both components and supportive participations from industry. For a trade to receive designation for compulsory certification, strong support by employers and workers in the trade are required. Attention must be paid to worker and public safety.

The Lieutenant Governor in Council has the authority under legislation to designate, redesignate, or rescind a trade as certifiable. Industry may petition the Minister of Career Development and Employment to have a trade designated.

Certification

Through legislation, there are two trade categories: compulsory certification trades and optional certification trades. Apprenticeship is compulsory in both trade categories, but certification is mandatory in compulsory trades only. A person cannot work in a compulsory trade unless that person is an indentured apprentice or holds a trade certificate in that trade. In optional certification trades, a person who has, in the opinion of the employer, the necessary skills to perform the work is not required to hold a trade certificate. However, if the person is engaged in *learning* the skills of the trade, he or she must indenture as an apprentice. Of the 52 designated apprenticeable trades, 17 are classified as compulsory trades. Persons employed in a trade that requires a journeyman certificate must hold a certificate in that trade.

In Alberta, a completing apprentice can qualify for a journeyman certificate by successfully completing the term of apprenticeship and passing the final period technical training provincial examination set by the board for the respective trade. The pass mark for the qualification examination is 65 percent. The certificate that is issued will state that the individual has successfully completed an Alberta apprenticeship program. Completing apprentices also write the Red Seal examination at the time that they write the qualification examination.

Access Initiatives

A potential source of skilled manpower that remained dormant was minority groups, who for the most part failed to participate in apprenticeship training. To tap this source of manpower in 1981, a special field unit, the Access Initiatives Branch, was established and given mandate to increase the participation of women, Native people, incarcerated people, persons with disabilities, immigrants, and visible minorities in apprenticeship training. These groups were designated by the federal government as requiring special needs to correct traditional imbalances.

At the end of 1990, approximately 1 in 11 apprentices were women. Ninety percent of them were registered in traditional trades for women: beautician, cook, landscape gardener, partsman, and printing and graphic arts. Three percent were registered in nontraditional construction trades: cabinetmaker, carpenter, electrician, insulator, motor mechanic, painter decorator, and welder. Of the total registration of 22,574 apprentices, Native people made up approximately 1 percent. Fewer than 0.1 percent were classified as disabled. Equal rights legislation precludes the compilation of statistics for visible minority participants in apprenticeship. Consequently, there are no accurate figures for this group. Promotional materials, both print and nonprint, are being made available to schools and service clubs throughout the province to provide detailed information on careers and technologies to increase the participation of minority groups.

Competency-Based Apprenticeship Training

Competency Based Apprenticeship Training (CBAT) began as a four-year pilot project at the beginning of the 1988-89 school year and concluded at the end of the 1992 school year. The technical training component for trades of carpenter, electrician, and welder were selected for inclusion because of the relationship of theory to practice for each of them when placed on a training continuum. *Welder*, because of the heavy emphasis this trade places on the practical, was placed at one end of the continuum and *Electrician* at the opposite end because of its more theoretical orientation. *Carpenter* falls in the middle of the continuum because of the balance between theory and practice found in the trade.

The technical training component for this trade is offered in the two larger technical institutes and two public colleges. The foundation of CBAT is the individualization of instruction through a program that has fixed entry, fixed content, and open exit. Fixed entry facilitates the scheduling of apprentices for periods of technical training and open exit accommodates self-paced learning by the apprentice. The practical (on-the-job) training component has not been changed because it is prescribed in the specific trade regulations.

Curriculum materials, pre- and post-tests, print and nonprint instructional materials, modules and learning activity packages were developed by tradesmen who were seconded by training institutions. These instructors worked under the direction and supervision of the program development officer responsible for the appropriate pilot project trade.

An independent consultant was contracted to evaluate the pilot project on a year-to-year basis. The final evaluation report was to be released when the project terminated in 1992.

Two of the major responsibilities for personnel of the division have been (1) to provide assistance to the instructors and institutions to resolve issues that are being identified during formative evaluation and (2) to initiate the delivery of the ensuing period of technical training for the three trades involved in CBAT.

One of the original purposes for developing CBAT was to identify ways to achieve reductions in support payments by having apprentices complete their technical training in less than eight weeks.

Registered Apprenticeship Program

The Registered Apprenticeship Program (RAP) is an innovative program offered to students in the secondary schools of Alberta under the combined participation of

- Local school jurisdictions,
- Alberta Education,
- Alberta Career Development and Employment Apprenticeship and Industry Training Division, and
- Local Business and Industry.

A unique feature of RAP is that should the students find themselves unsuited to apprenticeship work, they can move into a regular school program.

Those involved are considered full-time students and at the same time registered apprentices under the Apprenticeship and Industrial Training Act. Students who enroll can select one of the 52 designated trades as their trade of choice. Enrolling students must

- Be employed by an employer who is a journeyman or who employs journeymen.
- Register in any one of the 52 apprenticeship programs.
- Sign a Contract of Apprenticeship and have the contract registered with Apprenticeship and Industry Training Division.
- Fulfill the practical and theoretical components unless exemption is negotiated.

Once admitted to this program, students are treated as apprentices and receive supervision and instruction from a journeyman as well as an apprentice wage prescribed in the trade regulations. They are expected to work productively on the job site and supply their tools and work clothes. A student registered in RAP can accumulate apprenticeship hours by working partial days, full days, weekends, and during vacation and holiday periods. Up to 60 percent of each school year could be spent earning apprenticeship work experience requirements.

For admission to the Registered Apprenticeship Program, the student must be 16 years of age, meet the entrance requirements for the chosen trade, and complete all 58 compulsory credits for the high school diploma. Students enrolled in RAP will receive credit for work experience education. The school must monitor the work experience credits offered in the workplace. At the end of the program, the student graduates from secondary school with both a high school diploma and a significant number of apprenticeship hours toward achieving a journeyman certificate in the trade of choice.

The program offers employers access to a younger group of apprentices. It also gives employers the opportunity to establish community partnerships for education and training and to contribute to educational decision making. Employers who accept an apprentice under this program must pay apprentice wages as specified in the trade regulations.

Officials envision that the program will offer a way to develop and maintain a skilled workforce for the province, to bring about a decline in the school dropout rate by providing non-university-bound students with an alternative form of education, and to extend the working life of the younger journeymen.

References

Alberta Career Development and Employment. (undated). *Apprenticeship opportunities*. Edmonton, Alberta: Author.

Alberta Career Development and Employment. (1988). *The final report: Apprenticeship and industry training review committee*. Edmonton, Alberta: Author.

Alberta Career Development and Employment. (1988). *Apprenticeship and industry training review—Comments of the advisory panel on the review committee final report*. Edmonton, Alberta: Author.

Alberta Career Development and Employment & Education. (undated). *R.A.P. and you*. Edmonton, Alberta: Author.

Alberta Education, Curriculum Design Branch. (1991). *High school apprenticeship*. Edmonton, Alberta: Author.

Apprenticeship and Trade Certification Division. (1986). *Competency-Based Apprenticeship Task Force final report*. Edmonton, Alberta: Author.

Apprenticeship and Trade Certification Division. (1988). *Alberta's apprenticeship program*. Edmonton, Alberta: Author.

Apprenticeship and Trade Certification Division. (1988). *Competency-based apprenticeship training—A new approach*. Edmonton, Alberta: Author.

Apprenticeship and Trade Certification Division. (1988). *Competency-based apprenticeship training—Policies and procedures*. Edmonton, Alberta: Author.

Apprenticeship and Trade Certification Division. (1988). *Executive director's report and annual statis-tical review of apprenticeship and trade certification programs*. Edmonton, Alberta: Author.

Apprenticeship and Trade Certification Division. (1989). *Executive director's report on apprenticeship and trade certification programs for 1989*. Edmonton, Alberta: Author.

Apprenticeship and Trade Certification Division. (1990). *Principles of proposed legislation governing apprenticeship and occupational training*. Edmonton, Alberta: Author.

Apprenticeship and Trade Certification Division. (1991). *Executive director's report on apprenticeship and trade certification programs for 1990*. Edmonton, Alberta: Author.

Bell, D. W. (1984). *A report to the Honorable Ernie D. Isley, Minister, Department of Manpower, Province of Alberta on the delivery of apprenticeship technical training programs by individual employers*. Edmonton, Alberta: Alberta Manpower.

Berghofer, D. E., & Vladicka, A. S. (1980). *Access to opportunity 1905-80*. Edmonton, Alberta: Alberta Advanced Education and Manpower.

Canadian Labour Market and Productivity Center. (1990). *Report of the CLMPC task forces on the labour force development strategy*. Ottawa, Ontario: Author.

Dupre, J. S., Cameron, D. M., McKechnie, G. H. & Rotenberg, T. D. (1973). *Federalism and policy development: The case of adult occupational training in Ontario*. Toronto, Ontario: University of Toronto Press.

Department of National Defense. (1975). *Civilian recognition military tradesmen*. Ottawa, Ontario: National Defence Headquarters.

Employment and Immigration Canada & Alberta Career Development and Employment. (1987). *Canada-Alberta study on apprenticeship training*. Edmonton, Alberta: Author.

Graul-Follis, H. (1992). *Barriers to access encountered by women seeking employment in non-traditional occupations in Alberta*. Unpublished master's thesis, University of Alberta, Edmonton, Alberta.

Military/Civilian Training Accreditation Committee. (1975). *Survey of trades*. Ottawa, Ontario: National Defence Headquarters.

Rainsforth, R. (1991). *A descriptive study of the evolution of apprenticeship in Alberta to 1990*. Unpublished master's thesis, University of Alberta, Edmonton, Alberta.

Simon, F. (1963). *History of the Alberta Institute of Technology and Art*. Unpublished master's thesis, University of Alberta, Edmonton, Alberta.

Yee, T. L. (1977). *A description of the procedures used for civilian accreditation of military occupations in Canada*. Unpublished master's thesis, University of Alberta, Edmonton, Alberta.

Part IV:

What Might Be Done

17

A Proposal for Making Transition from Schooling to Employment an Important Component of Educational Reform*

Kenneth B. Hoyt

Introduction

In recent months, a major indictment of American living has surfaced with some regularity. It states: In no other industrialized country are the transitions from school to work left so much to chance as in the United States. This indictment contains too much truth to be ignored. Here, efforts are made to: (a) put the problem in preliminary perspective with reference to current K-12 educational reform initiatives in the education/work relationship domain; (b) discuss some of the major factors contributing to America's relative lack of success in solving the youth school-to-work transition problem; and (c) suggest possible solutions for making "transition from schooling to employment" an important component of educational reform in America.

Educational Reform and "Transition" Problem: An Initial Perspective

While most of the early educational reform proposals of the 1980s made reference to the need for America to become more competitive in the international marketplace, not one included "transition from schooling to employment" as a major component of reform pro-

*This chapter first appeared as an article in *Future Choices*, Vol. 2, No. 2, Fall 1990. Permission to use it granted by the Youth Policy Institute.

posals.[1] Most concentrated their proposals on efforts to improve academic achievement in communication, mathematics, and science.[2] We were warned that youth who fail to acquire such skills will have great difficulty finding employment. On the other hand, exactly how possession of such skills will *help* youth secure employment was never specified.

More recently, educational reform proposals have broadened the efforts to specify the kinds of skills employers need high school graduates seeking employment to possess.[3] While some variation in the names of recommended skills exists in these reports, they seem to center around three areas including: (1) academic skills, (2) reasoning/problem-solving skills, and (3) positive attitudes toward work and working coupled with productive work habits. The most comprehensive description of such skills can be found in a new book written by Carnevale, Gainers, and Meltzer.[4] Still, even though the specific kinds of skills employers are urging K-12 school systems to provide youth in the name of educational reform have been defined in a more precise manner, the topic of how youth are to actually use such skills in securing employment has not been a part of the reform discussion.

Three currently popular national proposals for relating the transition from schooling to employment now exist, only one of which is perceived by some of its proponents as directly tied to educational reform. The first is the Jobs for America's Graduates (JAG) program–a program that appears to be very similar to an earlier program called 70001 that is also still in operation.[5] JAG is a concentrated effort to work especially with disadvantaged high school seniors in providing them with job seeking/ finding/getting/holding skills and to actually assist them in securing employment. JAG does not seek to tie its operations to a broader, more comprehensive program of educational reform in the high schools where it operates. A second is a proposal from the National Alliance of Business (NAB) for the creation of what NAB calls Model Jobs Collaborative Programs aimed at guaranteeing jobs for participating secondary school youth when they graduate from high school.[6] This is, in effect, an extension of the Boston Compact program.[7] It does not pretend to be an educational reform proposal *per se*.

The third proposal–and one currently growing rapidly in popularity–is "work-based learning" as proposed by the U.S. Department of Labor (USDOL).[8] This program, now officially housed in USDOL's Office of Work-Based Learning, claims that its "apprentice-ship-style" approach is the best way for youth to *both* (1) acquire employability skills and (2) make a successful transition from schooling to employment. Much of the rationale for making such claims is documented in two recent reports describing highly successful programs of transition from schooling to employment in other developed countries.

One report describes programs in Sweden, West Germany, Great Britain, France, and Philadelphia, Pennsylvania.[9] The second report describes programs in England, West Germany, Sweden, and Japan.[10] In both documents, the importance of tying classroom learning directly to occupations via a concentrated period of work experience is emphasized. Great and growing interest is being expressed in devising and implementing some kind of "apprenticeship-American style" effort drawing from the successful experiences of these other industrialized nations.

Whether this is another educational reform proposal–or a proposal to create a completely new kind of educational system–is unclear. What is clear is that, at this point in time, only very limited attempts have been made to tie this form of USDOL-suggested reform to the broader set of proposals for educational reform developed during the 1980s. Both the practicality and the problems of inserting an "apprenticeship-style" work-based learning effort into the educational reform movement will be discussed later. We now turn to a discussion of some major reasons why the "transition" problem is currently greater in the U.S. than in other industrialized nations.

Special Schooling-to-Employment-Transition Problems Facing the U.S.

Problem #1: Higher education: A closer look at international comparisons

Unfortunately, neither the Nothdurft nor the GAO documents referred to above include specific data regarding the percentage of youth who pursue a four-year college/university degree program. The best estimates that could be found were from a 1987 reference.[11] The data indicate that the percentage of high school graduates who go on to college are:

- Sweden: 32 percent males; 43 percent females (p.38)
- West Germany: 21.5 percent (p.26)
- France: 28 percent (p. 24)
- Great Britain: 13 percent (p.17)

A U.S. Department of Education publication entitled *Japanese Education Today* indicates that 18 percent of Japanese high school graduates go on to four-year university degree programs.[12]

The U.S. Department of Labor reports that 38.9 percent of U.S. 1989 high school graduates were enrolled in four-year colleges and 21.1 percent in one- to two-year colleges in the fall of 1989.[13] When compared with major international competitors, it appears that American high school graduates are at least twice as likely to enroll in four-year college/university programs as are youth in these other nations. An even more startling contrast can be seen by noting that, even by the year 2000, only 23.4 percent of U.S. jobs are predicted to require a four-year college/university degree.[14] When almost 40 percent of high school graduates are planning to prepare themselves for jobs that will be available to only 23.4 percent of *all* employed workers, problems in the "schooling to employment transition" area are sure to be commonplace.

Kutscher has predicted that the surplus of college graduates in the U.S. that began in the early 1970s is expected to continue through the year 2000.[15] It seems apparent that the discrepancy between the percent of high school graduates entering college and the percent of jobs requiring a college education is much lower in other industrialized nations than it is in the United States.

Many who enroll in higher education leave prior to earning a baccalaureate degree. Thus, in the U.S.–as contrasted with other developed nations–the problems of transition from schooling to employment include very large numbers of college non-completers as well as high school graduates seeking immediate employment. The non-college-bound graduating high school seniors represent only a portion of the population to be considered.

One of the obviously significant factors is that, in all of these countries *except the U.S.,* youth desiring to enroll in four-year college/ university programs must pass a college entrance examination. A vast majority of youth in these countries (i.e., those who fail to take and/or to pass the college entrance exam) are well aware of their need to find alternative means of preparing for success in the world of paid employment. In the U.S., by contrast, the "American Dream," for most families, is that their children become college graduates. Readily available statistics make it clear that straight-line relationships exist between number of years of education and both (a) job earnings and (b) unemployment rates. For example, consider the following figures:

From *Education Week* (March 29, 1989) "Schooling and Earning":

Head of Household	Median Household Income, 1987
1-3 years high school	$21,165
4 years high school	$29,937
1-3 years college	$36,392
4 years college	$46,533
5 years or more college	$54,492 [16]

From *The Forgotten Half* Final Report (1988, page 126):

Educational Level Completed	Unemployment Rates Male	Female
1-3 years high school	11.2%	10.9%
4 years high school	6.7%	5.8%
1-3 years college	5.0%	4.0%
4 years college	2.5%	2.1% [17]

Faced with figures such as these, it is not surprising to find parents desirous of having *their* children prepare for and enter into college. Any alternative program aimed primarily at preparing students for immediate employment after high school is almost certain to be viewed as something for *"other* parents' children." The "right to try"–including the "right to fail"–is an essential part of the concept of "freedom of choice" in the United States. The creation of a national college admissions examination that all persons desiring to enter college/university settings must pass would be strongly resisted by most Americans. *Many* cases now exist of the "1 in 100" kind of person who battles the odds and successfully completes college.

As a result, the U.S. has, in effect, elected to build in a degree of purposeful inefficiency in its "transition from schooling to employment" system as the price to be paid for protecting individual freedom of choice. Until and unless this freedom is relinquished, it seems inevitable that the U.S. will, to some degree, continue to lag behind other industrialized nations in solving the "transition" problem.

Problem #2: The "secondary labor market" in the United States

Hamilton bases his call for an "apprenticeship" approach to solving America's "transition from school to employment" problem in part on the existence of a "secondary labor market" that most youth leaving the secondary school for employment are expected to enter.[18] According to Hamilton,

[Employers] . . . in order to curtail the costs of training new employees who soon quit for another job . . . have simply rejected teenage applicants, waiting until they have a few more years work experience before offering them career-entry positions and investing in their training.... [Now] because of the "baby bust," they can no longer ignore teenagers, simply allowing them to season in the secondary labor market." (p. 28)

Hamilton defines the "secondary labor market" as "jobs that pay little more than the minimum wage, offer no fringe benefits, demand few skills, are insecure, and lack advancement opportunities" (p. 22), and notes that many youth remain in such jobs until about age 25 when employers believe they are "seasoned" enough so as to justify investing some dollars in training them for various jobs. This view is reinforced by the recent USDOL publication *Work-Based Learning* by the following statements:

> [M]any young people who do not go on to a four-year college find low-paying, low-skilled employment with little opportunity for advancement.... Few high school graduates . . . are considered by the employer community to be ready for work. (p. 39)[19]

Part of the rationale behind suggesting the existence of a "secondary labor market" is found in the consistency of figures indicating youth unemployment rates to be consistently about three times as high as those of adults. Recent figures from USDOL's Bureau of Labor Statistics illustrate this with the following statistics:

Age Category	Unemployment Rate
18-19-year-olds	13.4%
20-24-year-olds	8.2%
25 years & over	4.1%[20]

Excellent examples of youth experiences in such jobs are found in a new publication of the Education Writers Association.[21] Youth jobs described in this publication fit Hamilton's description of the "secondary labor market" very well. Most of the youth described in this publication can be said to be persons who would like to "work" but are forced to settle for a "job."

It appears that in other industrialized nations conscious efforts are made to avoid plac-ing non-college-bound youth in the "secondary labor market." Instead, employers have joined forces with educators to provide youth with work experience which, when coupled with their formal schooling and employer training opportunities, enable most youth to secure career entry jobs leading to career ladder opportunities in the primary labor market.

If placement of non-college-bound youth in the "secondary labor market" has been largely the creation of employers, the question of willingness of employers to admit youth to entry-level positions in the "primary labor market" (i.e., jobs that provide some opportunity for advancement and for employer training) must be surfaced. This, in turn, raises the question of willingness of employers to accept part of the responsibility for helping youth make successful transitions from schooling to employment through "partnership" arrangements with the educational system. Are *both* employers *and* the K-12 school system prepared to change from being part of the "problem" to becoming part of the "solution"?

Until and unless this question is answered affirmatively, it seems unlikely that attempts to help non-college bound K-12 youth (a) see the importance of basic academic skills in occupational success, (b) acquire problem-solving skills, and (c) acquire positive work attitudes will be very successful. Even if youth were to learn such skills in the K-12 school system, many can expect to discover that the jobs they find in the "secondary labor market" are places where such skills are lost rather than gained—in other words, these skills simply aren't pertinent to success in such jobs. The continuing presence of a "secondary labor market" in the U.S. seems inevitable. The challenge will be to avoid making it the "primary labor market" for youth seeking employment immediately after leaving high school.

Problem #3: Diversity of opportunities for occupational preparation

An abundance of literature exists containing evidence that the American system of secondary vocational education has been only marginally successful in helping its students make the transition from schooling to employment. [22,23,24] If rough comparisons were made of U.S. secondary school vocational education graduates compared with non-college-bound high school graduates of other industrialized nations, the U.S. system would appear to be generally inferior. However, in view of the fact that, in most other industrialized nations, the period of occupational preparation extends beyond the traditional secondary school graduation schedule, it would appear to be unfair to make such direct comparison. For example, Nothdurft reports that:

> In Sweden—Upon completion of compulsory school at age 16, students choose from among 27 different courses in the "upper secondary system" ranging in length from two to four years.
>
> In Germany—Most young people complete their compulsory education at age 15 to 16 at the end of ninth grade and pursue an apprenticeship in a specific trade.
>
> In England—Compulsory education ends at age 16. This is now supplemented by the Technical and Vocational Education Initiative—a four-year program designed for youth 14-18 years old aimed at preparing youth entry into the occupational society.[25]

In each of these nations, some kind of "buffer" educational experience aimed directly at helping non-college-bound youth make a successful transition between the compulsory secondary school and employment is in place. Most K-12 education systems in the United States currently appear to leave it up to those youth seeking employment immediately after high school to "sink or swim" on their own—and it is clear that very large numbers "sink"!

Both the George[26] and the Nothdurft[27] reports describe comprehensive career guidance systems now operating in several other industrialized nations aimed at helping non-college-bound youth make a successful transition from schooling to employment. Yet, in the United States, the job placement function takes less of school counselors' time than any other major job duty.[28] The relative lack of attention to meeting career guidance needs appears to be due to a combination of (1) the lack of a wide diversity of career opportunities available to them and (2) the many non-career guidance duties typically assigned school counselors in the United States. In view of the fact that the career guidance movement originated in the United States—and that freedom of choice is a bedrock American value—it seems surprising to find that the career guidance function for non-college-bound youth appears to be a much higher priority for other industrialized nations than it is in the United States. There is clearly a need to reverse this situation.

"Apprenticeship—American Style" as a Possible Solution

Many strongly believe that experiential learning calling for some form of work experience is a valuable way for youth to acquire the kinds of worker skills employers seek. America's K-12 educational systems have, for many years, recognized this both in various kinds of work experience programs and in cooperative education programs. An important cornerstone of the career education movement consists of work experience aimed at providing youth with career awareness/career exploration opportunities. Some K-12 school system/private sector "partnerships" have, as part of educational reform efforts, created exemplary youth work experience programs. *Workforce LA* is a good example.[29] Many communities now operate industry-education councils using the system developed by the National Association for Industry-Education Cooperation. Various community youth organizations—for example, Junior Achievement; 4-H; Exploring Division, Boy Scouts of America—place major emphasis on using private sector persons as resources for helping youth learn about occupational possibilities in the world of paid employment.

There is nothing new about the concept of calling for private sector/education system efforts in general and work experience opportunities in particular as vehicles for use in helping youth make the transition from schooling to employment. What is relatively new are current calls for use of the concept of "apprenticeship" as a vehicle for solving youth schooling-to-employment transition problems.

At least three distinctly different "apprenticeship" proposals are currently being actively promoted. The largest is found in USDOL's Office of Work-Based Learning.[30]

While calling for retaining formal apprenticeship as industry-operated *programs,* strong pleas are made for expanding the apprenticeship *concept* of experiential learning to other kinds of learning opportunities as well. Part of this proposed initiative consists of industry/ USDOL partnership efforts to apply the apprenticeship *concept* (without calling it "apprenticeship") for use with adults in (a) entry-level training in non-apprenticeship occupations, (b) upgrading training in all occupations, and (c) as a career path for workers in lower skilled jobs. These new programs would be run by industries. The education system would, for all practical purposes, be ignored.

Work-Based Learning recommends that youth at risk of dropping out of school and non-college-bound high school graduates be enrolled in work-based learning environments "with clear and direct routes to successful career paths" (p. 42).[31] While not specifying who would operate the "work-based learning," USDOL recommends that the theoretical instruction required be provided by alternative high schools and community colleges. This effort would be separate and apart from (rather than a part of) the K-12 education system and thus clearly not associated with educational reform. The only place where the K-12 education system is recommended for use is in strengthening and expanding the current USDOL "school-to-apprenticeship" model now operating in about 400 sites and involving 1,500 students (p. 41).

A second "apprenticeship" proposal can be found in Hamilton's book *Apprenticeship for Adulthood: Preparing Youth for the Future.*[32] Unlike the USDOL proposal described above, Hamilton perceives what he calls a "comprehensive apprenticeship system" as an important and vital part of K-12 educational reform. He differentiates "school-based apprenticeship" (for use primarily in career exploration) from "work-based apprenticeships" that are specific and intensive in only one occupation. He envisions the creation of "work-based apprenticeships" for youth with clear occupational choices. Beginning in grade 11, the program operates under the 2 plus 2 concept originally proposed by Parnell.[33] By the end of

the program, participating youth would have: (a) a high school diploma, (b) an associate's degree, and (c) a certificate testifying to the possession of high-level skills. He acknowledges that this program best fits those preparing to be some kind of *technician.*

To better serve youth lacking the ability and/or inclination to pursue a technical education program requiring postsecondary education, Hamilton proposes three kinds of work-based apprenticeship programs including: (a) one that "begins in high school and concludes a year or two after graduation," (b) one for high school dropouts that will help them acquire a GED certificate, and (c) one for high school graduates who elect to enter into an apprenticeship following graduation. While he fails to indicate who is to operate and/or pay for these programs, it looks as though he must be assuming this to be some kind of education system/community collaborative effort. Clearly, Hamilton perceives "Apprenticeship—American Style" as a major new component of the total educational reform movement.

Still another approach to development of a youth apprenticeship system has been proposed by Lerman and Pouncy.[34] Under their proposal, students would, in grade 10, be offered a choice between pursuing a job apprenticeship or remaining in a purely academic track. Each student choosing the "apprenticeship" route would be required to sign a formal contract with a specific employer. These students would enter a three-year apprenticeship beginning in grade 11 with at least 75 percent of the third year spent in on-the-job-activities. Obviously, high school for such youth would be extended one year beyond its current K-12 format.

If successes of the "apprenticeship" approach in other industrialized nations are used as an indicator, all three of these proposals appear to hold promise for alleviating the current situation that finds many recent high school graduates floundering in the "secondary labor market" with no clear means available for securing entry level employment in a firm or organization holding some hope for career advancement. Among the obviously key and important questions that must be asked—and answered—before some kind of "apprenticeship" approach is endorsed as a national "solution" are:

1. As Hamilton pointed out in his book (p. 160), "apprenticeship" programs best fit those preparing for jobs as "technicians" that require 12 years of postsecondary education.[35] Since, even by the year 2000, only 21 percent of occupations are expected to fall into this category[36], how does the "apprenticeship concept" fit those occupations requiring only a high school diploma or even less? Are all "apprenticeships" to be for jobs in the "primary labor market"?

2. How is the optimal time required to provide youth with the specific job skills associated with each "apprenticeship" experience to be determined? How is the great variability in time requirement involved to be taken into account in program operation?

3. What kinds of provisions, if any, are to be made to accommodate college "stopouts" in the proposed "apprenticeship programs"?

4. Who is going to have operational control over the "apprenticeship" operation? The K-12 school system? The community college system? Employers? Labor unions? USDOL offices? Some new kind of organization yet to be created by the federal bureaucracy?

5. What assurances can be made that the time each youth spends performing job tasks at an employer's place of business is devoted to equipping the youth with occupational skills—as opposed to serving as a source of free and/or very cheap labor for the employer? To what extent is it contemplated that organized labor will have a voice here?

6. How much pay—if any—is to be provided for those youth who participate in the "apprenticeship" programs? Who is to make these determinations? What non-financial incentives can be offered?

7. Will opportunity to participate in some kind of "apprenticeship" be made available to *all* high school graduates? If so, who, eventually, will occupy jobs in the "secondary labor market"? Will employers choose youth—or will youth choose employers—or both? Will "creaming" in any form be allowed?

8. What assurances will participating employers be asked to provide with reference to their willingness to place youth who successfully complete an "apprenticeship" in entry-level jobs holding clear potential for advancement and/or further employer training?

9. Is requiring youth to make firm occupational decisions before they are ready and able to make reasoned, mature career choices a price worth paying in exchange for increased assurances they will be able to make successful schooling-to-employment transitions?

10. Are "apprenticeship" programs to be installed as a component of educational reform? Or are such programs to operate independent of current educational reform proposals aimed at better preparing today's youth for successful participation in tomorrow's occupational society?

Of the 10 questions raised above, the last 3 are, by far, the most serious. If an "apprenticeship work-based learning" approach is to become a generally endorsed youth "transition from schooling to employment" policy, *it is absolutely essential that Question 8 be answered in a satisfactory manner.* Assuming this can and will be done, the remainder of this chapter will be devoted to an attempt to suggest a series of activities which, if combined with "apprenticeship" approaches, will enable both Question 9 and Question 10 to also be answered in a positive fashion.

Tying "Apprenticeship," "Employability Skills," and "Career Development" to Educational Reform

Career Development and the "Apprenticeship System" Concept

Career development theorists are in strong agreement that most youth are not ready to make reasoned long-term occupational decisions before age 20.[37, 38, 39] Research in career decision-making confirms this element of career development theory.[40, 41, 42] While, of course, youth at almost any age *can* make occupational decisions if forced to do so, their readiness to make such decisions based on clear and accurate understanding of themselves and their occupational alternatives coupled with the skills of career decision making is quite a different matter.

There is ample evidence that career development can be speeded up to some extent by proper kinds of interventions. Campbell, in reporting on a met-analysis of a wide variety of studies aimed at assessing the effectiveness of career development, reported that : (1) 26 of 30 empirical studies reported positive results in the "personal and work skills" (including work values) category; (2) 27 of 34 empirical studies reported positive results in the "career planning" category; and (3) 31 of 44 empirical studies reported positive results in the "career awareness and exploration" category.[43] It seems clear that comprehensive career guidance programs can be effective in helping youth move toward career maturity.

The American School Counselor Association has issued a strong policy statement supporting the role of the school counselor in career guidance.[44] There is now evidence indicating that, while career guidance is still not a high priority for school counselors—and job placement continues to be a low priority—interest of school counselors in career guidance is increasing.[45] There is also good evidence that high school students look to school counselors for help in career development.[46]

While the school counselor is a key person in career guidance, it is important to remember that comprehensive K-12 career guidance programs also include important roles and responsibilities for classroom teachers, parents, and a wide variety of community agencies/organizations.[47] A community team effort is needed.

Need for career development assistance today is certainly not limited to youth. Recent data indicate, for example, that: (1) almost 4 in 10 of currently employed adult workers expect to leave their current jobs sometime in the next three years[48] and (2) plant closing and corporate downsizing have displaced about two million workers a year since the 1970s.[49]

The need for community career development assistance centers serving both youth and adults is clear.

If an "apprenticeship" style "work-based-learning" approach to solving the "schooling to employment transition" for both youth and adults is to be endorsed, it is absolutely essential that it be accompanied by strong and vigorous efforts to make high quality career guidance assistance available to all persons. Without assurance that such efforts will be made, serious questions must be raised regarding the desirability of asking American citizens to give up part of their freedom to make career choices in exchange for assurance of job placement.

Improving Educational Productivity: An Approach to Educational Reform

The wisest path to follow is often hidden from those searching for it because it is too obvious. This may well be true for many of the approaches for reforming American K-12 education put forth by private sector persons during the decade of the 1980s. Two recent documents provide hope that things are improving. One of these publications was produced by USDOL's Commission on Workforce Quality and Labor Market Efficiency.[50] It says:

> [T]he greater efforts of students (from other industrialized nations) account for much of the shortfall in American students' achievement . . . [T]here can be no doubt that increased effort by American students would contribute significantly to increased educational achievement . . . [M]any students lack sufficient incentives to inspire their whole-hearted engagement with learning.(p. 8)

Of all the contributions that the business community makes, the most important one is to help students understand the world of work and its relationship to what is learned in school (p. 9). The second publication is an "Issue Statement" recently released by the Minneapolis Youth Trust.[51] It says:

> The work readiness skills, habits, and attitudes needed by the employer are the

same as those which are needed by the family, school, and community. (p. 1) ... The classroom is the workplace for students, where they should learn the work skills, habits, and attitudes directly relevant to later success. (p. 2)

It seems clear that improvement of educational productivity is prerequisite to nationwide improvement of business-industrial productivity. It is equally clear that it is fruitless to expect high school graduates to possess positive work habits helpful in finding employment if they have spent their K-12 years practicing negative work habits in their school work. Both pupils *and* their teachers are—or at least should be—legitimate "workers" in the workplace called the "classroom." If each is to be a maximally productive worker, the basic rules of increasing productivity in any workplace (including classroom) must be applied. These include:

1. Show the worker the importance of the work tasks to be performed (e.g., how the subject to be learned is used in occupations).
2. Reward positive work efforts when they occur (e.g., provide recognition to pupils who do their best on an assignment).
3. Provide workers (teachers as well as pupils) power to determine their work style compatible with their willingness to accept accountability for their actions.
4. Introduce variety into the workplace (e.g., combine textbook and experiential learning).
5. Encourage teamwork among workers with shared responsibilities.
6. Encourage and reward the practice of productive work habits.

Application of these basic rules both to "pupils as workers" and to "teachers as workers," if supervised by professional educators who use private sector persons as productivity consultants, would almost surely result in a substantial increase in educational productivity. Ample evidence supporting this claim was accumulated during the decade of the 1970s as part of the career education movement. A meta-analysis of that literature summarized those studies demonstrating the effects of a career education treatment on increasing academic achievement as follows:

[D]uring the decade . . . 93 outcome studies assessing the impact of career education on gains in basic academic skills were identified. . . . [O]f these, a total of 31 produced statistically significant differences. . . favoring pupils who had been exposed to a career education treatment. . . . It is concluded that career education can . . . serve to improve pupil acquisition of basic academic skills at the elementary school level. (p. 234)[52]

In this same paper, statistically significant findings demonstrating the ability of career education to increase other aspects of educational productivity and career development can be summarized as follows: (1) increased use of productive work habits—10 of 55 studies; (2) developed positive work values 14 of 108 studies; (3) increased pupil understanding and appreciation of private enterprise system—14 of 16 studies; (4) developed skills in self-understanding of career interests and aptitudes—72 of 200 studies; (5) developed skills in understanding educational and occupational opportunities—156 of 311 studies; (6) developed skills in career decision making—68 of 134 studies; and (7) developed job seeking/finding/getting/holding skills—12 of 24 studies.

Certainly, such findings make it clear that there is no need for youth to leave the classroom and enter into an employer's job setting in order to be exposed to and to acquire productive work habits, positive attitudes toward work as part of total life-style, and/or increased understanding and appreciation of the private enterprise system. Clearly, these skills and attitudes *can,* given proper involvement of private sector resource persons, be provided within the K-12 school system.

It has often been observed that there are far too many persons—both youth and adults—looking for "jobs" and far too few looking for "work." American education can, using the right kinds of positive partnerships between educators and private sector persons, help each youth discover "work"–paid and/or unpaid–as an important and meaningful part of total lifestyle. If youth are to leave the K-12 school system with a sincere desire to find work in the jobs they secure, it will be essential that they have found work in their "job" as "pupils." If we wait until the K-12 schooling period is finished before attempting to help youth first discover "work," it will be a matter of too little too late. That is why this chapter is called "Transition From Schooling to Employment" rather than "Transition From School to Work." So long as people continue to think in a "transition from school to work" mentality, they miss the essential point of the importance of viewing the classroom as a workplace and both pupils and teachers as workers.

This effort must begin much before the apprenticeship period. As a matter of fact, it is essential to recognize that it must begin in the early elementary school years when pupils are acquiring both work habits and work values as they attempt to master basic academic skills. Such efforts are now in place in hundreds of K-12 school districts scattered throughout the nation. Most represent endeavors in which the school system and the broader community–including the business community–share authority, responsibility, and accountability in a truly collaborative relationship. They are, almost without exception, regarded as educational reform efforts in the communities where they operate. They have been given such names as "employability education," "work-readiness education," "education/work initiative," and "career education." It matters little which name is used. It only matters that the effort exists at a level that can produce positive results. If this is to happen nationwide, it must once again become an important national youth policy.

Concluding Remarks

There seems to be no doubt that "transition from schooling to employment" problems are currently being solved less well by U.S. policy makers than by their counterparts in other industrialized nations. Based on the available evidence, it is easy to see why the "apprenticeship concept" as seen in various forms of work-based learning has great appeal as a possible solution to this problem.

If conceptualized as a supplementary program to be added to existing experiential learning aspects of vocation education, the chances of improving the effectiveness of the total vocational education program through insertion of an "Apprenticeship–American Style" component appear to be good. Such a proposal should be deserving of positive consideration. If, on the other hand, an "apprenticeship" approach operated by USDOL is conceptualized as a substitute for vocational education programs operated by K-12 school systems, serious objections would surely be raised.

An "Apprenticeship–American Style" approach must, if the American value of freedom of choice for all citizens is to be retained, be accompanied by strong programs of career development–including career awareness, career exploration, career planning, career decision making, and career placement. If the total effort is to operate in the most efficient and effective manner possible, it must also be tied very closely to programs designed to improve educational productivity through the educational reform movement in American K-12 education. The challenges are as clear as they are important. Let us hope they will be accepted by those who make and implement youth policies in America.

Notes

[1]Hoyt, K. (1989a). *Counselors and career development: A topic in educational reform proposals.* Bloomington, IL: Meridian Education Corporation.

[2]U.S. Department of Education & U.S. Department of Labor. (1988). *The bottom line: Basic skills in the workplace.* Washington, DC: Office of Public Information, U.S. Department of Labor.

[3]Barton, P. (1990b). *Skills employers need: Time to measure them?* Princeton, NJ: Policy Information Center, Educational Testing Service.

[4]Carnevale, A., Gainer, L., & Meltzer, A. (1990). *Workplace basics: The essential skills employers want.* San Francisco: Jossey-Bass Publishing Company.

[5]*Jobs for America's graduates.* (1989). 1989 Annual Report. Alexandria, VA: Jobs For America's Graduates, Inc.

[6]National Alliance for Business. (1989). *Who will do the work? A business guide for preparing tomorrow's workforce.* Washington, DC: Author.

[7]Mann, D. (1987). Business involvement and public school improvement. *Phi Delta Kappan* 69 (2), 123-128.

[8]U.S. Department of Labor. (1989a). *Work-based learning: Training America's workers.* Washington, DC:

Employment and Training Administration, USDOL.

[9]Nothdurft, W. (1989). *Schoolwork: Reinventing public schools to create the workforce of the future.* Washington, DC: The Brookings Institute.

[10]U.S. General Accounting Office. (1990). *Training strategies: Preparing non-college youth for employment in the U.S. and foreign countries.* GAO/HRD 90-88. Washington, DC: Author.

[11]George, R. (1987). Youth policies and programs in selected countries. Youth and America's future. Washington, DC: Wm. T. Grant Foundation Commission on Work, Family, and Citizenship.

[12]U.S. Department of Education. (1987). *Japanese education today.* Washington, DC: Superintendent of Documents, U.S. Government Printing Office.

[13]Bureau of Labor Statistics. (June 26, 1990). Sixty percent of 1989 high school graduates enrolled in college. USDL 90-326. *News.* Washington, DC: U.S. Department of Labor.

[14]U.S. Department of Labor (1989b) Occupational employment. *Occupational Outlook Quarterly 33* (3), 28-37.

[15]Kutscher, R. (September, 1987) Projections 2000: Overview and implications of the Projections to 2000. *Monthly Labor Review.* Washington, DC: Superintendent of Documents, U.S. Government Printing Office.

[16]*Education Week.* (March 29, 1989). Schooling and earning. Washington, DC: Education Week.

[17]*The forgotten half: Pathways to success for America's youth and young families.* (1988). (p.126) Washington, DC: William T. Grant Foundation Commission on Work, Family, and Citizenship.

[18]Hamilton, S. (1990). Apprenticeship for adulthood: Preparing youth for the future. New York: The Free Press.

[19]*Work-Based Learning,* op. cit.

[20]Bureau of Labor Statistics. (June, 1990) The employment situation: June, 1990. *News.*Washington, DC: U.S. Department of Labor.

[21]Education Writers Association. (1990). *First jobs: Young workers in a changing economy.* Washington, DC: Author.

[22]Meyer, R. (1981). An economic analysis of high school education. In *The federal role in vocational education: Sponsored research.* Washington, DC: National Commission for Employment Policy.

[23]Campbell, P., & Basinger, K. (1985). *Economic and noneconomic effects of alternative transitions through school to work.* Columbus, OH: National Center for Research in Vocational Education, Ohio State University.

[24]Wirt, J., Muraskin, L., Goodwin, D., & Meyer, R. (1989). *Final report: Volume 1–Summary of findings and recommendations.* National Assessment of Vocational Education. Washington, DC: U.S. Department of Education.

[25]Nothdurft, op. cit.

[26]George, op. cit.

[27]Nothdurft, op. cit.

[28]Chapman, W., & Katz, M. (1981). *Survey of career information systems in secondary schools.* Princeton, NJ: Education Testing Service.

[29]*WORKFORCE LA.* (1990). A partnership of the IEC of California, Los Angeles Unified School District, & LA Community College District. Los Angeles, CA: Industry-Education Council of California.

[30]*Work-based learning,* op. cit.

[31]*Work-based learning,* op cit.

[32]Hamilton, op. cit.

[33]Parnell, D. (1986). *The neglected majority.* Washington, DC: The Community College Press.

[34]Lerman, R., & Pouncy, H. (March, 1990). *Why America should develop a youth apprenticeship system.* Policy report no. 5. Washington, DC: Progressive Policy Institute.

[35]Hamilton, op. cit.

[36]*Occupational employment,* op. cit.

[37]Brown, D., & Brooks, L. (1990). *Career choice and development* (2nd ed.). San Francisco: Jossey-Bass.

[38]Herr, E. & Cramer, S. (1988). *Career guidance and counseling through the life span* (3rd ed.). Glenview, IL: Scott, Foresman.

[39]Super, D. (1957). *The psychology of careers.* New York: Harper & Row.

[40]Jepson, D. (1989). Antecedent events to adolescent career decision processes. *Guidance & Counseling 4* (5), 5-14.

[41]Olson, C., McWhirter, E., & Horan, J. (1989). A decision-making model applied to career counseling. *Journal of Career Development, 16* (2), 107-117.

[42]Walsh, D. (1987). Individual variations within the vocational decision-making styles. *Journal of Counseling Psychology 27* (6), 581-588.

[43]Campbell, R., Boyle, J., & Bhaerman, R. (1983). *Enhancing career development: Recommendations for action.* Columbus, OH: National Center for Research in Vocational Education, Ohio State University.

[44]American School Counselor Association. (1985). The role of the school counselor in career guidance: Expectations and responsibilities. *The School Counselor, 32* (3), 164-168.

[45]Engin, H., & Noeth, R. (1983). Assessing quality in career guidance programs: One state's approach. *Vocational Guidance Quarterly, 32* (2), 80-88.

[46]Hutchinson, R., & Reagan, C. (1989). Problems for which seniors would seek help from school counselors. *The School Counselor, 36* (4), 271-280.

[47]Gysbers, N., & Henderson, P. (1988). *Developing and managing your school guidance program.* Alexandria, VA: American Association for Counseling and Development.

[48]Hoyt, K. (1989b). Policy implications of selected data from adult employed workers in 1987 Gallup career development survey. In Brown, D., & Minor, C. (Eds.), *Working in America: A status report on planning and problems.* Alexandria, VA: National Career Development Association.

[49]National Planning Association. (1990). *Preparing for change: Workforce excellence in a turbulent economy.*

Recommendation of the Committee on New American Realities. Washington, DC: Author.

[50]U.S. Department of Labor. (1989c). *Investing in people: A strategy to address America's workforce crisis.* Commission on Workforce Quality and Labor Market Efficiency. Washington, DC: U.S. Department of Labor.

[51]*Issue statement.* (1990, July). Minneapolis, MN: Minneapolis Youth Trust.

[52]Hoyt, K., & High, S. (1982). Career education. In Mitzel, H. (Ed.), *Encyclopedia of educational research* (Vol. 1, pp. 231-241). New York: Free Press.

18

Improving
the School-to-Employment Transition
for the Forgotten Half

Albert J. Pautler, Jr.

The William T. Grant Foundation used the term "the forgotten half " to describe young people who do not have a college education. The foundation's publication *The Forgotten Half: Pathways to Success for Youth and Young Families* (1988a) tried to focus attention on the educational preparation of all youth–not just those planning to attend college after completing high school.

The reform movement in education has not centered much attention on the approximately 20 million young Americans who are not likely to attend college, according to the Grant Foundation report. This lack of attention to the non-college-bound student raises questions regarding the transition of such students to work (employment) after high school graduation.

In the June 1990 issue of *Phi Delta Kappan,* Anne Lewis (1990, p. 748) stated: "This June, schools across the country will be touting the college attendance rate of the graduating class as an indicator of their success. In Junes of the future, perhaps schools will consider the employment rate of graduates an equally good indicator."

I seriously doubt that this will happen unless state policymakers mandate such a reporting policy and hold school districts accountable for the school transition of all graduating students.

It does not appear that one can separate the label that the Grant Foundation applied to "the forgotten half" from the issue of the "school-to-work transition." School-to-work transition occurs for all individuals who seek work, but the time of occurrence varies. For some, it will occur after they have dropped out of high school. For others, it may take place after high school graduation; after community college, college, or university graduation; after graduate studies; or someplace in between these levels. The transition may also involve the selection of a military career.

None of this is a new issue. The National Commission for Manpower Policy in 1976 published a collection of policy papers titled *From School to Work: Improving the Transition,* which dealt with issues addressed in this chapter. The focus of national concern should be on the one-quarter to one-third of young people who face major hurdles in making the transition from school to work. Most youth can make the transition without special assistance, although many could profit from improved linkages among schools, employers, trade unions, and other critical institutions.

Particular economic conditions and employment opportunities are unique to the present time frame, but the two basic concerns of "the forgotten half" and the school-to-work transition remain of major significance to educational policymakers.

School-to-Work Transition

Figure 1, showing the school transition, presents in a very simple manner the transition options of those students who complete school. It depicts the three most obvious exit paths for graduates: school-to-school transition, school-to-work transition, and–obviously the least desirable–a transition from school to unemployment or underemployment. This model applies equally well in secondary, community college, college, university, graduate, and private trade school settings. In this chapter, the discussion will center only on secondary-level programs.

Those students who decide to drop out before high school completion or are pushed out are also indicated on the model in Figure 1. As an ideal, educators should do whatever they can for those dropping out before graduation. Many of these dropouts find their way into programs sponsored by the United States

Department of Labor, such as Job Corps or Job Training and Partnership Act (JTPA) programs. They may eventually finish high school level programs. While I am concerned with these dropouts, I will limit myself here to those who do in fact complete high school. (It should be pointed out at this time that about 25 percent of young people nationwide still do not graduate from high school.)

An article in *Teacher Magazine* (1991) states that a recent report by the Heritage Foundation describes the United States dropout problem as grossly exaggerated. This is based on the fact that, according to the Heritage Foundation, when adults are counted, 87 percent of Americans do complete high school or its equivalent by age 24. This is encouraging if the data are correctly reported, but, it still causes problems for a period in the lives of dropouts who do go on to finish high school or its equivalent by age 24.

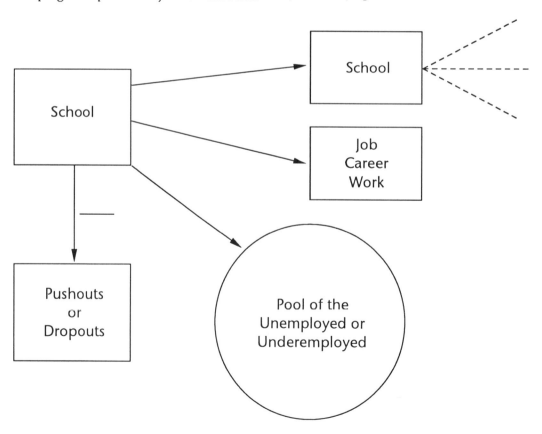

Figure 1—School Transition Model

Pautler and Skobjak (1979, p. 498), writing in *Educational Leadership*, stated that "high schools should be as concerned about placement of students who do not go on to college as with those who do." Little, if any, evidence seems to exist that secondary school administrators have a data base to support such transition experiences of high school graduates. Ample evidence appears of the number of students who graduate every year from high school and continue on to formal postsecondary education. As previously indicated by Anne Lewis, most school districts are very proud of their percentage of graduates who continue formal education, and this percentage is reported to the public. Little if any mention is made about those graduates not planning to pursue formal education immediately after graduation.

Seldom does a school district make an effort to conduct a two- or four-year follow-up of graduates to determine their success in college or their transition-to-work experiences. No clear policies or practices seem to exist concerning accountability of graduates other than awarding of high school diplomas. The educational system is less accountable to the taxpayers on this issue than are automobile manufacturers or any other product-orientated industry.

New York state has some 700 school districts that graduate a senior class each year. A fall 1989 report, *Distribution of High School Graduates and College-Going Rate*, indicates that 75.8 percent of public high school graduates were entering some form of formal postsecondary education. This total includes four-year and two-year colleges and other postsecondary schools. The data is as reported by school principals in the fall of 1989. The basic question that follows is what percentage of these graduates will in fact complete their educational programs at the postsecondary level. It would be interesting to find out how many of the principals involved know the "survival rate" of their college-going graduates two or four years after graduation from high school.

In addition, while the paragraph above addresses the reported 75.8 percent of 1989 New York state high school graduates who entered some form of postsecondary education, what about the other 24.2 percent of the graduates not accounted for? What experiences did *these* young graduates face in moving on with their lives?

Each year, high school graduates are "transitioned" into the next phase of their career development. The point we must pursue is how well prepared are these graduates for their transitional experiences and how well informed about their experiences are the school districts from which these young people graduated?

It is common procedure for vocational education high schools and area vocational centers to conduct follow-up studies of graduates. These studies also report data on the percentage of vocational graduates who attend postsecondary programs. This data is relevant to discussions of how well vocational graduates do in making their transition from school to work.

Hoyt (1990), writing in *Future Choices*, prefers to use the term *school-to-employment* rather than *school-to-work*. He feels that if students think about a transition from school to work, they will not think of school as a "workplace"—which is really the function school serves for students.

The Forgotten Half

Selvin and others (1990) conducted a study for the National Center for Research in Vocational Education in three high schools located in three California schools districts. They reported that at all three schools, the guidance and placement systems seem to concentrate on college-bound and severely troubled students, almost ignoring non-college-bound, untroubled students.

According to the William T. Grant Foundation Commission on Work, Family, and Citizenship's *Forgotten Half* report (1988b), the 20 million non-college-bound young people who comprise the forgotten half are the people who will build our homes; drive our buses; repair our VCRs, stereos, and television sets; and maintain and service our offices, hospitals, schools, and so forth.

Some key statements from the Grant Foundation Commission and from the December 1988 issue of *Phi Delta Kappan,* are worth noting:

- Between 1973 and 1986, families headed by persons between the ages of 20 and 24 experienced a 27 percent drop in median real income.
- The young family as a societal institution has become dangerously unstable, besieged by declining rates of marriage, higher rates of single-parent households, absentee fathers, a severe shortage of affordable housing, and increasing poverty.
- Between 1974 and 1986 the marriage rate of males between the ages of 20 and 24 fell from 39 percent to 21 percent. At the same time, the number of young families headed by a single female increased.
- It is estimated that these young families would have to pay 81 percent of their total income to afford adequate rental housing in 1987.

The Grant Foundation report has attempted to focus the attention of the nation and educators on the fact that society in general has become preoccupied with college as the only proper route to success. Data do support the fact that the more education one has, the higher his or her lifetime earnings will be.

Recently, a General Motors plant manager speaking in my class at the university was asked about the preparation needed for high school graduates seeking employment at the plant. He stated: "We will need high school graduates with a college education." The technology of assembly line work has been upgraded to such an extent that more qualified employees are needed to operate and manage the specialized equipment involved. Many essential occupations do not require a college education at the present time. Some may require technical training beyond high school that might be possible through apprenticeships or on-the-job (OJT) training programs. It is essential that we have well-prepared people for positions as carpenters, electricians, plumbers, automotive and diesel mechanics, machinists, welders, chefs, computer operators and service staff, appliance repair technicians, medical and dental support staff, retail sales staff, and so forth.

We must consider the educational preparation program that those not planning on attending college will need to have to be successful in our society. It is this group that the Grant Foundation has labeled as the "forgotten half."

Combining the Issues

The two issues of major concern are: First, educators must consider the importance of the Grant Foundation report and the issue of the so-called "forgotten-half" students, the high school graduates not planning to attend college. Second, serious consideration must go to the kind and quality of attention given to those high school graduates not planning to attend college after high school completion.

When these issues are combined and examined in some detail, it raises questions concerning how well prepared high school graduates are in terms of skills needed for employment. This involves questions dealing with both cultural and technological literacy as well as basic skills in English, math, communication, writing, and critical thinking. Simply stated, it involves all the things that business and industry leaders tell educators they need in young people attempting to enter the work force. Can the present curriculum in most schools address the societal needs of both preparation for college and preparation for employment after high school graduation?

From a variety of sources, it seems safe to state that as of 1991 the following statements are true: (1) The best estimate of those not finishing high school by age 19 is approximately 25 percent in the United States. (2) Census data and the condition of education indicate that 86 percent of those age 25-29 have a high school diploma (U.S. Department of Education, 1991). (3) As recently as 1987, about 87 percent of high school graduates enrolled in two- or four-year colleges. (4) The college completion rate of those ages 25 to 29 is about 25 percent. (5) What about the other 75 percent?

If the five items above are correct, it appears safe to say that about 25 percent of the population of the United States completes a college degree. We can consider the other 75 percent what the Grant Foundation calls the forgotten half.

What Can School Districts Do?

I don't want to be accused of bashing public or private schools. But I do want to encourage educators to give equal attention to all students, not just those planning to attend college or postsecondary education. It seems safe to assume that many school districts measure their success in terms of the numbers of graduates who are accepted for college on high school graduation. During May, June, and July, we rather commonly see newspaper items regarding the college acceptance rate of high school graduates. This is fine, and all may be proud of the accomplishments of the graduates. But, if 65 percent are accepted and planning to attend college, please don't forget about the other 35 percent. The 65 percent in the example will make a transition to college, what happens to the others?

Based on an informal survey of several districts, I could not locate any district that maintained or even attempted to maintain a data base on the transition experiences of graduates one, two, three, or four years after graduation. High school graduates seem to flow into a nationwide pool of graduates and remain there forever.

Ideally, for purposes of accountability and curriculum adjustment, it seems reasonable that school districts would want to do follow-up studies of high school graduates several years after graduation. This would allow them to better determine the longer-term experiences of graduates in making their transition from high school to college or to employment.

Such a data base could prove very helpful in making curriculum adjustments and improvements that would benefit all students, and not just those who succeed in completing college-level programs.

References

Hoyt, K. (1990, Fall). A proposal for making transition from schooling to employment an important component of educational reform. *Future Choices*, pp. 73-86.

Lewis, A. (1990, June). Remembering the forgotten half. *Phi Delta Kappan*, pp. 748-749.

National Commission for Manpower Policy. (1976). *From school to work: Improving the transition*, p. iv. Washington, DC: Author.

New York State Education Department. (1989). *Distribution of high school graduates and college-going rate*. Albany, NY: University of the State of New York.

Pautler, A., & Skobjak, Bernadette. (1979, April). Transition from school to work. *Educational Leadership*, pp. 498-501.

Selvin, M., et al. (1990). *Who gets what and why: Curriculum decisionmaking at three comprehensive high schools*. Berkeley, CA: National Center for Research in Vocational Education.

Teacher Magazine. (1991, January). p. 25.

U.S. Department of Education. (1991). *The condition of education 1990*. Washington, DC: Office of Educational Research and Improvement, U.S. Department of Education.

William T. Grant Foundation. (1988a). *The forgotten half: pathways to success for America's youth and young families*. Washington, DC: Author.

William T. Grant Foundation. (1988b, December). The forgotten half: Pathways to success for America's youth and young families. *Phi Delta Kappan*, pp. 275-289.

19

Improving Transition Experiences

Charles R. Doty

This chapter is written to present possibilities for easing the school-to-work/life transition. Possibilities rather than answers, because I know from experience that no definitive answers exist. Two questions serve as a guide in writing the chapter: What has been recommended for programs of transition based on research? Where are the sources that can be examined in depth for designing transition programs? To answer these, I will discuss the following: the purpose of school-to-work transition; the impetus for such programs; restructuring education; school/life reality; the different realities of female and male students; my own recent research; other international research; transition program traits; special needs student transitions; skills required by today's workforce; and guidance and counseling. Last, I list my observations of what a young person should know and be able to do. These might make students think and plan for the future.

Purpose of School-to-Work/Life Transition

Feichtner (1989, p. ix) wrote that the purpose of school-to-work/life transition programs is to provide persons with experiences that will help them develop skills and attitudes needed to secure and keep employment, to secure and maintain a meaningful adult life style, and to develop positive social interactions. Transition is an ongoing process that focuses on personal characteristics, training needs, and options of an individual that result in the development of realistic long-range goals and in the selection of appropriate programs and services to achieve those goals.

Those who design transition programs should place Feichtner's purpose on the wall above their desks. They should refer to that purpose every day and ask: "Am I straying from that purpose?" They should also realize that transition programs should be for everyone, not just non-college-bound or special needs students. While working at a university, I have had more than one senior or graduate student, almost in tears, say in desperation, "I don't even know how to apply for a job. Can you help me?"

Impetus for Transition Programs

In 1989, the nation's governors and president adopted a set of national goals. The Council of Chief State School Officers (CCSSO) developed an agenda to implement the goals and called on the U.S. administration to support their agenda. One item on the agenda was a request for investment in school-to-work transition programs (Lewis, 1990).

Clark Kerr, in the preface of *From School to Work* (Barton, 1990, p. 3) described the problem with which the president and others were concerned: All industrial societies create two difficult life transition points. One involves young people moving into the workforce, and the other involves older people moving out of the workforce. In earlier agricultural societies, such transitions were more gradual and more fully cared for within the family and local community. Now, more people are on their own in making these transitions into and out of the workforce. And the record of the U.S. in helping these transitions is among the worst in the entire industrial world.

At this point, there are several plans and some effort to make the transition from school to work and life easier. Proposals range from involving parents in the educational process, school-business partnerships, and experiential programs (e.g., cooperative education; apprenticeship; mentoring; shadowing; basic skills programs for math, language, and science; ethics instruction; geography instruction; and so forth). In effect, proposals are coming from every institution of human society—governmental, economic, familial, religious, and educational. Many of these proposals focus on some narrow aspect of knowledge. These plans and efforts have originated to ensure national survival, preserve or eliminate beliefs, control population growth, sell products, and so forth. What must be questioned in the motives is whether society is structuring the public school system to develop each person to his/her full potential or to develop each person to serve some vested interest. Whatever the purpose, there is one conclusion that can be drawn. No one institution of society can save that society, all institutions must cooperate.

The theory behind American education is that free public education should be required for all citizens so that a democratic society can be maintained. (The term *theory* should be defined before further discussion as a statement describing an environment and a prediction of some event or behavior occurring as a result of that environment.) The historic free public education included academic, general, and vocational components, at least to grade 12. The recent changes in public education seem to include only the academic component based on an apparent need to produce scientists for the United States to maintain competitiveness in the world economy. One might restate that the present theory behind American education is that free public education (academic education) should be required of all citizens so that more scientists will be developed for the U.S. to be competitive in the world economy. Whether this latter theory is correct or not, the concept of transition to work will require a restructuring of public education.

Restructuring Education

Implicit in the school-to-work-transition concept is restructuring education based on an assumption that schools are failing. Bracey (1991) in *Phi Delta Kappan* accuses the critics of education of being in error when they state that America's schools have failed (i.e., "The Big Lie"). Bracey backs his accusation by citing extensive research and analyzing the methodology used in the research. For example, he reports that the number of students taking the College Board Advanced Placement test rose from 90,000 in 1978 to 324,000 in 1990. Yet the scores decreased by only eleven one-hundredths of a point even though the percentage of Asians who took the test tripled, the percentage of Blacks doubled, and the percentage of Hispanics quadrupled. That is, the effect of thousands of persons from different cultural and economic backgrounds barely changed the scores. Based on such examples, Bracey concludes that American schools are doing better than they ever have and are even doing better than some indicators show.

Bracey further states that American schools may be overeducating the country's citizens. Such overeducation creates problems, such as persons avoiding certain jobs and developing social snobbery toward those who do take them. When discussing overeducation and education for work, Bracey states that the fact is that the schools are producing persons at about the numbers needed for the workforce—a situation he describes as "a good thing."

Bracey's analysis of business and industry training reveals that expenditures rise drastically for the more skilled jobs (15 percent of money for training is spent for unskilled and 65 percent for jobs requiring a college education). Only 5 percent of employers foresee increasing skill requirements for jobs, which probably accounts for this expenditure difference. His conclusion is that training in business is not to increase the ability of unskilled and skilled workers but to upgrade the highly educated personnel. He does mention the Hudson Institute's conclusion, based on the same business and industry training and future skill assessment data, that the only way for the U.S. to become more competitive is to increase the skill of non-college-bound students. Bracey does not advocate the status quo but believes that changes can be made without condemning schools. Such changes should be made by looking at the statistics available with some intelligent perspective. The statistics are available, he says, to anyone interested in seeking the truth.

What Bracey examined that the statistics may not reveal is the recent restructuring of kindergarten through the twelfth grade to a college preparation curriculum–although he did detect overeducation in his analysis. Bracey's "good thing" may be a "past thing." This restructuring has virtually eliminated the comprehensive high school (as previously stated), by eliminating general education and vocational education plus practical arts such as art, music, home economics, and industrial technology. Full-time and shared-time vocational secondary schools have become the recipients of special education students, "push outs"–meaning those who have deviant behavior or who will not score well on the standardized tests that seem to represent society's measure of a school's "quality," plus JTPA and welfare recipients. Thus, non-college-bound students and others of average and above-average ability are avoiding, or being prevented from going to, vocational schools. This recent restructuring has virtually eliminated education concerned with cognitive, affective, and psychomotor learning, through which non-college-bound and other students' work skills might increase. The assumption underlying the restructuring was that students could go to postsecondary education such as a private technical or trade school, or community/technical college. No one seems to have questioned that many could not afford such postsecondary education and no one has advocated that thirteenth and fourteenth grade levels be added at free schools such as is done in California. Nor was consideration given

concerning people in rural areas who would be more disadvantaged than urban and suburban people due to a lack of availability of such schools. Thus, transition has been made even harder for future students.

Smith (1983) in his excellent report to the Ford Foundation, *Institutionalizing the School to Work Transition*, reviewed major programs for transition, cited conditions necessary for transition programs, and concluded that such programs should be institutionalized (i.e., be made an integral part of education, not an add-on for the students who have not been prepared for their futures until their senior year in high school). He acknowledges that institutionalizing means restructuring education, a slow process and one that requires leadership at all levels. One of his key recommendations is that if school-to-work transition programs are to represent more than a glancing blow at solving transition problems that deserve far more attention, the programs must affect materially the way schools behave. Smith's final conclusion is that an incentive-based, partnership-based, locally operated, and federally funded effort to stimulate the school-to-work process is necessary and makes sense. The federal government must make school-to-work transition programs a national priority, but the local and state governments must be equal partners in the planning and implementation, a caution also stated by the General Accounting Office (1990) and Barton (1990).

Common elements Smith cited for transition programs include an intervention agency which is independent, outside the entity that establishes the program and introduces the program into schools; a private sector board of directors or advisory committee that brings the world of business into the classroom and translates its commitment into active support for the program; a curriculum package concentrating first on teaching job preparedness and job retention skills and second on building self-esteem and self-confidence; and a job placement function that works to induce private sector employers to hire certain youth part time while they are in school and full time upon graduation. Smith identified remedial academic instruction as a missing element in programs examined, which must be included in any program.

The private sector can be involved as cited by Smith by making frequent visits to observe students to determine changes in self-image, motivation, and assertiveness; hosting student field visits to help the students gain perspective on their abilities and to acquaint them with particular work environments; appearing with students on civic club programs; and committing to hire as many students as possible. Delaware's Jobs for America's Graduates, Richmond, Virginia's Partnership Project programs, and Boston's Boston Compact were identified as models for transition programs.

To institutionalize, Smith described four basic stages. First is the establishment of a partnership agreement involving the intervention agency, the private sector, and the schools that specifies the goals and plan for institutionalization; second is acceptance by the schools of being responsible for teaching the curriculum and preparing students for employment according to the agreement; third is acceptance by the state and local community that they will provide funding; and fourth is assimilation of the school-to-work curriculum into the academic curriculum and integration of academic and vocational offerings.

Problems identified by Smith for institutionalization include determining whether to give academic credit for school-to-work participation, whether to provide students with part-time jobs or enroll them in career clubs, whether to enroll only economically disadvantaged students or a mix, and who should be responsible for job placement.

Barton (1990, 1991), who is the director of the Policy Information Center at Educational Testing Service (ETS), is very concerned with restructuring education. Using extensive research conducted by ETS, Barton identified and recommended several features for improving the school-to-work transition at the high school level.

- First is integrating academic and vocational education in every school district. Barton acknowledges the "split" between academic and vocational education and recommends healing the split with a new pedagogy in which traditional academic skills are embedded in applied settings with both types of teachers working together. He cites the Southern Regional Education Board multi-year experiment in 13 states for integrating vocational and academic curriculum for students in vocational education; team teaching with academic and vocational teachers as at Montgomery County Joint Vocational School in Dayton, Ohio; four-year tech vocational magnet schools such as the Shenley High School in Pittsburgh; and organizing instruction around occupational clusters as in Dauphin County Technical School, Harrisburg, Pennsylvania.

- Second, collaborative occupational education efforts between school systems and employers should exist, in which schools provide theoretical education concerning occupations and employers provide practical instruction at the work site. Collaborative programs could be year round, with students rotating to various business and industrial sites for preapprenticeship, cooperative education, or short-term experiences (e.g., shadowing).

- Third, students should receive a record that documents their employment-related skills (work readiness)—such as those involving thinking, reasoning, analysis, creativity, problem solving, reliability, responsibility, and responsiveness to change—as well as a formal curriculum report. Barton noted that employers care much less about academic achievement than work readiness attitudes and abilities. He cited the ETS Worklink Project and JOBTAP, which assess work-related skills, as a possible component in this documentation process.

- Fourth, every student should have access to community-based occupational counseling and employment services. State employment services, business organizations, and nonprofit organizations should work in partnership with schools to provide such services in conjunction with school occupational counselors. Delaware's Jobs for America and Massachusetts's Boston Compact are cited as two working systems.

Four states were reported to be planning the institutionalization of school to work and life at a statewide December 1991 meeting conducted by the New Jersey Employment and Training Commission. This commission, representing one of the four states, has produced a statewide plan to connect disparate elements of the workforce readiness system into a "knowledgeable and articulated continuum of services" that bridges gaps that have traditionally separated institutions and programs, people and jobs. Further, the plan aims to create a continuum of work education from kindergarten through adulthood. It follows four guidelines: (1) The system will be consumer based and market driven. (2) There will be an accountability and evaluation system. (3) All people will achieve fundamental literacy and basic skills. (4) All people will be fully developed and utilized.

Some of the components of the New Jersey system will involve a comprehensive career development program to provide students with knowledge that will allow them to make informed decisions about the world of work. Establishment of graduation requirements will assure inclusion of competencies and foundations, such as those recommended in the U.S. Department of Labor's Secretary's Commission on Achieving Necessary Skills (SCANS) report. Plans for the system also include: (1) An option for students to have portfolios containing reports of achievement of knowledge and skills. (2) Expansion of work-based learning activities that will include linkages between community colleges, adult learning centers, technical and proprietary schools, and work-based training initiatives. (3) Oversight for proprietary schools. (4) Occupational education and training programs that are competency based and have an open entry/open exit curriculum. (5) A teacher and counselor inservice training program to ensure these professionals have the knowledge to conduct comprehensive career development programs K-12. (6) A career development curriculum in teacher education programs in higher education. (7) Expansion of apprenticeship. (8) An early warning system to identify employer

human resource needs. (9) An Automated Labor Exchange System (ALEX), to be accessible to all levels of educational institutions, and Career Information Delivery System (CIDS), to be placed in adult vocational education schools and adult centers. Directories that include availability of work preparation programs and data on the success of people who have participated in these programs are to be published.

Concerning reconstruction of education, an advertisement for a United Kingdom publication, *The Vocational Aspect of Education*, stated that education for occupations is mainly a postsecondary provision but that that situation is fast disappearing as societies realize the potential for work-oriented studies for general education purposes at lower levels. In developing countries, schooling can only obtain funding and resources if education relates directly to national economic needs. The question is: Why should the United States public school system be different than that of other countries?

School-Life Reality

Giroux and Freire (1991) edited a publication titled *Learning Work: A Critical Pedagogy of Work Education* by Simon, Dippo, and Schenke. An advertisement for this publication indicated that increasing attention is paid to the idea that education should include some type of vocational or career-related training. Further, concerns have arisen over how best to implement such programs to meet the needs of teachers, students, and community.

The idea that education should consider the world of work as a "new idea" shows the distance that some people have grown from the real world. It is to be hoped that the book does indeed help the reader develop a viewpoint of a pedagogy that will produce a clear and principled curriculum of work education. It is also to be hoped that the curriculum will meet the needs of students first, the community second, and teachers last.

Male and Female Realities

Many educational programs fail because they seem to forget the people for whom educators are designed. Therefore, those who design school-to-work programs must keep in mind the student and what the student will face on leaving school. In 1986, the Consortium for Educational Equity at Rutgers University studied statistics related to the future that youth might face. After studying statistics such as *Youth Indicators of 1991* and *1990 Condition of Education* by the U.S. Department of Education, and *America's Choice: High Skills or Low Wages* by the Commission on the Skills of the American Work Force, the following summary by the consortium seems to offer appropriate guidelines for planning school-to-work (and - life) programs. Program planners should tack the table printed below on their wall.

Recent Research

Doty and Hirsch (1991) conducted a study titled *Follow-Up Study of Non-College-Bound xxxxxxx County High School Graduates, June 1990, New Jersey.* (The title excludes the name of the county involved at the request of school administrators.) The county studied has the fourth highest per capita income in the United States. Twelve high schools that no longer can be classified as comprehensive (i.e., they offer only college preparation and some general education) and one full-time vocational school provide secondary education for the county. The study was initiated because the superintendent of the vocational school was concerned with the well-being of students who indicated before graduation that they were not planning to attend college but would seek full-time employment instead. No existing data on the non-college-bound existed for the county.

All 13 secondary-level schools participated in the study. The schools identified 408 non-college-bound graduates. A mailed survey and telephone survey yielded data from 198 of them, a 48.5 percent return, during March 1991 (9 months after graduation). During this month, unemployment was 6.8 percent in New Jersey and the U.S. was preparing for the Gulf War. Of these 198 graduates, 10 were in military service, 13 were reported by parents as being in school, 150 were employed, and 35 were unemployed.

When the high school majors were examined, general education majors fared better in percentage of employment than those in college prep and vocational education by 85 percent, 77 percent, and 61 percent respectively. However, the general education majors

Table 1—Differing Expectations for Females and Males

A girl graduating from high school in the next several years will face:	A boy graduating from high school in the next several years will face:
• The absolute certainty of encountering situations where she would benefit substantially from being aggressive and competitive.	• The absolute certainty of encountering situations where being aggressive and competitive is damaging.
• The absolute certainty of working for pay outside the home—on the average for almost three decades of her life.	• The virtual certainty of having a wife who will work for pay outside the home for most of their married life.
• An almost even chance of divorce.	• An almost even chance of divorce.
• Virtual certainty that she will retain custody of her children if she is divorced and has children.	• Strong probability, in case of divorce, of having to contribute to two households.
• Virtual certainty that if she is a single custodial parent, she will have the financial responsibility for herself and her children.	• Strong possibility of being called on in his working life to exercise skills and attitudes that have traditionally been associated with women.
• A strong possibility of being called upon in her working life to exercise skills and attitudes that have been associated with men.	• Strong possibility of conflict between career and family obligations.
• A strong probability of conflict between career and family obligations.	• Strong probability of having to work under a women's authority.
• A strong possibility that she will earn on average 68 cents for every dollar earned by a man.	• Significant possibility of having a wife who earns more than he does.
	• Strong probability that his wife will encounter sexual harassment on the job.
	• Small but increasing possibility of becoming a single parent with sole or joint custody of his children.

included many practical arts courses. Further analysis revealed that those graduates with variations of study—for example, industrial arts/college preparation, industrial arts/general education, vocational education/general education, and vocational education/industrial arts were all employed. When graduates were asked what courses of study were most helpful in seeking work, the top four courses were, in order of importance, math, vocational education, cooperative education, and industrial arts. Beginning salaries were equivalent regardless of major and and ran to the low end of the spectrum, as might be expected for high school graduates.

Those sources graduates used to find a job were friends and relatives, want ads, cooperative education, and self initiative. Teachers, guidance counselors, schools, and private agencies were insignificant as sources for obtaining jobs. In other words, I conclude that the schools have become removed from the world of work.

Almost 16 percent (15.93 percent) of those employed indicated they were not prepared by their high school education to enter the world of work, and 5.49 percent of the unemployed indicated they were not prepared. Those who considered themselves unprepared had majors in college preparation (31.82 percent), general education (25.71 percent), business education (23.82 percent), and vocational education (22.50 percent). The majority response as to why they were not prepared was that they had not been taught enough.

Graduates were asked if they would conduct their high school education differently if they could be freshmen again. Of the 182 people who responded, 77 (42.04 percent) said they would not do anything differently; 60 of these were employed and 17 were unemployed. One hundred and four (56.83 percent) reported they would do their education differently; 87 of these were employed and 17 unemployed. Two were undecided. To summarize, the majority of graduates would do their high school education differently. Fifty-three (54.64 percent) of 104 graduates would "try harder;" 25 (25.76 percent) would either go to vocational school or take business or trade courses; and 9 (9.28 percent) would take a college preparation program. Ironically, only

two of these graduates would take mathematics, an area identified by many graduates as helping in obtaining a job and one in which most graduates felt they were lacking. Evidently many graduates would still avoid taking mathematics even though they know mathematics is an essential area of knowledge.

When graduates were asked about continuing their education, of those employed (147 people), 62 (34.25 percent) were continuing their education and 13 (7.18 percent) were planning to begin school next year. That is, 41.43 percent of those employed were continuing their education. Seventy-three employed graduates were not continuing their formal education. Of 33 unemployed, 20 were continuing their education. In effect, 55 percent of the 1990 non-college-bound graduates were continuing their education in some formal manner. Enrollment was in universities (3 people), community colleges (38), technical institutes (16), trade schools (10), business institutes (6), and truck driver school (2).

The unexpected major finding was a hostility toward schools, especially toward guidance counselors. For example, some said, "Once the guidance counselor found out that you were [or my child was] not planning to apply for college, they forgot you." This comment summarizes the attitude found among students and parents who answered the survey.

Even more unexpected was a follow-up meeting in which the principals and guidance counselors were invited to a free breakfast for the results of the study to be presented. Only one principal attended, in addition to one assistant principal (from a school that refused to participate), and four guidance counselors from two other comprehensive high schools plus the guidance counselors and principal from the vocational school. The perception of the researcher was that two of the high schools sent guidance counselors and an assistant principal to unreasonably criticize the study. With the exception of the vocational school personnel, one high school represented by the principal, and two high schools represented by a guidance counselor, there seemed to be little concern for the non-college-bound students. (Incidentally, the major reason the other guidance counselors said they could not attend was that they were completing applications for college for their students.)

International School-to-Work Efforts Research

The U.S. General Accounting Office (GAO) conducted a review of U.S. education and training strategies (1990) to identify likely weaknesses and examine the strategies of England, the Federal Republic of Germany, Japan, and Sweden for preparing non-college-bound youth for employment. The GAO found significant similarities in the approaches of the four countries that seem relevant to shortcomings in the U.S. strategy for non-college-bound youth. These countries emphasize student effort rather than ability and share the expectation that all students will attain the academic skills necessary to perform effectively in the workplace or in postsecondary education. There is no assumption that many students will lag behind; schools and the employment community play a more active role in guiding the transition from school to work, including providing an orientation to the world of work that is integrated into the school curriculum; training is documented by certification of achievement of competency on nationally determined skill levels; and governments make an extensive investment in remedial education, training, or job placement for jobless out-of-school youth.

Some foreign countries emphasize taking steps to give all students an equal start. For example, they avoid grouping youth by ability in early grades, devote special attention to students with learning difficulties, allocate similar resources to all schools (with additional resources going to vocational schools for equipment), supplement poorer areas, and maintain a well-paid teaching force. Japan expects students to value the performance of the entire class, thereby helping classmates to not lag behind.

Each foreign country has in place a structure that smooths the transition from school to work by giving students occupational information and guidance while in school and by combining schooling with work experience. Employers provide structured work experiences for secondary students in many countries, apprenticeship for most youth in Ger-many, and formal school-employer linkages for job placement of most youth in Japan. England in 1983 began the Technical and Vocational Education Initiative for secondary education to prepare youth for a "better working life by making what they learn at school, and the way they learn it, more relevant to the world of work." The initiative addresses relating the curriculum to the world of work, teaching students workplace skills such as teamwork and problem solving, and work experience.

Germany provides courses in the seventh, eighth, and ninth grades for orientation to the world of work, one to two weeks of work experience, field visits, and employment office information on occupational information. Sweden provides early work orientation from ages 7 through 15 by completing 6 to 10 weeks of work orientation. Students in vocational fields in the first and second years of high school spend 10 percent of their time at a work site. Germany also provides apprenticeships that represent 20,000 occupations. In England, special teachers work with "career offices" from employment agencies to give students job information and placement assistance.

The GAO found that the U.S. has a worldwide reputation for giving youth extensive opportunities to attend college, while at the same time providing inadequate preparation for employment of non-college-bound youth. The GAO concluded that approaches used by foreign governments have possibilities for improving U.S. education and training, though it cautions that implementation must be tailored to the United States' social and political characteristics. This same caution is made by several authors. Barton (1990) stated that there needs to be a national policy for transition, but implementation must be planned at the state and local levels rather through a national master plan.

There is a strong opinion by elitists in the U.S. that public schools should be modeled after foreign systems. One major component of some of those systems is *tracking*. Tracking does not give a person a second chance, which we tend to do in U.S. education. Tracking is repugnant to American citizens and should be avoided.

Based on the practices of foreign countries,

the GAO recommended policy directions that included expanding preschool and early intervention programs such as Head Start to help more needy youth; expanding compensatory programs such as Chapter I throughout the school year so that continuing special support will maintain student progress; and providing adequate education resources for all children as a means to improve their opportunity to achieve academic skills competency.

The GAO further recommended that all levels of government should promote school-employer linkages, particularly to expand combined education and work (apprenticeship-type) programs and to help youth obtain suitable entry-level employment. It called for standards and competency certification that can be applied to school and industry training programs.

Harrison and McLeish (1987), at the European Centre for the Development of Vocational Training, produced a handbook for practitioners to reinforce initiatives to assist youth in transition from school to working and adult life. In their examination of transition programs, they discovered many similarities of thought and practice.

In all programs, (1) achieving demands from national and local levels is the responsibility of the local community; (2) each program resulted from collaboration that did not come about until unemployment and radical economic changes forced people to respond; and (3) program initiators recognized that the transition to work is a part of a much larger process of transition to adult life. Based on these three similarities, Harrison and McLeish concluded that (1) the entire community should have as a firm goal ensuring that all youth, not just those identified as at risk, have access to an integrated range of transitional instruction and services taking into consideration local needs and local resources; (2) youth should have the best means of preparing themselves for life within rapidly changing economic and social conditions; and (3) the most cost effective use of instruction and service should be guaranteed.

Concerning the needs of youth, Harrison and McLeish state that transition programs must (1) provide students with easy access to information and advice concerning education,

training, employment, and social and personal issues; (2) ensure the immediate as well as the long-term relevance of what students learn and do; (3) be designed and organized by properly trained staff; and (4) address the question of social status concerning education and jobs to prevent future anger. The authors conclude that a transition program must (1) give a clear explanation about the range of educational and vocational choice available within the context of student ability and economic status; (2) have a commitment to acquire employment suitable to the students' education and ability; (3) use national and local funds to ensure that all youth have reasonable equality of opportunity regardless of where they live (including rural or inner city areas); and (4) provide a clear statement by states of guaranteed personal equality of opportunity during transition.

Local, state, and national resources must be used to design local initiatives that match the preferences of youth to the real opportunities of the labor market. For local planning to be cost efficient and effective, higher governing bodies must encourage local planning by funding, provide services via existing agencies, publicize programs, and provide economic and social information. In addition, young people must recognize that the labor market will not adjust itself to accommodate them, but rather that they must adjust to the needs of business and industry.

Hamilton (1986), in his article "Excellence and the Transition from School to Work," asked how young people move from school to work. His investigation of the literature and West German programs gave him insights into the problems of transition. Among them is the fact that employers do not hire high school graduates because they consider them irresponsible and poor risks—yet a few years later employers hire the same people, who still possess the same knowledge and skills they had when they graduated from school. Failing to find early employment leads to "floundering," which explains why so few believe the slogan "To get a good job, get a good education." High school graduates and dropouts hold the same type of jobs; the dropouts are simply less likely to obtain a job. Not until some time later does a high school diploma make any difference in obtaining a real job, one with a career ladder.

Hamilton concludes that the labor market conditions that lead to floundering make anyone inaccurate who blames either young people or high school vocational programs for vocational graduates' employment instability, low wages, and difficulty with beginning a career. He believes that 18-year-olds can step into adult careers given the opportunity and education. The education he recommends comes partially via vocational programs, and he agrees with the National Commission on Secondary Vocational Education recommendation to resist reforms that would eliminate vocational education and replace it with purely academic education. He points out that the Germans have a name for a malady called *Schulmudigkeit*, or "school weariness". The German system recognizes the problem and provides a solution by using workplaces as learning environments that connect academic instruction to the reality of working life.

Hamilton concluded that the American system should not be designed to produce skilled workers in high school but should instead enlist employers and nonprofit organizations to provide experiential education to motivate students for academic learning, which is required by employers. Educators should also exploit vocational education for academic purposes. This strategy would place students in the position of workers and learners—a role they will have as adults, as well.

The Organisation Economic Cooperation and Development (OECD) conducted a study (1983) of the transition experiences of handicapped adolescents. This study looked at programs in France, Norway, Sweden, Italy, and the United Kingdom. Unfortunately, the major finding was that the provision for the "handicapped school leaver" is the most deficient aspect in all school systems. In particular, insufficient numbers of career education teachers and counselors were found to conduct transition programs properly. However, in the overview of the project, three conclusions were given for the most effective way to provide transition for handicapped adolescents.

First, the acquisition of basic skills of lit-eracy and numeracy together with personal development for relating with others (i.e., social skills) is essential. Particular emphasis must go to teaching communication skills because of the restricted life many handicapped students have after school hours. In the final years of school, students must be given the opportunity to go into the community to develop confidence in coping with transportation, shopping, and so forth. Knowledge of financial procedures such as banking, job and pension benefits, and community and social services must also be taught.

Second, programs must include the introduction of cultural, leisure, and recreational activities that can be pursued after leaving school. Schools in many countries were found to provide a bridge that allows young people to continue their participation in youth or sports organizations after leaving school.

Third, during the final two years of school, students should gain familiarity with the world of work through career education that informs them of available opportunities in a realistic manner and through individual career counseling. Career education and career counseling are described as "universally acknowledged" for transition programs. The OECD report states that multidisciplinary reassessment is central to individualized career planning (ICP). Those responsible for reassessment and ICP should include people inside and outside the school.

Transition Program Traits

Cheek (1991) gave five traits of successful transition programs. First, students go through the career development stages and receive exploratory experiences, assistance with planning, and job preparation. Second, students are selected and placed in programs that meet their employment objectives and the corresponding requirements for success. Third, school-community cooperative efforts give students real-life observation and work experience and technical expertise. Fourth, vocational guidance and job search assistance are provided, and follow-up studies determine labor market demands and program effectiveness. Fifth, students obtain strong academic preparation.

Pullis (1991), in describing school-to-work transition programs for students with emotional/behavioral disorders identified six components, representing a consensus among professionals from a variety of disciplines: (1) comprehensive services that include all aspects of independent adult living; (2) early access (beginning no later than the junior high school year); (3) school program content that includes (a) functional academics that teach literacy, vocational knowledge, health, citizenship, basic life needs, (b) career/vocational programs including career exploration, specific vocational skills development, on-site supported training and job support, (c) living skills for independent living such as transportation, health/social services and leisure, and (d) integrated social/self-management skills (e.g., interpersonal relationships, personal growth and development of self-control/responsibility); (4) case management by an individual/agency to monitor each person through school and into adult life; (5) family focus to involve the family in planning and implementing transition; and (6) interagency cooperation in which state- and local-level mechanisms for decision making are made regarding funding, coordination of services, and continuum of options, all which are cost efficient.

Feichtner (1989), in *School-to-Work Transition for At-Risk Youth*, identified four principles for successful programs: (1) Several transition options must exist and be identified. (2) Services must be articulated to avoid duplication and omission. (3) Systematic procedures must be available for prescribing services and instruction appropriate for each person. (4) A system must be available for tracking large amounts of information.

Feichtner found several program and service barriers that compound the societal barriers confronting at-risk youth. There is no mandated systematic process for providing school-to-work transition services, especially for disadvantaged persons and those with limited English proficiency. Case managers are lacking for disadvantaged and LEP persons. Career exploration is lacking in middle schools. Agencies are not coordinating their efforts. Parents and consumers are confused about transition programs. Parents are not involved

enough. There is a shortage of adult service programs, especially in rural areas. There is no system to manage the information needed to make intelligent transition decisions and evaluate outcomes and costs.

Baiocchi (1991) identified 10 key attributes for success that must be incorporated into transition instruction: (1) know yourself, your skills, abilities, and limitations; (2) assume responsibility for your career (according to Baiocchi the single most important guideline for managing a career); (3) make a commitment by dedicating yourself (i.e., by being loyal to your job); (4) continue to learn by making up your mind that lifelong learning is essential to career success; (5) manage upwards by finding what your supervisor wants and helping the supervisor achieve these goals; (6) think ahead and set goals; (7) know more than you have to (how many times have you said or heard someone else say, "Do I have to know this or is it only school that expects this?); (8) do more than you have to; (9) understand the company's culture, its rules, and rewards system; and (10) maintain a balance between work, family, and friends.

Baiocchi's identified principles may be the hardest to teach. As observed by Sir Joshua Reynolds, a noted eighteenth-century philosopher and artist, "There is no expedient to which a man will not resort to avoid the real labor of thinking." Certainly, people will have to think to manage a career.

Models that Link School and Work

Programs for transition have been described previously. The March 1991 issue of *Vocational Education Journal*, devoted to the school-to-work transition, cites six models that are being financed by $10.5 million from the Department of Labor. (Information on these programs is available from the Office of Work-Based Learning, Employment and Training Administration, Department of Labor, Washington, DC 20201 (202-535-0540). The models are (1) the Pennsylvania Department of Commerce's curriculum for the metalworking industry; (2) the Los Angeles Unified School District, which links three major employers in telecommunications, banking, and public service to public schools; (3) the Boston Private Industry Council for careers in health care; (4) the Maryland Department of Economic and Employment Development, which has three projects concerning manufacturing technology, replacing high school general education with technical skills education, and preventing dropouts via career education and apprenticeship; (5) the National Alliance of Business with projects in San Francisco in banking and in DuPage County, Illinois, in appliance service repair; and (6) the Electronics Industry Foundation.

The National Center for Research in Vocational Education issued a report titled *Exemplary Urban Career-Oriented Secondary School Programs* (Benson, et al., 1990). While transition is not mentioned in this publication, the emphasis implies transition to work as well as college entrance. Schools in the metropolitan areas of New York, Chicago, and Los Angeles are described (e.g., New York's Aviation High School and the entrepreneurship program at Jan Addams High School; Chicago's High School for Agriculture Science and George Westinghouse Vocational High School; and Los Angeles's Downtown Business Magnet School and secondary math-science center at Marbonne Senior High School).

Transition Information for Special Needs Students

The Center on Education and Training for Employment conducted a project titled NETWORK to fulfill mandates of two 1990 federal acts: the Carl D. Perkins Vocational and Applied Technology Act and the Individuals with Disabilities Act (IDEA). The project's goal was to develop guidelines for school and agency personnel, parents, and employers to coordinate their support services to help youth with disabilities successfully complete the transition from school to work. The Targeting Employment Series was the result. Publications in that series include *Network for Effective Transitions to Work: A Transition Coordinator's Handbook*, a comprehensive guide for planning and implementing a transition program; *The Job Placement Assistance Kit*, for marketing students; *Work Skills Profession Set*, a resource manual on orientation to the world of work;

The Employer's Choice Professional Set, a multimedia set of materials for preparing students to meet employer hiring and retention standards; *Employment File*, tools for students applying for jobs; and *Transitions, Special Needs, and Vocational Education*. Videocassettes include *A Waiting Workforce*, for awareness teaching, and *Discovering an Untapped Work Force*, on employment success stories.

A major source of information concerning the transition from school to work has been sponsored by the U.S. Department of Education's Office of Special Education Programs, Office of Special Education and Rehabilitative Services. This project, called the Transition Research Institute at Illinois, is being conducted at the University of Illinois, College of Education. Yearly annotated bibliographies have been produced (Leach, et al., 1986, etc.; Harnisch, et al., 1989) that provide information on attitudes toward employment, career guidance, community integration, independent living, interagency cooperation, job placement, model programs, evaluation, rehabilitation counseling, transition models, vocational education, training, and so forth. Approximately 1,200 references are given, grouped under specific areas. Although the focus is on special education students, the principles may apply to all students. The project currently focuses on strategies to improve transition for special education youth (Chadsey-Rusch, 1988).

The National Center for Research in Vocational Education conducted a $4 million project to assist state and local administrators working with special needs youth and adults in their efforts to strengthen the transition to workplace and continuing education programs. One publication (Kallembach, 1989) from that project provides extensive information concerning literature on the school-to-work transition, assessment, career guidance and counseling, curriculum and instruction, interagency coordination, legislation, parental involvement, placement, personnel development, journals, newsletters, agencies, associations, centers for information/services, clearinghouses, computer-based information networks, data bases, transition projects, and research consortiums.

Skills Required by Today's Workforce

The most impressive publication concerning what skills are required by today's workforce is *Workplace Basics* by Carnevale, Gainer, and Meltzer (1990). This book resulted from a three-year, nationwide study by the American Society of Training and Development (ASTD) and the U.S. Department of Labor. Included in the text are required skills and suggestions on developing curriculum. The authors concluded that the essential skills needed by the workforce exceed the basic skills of reading, writing and computations. The economic importance and theoretical basis is explained for 16 basic workplace skills. Reference to other research is also made throughout the text to confirm or repudiate the findings of this study. Among the basic skills are foundation skills—learning to learn; technical competence skills—reading, writing and computation; communication skills—speaking, listening; adaptability skills—problem solving and creative thinking; developmental skills—self-esteem, motivation/goal setting; group effectiveness skills—team work and negotiation; influencing skills/organizational effectiveness and leadership skills—the skills needed to "navigate" in an organization, assume responsibility, and use personal strengths to complete a task; personal management skills; employability skills; and individual career planning skills.

Phillipi (1989) conducted extensive research in identifying basic skills for work. He concluded that workers need flexibility and "retrainability"—in other words, they need to know how to learn and to continue to learn throughout their lives. He states that school-to-work curriculum usually attempts to motivate secondary students to remain in school until graduation by offering part-time work and job placement. Pre-employment programs operate with the same instructional components and experiences, substituting a basic skills or GED preparatory section of curriculum for the secondary school student's academic classes. Instruction is designed to help students obtain jobs by teaching employability skills. However, such instruction seldom addresses the issues of the ongoing use of learning skills required for retaining a job. Phillipi recommends refocusing curriculum on basic skill requirements for successful performance and retraining on the job, which would enable students to become lifelong productive members of society. He notes that research has demonstrated that occupational skill applications differ significantly from traditional basic skills taught in the classroom. He gives occupational skills for reading, writing, computation, and problem solving, along with references for further investigation by the reader.

Phillipi suggests a five-point plan for educators to implement transition from school or employment training to the workplace for at-risk students. First, select targeted jobs in the community for/with students. Second, meet with local employers who currently offer these jobs or who project job openings in the near future. Have the employers identify critical job tasks for entry-level and mid-level promotable employees, based on organizational job productivity, accuracy, and safety records. Third, conduct literacy task analyses of four to six critical tasks for targeted positions through observation/interviews of competent workers. Fourth, develop lessons based on the analyses. (Estimate 10 hours of instruction per critical job task, and four to six tasks taught in a 12-week unit of instruction.) Fifth, follow up students' job performance with employers' evaluations, and visit work sites to observe changes in the workplace.

Hall's (1986) concern that work is central to understanding social order and social dynamics caused him to analyze work, define work, and identify forms and elements of work. He defined work as the effort or activity of an individual to provide goods or services of value to others (p. 13). Other writers have described work as that which gives an individual meaning and sustenance for life. Some even say that work a person does defines what what that person is.

Forms of work Hall identified are executive, professional, white collar, blue collar, service, skilled, unskilled, farm work, and housework. Following these descriptions of form, Hall explains the dimensions of work as individual, horizontal, vertical, gender, age, race and ethnic, organizational, power and institutional.

Examination of Carnevale, et al., Phillipi, and Hall provides a perspective of work and enables us to begin questioning the present curriculum. The questioning will probably result in a need for revision of curricula. I do not try in this chapter to specify new curricula, but rather suggest seeking the existing curriculum via the National Curriculum Network, Vocational Education Consortium of the States, Center for Occupational Research and Development, National Occupational Information Coordinating Committee, commercial publishers, and so forth.

Guidance and Counseling

Barton (1991) identified five obstacles that today's students face in receiving proper guidance and counseling: High school counselors work a disproportionate amount of time counseling the college bound; job placement is almost nonexistent (only 6 percent of high school counselors spend more than 30 percent of their time helping students find jobs); academic skills taught in school are often insufficient for the workplace; graduates usually have no way to demonstrate employment potential; and large firms that offer career paths to well-paid jobs no longer hire new high school graduates.

The importance of career/vocational guidance is certainly not being overlooked internationally. Several international conferences have been held; in particular, note the international conferences sponsored by Ashiya University in Japan.

The National Occupational Information Coordinating Committee (NOICC) developed *National Career Development Guidelines* due to changes in the economy and attitudes of employers and employees, as well as conditions found by such authorities as Barton. NOICC recognized that career development must be a comprehensive, systematic program available to all youth and adults throughout their life span. The guidelines are a competency-based approach to career development that serves as a blueprint for states, schools, colleges, and universities, and human service agencies to plan quality career guidance and counseling programs.

The guidelines have three major compo-

nents: competencies and indicators that describe the outcomes of career guidance and counseling programs; needed administrative support, physical facilities, and materials and equipment; and competencies needed by counselors and other staff to deliver career guidance and counseling programs. Competencies for students include self-knowledge, educational and occupational exploration, and career planning. Five handbooks have been developed for use in local planning in elementary, middle, high schools, postsecondary institutions and community and business organizations. (The guidelines can be obtained from the NOICC Training Support Center.)

In addition, NOICC developed and recently revised the Improved Career Decision Making Curriculum (ICDM). ICDM is designed to train counselors on sources of labor market information and their use in the career development process. The curriculum has 12 modules that include: "What Is Information and How Can We Access It?" "CIDS Occupational Projections," "Specific Needs of Adults, Women and Teen Parents," "Persons with a Disability," and "Children at Risk." (For information, contact the Vocational Studies Center, University of Wisconsin-Madison, 964 Educational Sciences Bldg., 1025 West Johnson St., Madison, WI 53706; telephone (608) 263-3696.) (*NOICC Training Support Center Bulletin*, Spring 1991)

Canada is launching a national career development program based on the estimate that 100,000 people are providing career counseling in Canada with marginal training in theory, curriculum knowledge, organization, and delivery techniques. Technology will be used extensively in this program (for example, videodiscs are being prepared to encourage occupational exploration and career planning). An allocation of $5.4 million has been made for the program. (Information is available from the Executive Director, Canadian Guidance & Counseling Foundation, Suite 202, 411 Roosevelt Ave., Ottawa, Ontario K2A 3X9, Canada.) (*NOICC Training Support Center Bulletin*, Spring 1991)

The Carl D. Perkins Vocational Education Act, P.L. 101-392, authorizes $20 million for career guidance and counseling programs, $15 million for community-based organizations,

$10 million for business/labor/education partnerships, and $9 million for community education. All of these programs have facilitating the school-to-work transition as their main goal. Strong guidance and counseling programs are required in these and other programs cited in this law. Unfortunately, most guidance and counseling programs are designed for college guidance and for counseling related to personal problems. In addition, college and university programs that produce guidance and counseling teachers focus on counseling psychology. People emerging from the college and university counseling psychology programs have little or no knowledge of vocational/career guidance or of the world of work as observed by me.

I recommend the NOICC Guidelines and ICDM as a way to improve the school to work transition. I also recommend that guidance counselors have at least three years of full-time work experience outside education before being employed in public or private education, to familiarize them with business/industry work requirements. A third recommendation involves restructuring college and university guidance and counseling programs to educate counselors to conduct vocational/career guidance.

Conclusion

The possibility of fully integrating quality school-to-work transition programs and services into the nation's public schools is very poor, in my opinion. To my knowledge, college and university teacher/administrator/educator faculty have the preparation of students for the world of work as the last thought on their minds, if they think of it at all. Faculty discussions concentrate on theory, philosophy, state certification requirements, administrative details and preparation of students to fulfill education requirements for graduation or further education. In 25 years as a university faculty member, I have never observed discussion of the preparation of youth for work at a school of education faculty meeting. Perhaps a reason for this lack of concern is that most faculty have never had a full-time job outside education, and many have never taught or administered in the schools for which they are preparing teachers and administrators, who

will be educating the youth of the nation. Another reason may be that the single criterion of success of schools is the number of high school graduates going to college. Consider the Doty and Hirsch study (1991) in which no data on non-college-bound youth was available from 12 "comprehensive" high schools in one of the richest school districts in the nation. As long as those teaching and administering the schools of this nation (who have little or no experience in business and industry) control the curriculum, school-to-work programs and services will only exist when the U.S. Congress funds such programs. With federal level funding removed, the curriculum returns to *academic* business as usual. Further research will remain concentrated on what occurs in the classroom rather than outside school and on questions concerning why schools are or are not incorporating into the curriculum what students need to know after leaving school. Therefore, the author recommends that all future teachers, guidance counselors, administrators, and college/university teacher educators have at least three years full-time work experience outside any educational institution before being allowed to enter public education.

Last, having reviewed the literature, interviewed hundreds of people, and conducted research, the one concept that seems outstanding in importance for helping every person make a good transition into work and life—and notable for not being mentioned anywhere—is helping each student have a dream. For without a dream (or goal) for life, people just drift, or as one person said, "flounder." Teachers and administrators might adopt a philosophy for teaching to help make the transition to work and life easier, a philosophy that I try to achieve: "Every child is the hopes and dreams of someone—make that someone you."

Thinking Exercises

The following observations resulted from my interviews with people from more than 20 states in many different occupations. I asked: "What should a young person know and/or be able to do when entering the world of work?" The responses could stimulate a very useful discussion.

- A person should know that a career is worth what it costs. In other words, if you don't invest effort, time, and money in a career, don't expect to have a good one.
- You only work for yourself, not someone else.
- The key to success is knowledge and work.
- You are worth what you know and what you can do for others.
- A question a person better ask is, what can I do that someone else will pay me money for doing?
- I don't know anyone who has a good life who didn't have to work hard.
- A good job is working for yourself, not someone else.
- If a person wants something, that person is going to have to work to get it. No one is going to give you anything. And you are not going to win the lottery—so don't day-dream.
- A person must learn to take risks.
- The more you know, the more flexible you are to meet change in life. We have too many people who have not continued their education to be able to change, and they have become bitter, unemployed people.
- You'd better make up your mind that you will have to go to some type of school all your life. For example, I have seen so many people join the armed service so they would not have to go to school—then they spend 25 percent of their time in the service going to school. The same would hold true if they obtained a job in some company.
- Peer pressure can ruin your life. Think for yourself. Ask yourself what you want from life.
- There is only one person who can make decisions about your future—you. This is what freedom is all about, the opportunity to take responsibility for one's self. Most people rely on someone else to make decisions and are very unhappy.
- The one thing I have learned after a lifetime is to prepare yourself so that you do not allow decisions about you to be made by someone else. For example, if

you do not learn math, someone else is going to be able to decide that you are not going into engineering school. You have lost your power to make decisions for yourself.
- A person must live conservatively and invest money early in life in sound investments (e.g., stocks) in order to have comfort in life.
- Don't turn down a job offer because you do not think you can succeed. The job offer has been made because you have been judged as capable of succeeding.
- The old saying "It's not what you know but who you know" is only half correct. Knowing someone may help you get the job, but you better know how to do the job or you will be fired.
- Honesty is the best policy. But it is hard to be honest at times when so many people are caught lying, such as the president of the United States. Keep your self-respect and stay honest—and stay out of jail.
- Confidence should be based on competence, not ego. Ego will only cause a person to fail.
- Persons who have "pride" usually have nothing else.
- Every job is useful and no job is better than another. If there were no waitresses how would you be served in a restaurant?

References

Baiocchi, D. P. (1991, Fall). Ten key principles of career success. *The Wall Street Journal, Managing Your Career,* pp. 5-6.

Barton, P. E. (1990). *Policy information report: From school to work.* Princeton, NJ: Educational Testing Service. (ERIC Document Reproduction Service No. ED 320 947)

Barton, P. E. (1991). The school-to-work transition. *Issues in Science and Technology, 7*(3), 50-54.

Benson, C. S. (Project Director). (1990). *Exemplary urban career-oriented secondary school programs.* Berkeley, CA: National Center for Research in Vocational Education.

Bracey, G. W. (1991, October). Why can't they be like we were? *Phi Delta Kappan, 7*(2), 104-117.

Bulletin. (1991, Spring). Salem, OR: NOICC Training Support Center (875 Union St., N.E., Salem, OR 97311; telephone: 503-378-8146).

Canadian Guidance & Counseling Foundation. *Creation and mobilization of counseling resources for youth project.* Ottawa, Ontario: Author.

Carnevale, A., Gainer, L. J., & Meltzer, A. S. (1990). *Workplace basics: The essentials employers want.* San Francisco: Jossey Bass.

Chadney-Rusch, J. (1989). *Project directors' annual meeting: Secondary Transition Intervention Effectiveness Institute.* Champaign, IL: University of Illinois. (ERIC Document Reproduction Service No. ED 318 167)

Cheek, G. (1991). What students really need: A 'work to work' transition. *School Shop / Tech Directions, 51* (4), 17-19.

Consortium for Educational Equity. (c1986). *72 is not enough: Did you know?* New Brunswick, NJ: Rutgers University.

Doty, C. R., & Hirsch, L. S. (1991, October). *Follow-up study of non-college-bound xxxxxxx county high school graduates, June 1990.* Unpublished research report, Rutgers University, New Brunswick, NJ. (ERIC Document Reproduction Service No. ED 351 548)

Edwards, J. P., Kimeldorf, M., & Bradley, C. (1988). *Secondary school to work transition research project emphasizing transition to work and leisure roles.* Portland, OR: Portland State University. (ERIC Document Reproduction Service No. ED 312 804)

Feichtner, S. H. (1989). *School-to-work transition for at-risk youth.* Information Series No. 339. Columbus, OH: ERIC Clearinghouse on Adult, Career, and Vocational Education. (ERIC Document Reproduction Services No. ED 315 666)

Final report on sixth international conference on vocational guidance. November 2-4, 1988. (1989). Ashiya, Hyogo, Japan: Secretariat of the International Conference on Vocational Guidance, Ashiya University. (Available from Secretariat of the International Conference on Vocational Guidance, Ashiya University, 13-22 Rokurokusocho, Ashiya, Hyogo, 659 Japan)

General Accounting Office, Division of Human Resources. (1990). *Training strategies. Preparing noncollege youth for employment in the U.S. and foreign countries.* Report to Congressional Requests. Washington, DC. (ERIC Document Reproduction Services No. 321 096)

Giroux, H. A., & Freire, P. (Eds.). Simon, R. I., Dippo, D., & Schenke, A. (1991). *Learning work: A critical pedagogy of work education.* Westport, CT: Bergin & Garvey.

Going to work. (1990). Madison, WI: Vocational Studies Center, University of Wisconsin. (ERIC Document Reproduction Service No. ED 304 523)

Hall, R. H. (1986). *Dimensions of work.* Beverly Hills, CA: Sage Publications.

Hamilton, S. F. (1986, November). Excellence and the transition from school to work. *Phi Delta Kappan, 68,* 239-242.

Harnisch, D. L., & Fisher, A. T. (1989). *Transition literature review: Educational, employment and independent living outcomes: Vol. 3.* Champaign, IL: Intervention Effectiveness Institute, University of Illinois. (ERIC Document Reproduction Service No. ED 315 984)

Harrison, J., & McLeish, H. (1987). *Young people in transition—The local investment. A handbook concerning the social and vocational integration of young people: Local and regional initiatives.* Berlin, Germany: European Centre for the Development of Vocational Training. (ERIC Document Reproduction Service No. ED 316 729)

NOICC Training Support Center Bulletin. (1991, Spring). (Available from NOICC Training Support Center, Oklahoma SOICC, Dept. of Vocational Technical Education, 1500 West 7th Ave., Stillwater, OK 74074; telephone: 800-654-4502).

Organisation for Economic Cooperation and Development. (1983). *The education of the handicapped adolescent: The transition from school to working life.* Paris, France: Centre for Educational Research and Innovation. (ERIC Document Reproduction Service No. ED 237 213)

Philippi, J. W. (1989). School to work transition for at-risk populations: How to bridge the gap. Paper presented at the Annual Convention of the International Reading Association, New Orleans, LA. (ERIC Document Reproduction Services No. ED 317 738)

Pullis, M. (1991). No bridges over troubled waters: Transition services for students with emotional/ behavioral disorders. *Missouri LINCletter, 14*(2), 1-4.

Realities of the future for males and females. (1991). *Gender Equity Notes.* New Brunswick, NJ: Consortium for Educational Equity, Rutgers University.

SETC Planning Committee. (1991, October 2). *White paper on New Jersey's united plan for the workforce readiness system.* Trenton, NJ: New Jersey State Employment and Training Commission.

Smith, R. C. (1983). *Institutionalizing the school to work transition.* Chapel Hill, NC: MDC, Inc. (ERIC Document Reproduction Service No. ED 246 140)

The Vocational Aspect of Education: A Journal of Vocational Education and Training. (Available from Triangle Books LTD, P.O. Box 65, Wallingford, Oxfordshire OX 10 OYG, United Kingdom).

Transition from school to work. Missouri LINC module. (Revised 1989-1990). Columbia, MO: University of Missouri. (ERIC Document Reproduction Service No. ED 321 145)

Vocational Technical Education Consortium of States (VTECS). ACROS. Decatur, GA: Author. (VTECS catalogs of job analyses available on computer disks, Automated Cross Referencing Occupational System [ACROS], $75 per set or $10 per search. Telephone: 800-248-7701, or write VTECS, Commission on Occupational Education Institutions, Southern Assn. of Colleges and Schools, 1866 Southern Ln., Decatur, GA 30033-4097).

20

The Role of Guidance Counselors in Improving School-to-Employment Transition Experiences

W. John Kozinski

In the last decade of the twentieth century, the vocabulary of the new technology and the workplace continues to expand rapidly. *Statistical quality control, participative management, customer service,* and *just-in-time production* are just a few of the new concepts shaping the world of work. Will employees now entering the workplace bring with them skills that will allow them to compete and prosper in the new global economies? What role will schools, and more specifically the high school guidance counselor, play in improving school-to-employment transition? Contrary to current popular beliefs, in the 1990s the United States will face a human capital deficit among both new and experienced workers. This shortage of workers threatens business and industry's economic competitiveness and will act as a formidable barrier to the individual opportunity of all Americans.

The United States presently faces a startling demographic dilemma which is not likely to dissipate soon. The pool of 16 to 24 year olds, which has always been the source of new workers, is shrinking, and as a result industry and business will have to hire less-qualified workers to fill the entry-level workforce. The current surplus of well-educated job seekers anxious to begin new jobs will evaporate. In the near future, there will likely be further shrinkage in the number of well-educated young Americans seeking jobs.

This imminent demographic development is on a collision course with the idea that employees can quickly adapt to new technologies. Also, the ability of employees to acquire new skills is now recognized as an indispensable ingredient in employers' ability to retain a competitive edge in a global economy.

It is becoming increasingly apparent that there exist serious deficiencies in basic workplace skills. These skill deficiencies constitute significant barriers not only to entry-level employees, but also experienced employees, as well as dislocated workers attempting to adapt to technological change.

Perhaps those most affected by deficiencies in workplace skills are minority youths in the inner city who must struggle especially hard to join the economic mainstream. Many inner-city high school students in America are members of a minority group. They require the most attention from schools and industry, because they will form the backbone of the future workforce.

Diverse Roles of Guidance Counselors

In education today, there is considerable confusion concerning (1) the proper role of education in society, (2) the concrete responsibilities the educational system should shoulder, (3) the place of counseling, and (4) the nature of guidance.

School counseling emerged from early vocational guidance efforts and is a purely American invention. The need to place people in the labor force of the early twentieth century and to provide moral guidance gave school counseling its start. In the 1920s and 1930s, standardized testing programs assisted counselors with the job placement process. Also added to the tasks of the school counselor at that time was the enforcement of compulsory attendance laws.

When the Russians launched Sputnik in 1957, American's educational system was awakened. Encouraging academically talented students became a high national priority, and emphasis went to college placement. In addition, the National Defense Education Act gave many classroom teachers the opportunity to return to college and be trained as school counselors in quickly assembled counselor education programs. Many of these programs lacked common purpose, coherent philosophy, and the development of relevant skills. A highly touted counseling approach was the client-centered therapy that used a one-to-one approach. Newly trained counselors reentered their school setting to encounter teachers and other educators who saw them as having an abundance of free time to assume the paperwork associated with college admissions. In many instances the school principals further burdened the counselors with quasi-administrative work related to the day-to-day operation of the school.

In 1959, in the book *The American High School Today,* James B. Conant advocated large comprehensive high schools. He also advocated appointing one full-time counselor for every 250 students, a number that still serves as a guide in many school districts. Conant's ideas had a tremendous impact on public schools across the United States. The consolidation of small school districts into larger ones caused a disruption of many natural communities. The newly created large high schools resulted in a depersonalized atmosphere, which created new problems.

The 1960s, along with the war in Vietnam and the struggle for civil rights, introduced great social change. Increasingly, the public viewed schools as an instrument to restructure society. With the heightened social awareness of the civil rights era, many looked to guidance counselors to reduce the effects of stereotyped choice making in regard to career selection. The "do your own thing" attitude and the rapid increase in drug use among high school students caused a rise in conflict among students, parents, and school staff. Group sessions, as an alternative to one-to-one counseling, gained credibility. Early intervention and prevention began to be discussed, and elementary school counseling came into existence.

The 1970s brought increased federal legislation on issues affecting education: busing-related legislation, the Career Guidance and Counseling Act, Title IX, antidiscrimination legislation, and the most far reaching in its impact, Public Law 94-142. P.L. 94-142 legislated, among other things, the mainstreaming of special education students. The seventies and the eighties also brought along further development of early intervention and prevention. Teachers and counselors gained access to volumes of new research materials on decision making, career education, substance-abuse prevention, and self-development.

Over the years, the role of the school counselor moved from one of advisor, to one of therapist, to the present one of facilitator/problem solver/decision maker/personal development educator.

Currently, the New York State Department of Education is in the final stages of implementing its Regents Action Plan, a plan for state reform of education. The plan encompasses educational laws, rules of the Board of Regents and the Regulations of the Commissioner of Education. The plan details guidance and counseling in this way:

1. Each nonpublic secondary school shall provide a guidance and counseling program to students in grades 7-12.
2. Each public school district shall have a guidance program for all students.
3. In grades 7-12, the guidance program shall include an annual review of each student's educational progress and career plans. This review by certified licensed school counselors must take place with students individually or in small groups. The program must also

include instruction at each grade level to help students learn about careers and career planning skills. It is conducted by a school counselor or by teachers in cooperation with school counselors. Advisory and individual or group counseling assistance must be provided to enable students to benefit from the curriculum, to help them develop and implement postsecondary education and career plans, and to help students who exhibit any attendance, academic, behavioral, or adjustment problems. Parental involvement should be encouraged and should include activities which enable parents to work with their schools in achieving desired student outcome.

4. Each school district shall develop a plan which describes how the district will comply with the regulation.

As prescribed by the above regulations, the Buffalo Public Schools have developed a K-12 guidance plan of their own. The plan sets forth a comprehensive program based on developmental learning theory and established principles and practices of guidance and counseling. It prescribes the delivery of services to all students including special education pupils. This plan is designed to maximize the educational and career development of students and to provide them with the knowledge and ability to make life and career decisions which will be fulfilling and productive.

Buffalo's K-12 guidance program uses the Three-C guidance model for delivery of services.

- **C1—counseling** –is the most intense part of this model and includes individual and small group counseling with students.
- **C2—consultation** –is less intense and involves consultation and dialogue with significant others in the student's life to assist the student in goal setting, problem solving, and decision making.
- **C3—coordination** –is the least intense component and involves planning and coordinating a variety of guidance programs for and with school and community organizations.

In sum, the Buffalo Public Schools' Guidance Program aims at helping the student become informed, aware, and fully able to exploit the many aspects of the school's services, functions, and related institutions. In the best instance, the student will learn to make sound choices and reach realistic decisions, which will contribute to success in after-high-school endeavors.

Career and Vocational Guidance

The principle factor which confronts all senior high school students is the reality of the rapidly approaching transition from high school to the independence of young adulthood. Like other factors in decision making, reality is here defined as the many alternatives facing the individual on the threshold of postsecondary school life and the consequences the alternatives chosen will have on the individual's life.

Edwin Herr (1979) identifies six possible scenarios facing students as they leave high school:

1. Selecting a post high school or technical school to pursue a skilled specialty.
2. Gaining acceptance to a college and selecting a field of study that will have great implications for later vocational endeavors.
3. Converting part-time work experience while in school into full-time employment after graduation.
4. Entering the labor market by taking a first full-time job.
5. Contemplating military service, marriage, combining work and continuing education.
6. Entering an apprenticeship program.

In spite of this variety of options, for a number of students none of these possibilities will seem appealing and the future will feel like a threat or trauma. For some, thinking about the future beyond high school represents a confrontation that will result in indecisiveness. Other students will find the burden of decision-making too great and will try to avoid or postpone making important decisions. Since individual high school students will have different levels of career maturity, career guidance activities must rest on the assumption that many young people will require special assistance with coping effectively with the process of selecting an occupation and establishing a "career."

Career guidance activities must have three areas of emphasis: stimulating career development, providing treatment, and aiding placement. The last area refers to student movement from high school to the world of adulthood. It must be recognized that in terms of career development some senior high school students will be more mature than other high school students. Whichever of the three areas of career guidance emphasis is implemented, a counselor must know where the student stands in career development and which needs to meet at a given time. The treatment of needs may include providing reassurance, information, reality testing, emotional release, attitude clarification, or work exposure.

According to popular wisdom, Freud in his later years defined maturity as the "capacity to work and love." Some 50 years earlier, the Russian writer Leo Tolstoy suggested that "one can live magnificently in this world if one knows how to work and how to love, to work for the person one loves and to love one's work" (Troyat, 1967). Since the capacity to work is fundamental to growth during the adult years, career development programming is vital and is the ultimate concern with helping young people to discover and pursue their work. Holland (1974) details four kinds of vocational problems and addresses how most people cope with them during their lifetime:

1. They must decide what occupation to enter, or take a job by default due to poverty, prejudice, lack of education, and so forth.
2. They must secure the training required to enter their chosen occupation, or by default enter whatever occupation is available.
3. They must learn to cope with a lifetime of job changes, when to move sideways or upward, how to cope with involuntary job changes, and when to taper off or retire.
4. For each job held, a person must learn to cope successfully with the work itself, fellow workers, supervisors, and subordinates.

In summary, every job presents occupa-tional, interpersonal, and emotional problems that can lead either to achievement, support, and satisfaction, or to lack of fulfillment, failure, and alienation. Schools and the counselor community *must* provide appropriate career education, especially in American cities. Career education, with its obvious relevance, immediate practicality, and extended options offers the best chance to make secondary education more responsive to the economic and social needs of all students, especially those in the minority population.

Over the years, many career education models have been devised. Many of them have been extended from kindergarten to graduate school. The United States Office of Education (1976) developed a school-based comprehensive career education model. The original goals of the school-based model were to develop within each student the following traits: (1) a sense of purpose and direction; (2) a concept of self, which is in keeping with a work-oriented society; (3) basic skills and knowledge; (4) positive attitudes toward work, school, and society, and a sense of satisfaction resulting from successful experience in these areas; (5) personal characteristics of self-respect, self-reliance, perseverance, initiative, and resourcefulness; (6) a realistic understanding of the relationships between the world of work and education; (7) a comprehensive awareness of career options in the world of work; (8) the ability to enter employment in an appropriate occupation at the productive level and/or to pursue further education.

These goals are progressively sequenced, starting with career awareness in the elementary grades, career exploration in the junior high school, and career preparation in the senior high school grades. Table 1 shows a graphic representation of the matrix of elements used in the school-based model.

Career education has shown that no single group of educators accomplishes all of the objectives in the complex delivery system. But no other group of specialists is more important to the goals of career education than guidance personnel. Other representatives of the school, community, or family may ignite a spark of career awareness. However, it remains the central task of career guidance to help indi-

Table 1—Comprehensive Career

Elements of Career Education		Element Outcomes Education
Career awareness	K----------12	Career identity
Self-awareness	K----------12	Self-identity
Appreciation attitudes	K----------12	Self-social fulfillment
Decisionmaking skills	K----------12	Career decisions
Economic awareness	K----------12	Employment skills
Employability skills	K----------12	Career placement
Educational awareness	K----------12	Educational identity

viduals identify their career options, understand implications, plan the educational experience necessary to achieve their goals, and sharpen the decision-making process. In 1973, a joint position paper of the Commission of the American Vocational Association and the National Vocational Guidance Association (Commission on Career Guidance and Vocational Education) recommended and outlined the responsibilities of what they called the guidance team. This team would comprise counselors and related specialists. Their responsibilities would be to:

- Coordinate the career guidance programs.
- Provide staff with the understanding necessary to help each student obtain a full competency-based learning experience.
- Coordinate the acquisition and use of appropriate occupational, educational, and labor market information.
- Help staff plan for sequential student learning experiences in career development.
- Identify and coordinate the use of school and community resources needed to facilitate career guidance.
- Coordinate job placement programs for the school and provide for job adjustment counseling.
- Provide individual and group counseling and guidance to students to stimulate and continually interrelate their experiences, knowledge, understanding, skills, and appreciation as they grow and develop throughout their lives.

Skills Sought by Employers

In the 1990s, significant economic, social, and demographic changes will strongly affect the nation's schools, families, and workplaces. Because of these developments, there is renewed interest in the acquisition of basic skills. The National Commission on Excellence in Education titled its report on the need for educational reform *A Nation at Risk: The Imperative for Educational Reform*. The report pointed out that an inadequacy in basic skills will hamper the labor force in adapting to the new changes which new production technologies bring forth every day.

The two separately listed national problems–inadequate schools and economic competitiveness–are closely intertwined. They contain a common theme: the importance of basic skills and the need for concerted national effort to address the nation's competitiveness in a global market economy. Hardly a day passes without a newspaper or magazine referring to the competitiveness issue or the ineptness of our schools. A Labor Department study recently stated that half of all American students do not have sufficient skills to successfully enter the job market, even in an entry-level, blue-collar job. These skills include the ability to read diagrams and manuals, to write memos that justify expenses or interpret graphs, to maintain numerical records and interpret statistics, to reason how these things fit together, and to work with other people to solve daily problems in the world of business and industry (Rankin, 1991).

Students who begin to acquire basic skills early in their educational career do better in school, at work, and in other areas of their lives. They will more likely perform well in school, earn a high school diploma, enroll in and complete college, work more hours, earn higher wages, be more productive workers, and avoid bearing children out of wedlock.

Conversely, those who lack basic skills will more likely be school dropouts, jobless, teenage parents, on welfare, and involved in crime (Berlin and Sum, 1988). In short, basic skills play an important role in the future well-being of workers, families, businesses, and the nation itself.

Our nation has already taken the first steps toward addressing basic workplace skills deficiencies. The combined voices in education, business, and government are joined increasingly in a dialogue aimed at repairing the damage done and meeting the challenge of basic skills deficiencies.

Employers are beginning to see that to retain competitiveness they must help current and future workers achieve competence in workplace basics. More and more, American business will no longer enjoy the luxury of selecting skilled employees from a large labor pool. Less-skilled employees will be hired and employers will have to help build individual competencies in the basics.

New technologies have created both opportunities and problems for employers. The employer's competitive edge relies increasingly on how effectively and efficiently workers and machines are integrated into the production cycle. Success depends on how quickly workers can accumulate new skills, and the acquisition of technical skills requires a solid grounding in the basics. While advancing technologies may eliminate some jobs, they also increase the range of skills needed to perform jobs that remain.

Many employers say that the most important skills for any employer are the three "R's": reading, writing, and arithmetic. However, with further probing, we find that businesses seek good basic academic skills and much more. They believe that basic workplace skills deficiencies are beginning to affect their bottom line. Thus, it is pertinent to know the nature of these skills. A U.S. Labor Department report, *Workplace Basics: The Skills Employers Want* (1988), identifies seven skills prescribed for a well-rounded worker who can acquire more sophisticated skills as necessary:

- Foundation–knowing how to learn
- Competence in reading, writing, and computation

- Oral communication–listening and speaking
- Adaptability–creative thinking and problem solving
- Personal management–self-esteem, goal setting, motivation, and personal/career development
- Group effectiveness–interpersonal skills, negotiation, and teamwork
- Influence–organizational effectiveness and leadership

The accumulation of knowledge is respected and encouraged, but students rarely learn the principles that prepare them to apply information effectively. Knowing how to learn is the most basic of all skills, because it is the key that unlocks future success. An individual who knows how to learn can achieve competence in all other basic workplace skills from reading through leadership. Without this skill, learning does not progress as rapidly and as efficiently.

The three basic academic skills–reading, writing, and computation–have always been recognized as the key ingredients to success in society and the workplace. But today's world of work involves interaction with sophisticated, computerized machines that require good reading skills for efficient use, thus making acquisition of those skills more important and complex. In a traditional school setting, reading instruction is often designed to teach discrete reading skills in isolation, for the purpose of increasing a student's ability to follow directions or memorize data for future recall. Reading skills in the world of work take on a different form. They require the reader to analyze information, to summarize it and to monitor his or her own comprehension of the reading task. The traditional approach to teaching writing is based on description and on the articulation of learned responses concerning facts and events. Conversely, workplace writing requires analysis, conceptualization syntheses with clear articulation of points and proposals. Similarly, in schools mathematical instructions are presented sequentially, beginning with fundamental concepts and working through to higher level operations such as geometry and algebra. In the workplace, these math skills are taught contextually to reflect their actual use on the job; instructional materials simulate specific job tasks, and emphasize problem identification, reasoning, estimation, and problem solving.

Writing, reading, and computing are essential communication tools, but it is through listening and speaking that people interact most frequently. Recent studies indicate that only job knowledge ranks above listening and oral communications skills as a factor for workplace success.

Problem-solving skills and creative thinking hold the key to any organization's ability to achieve its strategic objectives. The level of these skills quickly determines how a company can improve productivity and competitiveness. Problem-solving skills include the ability to recognize and define problems, invent and implement solutions, and track and evaluate results.

An individual's productivity and effectiveness in the workplace can be linked directly to positive self-esteem and successful personal management. A good self-image relates to the ability to take pride in one's work. The capability to set goals and meet them helps an individual increase production quotas and meet deadlines. Career development and personal skills become apparent through the pursuit of higher training and education.

The use of teams in the workplace has steadily increased in the last decade. The team approach is linked to increased productivity and product quality, as well as an increased quality of work life. Whenever people work together, the success of the group depends on effective interpersonal skills, focused negotiations, and a sense of group purpose.

Employees' effectiveness in an organization rests on their actions that affect the organization and its strategic objectives. A skilled worker can function as a master problem solver, an innovator, and a team builder. Businesses that cultivate organizational effectiveness and employee leadership skills will succeed in tomorrow's workplace.

The School-to-Work Transition: What Can Be Done?

Some scholars have defined adolescence as an artifact of a changing economic scene.

Before the Industrial Revolution, young people were expected to take on adult responsibilities much earlier. But at the turn of the century, child labor laws put an end to the economic exploitation of children. In addition, workers were plentiful in relation to available work, and as the workplace demanded a better prepared labor force, young people were, in effect, declared surplus. The extended educational system was put in place to teach them but also, in part, to occupy their time outside the economic market. This period of extended learning has grown longer and longer. Today, the youth-to-adulthood transition for many young people lasts into the mid-twenties and beyond.

A universally recognized guideline in America holds that a college education provides the best route to economic security and prosperity. From elementary school on, parents, teachers, and others encourage students to strive for a college education. Clearly, college experience will pay off handsomely for many graduates. However, a college degree is not the only way to develop the talents of tomorrow's workforce. A 1988 report, *The Forgotten Half,* estimates that approximately 20 million youth between 16 and 24 years of age will not have the opportunity to gain a college education. They will enter a work environment that, in most cases, is hostile to those without experience, training, or postsecondary education. Currently, many opportunities for financial assistance are available to those choosing the college path, but very little is done for those who do not go on to postsecondary education. However, non-college-bound youth also aspire to success—to a career in a workplace that offers economic security and the ability to raise a family and become productive members of the community. However, these young people will receive very little help from any quarter in making the transition from school to work. This will result in economic hardship for many, reduced productivity for the nation, and a waste of human resources. On the economic scale, the earning potential of non-college-bound youth has deteriorated. Their real earnings dropped 28 percent from 1973 to 1986, and the gap between their earnings and those of college graduates widened (Barton, 1990).

The federal budget cuts of the 1980s eliminated job counseling services in many high schools. For more than two decades, the federal government provided in-school testing, counseling, and job placement services for high school seniors as part of the Public Employment Service. At its peak in 1963, this program served 600,000 students in more than half of the nation's high schools. Recently, the U.S. Department of Labor has assigned a high priority to improving the school-to-work transition. Its employment and training administration has established a new Office of Work-Based Learning, to serve as a focal point for the department's job and training partnerships with the private sector. One of its principal tasks will be to assist young people with their school-to-work transition so they can move into productive careers and upgrade their skills.

In the past, school counselors were the primary school personnel who delivered career counseling services. However, school counselors have become a target for criticism by both insiders and outsiders. Outsiders complain that they are biased towards non-college-bound youth. Insiders complain that the numbers of students per counselor is too large, and that the weight of noncounseling administrative duties renders their jobs impossible. Among youth-serving and social service agencies and some high schools, a new type of counselor is emerging. In several cities, counseling services use the school-to-work approach for training the dropout prone or high-risk students and to help keep them in school.

Barton (1990) identifies several innovative initiatives at the state and local levels:

- Missouri's employment service has assigned a full-time career counselor to each vocational-technical high school. The counselor provides instruction in pre-employment skills, and job search help.
- The Arizona Employment Service provides two career development and job placement services for in-school and out-of-school 16-to-21-year-olds. This program is co-sponsored through the State Education Department and the Job Training Partnership Act.

- The Rhode Island Job Service operates a program for high school seniors on a statewide basis. It is a career exploration and job skill and search instruction program.
- In New York state, the Youth Opportunity Centers together with a program called the New York City Partnership, provide high school students with computerized occupational information, job search workshops, and a resource center to develop career plans. The counselors develop full- and part-time work for current students and graduates.

Most developed countries have highly structured institutional systems to help young people make the transition from school to work—this is not a matter left to chance. Germany does it through an apprenticeship system, combining classroom work and on-the-job instruction. In Japan, schools themselves refer students to employers. In other developed countries, there is a strong employment counseling and job placement function within the school system. In the United States, there are schools that have developed good linkages to the world of work. These are found in the guidance offices of vocational schools or a natural operation of cooperative education programs. In addition, computerized career information programs have been installed in many of these schools. The number of distinct job titles found in business, industry, and government is enormous. Yet students' knowledge about these jobs is limited. These user friendly, computer-driven programs give young people access to information regarding future careers.

In spite of these various attempts to provide career information and assistance for young non-college-bound youth, the current situation needs much improvement. In a national study authored by Chapman and Katz (1981), the high school counselor's role in *employment* counseling plays a minor role in his or her busy schedule. Helping students choose their school courses receives the most attention from counselors, followed by college selection and the admission process, followed by attendance and discipline problems. Next comes assistance in occupational choices and career planning. Dead last is job placement.

While in some schools counselors do help non-college-bound students, their primary services are clearly directed to other functions.

The last decade brought to American education reforms that targeted content, and transition-to-work themes disappeared from the high school curriculum. In the last decade of this century, schools and counselors must again focus their resources to help the youth of America bridge the school-to-work transition in a radically new global economic system.

References

Barton, P. E. (1990). *From school to work*. Princeton, NJ: Educational Testing Service, Policy Information Center.

Berlin, G., & Sum, A. (1988). *Toward more perfect union: Basic skills, poor families and our economic future*. New York: Ford Foundation.

Buffalo Public School System. (1988). Kindergarten through twelfth grade guidance plan. Unpublished report, Buffalo, NY: Board of Education.

Chapman, W., & Katz, M. R. (1981). *Survey of career information systems in secondary schools*. Princeton, NJ: Educational Testing Service.

Clyde, J. S. (1979). *Computerized career information and guidance systems*. Columbus, OH: National Center for Research in Vocational Education.

Coleman, J. S. (1974). *Youth: Transition to adulthood*. Report of the Panel on Youth of the President's Science Advisory Committee. Chicago: University of Chicago.

Commission on Work, Family and Citizenship. (1988). *The forgotten half: Non-college youth in America*. Washington, DC: William T. Grant Foundation.

Conant, J. B. (1959). *The American high school today*. New York: McGraw Hill.

Eurich, A. C. (1981). *Major transitions in the human life cycle*. Lexington, MA: D.C. Heath.

Herr, E. L., & Cramer, S. H. (1979). *Career guidance through the life span*. Boston: Little Brown.

Herr, E. L. (1977). *Guidance and counseling, vocational education research and development*. Columbus OH: National Center for Research in Vocational Education.

Holland, J. L. (1973). *Making vocational choices: A theory of careers*. Englewood Cliffs, NJ: Prentice-Hall.

Hoyt, K. B. (1990, Fall). *A proposal for making transition from schooling to employment an important component of educational reform. Future choices*. Washington, DC: Youth Policy Institute.

National Commission on Excellence in Education. (1983). *A nation at risk: The imperative for educational reform*. Washington, DC: U.S. Department of Education.

Office of Career Education. (1976). *Career education in the public schools 1974-1975. A national study*. Washington, DC: Author.

Pautler, A. J., Jr. (Ed.). (1990). *Vocational education in the 1990s: Major issues*. Ann Arbor, MI: Prakken Publications.

Rankin, R. A. (1991, July 3). U.S. students lacking real-world job skills, labor study concludes. *Buffalo News*.

Troyat, H. (1967). *Tolstoy*. New York: Doubleday.

U.S. Department of Labor, Employment and Training Administration. (1988). *Workplace basics: The skills employers want*. Washington, DC: Author.

21

Curriculum Considerations to Improve School-to-Employment Transition

David J. Pucel

In the final analysis, curriculum is what schools offer to students in the form of courses and other experiences to prepare them for the future. If curriculum is developed with the view that preparation for employment is important, school-to-employment transition can receive constant reinforcement. However, there has been a continuing historical debate about the major purposes of schools and the role of preparation for employment in America. The debate has focused on which type of education will best prepare students for the future. Within this debate, education for employment has traditionally received relatively low priority.

The Past

Historically, schools have not emphasized education for employment. As a consequence, the federal government has had to provide incentive subsidies to states and to local school districts to include education for employment in the curriculum. Large-scale subsidies began in 1917 with the passage of the Smith-Hughes Act and continued with subsequent legislation in the form of reimbursement for teacher equipment and related expenses for "vocational education" programs. Originally, programs were subsidized to provide training that focused on preparing students for specific occupations. The occupations centered around the home, farm, and industry. Later, the range of occupations was broadened to include essen-

tially all occupations that required less education than a baccalaureate degree. Curricula were most often developed around specific job skill requirements, and many believed that the best way to train people was to use the types of equipment and materials they would encounter on the job or in the home. Training usually focused on the hands-on activities performed on the job, along with knowledge needed to perform the activities. If a problem occurred with the curriculum, "the traditional way to address such problems [was] to upgrade equipment and tailor the curriculum more closely to the needs of employers" (Rosenstock, 1991, p. 434). Since such training took a substantial amount of time, students were expected to enroll in their vocational programs for approximately three hours a day.

During this same time period, there was a recognition that students, other than those who wished to receive specific job training, also required some orientation to the types of skills and knowledge found in employment. Therefore, additional general education counterparts to vocational education programs were included in the curriculum. Those programs were viewed as part of the general education curriculum for all individuals. They included subjects such as industrial arts (technology education), business education, and home economics. The purpose of these programs was not to prepare students for jobs, but to provide them with general skills, occupational awareness, and career exploration. Often these programs contained content that sampled various occupational skills. Because participation in one or more of these programs was mandatory for most students as part of their high school education, students received some skills that facilitated school-to-employment transition.

During the 1970s, an attempt was made to reorganize schools and to develop curricular innovations to foster school-to-employment transition. The movement became known as "career education" (Hoyt, 1982; Marland, 1971). It recognized the need to start the process of thinking about and preparing for careers early in life. It fostered occupational exploration and awareness for all students throughout the curriculum. Although it had the support of the federal government, it eventually disappeared as a movement. However, the concept of transition from school to employment was further clarified and made more visible.

With further rapid changes in society from the industrial age to the information age, the composition of the workforce changed and the amount of training and breadth of education needed for adequate preparation for new jobs increased. The wisdom of having specific job training for employment in K-12 schools was increasingly questioned as the best approach to high school preparation for employment. Some argued that students were spending so much time in vocational programs that they could not take the academic subjects they needed for future success. Others argued that specific job training in the high schools could not adequately prepare students for employment. They called for delaying such job specific training until after high school. Some said that the types of employment-related skills that would be most useful to the widest range of students were not specific job skills but more generic skills. The final result has been a continual decrease in the commitment to prepare students for specific jobs through traditional K-12 vocational education programs. With this reduced commitment there has been a reduction in federal subsidies for job-specific vocational training programs in high schools.

Within the current debate of the purposes of schools, the debate over the role of vocational education and preparation for the school-to-employment transition is again a focal point of education reform. Some continue to believe that schools should focus on preparing students for general living and that the best way to do that is to give them a liberal education. Some believe that schools should concentrate on math and science to prepare students to enter a world facing technological competition and that the best way to do that is to teach students the basics of math and science. Still others believe qualification for employment is an implied promise of education and would, therefore, focus on implications for future employment. As the debate continues, the role of vocational education is evolving. Vocational education attempts to define the unique role it might play within the current context of reform.

Contextual Influences

A number of important events have occurred that are impacting vocational education and creating a new view of preparation for employment. Recent critics of education have expressed concern that students should be better prepared in basic skills and traditional academic subjects (e.g., Carnegie Task Force, 1986). They suggest that students in the United States are falling behind students in other countries. This group has influenced policymakers to include in the curriculum more rigorous requirements for academic courses and foreign languages. These new requirements have occupied most of the curricular space, and other subjects like vocational education, music, and art have been forced to compete for what remains. Recently there has also been an increasing belief that education must be functional in preparing youth for everyday living and employment. Concentrating on rote learning and testing of isolated skills is becoming viewed as an insufficient basis for education. This movement has not minimized the need for academic skills; however, it is concerned about how they are taught. Newmann summarizes this new concern around what he calls "authentic achievement":

The kinds of skills required to earn school credits, good grades, and high scores on typical tests are often considered trivial, meaningless, and contrived—both by students and adults. In contrast, a "restructured" vision of the goals of education seeks to evaluate performance activities that are worthwhile, significant, and meaningful: in short, activities that are authentic. (Newmann, 1991, p. 459)

The emphasis on academics and the need for authentic experiences was viewed by some as an excellent opportunity for academic and vocational education to cooperate. This has brought about a movement toward integrating academic and vocational education. Initial discussions of this concept seemed to focus on teaching academic skills in a vocational education context. Models were proposed where an academic teacher (e.g., math teacher) and a vocational education teacher would work together to develop real applications of the academic (e.g., math) content. Using this model, work-related examples are developed to demonstrate applications of academic subjects. This movement provides an excellent approach to making academic subjects more relevant to everyday life and employment. However, it tends to suggest that there is no unique content related to preparation for employment that should be taught. Preparation for employment is approached solely through the demonstrated relevance of academic subjects during employment. This approach has had a great deal of appeal because it functionally relates academic subjects to the real world. The following quote exemplifies this model:

> Pursuing integration with academic education requires us to adopt a different view: that vocational education is a different way to learn the same academic concepts and skills that nonvocational students learn. Vocational teachers see students demonstrate competence, thinking ability, and creativity in a vocational setting that some of them are unable to demonstrate in an academic setting or on a standardized test. (Rosenstock, 1991, p. 435)

The America 2000 plan proposed by the Bush administration for revising American schools acknowledges not only that subject matter should be taught in a way that allows students to see its functional use, but that there exists a unique body of content related to preparing students for their transition from school to employment. That plan required the Secretary of Labor to establish the Secretary's Commission on Achieving Necessary Skills (SCANS) for employment. The report produced by the commission (U.S. Department of Labor, 1991, p. xv) presented a list of five competencies and three foundation skills necessary for employment (see Table 1). The

Table 1—SCANS Competencies and Foundation Skills

Competencies effective workers can use:

Resources—allocating time, money, materials, space, and staff
Interpersonal Skills—working on teams, teaching others, serving customers, leading, negotiating, and working well with people from culturally diverse backgrounds
Information—acquiring and evaluating data, organizing and maintaining files, interpreting and communicating, and using computers to process information
Systems—understanding social, organizational, and technological systems, monitoring and correcting performance, and designing or improving systems
Technology—selecting equipment and tools, applying technology to specific tasks, and maintaining and troubleshooting technologies

The foundation competence requires:

Basic Skills—reading, writing, arithmetic and mathematics, speaking and listening
Thinking Skills—thinking creatively, making decisions, solving problems, seeing things in the mind's eye, knowing how to learn, and reasoning
Personal Qualities—individual responsibility, self-esteem, sociability, self-management, and integrity (U.S. Department of Labor, 1991, p. vii)

commission indicated that "[t]he message was universal: good jobs will increasingly depend on people who can put knowledge to work. . . . Thus, the (SCANS) competencies and the foundation should be taught and understood in an integrated fashion that reflects the workplace contexts in which they are applied." The report also acknowledged that "schools do more than simply prepare people to make a living. They prepare people to live full lives. . . ." (p. v). Consequently, they also emphasize the importance of skills other than those necessary for employment.

What should a new curriculum designed to facilitate the transition from school to employment look like in light of past experience and these new forces trying to shape education? The shifting composition of the workforce, the amount of skill required for adequate training, a belief that schools should concentrate on basic academic skills, the focus on authentic learning activities, and the belief that other general employment-related skills are more important in the curriculum than specific job skills have caused a drastic reduction in traditional job training vocational education as part of the K-12 curriculum in many states. At the same time, the general education counterparts of general business education, industrial arts, and home economics education have also been drastically reduced as increased math, science, social studies, and foreign language requirements have taken over space in the curriculum.

Curricular Modifications to Facilitate School-to-Employment Transition

It is within this new context that one must consider teaching students to make a more meaningful transition to employment. The notion is broader than only job-specific training. This does not mean that high schools should not provide job-specific training—for some it may still be an effective option. However, if one believes that all students must have better preparation to make a school-to-employment transition, other curricular options must also be provided.

Seven options appear below for modifying the K-12 curriculum to better foster transition

from school to employment. The options were derived by reviewing the current trends in thinking about schools, proposals for future modifications in school curricula, and information about the current employment environment. Some options relate to how current courses might be redeveloped and taught, and others to changes in the courses offered within the curriculum. Some options suggest that K-12 schools may need to cooperate with other educational institutions, agencies, and business and industry to provide the necessary options for students.

Option 1—Teach all subjects so students not only learn the basics but also discover how what they learn can be applied and used in real life. This basic premise of vo-caional education is now being adopted in the teaching of math, science, reading, writing, and so forth. It has been supported by the national mathematics association and the U.S. Department of Education.

Publishers now make materials available to teach academic courses in an applied fashion without compromising basic academic content. These materials teach the same content as traditional academic courses, but they do so based on real problems from everyday life or employment settings. This premise underlies the materials prepared by the Center for Occupational Research and Development (CORD) for teaching applied physics, mathematics, biology/chemistry, and communications. It also underlies the materials prepared by Paradigm Publishing in its series on math, reading, and writing for workplace success. This functional orientation to teaching academic content seems to have the advantages of increasing both student motivation to learn and the amount they learn, because the material is meaningful and not just content to be learned for learning's sake. This approach addresses the criticism leveled at schooling by Anthony Carnevale, chief economist and vice-president of the American Society for Training and Development, who has said:

American schooling sequesters students from the real world, breaks knowledge down artificially into theoretical disciplines, breaks disciplines down into component pieces, and demands that students commit fragments of knowledge to memory. Applications are reserved for pen-and-paper exercises at the back of the chapter. Interdisciplinary applications are rare, and applications in the context of working groups are even more rare. (Carnevale, 1991)

If curriculum was developed with the expectation that students should be able to clearly see how what they learn applies to real life, the emphasis on employment would naturally occur. Many of the academic skills taught take on meaning in relation to performing specific occupations. If examples of the application of skills make up an essential part of the curriculum development process, students can see how what they are learning can be applied in employment situations. They thereby increase their ability to make the transition from school to employment.

Option 2—Focus education on student outcomes. This is now being recognized as important throughout K-12 education. A national movement underway would require educators to specify student outcomes for the courses they teach and to focus instruction on those outcomes. This option is closely tied to Option 1 above, though it goes further by ensuring that what is taught is more functionally usable. One could teach the content described in Option 1 using real-life examples. However, each piece of content could still be organized around isolated basic skills. The emphasis on specifying student outcomes makes sure that basic skills are collectively focused on larger student outcomes. Often these outcomes are still specified in terms of learning a set of academic skills, but more and more the literature reflects a need to specify "authentic" outcomes and to develop curriculum in terms of what people can do after completing schooling.

Option 3—Include courses on interpersonal skills necessary for success in a work environment into the curriculum. The SCANS report clearly indicated that learning academic and job skills required in work environments is not sufficient to prepare students for employment. In addition, students must be taught interpersonal skills such as

how to work on teams, teach others, serve customers, lead, negotiate, and work well with people from culturally diverse backgrounds. Learning activities should teach students to operate a computer, tune-up a car, solve mathematical problems in such a way that they also require the application of interpersonal skills. Few teachers intentionally do so, because they have been given the primary goal of making sure students learn the "content." However, if new content in the form of interpersonal skills is also essential, educators must infuse the curriculum with it. Techniques are evolving and available to help educators identify, analyze, develop, and implement curricula to formally teach these skills (e.g., Pucel, 1989, 1991).

Option 4—Include activities throughout the curriculum that teach people to think and to develop personal qualities needed during employment. The SCANS report also clearly indicated that students need to creatively apply skills they learn to problem solving on the job, and that they need to develop personal qualities that will allow them to be trusted to work responsibly with little supervision. This also requires a change in the teaching of subject matter. The ability to think creatively, make decisions, solve problems, envision things, learn, and reason must be reinforced, regardless of subject content (De Bono, 1990). Personal qualities such as individual responsibility, self-esteem, sociability, self-management, and integrity also must be reinforced. This can be accomplished by changing the way lessons are structured and the way teachers view their roles. Rather than teaching content separately from teaching problem-solving and desired personal qualities, these things could be taught simultaneously throughout the curriculum. This would require changing the curriculum from focusing on drill and practice and memorization, to teaching content based on real employment applications through a problem-solving format.

For example, when teaching any type of content, students could be given sample job situations within which the content could be applied. They could then be taught to define the job problem to be solved using the content, plan a solution, implement the solution, and check to see whether the job problem was solved. This differs from presenting students with a problem, telling them what solution is necessary and teaching them to solve the problem. Using this latter model, students only learn how to solve problems after they have been defined and the solution identified. Using a problem-solving format during the teaching of other content also differs from separating problem solving and creative thinking into separate courses and teaching content such as math, science, computer, or auto mechanics skills applications separately. Problem solving and creative thinking are often most effectively taught in the contexts within which students will be expected to solve problems.

Teaching students using problem solving within the context of real job problems also lends itself to teaching personal qualities desired on the job. Instead of having students function as passive learners who are expected to internalize the content teachers put before them, the curriculum becomes more experientially based. Students must actively interact with the content around real-life applications designed to require them to work with others, and to be responsible to themselves and others. Success in experiencing the positive reinforcement of these qualities can also build self-esteem as students learn they can do something of value.

Option 5—Develop curricula that allow students to begin training for employment in high schools that are articulated with post-high-school specialized occupational training programs. This option is currently supported and encouraged by the federal government through the Carl D. Perkins Vocational and Applied Technology Education Act of 1990 and subsequent amendments. Again, the federal government has found it necessary to provide incentives to include preparation for employment in the K-12 curriculum. The new initiative is call tech prep. "Tech prep links high school curriculum with the curriculum of two-year community or technical colleges to produce skilled technicians of high productivity" (Hull, 1992). Tech prep programs combine the premises contained in Option 1 above with the belief that technical occupations require more job skill education than can be presented in high schools. There-

fore, tech prep calls for applied academic courses in high schools as well as courses in a variety of career clusters. Academic courses are taught around real occupational contexts with hands-on activities. In addition, students can choose courses in career clusters developed around groupings of occupations that require common skills and knowledge. Each career cluster has core courses developed around cluster commonalities that all students who have an interest in an occupation in the cluster take. In addition, students take specialty courses related to their specific occupation within the cluster. CORD recommends that the core courses constitute about 80 percent of the courses available in the cluster. "Nationally, four career clusters are prominent: engineering/industrial, information systems, health/human services, and art/humanities" (Hull, 1992, p. 19). Existing vocational program areas can also provide career-specific courses. Having completed a tech prep program in high school, a student should be able to go to a community or technical college to continue with training for a specialized occupation in a cluster and to obtain an associate degree. Success in this articulation between the high school and post-high-school institution requires substantial cooperative planning among the participating high schools and postsecondary institutions. Federal funding supports this planning effort.

Option 6—Provide opportunities for students to enter employment directly out of high school. Although most educators recognize that employment opportunities directly out of high school are limited, many students do attempt to enter employment at that point. Adopting a curriculum that assumes that everyone will go on to additional education seems to avoid reality. The most effective form of the curriculum to prepare students directly for employment is debatable. Some suggest that it should resemble the job-specific vocational training programs of the past, which were designed to prepare people for specific occupations. It is not likely that large numbers of traditional occupational programs that require students to enroll for three hours a day for multiple years will continue in K-12 schools. However, other methods for providing job training have been developed and are currently in use. One option, *cooperative education*, allows students to take part of their occupational education in the school and part in an actual employment setting under the direction of a cooperating supervisor. This option offers the advantage of serving students with a wide range of possible occupational interests and choices. It is not limited by the facilities within the school itself. In addition, co-op students can also take part in other curricular offerings in their schools.

Another method is to enter cooperative agreements with postsecondary institutions so high school students interested in specific job training can attend those institutions as part of their high school program. For example, Minnesota has passed a postsecondary options act that allows high school students to attend postsecondary institutions as part of their high school programs. This means that qualified students could take courses not available in their high schools at a university, community college, or technical college. Such arrangements give high school students access to a wide array of job training programs in postsecondary schools, and they can reduce the pressure on the high schools to staff and provide for job-specific training.

Option 7—Adopt a wider range of instructional strategies within courses. This is a general option that can apply in any or all of the previous options. To more effectively develop the previous options, a wider range of instructional strategies should be used. The notion that education is typically delivered in the school classroom and content is presented by the instructor needs modification. All of the skills needed to adequately prepare students for school-to-employment transition may not be most effectively delivered within the schools or by instructors.

One principle gaining wider use in developing instructional strategies is collaboration (Tindall & Gugerty, 1989). Collaboration can involve working with other disciplines within the school, other educational institutions, businesses and industries, or other agencies that have a common purpose. For example, collaboration may take the form of team curriculum development and teaching between voca-tional and academic instructors (Shelby & Johnson, 1988). High school students who wish more in-depth occupational training might take part in internships in cooperating industries or enroll in courses in community colleges.

Two other practices gaining wider usage are allowing for cooperative learning and more experiential learning (Johnson & Johnson, 1983). These require instructors to develop learning activities through which students learn together or from a set of experiences. Such learning activities offer much greater potential than instructor-directed activities for allowing students to develop the interpersonal skills, problem-solving skills, and personal qualities needed for employment. These learning activities allow students to become actively engaged in skill application.

Summary and Conclusions

The nature of the K-12 curriculum and the form of its delivery to students is changing. There is a growing belief that education should give students a command of the basics, and that students know how to apply those basics to the functional contexts in which they live and work. With this has come increased emphasis on the need to better prepare students to make the transition from school to employment. Pressure is being placed on traditional vocational and academic education to modify their curricula. Vocational education is being asked to broaden its perspective to include a wider range of employment-related skills than just the job tasks of the past. These include skills such as academic basics, interpersonal skills, problem-solving skills, and personal qualities necessary to work with others. Students must also develop an understanding of systems within which things get done on the job. At the same time, academic educators in areas such as math and science are being asked to teach the basics not through drill and practice but in the context of realistic problem solving. In this way, students can develop higher-order problem-solving skills by addressing real-world problems.

Both vocational education and academic education have begun to respond to this change and pressure. Tech prep demonstration projects are being funded throughout the United States. Each project requires a cooperative effort between academic and vocational education programs within the K-12 schools and with their counterparts in postsecondary institutions. Each project also requires the cooperation of the institutions' counseling staffs and administrations to better inform students and parents about opportunities. New ways of thinking about how to direct the efforts of both the academic and vocational education communities toward preparing students for employment are being encouraged. All of this activity seems clearly to indicate that the schools will increase their emphasis on school-to-employment transition. However, in the future that emphasis will take on a more pervasive and different form than it has in the past. It will become integrated into the basic fabric of the total curriculum.

References

Carnegie Task Force on Teaching as a Profession. (1986). *A nation prepared: Teachers for the 20th century*. New York: Carnegie Forum on Education and the Economy.

Carnevale, A. P. (1991). *America and the new economy*. Washington, DC: U.S. Department of Labor Employment and Training Administration.

De Bono, E. (1990). *Thinking skills for success*. Eden Prairie, MN: Paradigm Publishing, Int.

Hoyt, K. B. (1982). Federal and state participation in career education: Past, present and future. *Journal of Career Development, 9*(1), 5-15.

Hull, D. (1992, March). Tech prep: practical education for America's work force. *School Shop/Tech Directions, 51*(8), 17-19.

Johnson, R. T., & Johnson, D. W. (1983). Effects of cooperative, competitive, and individualistic learning experiences on social development. *Exceptional Children, 49*, 423-329.

Marland, S. (1971). Career education now. Speech presented before the annual convention of the National Association of Secondary School Principles, Houston, TX.

Newmann, F. M. (1991). Linking restructuring to authentic student achievement. *Phi Delta Kappan, 72*(6), 458-463.

Pucel, D. J. (1989). *Performance-based instructional design*. New York: McGraw-Hill.

Pucel, D. J., et. al. (1991). *Performance-based occupational affective behavior analysis (OABA)*. St. Paul, MN: Minnesota Research and Development Center, University of Minnesota.

Rosenstock, L. (1991). The walls come down: The overdue reunification of vocational and academic education. *Phi Delta Kappan, 72*(6), 434-436.

Shelby, S., & Johnson, J. (1988). Tying it all together. *Vocational Education Journal, 63*(2), 27-29.

Tindall, L. W., & Gugerty, J. J. (1989). Collaboration among clients, families and service providers. In D. E. Berkell & J. M. Brown (Eds.), *Transition from school to work for persons with disabilities*. White Plains, NY: Longman.

U.S. Office of Elementary and Secondary Education. (1991, June). AMERICA 2000: An education strategy. *The Outlook, 1*(4), 1-6.

U.S. Department of Labor. (1991, June). What work requires of schools: A SCANS report for America 2000. Washington, DC: U.S. Government Printing Office.

22

Partnerships
in the School-to-Work
Transition

Virginia H. Pease and George H. Copa

The United States competes with other highly industrialized countries for dominance in the global market, prestige in educational standards, and a high quality of life brought about through civic and corporate responsibility for others. Within this arena, and in comparative terms, the United States is seriously lacking in a national system of school-to-work transition for its young people. In other countries that compete with the United States, such as Germany and Sweden, a social contract exists that provides both a structure for transition-to-work experiences and people who serve as human bridges.

Until now, vocational education and vocational educators have served as the mainstays of any school-to-work programs that exist in most local communities in this country. During the last decade, as awareness has increased regarding the need to prepare all young people for work life, the question of how to go about doing so has grown more common. Vocational education must guide public discussion on school-to-work transition and share its experience with partnerships.

As director and coordinator for two years of New Designs for the Comprehensive High School, we have brought current research about school (Copa & Pease, 1992) restructuring together with imaginative individuals from schools and the community. We have worked to create design specifications for the compre-

hensive high school of the future, including attention to school-to-work transition. This program of research and development is sponsored by the National Center for Research in Vocational Education. Our ideas about school-to-work transition and partnerships were stimulated by interactions in cities around the country with all parties involved: imaginative teachers and administrators, knowledgeable researchers, concerned community members, and students.

What we have learned is that partnerships are an essential part of successful school-to-work transition for young people. Neither schools nor workplaces can do the task themselves for reasons of authenticity, resources, equitable support, and infrastructure. We need a newer vision for partnerships in the school-to-work transition to help us go forward.

There was a time when employers stuck to their own business and schools tended to the three R's. This was the era when non-college-bound students were expected to fall out of school and fall into local jobs. The blue collar workforce made room for the boys. The girls joined pink collar workers in offices and retail shops. Partnerships between schools and businesses were limited to vocational education; the adopt-a-school model of partnership had not begun.

More recently, school resources have been more limited, and graduates were expected to know more about "workplace basics." Partnerships between schools and other organizations increased in number primarily to extend resources and to link lessons to the real world. As the process continues, the goals of schools will turn even more sharply in the direction of student learning for a complex, interdependent world.

In its 1988 report *The Forgotten Half*, the W. T. Grant Commission on Work, Family and Citizenship concluded that young people today need to prepare for a different experience and that the institutions in our communities have not responded adequately. Efforts to increase school success that do not consider the broader context of families, communities, and workplaces will not likely make a substantial difference for young people. It is now urgent that communities open new pathways to success to provide a fair chance for non-college-bound youth.

This chapter attempts to describe a newer vision for partnerships in the school-to-work transition that blends what we've learned about schools, high- and low-performance workplaces, and partnerships. It is organized in the following sections: (a) meaning of the concepts of transition to work and partnership, (b) dimensions of quality in school-to-work transition, (c) functions of partners in a quality transition, (d) potential partners for these functions, and (e) guidelines for partnerships for transitions.

The Concept of Transition to Work

Transition from school to work needs careful definition before further discussion about desired qualities, presumed effects, or values of a smooth transition. A standard college dictionary defines *transition* as a progression from one state, stage, place, or subject to another; it is characterized by change. The Latin root word *trans-* means across, beyond, through, so as to change.

Transition from school to work seems to have two identifying features. First, there are two different, expressed states—a before and an after. In this case, the before is *as student*; the after state is *as worker*. Second, there is some form of bridge between the two states—

the passage over which change is produced.

Do these two features capture enough of the concept that we can identify real transitions to work and distinguish them from other educational concepts? In *An Introduction to the Analysis of Educational Concepts* (1978), Soltis suggests that if our definition meets the test of necessary and sufficient conditions, it will serve for discussion purposes.

The necessity test asks whether we can have a transition to work without one or the other of the features. The first feature to test is the *two states*. For example, can there be a transition to work characterized by a change, producing passage, but involving only one state? The requirement to change brings about the need for a different state. One state of being cannot change and still maintain its identity (in a mathematical sense, identity means sameness).

The second feature to test is the *passage*. Can there be two different states (*worker* and *student*) without the passage? This is a more difficult condition to test. Young people can carry more than one identity at the same time. For instance, today a young woman can be a student, paid worker, sister, volunteer, roommate, and teammate. We must somehow qualify our meaning further. Young people who take their jobs seriously usually say things such as "I have to work today" or "I've been working here for six months." They express their work status in declarative statements. Therefore, we added the qualifier *expressed* passage to our meaning of transition to work. With the qualifier, both features are found to be necessary.

The sufficiency test can be met if we can differentiate transition to work from other educational concepts with the two features described above. If so, we will have a useful meaning. If not, we missed important features. One way to test for sufficiency involves examining the literature on transition to work to see whether other defining features may be helpful.

The transition-to-work literature base from the United States appears to have two main subgroups: (1) descriptions of current youth and work situations in terms of schools, demographics, economic activity, and the relationship between education and employment, and (2) details about the goals, activities, results, and recommendations from government programs such as job training (e.g., Job Training Partnership Act (JTPA)), vocational equity, special education, and dropout prevention. This literature suggests that *program* may be another feature to test.

We can test for sufficiency by asking: Is *program* another feature that distinguishes the concept of transition to work? A second look at the literature shows many instances of well-financed, -planned, and -staffed transition-to-work programs that have not produced work for young people. Empirical evidence tells us that most young people in the United States eventually go to work—if work opportunities exist—without benefit of a planned program. Therefore, *program* is not a sufficient feature of this concept. Our first set of two proposed features seem to hold.

Let's look at the contrary, at what is *not* school-to-work transition. Transition to work is identified by the features of (a) two different, expressed states (a before and an after) and (b) existence of some form of bridge between the two (the passage over which change is produced). These features help to distinguish transition to work from other educational concepts such as work readiness, career education, vocational education, and out-of-school government-sponsored job training, such as JTPA.

Work readiness in states like Wisconsin (Poole, 1988) has the goal of having students assimilate information about, and an orientation toward, work. At best, the information and orientation are provided formally in schools by teachers or counselors, informally at home, through peer groups, or through the information media. The young person participates as a student, not as a worker. Work readiness programs emphasize qualities desired in workers, labor market information, and ways to secure initial employment. A young person will not likely adopt the identity of *worker* or be changed by the knowledge of the passage. Work readiness is just a part of the transition to work.

Career education preceded work readiness programs in schools. Traditionally, career education was a program of study dealing with careers that had the goal of bringing together students' interests and knowledge of career opportunities. As with work readiness, the young person participates as a student, not as a worker. There are opportunities to hear the stories about careers as experienced by older workers. One of the current impetuses for transition-to-work policy and programs comes from the failure of career education—even in its best forms of implementation—to make a difference in young people's search for initial employment. Career education has been informative, but not transformative.

Vocational education provides a third method for bringing together young people, school, and work. Under certain conditions, vocational education comes close to the desired features of transition-to-work programs. To do so, it must include work experience, require complex knowledge and skills, and offer a related class to discuss issues related to becoming a worker. Vocational education as a program ends when the student leaves school. Young people must complete the journey of becoming workers on their own, unless their work supervisor or trainer knows about the needs of beginning workers and provides support.

JTPA, as an example of government-sponsored job training, takes form as an out-of-school program that has as its goal the transition to work for young people in special trouble. JTPA deals with young people as low-income citizens, possibly as parents, as students (once they enter the program), and as workers (often offered work in subsidized form). JTPA is one transition-to-work model that is characterized by the special circumstances of its participants and by the available work.

While the concepts described above do not fully match the proposed features of school-to-work transition, they provide ideas that help to describe a desirable state of affairs and the current status of young people who are on their way to becoming workers. The above concepts indicate that we give serious consideration to understanding what is meant by work, who we include when we are discussing workers, and ways to provide challenging, complex work experiences.

The Concept of Partnership

Again using Saltis (1978) as a reference we ask: What features must a relationship have to be called a partnership?

Drawing from a recent review of literature on partnerships (Karls, Pease, Copa, Beck, & Pearce, 1992, pp. 10-11), we find that the defining features involve two or more entities (partners) and some type of mutually beneficial relationship. Partnerships include (a) some level of cooperative effort; (b) shared goal, vision, or enterprise; (c) mutual respect and trust; (d) contributions of particular talents, experiences, perspectives, and resources; (e) shared power; and (f) shared accountability. In our context, the sharing is around young people making an effective transition from school to work.

In defining the concept of partnership, we can also ask the question: What are the basic different meanings of partnership? This approach is particularly useful in reference to partnership because it seems to have several meanings. From a functional perspective, a typology of partnerships in the context of private sector involvement with vocational education is proposed by Maurice (1984, pp. 8-9). He describes different types of involvement as a continuum of means through which mutual benefits are realized. The levels of relationships he describes range from *separation* to *cooperation* to *integration*. Along the continuum, the partners increase the amounts of shared information and resources, the joint authority for planning and responsibility, and the willingness to change organizational structure to accomplish objectives.

Partnerships also vary in terms of the motivations for participating in the partnerships. Jones and Maloy (1988) found that most partnerships of divergent motivations result in assumptions of *obliged to*, *ought to*, and *want to*. They define *obliged to* as conveying top-down pressure for organizational collaboration, such as court orders, funding conditions, or state policy requirements. *Ought to* prevails where leaders sense their organizations will benefit from partnership in some undetermined way. *Want to* describes organizations that anticipate gains from involvement in proposed joint activities (Jones & Maloy, 1988, p. 50). Mixed motivations between partners might result in open conflicts, passive forms of resistance, or confusion. Jones and Maloy suggest that the ideal partnership situation occurs when want

to/want to motivations prevail. This analysis suggests that the mutual benefit feature of partnerships is related to motivations.

The conceptual analysis of partnership given above is designed to cause reflection on the meaning held for partnership as it is used in relation to school-to-work transition. The point is that while partnerships have some common features such as two or more partners and a mutual benefit, they can vary quite considerably in degree of intensity and motivation.

Dimensions of Quality in School-to-Work Transition

Having definitions of the concepts of school-to-work transition and partnership proves helpful because it provides some foundation for thinking seriously about desirable experiences for young people who are becoming workers, and about the partners who might support their journeys. In the section that follows, we attempt to describe briefly a desired state of affairs for school-to-work transition that would mutually benefit students and all partners. Then, we attempt to explain the present state of affairs as we hear it described by those experienced with transitions and partnerships, and we share our understanding of the research base on school-to-work transition.

Desired State of Affairs

In an ideal United States, a social contract would exist that guarantees each young person an opportunity for a transition to work. The opportunity would have characteristics of being highly literate, highly skilled, highly enlightened, and highly personalized. The journey from school to work would be understood for what it was—a typically American representation of progress and contradictions—rather than a straight, upward sloping passageway. Knowing its uniqueness allows for preparation. Ideally, it would be understood that transition is a "today" phenomenon for young people, and not a "tomorrow" event. A description of the desired state of affairs in transition from school to work follows.

Highly literate. Students in school would envision themselves as serious students who are preparing for a third wave, symbol-rich economy (Toffler, 1990). They would learn to perform work in a complex human and technological environment. They would be knowledgeable and critical in their approach to work and able to understand the concerns of unemployment.

Highly skilled. Schools would be viewed as important but imperfect places. Because they are imperfect, compulsory attendance within the building would be replaced by compulsory participation in an educative environment. While traditional classes might work well for basic symbolic literacies, workplaces would serve as important alternatives for learning technological literacies, problem construction, and applications of symbolic systems.

Highly enlightened. Ideally, the value of learning to become a worker in a workplace would help expose the artificiality of the social and institutional constructions of adolescence in the United States. Students would begin to envision themselves as serious workers with a responsibility to improve treatment of their age-group peers. A critical orientation to curriculum would help prepare students to use their understandings of school, work, and community to act in ways that improve the possibilities in the future.

Highly personalized. Becoming a worker would ideally be personalized. The desired state of affairs would include choices. There would be a multitude of differently complex and important jobs for which to aim. Reasonable accommodations would be made so that every young person would be treated as willing to work, able to learn, and capable of success.

The journey. Transition from school to work would be thought of as a journey. The journey would be recognized for what it is; a variation of several attributes. Journeys are smooth and rough, long at points and short at others, and often lonely. Journeys can be costly if poorly planned; some are spontaneous and begin without a destination. The quality of the ideal transition to work would be measured by the satisfaction of the young person who is becoming a worker and by the quality of care provided to the young people who are still in transit.

The Present State of Affairs

In contrast to this desired state of affairs for transition from school to work, the current state in the United States can at best be described as an agglomeration of programs and individual experiences (Office of Adult and Vocational Education, 1991; General Accounting Office, 1991; Hamilton, 1992). Programs that exist usually serve youth with special troubles, but offer far too few places for all who want to participate. At the state level, Wisconsin and Oregon have school-to-work legislation as an umbrella for myriad programs and individual efforts (W. T. Grant Foundation Commission on Work, Family, and Citizenship, 1991). Business partnerships are primarily focused on an overall goal of improving the quality of the public education organization (Levine, 1988). Local communities and individuals help with transition to work as important happenstance. Families seem to be the mainstays (Olson, 1990).

In the present state of affairs, being unemployed can mean more than one thing. The temporary-help firms have shown by example that almost everybody who wants to work can be placed in a job of some type. The unemployment problems for young people seem to be caused by more than a lack of work (Packer & Wirt, 1991; Osterman, 1989; Hamilton, 1990). There are limited points of career entry into the primary labor market or within young people's range of geographic or ability accessibility. The influence of technology has even more dramatically impacted the face of work and unemployment for young people.

Schools today are most typically structured and outfitted to offer transition-to-work programs for some selected students (W. T. Grant Commission on Youth, Family, and Citizenship, 1988). For students with college-educated parents who have the means and ability to attend college, the notion of work is defined through career education and guidance, but actions are deferred until leaving college. Students with identified disabilities have the right by law to have a transition-to-work plan that is enforceable.

The majority of young people have no formalized transition-to-work system that supports and educates them in the journey to becoming a worker. Benefiting from contacts, an expanding economy, or luck, some students set out on the journey to become a worker, find their way, and reach a destination in a reasonable amount of time with their illusions about work intact. Others wander into the moratorium of the secondary labor market until they are in their twenties (Osterman, 1989). Discouraged, they attempt to sustain illusions about careers by returning to school for additional training. The transition to work is not completed until the young person understands the realities of the capitalist economy, the fickleness of the labor market, and the apparent value of being an adolescent.

Some young people quickly lose their illusions. Disabled youth discover that the path to work's door won't accommodate a wheelchair or that the personnel official doesn't understand sign language. Young women, raised on sex-biased and misleading career information, face the reality of sex-stereotyped jobs and glass ceilings at an early age. Teen parents learn early that the benefits of low-wage jobs don't cover the real costs of working. Young black, Hispanic, Native American, and recently immigrated people are systematically structured out of work by business managers and owners who are still typically white, and mostly male. Some of these young people may be within reach of a caring friend or teacher, community support network, or job training program. With assistance they may get back on their journey and become workers. Others may never recover the way and will grow less employable.

Problem Areas to Be Addressed

When the desired state of affairs and the present state of affairs are examined closely, we can begin to see sources of frustration for those approaching or in the transition from school to work. The differences between the ideal and real causes problems or concerns. The problems arise from ideologies about adolescents, education, and work that sustain unexamined assumptions, tolerate untested beliefs, and reproduce paternalism and bureaucracy.

What follows are five problem areas that we propose as needing further investigation if

improved school-to-work transition is an ultimate goal.

System to Support the Programs Is Missing

As educational professionals, we seem to know what makes good school-to-work transitions. The research base offers lengthy descriptions of the specific elements of successful programs. We know many young people who found initial employment and became good workers. From our experience, we also know that in the United States the intention and the money is lacking to support job training and education programs for all young people who want to participate.

An investigation of secondary education in countries considered economically competitive with the United States revealed strong support for strengthening the systems of transition to work in these countries (Donahue, Copa, & Pease, 1992). During the decade of the 1990s, the challenge is to find out *if* communities and states in this country have an equal will to support a more over-arching social contract with our young people.

If there is to be organized and sustained effort on the transition issue, effort should be directed at the system level. The individual efforts of families, friends, and teachers will continue (Minnesota State Council on Vocational Technical Education, 1993).

We'd Better Rethink the Student Experience

In the United States, the common identity of a young person is as a *student* until the midteen years. Young people are kept away from full-time, paid work by a government system of compulsory common schooling and child labor laws (Stacey, Alsalam, Gilmore, and To, 1988). Schools are run as compromises between rigorous expectations for a few and unspecial treatment for the rest (Sizer, 1991).

The current state of affairs can be improved by appreciating all students as effective learners, constructors of knowledge, and producers of products. Some restructured school designs are moving toward a thinking curriculum for all (Packer & Wirt, 1991), guided by the metaphor of student as worker, where *worker* refers to "working the mind" (Sizer, 1991). Regrettably, vocational educators have often been reluctant (or have not been asked) to share their unique and important perspective on the meaning of *work* that integrates working the mind and working the hands. The invisible wall that seems to separate vocational and academic educators in many schools has inhibited a truly engaging, relevant, and lively discussion about the goals, expressions, and representations of student learning.

We Misunderstand the Nature of Work

As early as sixth grade, most students hear and believe that a good education is important to getting a good job. Not thinking critically, they also tend to believe the converse: that a good job results from a good education. As they get older, three-fourths of the students take on part-time, paid work before leaving school. What they discover is that the alleged connections do not hold in the secondary labor market. Good educations do not necessarily produce good jobs. High skills do not yield high wages. Jobs do not give them adult status and respect.

The effect appears in frustration over the way things are, false hopes about what might be possible, and self-defeating behavior that is part of the transition that can be a catalyst for understanding. Feeling ever less valued, young people are involved in costly mistakes and can drift toward resignation or hopelessness. Career self-direction is beyond their control and good jobs are more a matter of connections, luck, and current economic conditions (Osterman, 1989).

In most school curricula, young people spend more time studying the values and morals of Greek and Roman mythology than the mythology of the workplace. More effort goes to telling them what employers expect than to helping them raise questions about their own work experiences. To be fully prepared to become workers, students need to examine critically myths such as:

1. Adolescents are our most valuable natural resource.
2. The United States cannot compete internationally without students achiev-

ing to world class standards.
3. Economic competitiveness is threatened by the current demographics of the workforce (i.e., increasing numbers of women, minorities, disabled).
4. Higher student achievement in core subjects has a positive employment effect.
5. Free enterprise can best solve the education and training problems.

The values and morals of the workplace myths need to be understood in the context of twenty-first century capitalism (Reich, 1992; Carnevale, 1991).

Our Journeys Need Smarter Starts

Programs for school-to-work transitions have often been built on the current practice of career education. Career information that is fresh, relevant, and focused on young people's futures in the community works well as a part of the transition system. In many situations though, career education has possibly created more illusions about work and done more harm to students—women and minorities in particular—than the benign neglect of bookish academic learning.

Career education has three major flaws that may be too much to overcome. First, the notion of a career is limited to certain gender, socioeconomic, ability, and ethnic groups— and to people older than 22 years of age. Career models tend to assume that careers follow a linear path, at least for some individuals. Evidence that women consider career decisions in the context of other relationships did not enter the theoretical base until the past decade. The notion of multiple careers is only now finding its way into the literature.

Next, research about careers and career development draws on a matching model first popularized in 1910 by the Boston Vocational Guidance Bureau. The model assumes that individual abilities predestined a person to some appropriate occupation. A good match would result from vocational testing and occupational data bases. The bureau developed data bases from the experiences of workers who were mostly white males.

Finally, career information that is typically used to develop school education programs comes from government occupational data banks that are incomplete, out of date, and biased toward an economy that Toffler (1990) identified as a second-wave, smoke-stack economy. Government funds have been lacking to maintain and improve the *Dictionary of Occupational Titles.*

We've Neglected the Wisdom of Youth

Young people have often been excluded from discussions about transition from school to work. Their opinions, ideas, and experiences have been minimized. Young workers are often referred to as human capital or, worse, as economic warriors. The Commission on Work, Family and Citizenship urges adults to rethink their opinions about some young people:

> Unlocking the human potential of the Forgotten Half requires an essential ingredient, adult *respect*, which welcomes youth as companions in the search for solutions rather than as part of the problem. (W. T. Grant Commission on Youth, Family, and Citizenship, 1988, p. 4)

They should be respected as colleagues who bring both a wealth of abilities and a persistent hopefulness about the future.

In many communities, we seem to have forgotten the notion, often identified as Deweyian, that workers can improve workplaces. The history of work shows that this idea was promoted and fought over by populists, progressives, socialists, labor unions, social reformers, manual training enthusiasts, and liberal-minded educators. Enlightened transitions contrast sharply with other approaches to transition, based on human capital theory, that tend to conceptualize young people as a sort of human inventory for business enterprises and as economic warriors in an international competition for control of the world's resources.

Summary

The problem areas above have been described from the point of view of young people who will be making the school-to-work transition, rather than the educational and economic organizations that are part of a system. The experiences of young people were foremost in our thoughts as we analyzed the problem areas for common issues. By identifying common issues, we sensed there is potential to discover some new approaches to improving the present situation through partnerships.

New possibilities for partnerships became evident in the analysis. Young people need partners in their journey to becoming workers. Families and communities need the contributions that skilled, literate, and enlightened young workers can make. In these respects, partnerships aimed directly and long term at specific problems areas can make a significant contribution. What are the most vital functions for these partnerships?

Functions of Partners in Transition

The previous section has identified and described a series of problem areas that must be addressed to improve the transition from school to work. Using these problem areas as a focal point, who needs to talk and act together to better resolve these problems? Our view in this chapter is that their resolution can come through partnerships among schools and several other groups, organizations, agencies, and institutions. In addition, for these partnerships to grow significantly more effective, they must be functionally grounded in the problem areas described above. In other words, they must be specifically "designed down", or made functional in terms of the problems that need addressing. Too often missing in the literature and practice of partnerships is a specific functional context for partnerships that would guide their design, implementation, and evaluation as a strategy to improve young people's transition from school to work.

We see at least four functions in transition from school to work that partnerships can provide in addressing the problem areas: (a) an authentic learning setting, (b) a supportive community underwriting the risks of transition (care and respect), (c) resources for a more complete and rich transition learning process (d) a seamless and forgiving system for insuring continuing transitions (democratic infrastructure).

Authentic Learning Settings

Improving school-to-work transition will require providing a student experience which is more relevant to work and the transition to work with attention to smarter journeys for young people. A natural strategy to address this challenge is to expand the idea of the learning setting beyond the school to include the home, workplace, and wider community as places of learning. These additional learning settings provide for authenticity or contextualizing the learning process in terms of curriculum, instruction, and assessment. For this to work well, there must be close interaction and sharing among the partners to ensure learning supportive of a smooth transition. The characteristics of partnership noted above must all come into play.

Supportive Community

Improving school-to-work transition for young people will require tapping their wisdom in ways that communicate the idea of shared responsibility for transition and that ensure equitable attention to the diverse needs young people bring to the transition phenomenon. A natural strategy to realistically communicate to young people the idea of shared responsibility and to respond to their diverse needs again comes through partnerships with adults inside and outside the school who show care and respect. It is extremely important for the care and respect to be consistent from these adults—particularly regarding the commitment to listen to and involve young people as significant contributors and stakeholders in improving the transition process.

Providing Resources

More efficient use of existing resources and provision of additional resources can enhance the transition efforts. Resources can take a wide variety of forms. Perhaps most important is to ensure a curriculum that confronts misunderstandings about the nature of work, including myths about young people and the world of work. A curriculum that can address these tasks will require staffing and leadership from the many players in the transition process—again a functional service of partnerships. In addition to staffing, resources made available through partnerships with family, workplace, other educational institutions, and the wider community could include assistance in identifying needs; providing encouragement, guidance, and mentoring; conducting assessments; and ensuring political awareness and priority.

A Seamless and Forgiving System

Improving the transition will require more attention to the whole system as well as individual components of the transition support system. The whole system is formed by the underlying infrastructure of relationships between and among the players in the transition process, which provides yet another functional basis for partnerships. The players must somehow come together to develop a more seamless system, without gaps and needless duplication. A seamless system must provide first for attention to the needs of young people and after that for the needs of schools and workplaces. Second, the system must provide for smart first starts in the transition journey, as well as for multiple opportunities or chances to start again and again as the need arises.

Democratic ideals play an important role in developing this whole system or infrastructure. There must be attention to the provisions for freedom and shared responsibility of the players; for the complexities, unpredictableness, and frailties of human nature and our culture; for consensus and coalition building and falling away; and for attention to the needs of others in the interests of the common good and a stronger community.

Potential Partners[1]

We next turn to the partners and their contributions. As we listened to young people,

[1]The descriptions of the potential partners in this section was originally developed at length in the working paper by Karls, Pease, Copa, Beck, and Pearce as a part of the research project "New Designs for the Comprehensive High School" (Copa & Pease, 1992) sponsored by the National Center for Research in Vocational Education.

searched the literature base on transitions, and reflected on our own experiences, we identified some of the potential partners who make or could make significant contributions to the school-to-work transition. The most important and basic partnership element is adults' attitude toward young people. Potential partners include (a) family, (b) employers, (c) community at large, (d) postsecondary educational institutions, and (e) others within the traditional school system (i.e., students, staff, alumni, and feeder schools).

Family

Parents and families are consistently identified by young people as primary sources of information and insight about becoming a worker. Some parents and other family members have a broad exposure to the variety of jobs in the community and know where the job openings occur. In several schools, parents have volunteered to share their time by coming to school to discuss their own job situations, taking young students as interns for a brief period, and acting as volunteer counselor and mentor to another parent's teenager. These activities engage students, help to make learning in the classroom more relevant, and provide important links to the greater community.

Employers

Partnerships between schools and employers are already a significant trend. Traditionally, these partnerships were formed through vocational education to provide cooperative work placements and job training. Cetron and Gayle (1991) contend that their easiest forecast for the 1990s is the deep commitment and involvement between American business and schools. They conclude that this trend will be so strong that no school in need of help will go without resources or other help.

The benefits must go beyond expanded resources and real-world relevance. Partnerships for young people need to also address issues of equity and democracy. In their study of the rationale of public-private collaboration for work transition, Smith and Trist (1988) concluded that, given the looming shortage of skilled labor worldwide, the interests of the economy and of individual equity are converging as the need for better and more widely distributed skills grows. While there is no consensus about which institutions should handle which roles in workforce preparation, the process of civic collaboration will bring us good answers.

Community at Large

Schools and employers will need to turn to other partners from the community at large to give young people a sense of community and caring that is often currently missing. The community at large includes any number of agencies, institutions, and citizens. Community partnerships offer possibilities that extend the sense of care to young people as well as give them opportunities to develop prosocial behavior. Prosocial behavior covers a wide range of human actions: helping people in distress; donating time or energy to volunteer service organizations; attempting to reverse political, economic, and social injustice or inequality. The common thread among prosocial behaviors is the desire to promote the welfare of others, a characteristic of corporate social responsibility.

Postsecondary Educational Institutions

Postsecondary educational institutions are also important partners in a quality transition to work. Partnerships involving them can most effectively address the problems of students' current school experience. Their initiatives often involve the coordination of curricula at different levels; provide for a smooth transition between schools; or prepare a student with the skills needed to perform specific jobs. Often referred to as articulated programs, these partnerships incorporate the notion of mutual benefit. They can directly affect the lives of young people and the nature of the organization.

The contemporary definition of articulation is as a process, an attitude, and a goal when it relates to tech prep initiatives. Vocational education, the occupational programs in comprehensive high schools, area vocational schools, and joint vocational centers, can be closely and carefully aligned with related programs in technical or community colleges, or in a proprietary school. These programs offer occupational training, credentials, and linkages to employers.

Internal Partners

The potential partnerships mentioned above are generally considered external to the public secondary school. Other potential partners exist internally. These are partnerships with the other students and teachers in the school, and with feeder schools and school alumni.

Seeley (1985) notes that fundamental to sound educational policy is acknowledgement that students must be in partnership with the person who immediately teaches them. He concludes from examples within schools that strong partnerships incorporate a small scale, more voice and choice for students and teachers, more student responsibility, more teacher initiative, more parent involvement, and a greater emphasis on the school family.

Often, the familiar circle of internal partners supports the transition from school to work through example, actions, and attitudes. The cadre of slightly older siblings, friends, and acquaintances is the primary source of information about possible jobs, desirable occupations, and good supervisors.

The circle of internal partners is large enough to include the alumni of the school. The alumni of a school know the the school's culture, retain sentimental attachments, and can provide important links from the school to the external community and places of employment. They can serve as mentors, guest speakers, career counselors, peer tutors, and even teachers. Alumni play an important role in providing mentorships and scholarships for present students. Young people tend to turn to the other people in their world for information, guidance, and support during their first experiences with work and with their concerns about becoming a worker.

Guidelines for Partnerships

Partnerships to improve the school-to-work transition of young people need guidance by a set of attitudes and beliefs, as well as some sort of structure, if they are to be sustained past an initial flurry of activity. In addition, interactions within new partnerships will raise new questions.

Attitudes and Beliefs

Attitudes and beliefs are important. Partners must believe they have something to offer that can make a difference. They must also believe they can bridge different institutional and ethnic cultures for a specified purpose. They must display mutual respect and trust, which are often built through prior associations. Finally, they must be realistic about what they can accomplish.

Structure

Partnerships need a structure that can support a long-term relationship. The elements of such a structure would be (a) statement of common goals, (b) assessment of the partners' talents and willingness to share them, (c) comfortable forums that promote communication, (d) shared accountability and periodic evaluation, (e) celebrations of success, and (f) planning time to look at future collaborations.

Issues and Questions

As with any changes, moving toward partnerships will also raise a number of issues and questions. The study of partnerships indicates that we need to discuss among educators and their partners some of the following questions.

Motivation. The research indicates that sustained collaborative work must come with a *want to/want to* motivation. Can partnerships that are mandated by top-down pressure for organizational collaboration such as state policy requirements be successful in an atmosphere of *ought to* or *obliged to*?

Effort. Partners need to communicate well and have a history of cooperative association before the trust and groundwork are created for collaborative effort. Are schools and potential partners ready and able to commit the time and the training necessary to sustain collaborative partnerships? Why are schools often leery of forming partnerships with business and industry?

Diversity. Some of the most creative, effective partnerships involve unlike partners who approach goals and problems from their varying perspectives. How can the stereotypes and misconceptions held by educators and potential partners be stripped away so that effective partnerships can be formed? How can we deal with the ambiguity that naturally exists when people from different backgrounds want to work as partners?

Respect. Are educators willing to move from a service delivery model of education that speaks in terms of provider and client, professional and target audience, to a partnership model of education that speaks in terms of shared power, goals, and accountability?

Inclusion. Collaborative partnerships are not a quick-fix for educational improvement. How can we move from rhetoric to actually implementing collaborative partnerships? How do we find mechanisms for fair and equitable practices that involve all stakeholders in educational reform?

Summary

Recall that in this chapter transition to work means the movement from a state of being in school to functioning at work, with a supporting bridge between the two states. Partnership means a relationship among two or more institutions for their mutual benefit, often involving a common purpose. The common purpose of partnerships assumed in this chapter is to support the transition of young people from school to work.

In contrasting a desired state of affairs with the present state of affairs for the transition to work, a series of problem areas became evident as needing resolution if the state of affairs is to be improved. These problem areas are: (a) need for a system to support transition programs, (b) need to re-think the student experience in preparing for transition to work, (c) need to address young people's misunderstandings of the nature of work, (d) need for smarter starts for young people in the transition-to-work journey, and (e) need to respect the knowledge and contribution of young people in designing the transition support system.

In resolving these problems, a series of functions that necessitate partnerships among the school and other entities must be provided for. These functions include providing authenticity, equitable support, resources, and infra-structure. The partners considered most important in accomplishing these functions are family, employers, community at large, postsecondary institutions, and a group of partners internal to the school. Last, a series of guidelines and questions must be developed to maintain effective partnerships as an essential part of successful school-to-work transition for young people in the United States.

References and Suggested Reading

Carnevale, A. P. (1991). *America and the new economy* (Grant No. 99-6-0705-75-079-02). Washington, DC: U. S. Department of Labor.

Carnoy, M., & Levin, H. M. (1985). *Schooling and work in the democratic state.* Stanford, CA: Stanford University Press.

Cetron, M., & Gayle, M. (1991). *Educational renaissance.* New York: St. Martin's Press.

Christenson, L. C., & Mercer, J. W. (Eds.). *Making the first chance a real chance: Bridging education and work for all Minnesota youth and adults* (Report to the 1993 Legislature—Minnesota Task Force on Education and Employment Transition). St. Paul, MN: Minnesota State Council on Vocational Technical Education.

Commission on the Skills of the American Workforce. (1990). *America's choice: High skills or low wages!* Rochester, NY: National Center of Education and the Economy.

Copa, G. H., & Pease, V. H. (1992). *New designs for the comprehensive high school.* Berkeley, CA: University of California, National Center for Research in Vocational Education.

Donahue, T. R., Copa, G. H., & Pease, V. H. (1992). The comprehensive high school: An international perspective. In G. H. Copa & V. H. Pease, *New designs for the comprehensive high school* (Vol. II, pp. M-1-M-56). Berkeley, CA: University of California, National Center for Research in Vocational Education.

General Accounting Office. (1991). *Transition from school to work: Linking education and worksite training.* Gaithersburg, MD: U.S. General Accounting Office.

Hamilton, S. F. (1990). *Apprenticeship for adulthood: Preparing youth for the future.* New York: Free Press.

Hamilton, S. F. (1992). Growing a quality pool of human resources. In J. R. Yablon (Ed.), *Fostering a technologically adaptable workforce* (LCST Report No. 92-1) (pp. 113-115). Albany, NY: Legislative Commission on Science and Technology.

Hord, S. M. (1985). *Collaboration or cooperation: Comparisons and contrasts, dilemmas and decisions* (Report No. R&DCTE-R-3203). Austin, TX: Texas University, Research and Development Center for Teacher Education. (ERIC Document Reproduction Service No. ED 258 356)

Jones, B. L., & Maloy, R. W. (1988). *Partnerships for improving schools*. New York: Greenwood.

Learning partnerships: Lessons from research literature and current practice in secondary education. In G. H. Copa & V. H. Pease, *New designs for the comprehensive high school* (Vol. II, pp. G-4–G-51). Berkeley, CA: University of California, National Center for Research in Vocational Education.

Levine, M. (1988). Introduction. In M. Levine & R. Trachtman (Eds.), *American business and the public school* (pp. xiii-xxiii). New York: Teachers College Press.

Maurice, C. F. (1984). *Private sector involvement with the vocational community: An analysis of policy options*. (Information Series No. 281). Columbus, OH: Ohio State University, National Center for Research in Vocational Education.

Office of Vocational and Adult Education. (1991, March). *Combining school and work: Options in high schools and two-year colleges*. Washington, DC: U.S. Department of Education.

Olson, L. (1990, April 4). Parents as partners: Redefining the social contract between families and schools. *Education Week*, pp. 17-24.

Osterman, P. (1989). The job market for adolescents. In D. Stern and D. Eichorn (Eds.), *Adolescence and work: Influences of social structure, labor markets, and culture* (pp. 235-256). Hillsdale, NJ: Lawrence Erlbaum Associates.

Packer, A. H., & Wirt, J. G. (1991, September). *Restructuring work and learning*. Paper presented at the meeting of the Urban Opportunity Program Conference on Urban Labor Markets and Labor Mobility. Washington, DC: U.S. Department of Labor, Secretary's Commission on Achieving Necessary Skills.

Poole, V. (1988). *Education for employment*. Madison, WI: Wisconsin Department of Public Instruction

Reich, R. B. (1992). *The work of nations*. New York: Vintage.

Seeley, D. (1985). *Education through partnership*. Washington, DC: American Enterprise Institute for Public Policy Research.

Sizer, T. R. (1991). *Horace's school*. Boston: Houghton Mifflin.

Smith, T. J., & Trist, C. (1988). *Training and educating the work force in the nineties: The rationale for public-private collaboration* (Information Series No. 331). Columbus, OH: Ohio State University, Center for Education and Training for Employment. (ERIC Clearinghouse on Adult Career, and Vocational Education)

Soltis, J. F. (1978). *An introduction to the analysis of educational concepts* (2nd ed.). Reading, MA: Addison-Wesley.

Stacey, N., Alsalam, N., Gilmore, J., & To, D. (1988, April). *Education and training of 16- to 19-year-olds after compulsory school in the United States*. Washington, DC: Office of Educational Research and Improvement.

Stern, D., & Nakata, Y. (1989). Characteristics of high school students' paid jobs and employment experience after graduation. In D. Stern and D. Eichorn (Eds.), *Adolescence and work: Influences of social structure, labor markets, and culture* (pp. 189-209). Hillsdale, NJ: Lawrence Erlbaum Associates.

Toffler, A. (1990). *Powershift*. New York: Bantam.

W. T. Grant Commission on Youth, Family, and Citizenship. (1988). *The forgotten half: Pathways to success for America's youth and young families*. Washington, DC: author.

W. T. Grant Foundation Commission on Work, Family, and Citizenship, et al. (1991). *States and communities on the move: Policy initiatives to create a world-class workforce*. Washington, DC: Author.

23

New York State's Compact for Learning and Its Role in School-to-Employment Transition

Phillip J. Marron

Introduction

Recently, the New York State Board of Regents released a comprehensive reform program for its schools. The plan, which State Education Commissioner Thomas Sobol labeled A New Compact for Learning, is designed to fundamentally change the way schools operate and how they educate children. In simple terms, its target of producing improved educational outcomes is to be accomplished by providing greater flexibility in school governance, especially through the collaborative participation of numerous interested players. While the state's previous school improvement efforts expected increased results through mandates to schools, the compact represents a drastic philosophical shift in how to reach those goals. Schools always had the responsibility to produce results. Now they'll be given the authority to determine *how* to produce them.

Regents Action Plan

In 1984, the regents released the Regents Action Plan to Improve Education Results in New York, a comprehensive ten-year school improvement plan. Like other states' education reform efforts, this "first-wave" attempt was New York's scheme to strengthen the quality of education provided in its schools by setting higher expectations for its students. Among other things, this intensification model raised math and foreign language standards while instituting stricter graduation requirements.

To support the Regents Action Plan, the state legislature passed significant annual increases in aid to education. But despite its good intentions and the large sums of money dedicated, New York did not succeed in reforming its educational system. In effect, the initiative didn't change the way things worked. It just set higher goals, and then it focused on procedures to measure them. The state was simply watching its investment. After all, the more you spend for something, the more you expect to receive. And New York expected that increased expenditures for education would result in a corresponding increase in student outcomes.

A new ruler called Comprehensive Annual Reports (CAR) was designed to assess the state's "return on investment." After schools submitted specific kinds of data about enrollments, standardized test results, completion rates, and so forth, distinctive district profiles were produced. The measuring of one district against the others (and against itself before the action plan) was started. When concerns about educational outcomes became the center-stage topic locally, the CAR document provided a new script for interpreting each school's effectiveness.

Although these statistical accountings were

relatively informational and could have served as a reference for program improvements, their adoption was irregular. Schools that had "good stories" to tell publicized their CARs well and interpreted them as saying "Everything's OK; don't make any changes." In the case of some schools that had negative evaluations, the CAR numbers were at times accepted and improvements sometimes occurred. In other cases, however, administrators might have made "special interpretations" to portray their school's poor standings as "not too bad; especially when you look at XYZ School with worse numbers".

Excellence and Accountability Program

To many, the Regents Action Plan created more disparity than success. Now, the least able, mediocre, and at-risk students had greater challenges to meet. It's not surprising that New York initiated a new effort just five years later, the Excellence and Accountability Program (EAP). Borrowing from the Effective Schools movement, EAP focused on learning mastery following the premise "all children can learn." Targeting the concepts of equity and excellence as the essential ingredients of effective schools where outcomes are paramount, New York brought these elements together with a few others to create a new agenda to more effectively help children achieve their potential.

Grounded in objectives that are clear, simple, and manageable, Effective Schools promoted the gathering of small but credible amounts of test data to check for skills mastery. EAP, however, emphasized procedures and standards rather than focusing on results. It directed school districts to collect additional information for input into their CARs. Along with other new information, each district had to present comprehensive five-year education plans and make comparisons between their current status of accomplishment and previously adopted standards.

A New Compact for Learning

It is hoped that A New Compact for Learning will change these prescriptive formats. Unlike past innovation efforts that maintained specificity in directing schools regarding what to do and how to do it, the compact represents a shift in beliefs, philosophies, and paradigms about the role of the participants in the process. Although it begins somewhat in typical bureaucratic fashion by giving schools specific goals, such as the preparation of all high school graduates for college and/or employment, it differs significantly from its predecessors. Specifically, it promotes procedural freedom to the participants through local initiatives, support by means of relief from mandates (i.e., no more "Do it this way"), and encouragement through incentives and resources. Altogether, these factors are expected to nurture the participants' efforts to plan for and participate in making the specific improvements *they* deem appropriate and in selecting and developing the ideas and programs *they* think will succeed in their local schools.

The compact's architects recognized that schools have failed to bring about the educational results society expected. In assessing New York's (and the nation's) educational system, these writers readily detected a prevailing theme. School organization, curriculum, teaching methodologies, and governance hadn't changed significantly throughout the century. Without question, the gambit of education experts, from teachers and administrators in schools to researchers and scholars in private business and universities, viewed "the system" similarly.

Since many of the compact's proposals were developed with the assistance of business leaders, they are somewhat unique in education. After all, the managers involved used input from all the players on their teams and assumed the same variety of contributions in the compact. (Coincidentally, this approach has helped many American businesses regain their competitive edge in the world market.) Consequently, the sponsors of the compact hail it as an innovative approach to school improvement; a means by which schools can regain respect in society through marked improvements in their "products".

Under the compact, parents and other noneducators are asked to get more involved with educators, to take greater responsibility for children's learning by taking part in program planning and school governance. Borrowing from the African proverb "It takes a whole village to raise a child," the compact's authors envisioned a collaborative effort of administrators and teachers along with parents, higher education and cultural institutions, professional societies, health and social agencies, and businesses to achieve these objectives. Moreover, the compact calls for "people in all parts of the system to exercise initiative ... [and] take responsibility for and contribute to the education of children" (New York State Board of Regents, 1991, p. 19), particularly on a hands-on basis. But to assure this initiative, Commissioner Sobol directed every school district to develop and adopt a collaboration plan for school-based planning and shared decision making by February 1994.

Business's Role in the New Compact for Learning

The unique perspectives and potential contributions of parents, teachers, businesses, and others are both recognized and valued when these parties are encouraged to participate in educational program planning and school governance. Recently, Kuhn (1990) noted that business's most visible role in education consisted of providing scholarships, work-study programs or internships, teacher internships, and/or forming special relationships with schools. Known as "adopt-a-school" academies or partnerships, these bonds were usually "home-grown" deals or arrangements between local schools and local businesses.

The potential for success in partnerships between education and business (or education and other players for that matter) is limited by the participants' capacity for innovation, the quality of their concerted actions, and their willingness to "give and take." But considering that these affiliations are supposed to be characterized by shared responsibility with democratic input, concerns of imposed hierarchical control (i.e., school administrators curbing the process) must be considered and plans made for addressing consensus building and other relevant issues. Anticipating the potential for derailment, Commissioner Sobol directed school districts to develop and adopt a collaboration plan for school-based planning

and shared decision making. Besides these factors, Bruner (1991) stated that school/business collaboration efforts succeeded only when the partners remained focused on the goals of fulfilling the needs of educating children.

Woolhouse (1991) found that school/business alliances typically involve an exchange of resources between schools and businesses after an understanding is reached on specific school enhancement or enrichment outcomes. School/business coalitions are expected to support the compact's principles of focusing on results, aiming for mastery, and, perhaps, providing the means to achieve compact objectives. Indeed, the compact's writers confidently expect future participating businesses to actively share in the educational development of youth as others had previously done.

Farrar and Connolly (1990) documented past education and business collaborations. They specifically studied the Boston Compact Initiative, a substantial joint effort involving seven middle schools and almost 60 businesses in Boston, Massachusetts. As a result of those associations, both the schools' academic and extracurricular programs improved. In addition, school participants gained better understanding of the private enterprise system, and students and teachers learned about the requirements and expectations of the business world. In exchange, business people gained increased knowledge of the educational system. Other benefits also arose, including provision of adult worker literacy training. In short time, the agreements expanded to include colleges and universities—to the degree that business and postsecondary education collaborators outnumbered participating middle schools by three to one. Through school/business accords, the New Compact's creators anticipate similar developments to occur throughout New York.

In discussing what partnerships might achieve, we must distinguish between the types of resources that may be exchanged. Woolhouse referenced several—including information, knowledge, skills, expertise, and professional capability—that already existed or that might be generated and applied through cooperative actions. For example, the curriculum mastery and pedagogical skills of teachers could be made available to businesses, and business's managerial and technical know-how could be made accessible to administrators, teachers, and students. This reciprocal arrangement might take place through personnel exchange programs, teaching programs, internships, work study, or joint development initiatives.

Another possibility involves pooling, sharing, or joint use of capital investments in buildings, plants and equipment, hardware, software, transport and communication systems, and so forth. Projects or work experiences undertaken by students, teachers, and administrators in firms are another way of sharing both expertise and physical resources. These might include an allotment of scientific laboratories, classrooms, recreational facilities, retail stores, hospitals, construction sites, financial centers, manufacturing sites, and so forth. Further sharing could involve contributions in the form of grants, donations, endowments, summer jobs to students and/or teachers, pro bono and ancillary services, or other in-kind support.

Concerns about Forming Partnerships

A driving force must underlie the exchange of resources and the programs through which they are managed to provide a source of inspiration and energy that moves individuals and groups to want to do things that they are not already doing. That effort is generated by shared concerns and a shared vision of how to change things for the better. Successful partnerships must rely on the commitment of all players involved. While most members of society seem to endorse these unions, some are skeptical—especially some educators. Perhaps feeling threatened, they don't necessarily share the opinion that businesses have a sincere interest in schools.

A national audit of the motivating forces behind partnership activities by Krachai (1991) in the United Kingdom (UK) indicated that some compacts were embedded in economic philosophies and/or needs. Many businesses appeared to be concerned only with the present and future quality of the labor market and the need to have a better and more highly trained workforce. These immediate economic imperatives capped the potential of alliances that might have otherwise attended to more complex long-term issues, the issues that could condition and shape society in the future. However, several of those economic-biased relationships focused on immediate needs (e.g., financial benefits) and not necessarily on the greater issue of improved educational outcomes.

Businesses in UK partnerships that deviated from educational interests towards self-interest are not necessarily unique to Britain. It's not surprising since the majority of British partnerships were developed from United States models, especially the Boston Compact, a partnership program that was essentially concerned with employability issues. Nonetheless, British alliances differ significantly from those in the United States in how they're organized and funded. In providing most of the sponsorship, the British government organizes school/business alliances through a highly structured system of regional training and enterprise councils, local enterprise companies and education business partnerships and compacts (Tolfree, 1992).

Marjoribanks (1985) explained a popular theory of the purpose of education that embraced these attitudes. Known as functionalism, it viewed schools as serving two purposes. Structurally, they acted as agents of socialization by promoting loyalty towards the prevailing social system. From a technological perspective, education was seen as a working mechanism for providing a skilled workforce appropriate to an overexpanding economy.

Parsons (1959) presented similar views a quarter century earlier. He contended that education's role was to develop the appropriate skills and social attitudes in children required for an industrialized society's survival in the evolving world marketplace. Schools would assure every child an equal chance for success based on individual effort rather than through privileges afforded or denied because of social status. For that reason, Parsons saw education serving both a socialization and an individual development purpose. On the social level, schools helped assure an industrialized democracy through the development and maintenance of required skills and attitudes. On the individual level, schools enhanced the possibility that job placement and the distribution of income, prestige, and authority would be fair for everyone. Schools did away with each group's ascribed social status and instead, promoted individuals' achieved status.

While functionalism has been the dominant tradition in American and British educational governance, it is not without competition. Of its competitors, conflict theory appears the most prominent challenge. Neo-Marxists argue that business-supported schools reinforce social inequalities, contradict structural order, and reproduce both. In Neo-Weberian terms, if one social status group has power, it could determine what was valued and, thus, taught in schools. The subordinated social status groups end up disadvantaged in relation to the criteria set forth by the dominant group. Critical theorists view business as using its influence in education, albeit unknowingly at times, to suppress people from socially and economically disadvantaged backgrounds (e.g., minorities, women, immigrants) and to restrain their potential upward social movement. Berlin and Sum (1983) noted that many members of low socioeconomic groups place their hopes in education as they attempt to escape the problems that typically plague their communities (e.g., poverty, drug addiction, gang warfare, and unemployment), yet schools seem to "keep them in their place." As a result, some people see the educational system as promulgating the needs of "the haves" and ignoring those of "the have-nots."

Giroux (1983) agreed that the critical theorist vision holds that not everyone receives an equal opportunity to achieve success. He sought to determine what aspects of society influenced some people (i.e., those in power) to treat those different from themselves (i.e., those with dissimilar looks, cultures, or values) with disregard. He also noted that many of the majority professed functionalist-like values that legitimized economic class systems. At the same time, the subordinate groups seemed to exert little effort to "get ahead" compared with the dominant class. As a result, the majority continued to gain specific advantages over the minorities. Giroux saw those in power as trying to maintain their upper hand through the use of "hidden agendas" in the curriculum, their presentation of past experiences and future ambitions, and perpetuating their specific interests.

Conclusions

While the question of whether the motives of business are sincerely generous toward students, self-serving, or self-preserving may not be determined before each potential relationship is established, the intensity of those interests is quite high. Given the consensus opinion that America's business and government leaders express about the need for a highly competent workforce (McLaughlin, Verity, & Bennett, 1988; Carnevale, Gainer, & Meltzer, 1989) and the shortage of trained workers (Levitan, 1988; Employment Department Group, 1991), the interests of business seem unarguably genuine and bona fide. No doubt, the compact's planners weighed the fact that, in the past, some businesses had selfish interests in their dealings with schools. Yet, the compact's principle of "providing the means" champions the cause of equality that all Americans should uphold—not in terms of input, but of "equity of outcome" (New York State Board of Regents, 1991, p. 3).

For those reasons, school/business relationships must be recognized for their value and their development must be stimulated. The compact's supporters are convinced that collaboration between education and business and other interested groups *will* build a healthy society; promote the common objectives of developing human capability; serve all individuals, organizations, and communities equally; enhance the quality of life; be responsive to local, state, national and global interests; and contribute to the relevance and quality of initial education and lifelong learning.

Although these observations might be interpreted as criticisms of school partnerships, this isn't the intention. Mutual benefits and shared learning do, indeed, emanate from these bonds. Farrar found that relationships between education and business are generally believed to be good, useful, and worthwhile to both parties. In addition, since partnerships are about intentions, they derive their stature and attraction from what they achieve. In the end, the anticipation of new and improved outcomes, predicated perhaps on a simple notion Krachai described as "two plus two can make five" (1991, p. 133), will foster new alliances.

In closing, the desirability of close, productive, and harmonious pacts between education and business is hardly challenged. Schools involved in current and future relationships must have confidence in the scope, quality, and intent of their partnerships. After all, it is expected that these efforts will affect access to the hopes and expectations that schools probably could not attain for children otherwise. Further, it is anticipated that profoundly important goals can result from these relationships—not just by fulfilling each others' economic needs, but by improving the ways education is perceived, governed, and delivered.

References

Berlin, G., & Sum, A. (1983). *Toward a more perfect union: Basic skills, poor families, and our economic future.* Ford Foundation Project on Social Welfare, Occasional Paper No. 3. New York: Ford Foundation.

Bruner, C. (1991). *Thinking collaboratively: Ten questions and answers to help policymakers improve children's services.* Washington, DC: Education and Human Services Consortium.

Carnevale, A. P., Gainer, L. J., & Meltzer, A. S. (1989). *Workplace basics: The skills employers want.* Alexandria, VA: American Society for Training and Development.

Employment Department Group. (1991). *Labor market & skills trends.* Sheffield, Great Britain: Crown.

Farrar, E., & Connolly, C. (1990). *Improving middle schools: The Boston compact initiative.* Buffalo, NY: Buffalo Research Institute on Education for Teaching, State University of New York at Buffalo.

Giroux, H. A. (1983, August). Theories of reproduction and resistance in the new sociology of education: A critical analysis. *Harvard Educational Review, 53* (3), pp. 257-293.

Krachai, J. (1991). A new role for partnerships. In B. Gibbs, R. Hedge, & E. Clough (Eds.), *The reality of partnership* (pp. 133-145). Essex, Great Britain: Longman.

Kuhn, S. E. (1990, Spring). How business helps schools. *Fortune, 121* (12), 91-94.

Lacey, R. A., & Kingsley, C. (1987). *A guide to working partnerships.* Waltham, MA: Center for Human Resources, Heller Graduate School, Brandeis University.

Levitan, S. A. (1988). Beyond 'trendy' forecasts: The next 10 years of work. In E. Cornish (Ed.), *Careers tomorrow: The outlook for work in a changing world.* Bethesda, MD: World Futures Society.

Marjoribanks, K. (1985). Sociology of education. In T. Husen & T. N. Postlethwaite (Eds.), *The international encyclopedia of education research and studies* (pp. 4680-4700). Oxford, Great Britain: Pergamon Press.

McLaughlin, A., Verity, C. W., & Bennett, W. J. (1988). *Building a quality workforce.* Washington, DC: U.S. Departments of Labor, Education, & Commerce.

New York State Board of Regents. (1991). *A new compact for learning.* Albany: The University of the State of New York.

New York State Board of Regents. (1984). *Regents action plan to improve education results in New York.* Albany: The University of the State of New York.

Parsons, T. (1959, Fall). The school class as a social system: Some of its functions in American society. *Harvard Educational Review, 29* (4), 297-318.

Sobol, T. (1992). Making a new compact for learning a reality. *The Council Journal.* Albany, NY: New York State Council of Superintendents.

Tolfree, P. (1992, January/February). Year in industry scheme expands. *Partnership Points, 17,* p. 5.

Woolhouse, J. (1991). Partnership principles. In B. Gibbs, R. Hedge, & E. Clough (Eds.), *The reality of partnership* (pp. 3-23). Essex, Great Britain: Longman.

Special Section

Career Information Sources for Curriculum Development, Guidance, Vocational Counseling, and Career Education

Charles R. Doty

The information explosion has created knowledge gaps for everyone. I created this compilation to assist users to quickly locate the most useful information for planning and implementing education programs, specifically those components related to the school-to-work transition. The following information was gathered, and found useful, over several years when I taught graduate-level courses and conducted non-profit and profit consulting for private and public institutions. The compilation is organized using the following major areas:

Accreditation
Adult Career Education
Assessment
Associations
At-Risk Populations
Boy Scouts
Business Involvement
Career and Vocational Guidance
Certification
Computer
Consortium
Data
Decision Making
Education and Employment
Effects of Career Education
Entrepreneurship
ERIC Clearinghouse on Career Education
Family-Career Connection
Foundations
Health Careers
Individualized Career Plan Models
Job Information
Licensing

Limited English Proficient (LEP) Resource Organizations
National Curriculum Network
National Projects
National Sources
Parents and Career Education
Publishers of Career and Guidance Materials
Rehabilitation Counseling
Research Centers
Safety/Consumerism
Selecting and Using Career Education Systems
School-to-Work Transition
Special Needs
Standard References
Systems
Technology Literacy
Texts
Trends
Women
Work Ethic
Workplace Career Development
Youth Organizations

Accreditation

- Council for Accreditation of Counseling and Related Educational Programs
American Association for Counseling and Development
5999 Stevenson Ave.
Alexandria, VA 22304

Adult Career Education

- *Career development for undereducated adults in ABE programs* (Final report). (ERIC Document Reproduction Services No. ED 317 846)

- Imel, S. (1986). Adult education teacher's role in career planning. *ERIC Digest No. 55.* Columbus, OH: Clearinghouse on Adult, Career,& Vocational Education, Center on Education & Training for Employment

- Kerka, S. (1987). Adult career counseling—An interactive model: Overview. *ERIC Digest No. 65.* Columbus, OH: Clearinghouse on Adult, Career, and Vocational Education, Center on Education and Training for Employment.

Assessment

- Armed Services Vocational Aptitude Battery (ASVAB)
HQ USMEPCOM/MEPCT-E
2500 Green Bay Rd.
North Chicago, IL 60064-3094

- Botterbusch, K. F. (1987). *Vocational assessment and evaluation systems: A comparison.* Menomonie, WI: Materials Development Center, Stout Vocational Rehabilitation Institute, University of Wisconsin-Stout.

- Consulting Psychologists Press
577 College Ave.
Palo Alto, CA 94306
415-857-1444

- DeStefano, L., et al. (1987, May). *Review of student assessment instruments and practices in use in secondary/transition projects.* Champaign, IL: Illinois University. (ERIC Document Reproduction Services No. ED 291 170)

- National Assessment of Educational Programs
Box 2923
Princeton, NJ 08541
800-223-0267

Associations

- American Association for Counseling and Development
5999 Stevenson Ave.
Alexandria, VA 22304

- American School Counselors Association
5999 Stevenson Ave.
Alexandria, VA 22304

- American Vocational Association
1410 King St.
Alexandria, VA 22314

- Association for Advancement of the Mentally Handicapped
60 Prince St.
Elizabeth, NJ 07208
201-345-3040

- Association for School, College & University Staffing, Inc.
301 South Swift Rd.
Addison, IL 60101
312-495-4707
(publisher of *A Job Search Handbook for Educators*)

- Association of Computer-Based Systems for Career Information Clearinghouse
1787 Agate St.
Eugene, OR 97403

- Association of Counselor Education and Supervision
5999 Stevenson Ave.
Alexandria, VA 22304

- Center for Environmental Intern Programs
68 Harrison Ave., 5th Floor
Boston, MA 02111

- Commission on Precollege Guidance and Counseling
The College Entrance Examination Board
45 Columbus Ave.
New York, NY 10023-6917

- Counseling for Accreditation of Counseling Related Educational Programs
1215 Norman Hall
University of Florida
Gainesville, FL 32611

- Council for the Advancement of Standards for Student Services/Development Programs
American College Personnel Association
5999 Stevenson Ave.

Alexandria, VA 22304

- National Association of the Deaf
  814 Thayer Ave.
  Silver Springs, MD 20910

- National Association of Trade and Technical
  Schools
  P. O. Box 2006
  Annapolis Junction, MD 20701-2006

- National Board for Certified Counselors
  5999 Stevenson Ave.
  Alexandria, VA 22304

- National Career Development Association
  5999 Stevenson Ave.
  Alexandria, VA 22304
  703-828-9800

- National Science Foundation
  NSF/Forms and Publication
  1800 G. St. NW
  Washington, DC 20550
  202-357-7492

- New Jersey Career Development Association
  28 Summit Ave.
  Hackensack, NJ 07601-1263
  908-572-2420

At-Risk Populations

- Lowry, C. M. (1990). Helping at-risk youth make the school-to-work transition. *ERIC Digest No. 101*. Columbus, OH: Clearinghouse on Adult, Career, and Vocational Education, Center on Education and Training for Employment. (See also ED 315-666)

- ERIC Clearinghouse on Adult, Career, and Vocational Education. (1986). *Career education for at-risk population: A resource list from the ERIC Clearinghouse*. Columbus, OH: Center on Education and Training for Employment.

Boy Scouts

- Boy Scouts of America
  Exploring Division
  P. O. Box 152079
  Irving, TX 75051
  (or call the Office of Career Awareness Exploring, 214-580-2428)

- Pestel, A. (1990, November). Scouting program brings career awareness to schools. *School Shop/Tech Directions, 50*(4), 16-17.

Business Involvement

- ERIC Clearinghouse on Adult, Career, and Vocational Education. (1987). *Business involvement in career education: A resource list from the ERIC Clearinghouse*. Columbus, OH: Center on Education and Training for Employment.

- National Entrepreneurship Education Consortium
  Center on Education and Training for Employment
  1900 Kenny Rd.
  Columbus, OH 43210-1090
  800-848-4815
  (Cosponsored by the U.S. Small Business Administration and the Center on Education and Training for Employment)

Career and Vocational Guidance

- Boyle, K. K. (1983). *Career information in the classroom: Workshop guide for infusing the Occupational Outlook Handbook*. Columbus, OH: National Center for Research in Vocational Education. (ERIC Document Reproduction Services No. ED 231 985)

- *Counselor resource guide*. (1992, February). Available from Educational Development & Training Center, East Texas State University, Commerce, TX 75429, 800-356-3382; FAX: 903-886-5744, or telephone: 903-886-5623.

- Creation and Mobilization of Counseling Resources for Youth Project (A project similar to the U. S. National Career Development Guidelines project). Career guidance and counseling is the focus of this $5.5 million project including video disc development. Information available from Executive Director, Canadian Guidance & Counseling Foundation, Suite 202, 411 Roosevelt Ave., Ottawa, Ontario K2A3X9, Canada.

- *Final report on 6th International Conference on Vocational Guidance, November 2-4, 1988, at Ashiya University*. Available from Secretariat of the International Conference on Vocational Guidance, Ashiya University, 13-22 Rokurokusocho, Ashiya, Hyogo, 659 Japan.

- Magosis, J. H. (Ed.). (1973). *Career education*. Washington, DC: American Vocational Association.

- Halasz, I. M. (1988). *Trends and issues in*

career education 1988. Columbus, OH: Center on Education and Training for Employment.

- Hoyt, K. B., & Shylo, K. R. (1987). *Career education in transition: Trends and implications for the future.* Columbus, OH: National Center for Research in Vocational Education. (ERIC Document Reproduction Service No. ED 290 933)

- *New Jersey statewide validation of career and vocational guidance and counseling standards project. Final report.* (1988, February). New Jersey: Bayonne Public Schools. (ERIC Document Reproduction Services No. ED 290 894)

- National Occupational Information Coordinating Committee (NOICC). *Improved career decision making (ICDM) curriculum.* Program designed to train counselors on sources of labor market information and effective use in the career development process. For information, contact The Vocational Studies Center, University of Wisconsin-Madison, 964 Educational Sciences Bldg., 1025 West Johnson St., Madison, WI 53706; telephone: 608-263-3696.

- National Occupational Information Coordinating Committee (NOICC). (1989). *National career development guidelines project.* Washington, DC: Author. (Available from NOICC, Suite 156, 2100 M. St., NW, Washington, DC 20037; telephone: 202-653-5665; or Center on Education and Training for Employment, Publications Office, Box C, The Ohio State University, 1900 Kenny Rd., Columbus 43210-1090. Category A: *Guidance program planning,* 6 modules—$43; Category B: Supporting, 5 modules—$46; Category C: Implementing, 19 modules—$14; Category E: Evaluating, 2 modules—$14; complete series—$245.

- National career development guidelines. (ERIC Document Reproduction Services No. ED 317 874, ED 317 975, ED 317 876, ED 317 877, ED 317 878, ED 317 879, and ED 317 880)

- NOICC Training Support Center
  Oklahoma SOICC
  Dept. of Vocational Technical Education
  1500 West 7th Ave.
  Stillwater, OK 74074

800-654-4502

- Office of Career Education. (1979, September). *Career education programs that work.* Washington, DC: U. S. Government Printing Office.

- Walsh, W. B., & Osipow, S. H. (1990). *Career counseling: Contemporary topics in vocational psychology.* Hillsdale: Lawrence Erlbaum Associates.

- Yost, E. B., & Corbishley, M. A. (1987). *Career counseling: A psychological approach.* San Francisco, CA: Jossey-Bass Publishers.

Certification
- Commission on Rehabilitation Counselor Certification
  1156 Shure Dr., Suite 350
  Arlington Heights, IL 60004

- National Academy of Certified Mental Health Counselors
  5999 Stevenson Ave.
  Alexandria, VA 22304

- National Board for Certified Counselors
  5999 Stevenson Ave.
  Alexandria, VA 22304

Computer
- Association of Computer-Based Systems for Career Information (ACSCI) Clearinghouse
  1787 Agate St.
  Eugene OR 97403

- *Insight: The interactive career planning program.* (Available from Bytes of Learning Incorporated, 150 Consumers Rd., Suite 202, Willowdale, Ontario, Canada M2J lP9)

Consortium
- National Consortium of State Career Guidance Supervisors
  National Center on Education and Training for Employment
  The Ohio State University
  1900 Kenny Rd.
  Columbus, OH 43210-1090
  800-848-4815; FAX: 614-292-1260
  (Publishes National Career Guidance News)

Data
- Department of the Army. (1990). *Experience for hire: Closing the skills gap with army alumni.* (Available from Army Opportunities, Experience for Hire, P. O. Box 3219,

Warminster, PA 18974-9845)

- National Occupation Information Coordinating Committee
2100 M St., NW
Washington, DC 20037

- National Occupational Information Coordinating Committee (NOICC) Training Support Center. *Bulletin.* (Available from NOICC Training Support Center, Oklahoma Dept. of Vocational and Technical Education, 1500 W. 7th Ave., Stillwater, OK 74074-9906; 405-743-5197)

- New Jersey Occupational Information Coordinating Committee
Labor and Industry Bldg., CN 056
Trenton, NJ 08625-0056; 609-292-6904.
(Each state has its own occupational information coordinating committee.)

- Office of Personnel Management
Federal Job Information Center
1900 E. St., Room 1425
Washington, DC 20415

Decision Making
- Imel, S., & Kerka, S. (1989). Labor market information and career decision making. *ERIC Digest No. 83.* Columbus, OH: Clearinghouse on Adult, Career, and Vocational Education, Center on Education and Training for Employment.

Education and Employment
- Harrison, C. (no date). Education and employment. *ERIC Digest No. 50.* Columbus, OH: Clearinghouse on Adult, Career, and Vocational Education, Center on Education and Training for Employment.

- Lankard, B. A. (1990). Employability—The fifth basic skill. *ERIC Digest No. 104.* Columbus, OH: Clearinghouse on Adult, Career, and Vocational Education, Center on Education and Training for Employment.

Effects of Career Education
- Miller, J. (no date). Effects of career education on student achievement and retention. *ERIC Digest No. 32.* Columbus, OH: Clearinghouse on Adult, Career, and Vocational Education.

Entrepreneurship
- Association of Collegiate Entrepreneurs
1845 N. Fairmont

Ace Box 147
Wichita, KS 67208

- National Entrepreneurship Education Consortium
National Center on Education and Training for Employment
The Ohio State University
1900 Kenny Rd.
Columbus, OH 43210-1090

ERIC Clearinghouse on Career Education
- ERIC Clearinghouse on Adult, Career, and Vocational Education
1900 Kenny Rd.
Columbus, OH 43210-1090
800-848-4815.
(Paper and microfiche copies of microfiche documents (i.e., for EDs, are available from the ERIC Document Reproduction Service, 3900 Wheeler Ave., Alexandria, VA 22304-6409; 800-227-3742. Journals for EJs are available in many libraries, and article reprints can be obtained from UMI Article Clearinghouse, 300 North Zeeb Rd., Ann Arbor, MI 48106; 800-732-0616.

Family-Career Connection
- Miller, J. (no date). The family-career connection. *ERIC Digest No. 52.* Columbus, OH: ERIC Clearinghouse on Adult, Career, and Vocational Education, Center on Education and Training for Employment.

Foundations
- New Ventures in Education and Training
PAVE, The Education and Training Foundation, Non Profit Organization
208 N. Washington St.
Alexandria, VA 22314
703-683-0547

Health Careers
- Health Careers Guidance Clinic
College of Allied Health Sciences
Thomas Jefferson University
Edison Building/Ste. 706
Philadelphia, PA 19107
215-928-6294

- National Health Careers Information Hotline
800-999-4248
(Health Careers for You)

Individualized Career Plan Models
- Bhaerman, R. D. (1988). Individualized career plan models. *ERIC Digest No. 71.*

Columbus, OH: Clearinghouse on Adult, Career, and Vocational Education, Center on Education and Training for Employment.

Job Information

• *Job market: The career exploration aide.* (Available from AVA, Dept. JM1190, 1410 King St., Alexandria, VA 22314; 800-826-9972)

• Career Information Delivery System (CIDS)
New Jersey Occupational Information Coordinating Committee, CN 056
Labor Bldg., Rm. 1008
Trenton, NJ 08625-0056
800-222-1309

• Center on Education and Training for Employment. (1990, November). Job and career information: What you should know. *Centergram, 25*(11).

• Imel, S. (1990). Jobs in the future. *ERIC Digest No. 95.* Columbus, OH: Clearinghouse on Adult, Career, and Vocational Education, Center on Education and Training for Employment.

• New Jersey Department of Labor, Bureau of Occupational Research. *Employment projections. Volume IV: Occupational outlook for the counties of New Jersey, 1986-2000.* (Available from New Jersey Dept. of Labor, Bureau of Occupational Research, CN 383, Room 202, Trenton, NJ 08625-0383; data available on diskettes)

• New Jersey Occupational Information Coordinating Committee. (1989). *Jobs 1990 and beyond: Is New Jersey ready?* (Available from NJOICC, Labor Bldg., Rm. 1008, CN 056, Trenton, NJ 08625-0056)

• New Jersey Occupational Information Coordinating Committee. (1988). *New Jersey occupational outlook handbook.* (Available from NJOICC, Labor Bldg., Rm. 1008, CN 056, Trenton, NJ 08625-0056)

• New Jersey State Data Center/Business and Industry Data Center
Electronic Bulletin Board System
New Jersey Dept. of Labor, Labor Market & Demographic Research, CN 388
Trenton, NJ 08625-0388
609-984-2595/609-292-0076;
    FAX: 609-984-6833
(An on-line demographic and economic data system)

• *National business employment weekly.* (From the publishers of The Wall Street Journal, Dow Jones & Co., Inc., 420 Lexington Ave., New York, NY 10170; telephone 800-535-4800)

• Wagner, J. O. (1988). Locating job information. *ERIC Digest No. 85.* Columbus, OH: Clearinghouse on Adult, Career, and Vocational Education, Center on Education and Training for Employment.

Licensing

• Educational Testing Service
Center for Occupational & Professional Assessment
Princeton, NJ 08540
609-951-6086
(Occupational licensing test development is a priority of ETS)

• New Jersey Occupational Information Coordinating Committee. (1989). *Licensed occupations in New Jersey.* (Available from: NJOICC, Labor Building, Room 1008, CN 056, Trenton, N. J. 08625-0056)

Limited English Speaking (LEP) Resource Organizations

• ERIC Clearinghouse on Adult, Career, and Vocational Education. (no date). *Career education for the limited English proficient, Trends and issues: Alerts.* Columbus, OH: Author.

• National Association for Bilingual Education
1201 16th St., NW, Room 405
Washington, DC 20036
202-822-7870

• National Association of Vocational Education Special Needs Personnel
110 Rackley Bldg.
Pennsylvania State University
University Park, PA 16802
(affiliated with American Vocational Association, Special Needs Division)

• National Clearinghouse for Bilingual Education
11501 Georgia Ave., Suite 100
Wheaton, MD 20902
800-647-0123

• National Council of La Raza
20 F St., NW, 2nd Floor
Washington, DC 20001
202-628-9600

- Teachers of English to Speakers of Other Languages
  1118 22nd St., NW
  Washington, DC 20037
  202-625-4569

National Curriculum Network
The National Curriculum Network consists of six centers located throughout the nation to serve educators. Free computer searches concerning curriculum are available.

- East Central Center
  Sangamon State University, F-2
  Springfield, IL 62794-9243
  217-786-6375

- Midwest Center
  Department of Vocational and Technical Education
  1500 W. 7th Ave.
  Stillwater, OK 74074-4364
  405-377-2000, ext. 398

- Northeast Center
  New Jersey State Department of Education
  Division of Vocational Education
  Crest Way
  Aberdeen, NJ 07747
  908-290-1900

- Northwest Center
  Old Main—Room 478
  Saint Martin's College
  Lacey, WA 98503
  206-438-4456

- Southeast Center
  Research & Curriculum Unit
  P. O. Drawer DX
  Mississippi State, MS 39762
  601-325-2510

- Western Center
  University of Hawaii
  1776 University Ave.
  Wist 216
  Honolulu, HI 96822
  808-948-7834

National Projects
- National Science Foundation
  Forms and Publications
  1800 G St. NW
  Washington, DC 20550

- Transition Research Institute at Illinois
  113 Children's Research Center
  51 Gerty Dr.
  Champaign, IL 61820
  217-333-2325
  (Produces annotated bibliographies concerning school-to-work strategies for special needs students; also publications, audiovisual media, associations, projects. See ERIC Document Reproduction Services No. ED 315 984, ED 318 167, ED 321 096)

- The National Projects Branch
  Office of Vocational and Adult Education
  U. S. Department of Education
  Washington, DC 20202
  202-245-2614

National Sources
- *Counselor Resource Guide*
  EDTC
  East Texas State University
  ET Station
  Commerce, TX 75429
  903-886-5623 or 800-356-EDTC

- Office of Personnel Management
  Federal Job Information Center
  1900 E St., Rm. 1425
  Washington, DC 20415

- National Association of Trade and Technical Schools
  P. O. Box 20006
  Annapolis Junction, MD 20701-2006

Parents and Career Education
- Burge, P. L. (1987). *Career development of single parents*. Columbus, OH: Clearinghouse on Adult, Career and Vocational Education. (ERIC Document Reproduction Services No. ED 290 934)

- ERIC Clearinghouse on Adult, Career, and Vocational Education. *Career education for teen parents: Trends and issues alerts*. Columbus, OH: Center on Education and Training for Employment. (ERIC Document Reproduction Services No. ED 317 846)

- Kerka, S. (1988). Single Parents: Career-related issues and needs. *ERIC Digest No. 75*. Columbus, OH: Clearinghouse on Adult, Career, and Vocational Education.

- *Parent involvement in career education: Bibliography*. (no date). Columbus, OH: ERIC Clearinghouse on Adult, Career, and Vocational Education.

Publishers of Career and Guidance Materials

- A.C.T.
  P. O. Box 168
  2201 N. Dodge St.
  Iowa City, IA 52245
  319-337-1566
  (career assessment and exploration resources)

- American Honda Motor, Inc.
  Mail Stop 500-2C-llB 1919
  Torrance, CA 90501
  310-783-2000
  (customer communications and technical
    service procedures)

- American National Cattlewomen, Inc.
  P. O. Box 3881
  Englewood, CO 80155
  303-694-0313
  (cattle industry)

- American Vocational Association
  Dept. 1090AR
  1410 King St.
  Alexandria, VA 22314
  703-683-3111
  (books, videos, software, cassettes)

- Cambridge Career Products
  P. O. Box 2153
  Charleston, WV 25328-2153
  800-468-4227
  (videos, software, texts concerning guidance)

- Career Design
  P. O. Box 95624
  Atlanta, Georgia 30345
  800-346-8007 or 404-321-6100

- Careers, Inc.
  P. O. Box 135
  Largo, Florida 34649
  800-726-0441
  (career, guidance and life skills materials,
    books, software and videos)

- Career Pages
  P. O. Box 100
  Spring City, PA 19475-0100
  215-948-5615

- *Career Training*
  Journal of the National Association of
    Trade and Technical Schools
  2251 Wisconsin Ave. NW
  Washington, DC 20007
  202-333-1021

- *Career World Magazine*
  245 Longhill Rd.
  Middletown, CT 06457

- Chronicle Guidance Publications, Inc.
  P. O. Box 1190
  Moravia, NY 13118-1190
  800-622-7284
  (career/guidance/life/basic skills video career
    library)

- Conover Company
  P. O. Box 155
  Omro, WI 54963
  800-933-1933
  (computer-based career planning)

- Consulting Psychologists Press
  577 College Ave.
  Palo Alto, CA 94306
  415-857-1444

- Corporate Jobs Outlook
  P. O. Box 100
  Boerne, TX 78006
  800-325-8808

- Delmar Publishers, Inc.
  Two Computer Dr. W.
  Albany, NY 12205
  518-459-1150

- Drake Beam Morin, Inc.
  100 Park Ave.
  4th Floor
  New York, NJ 10017
  800-345-Jobs or 212-692-7700
  (publishes *Career Navigator*)

- EBSCO Curriculum Materials
  P. O. Box 281
  Chelsea, AL 35043-0281
  800-633-8623

- EDITS Publishers
  P. O. Box 7234
  San Diego, CA 92164
  619-222-1666
  (COPsystem, career guidance assessment
    program)

- Education Associates, Inc.
  8 Crab Orchard Rd., P. O. Box Y
  Frankfort, KY 40602
  800-626-2950
  (life skills, employability skills, basic skills)

- Educational Design, Inc.
  47 W. 13th St.
  New York, NY 10011
  800-221-9372

- Educational Development and Training
    Center
  East Texas State University
  Commerce, TX 75429
  1-800-356-EDTC, 214-886-5624, or 886-6147

- Educational Technologies, Inc.
  1007 Whitehead Rd. Ext.
  Trenton, NJ 08638
  609-882-2668
  (computerized aptitude and interest assess-
    ment for 66 work groups)

- Electronics Industries Association
  2001 Pennsylvania Ave., NW
  Washington, DC 20006
  202-457-8715
  (consumer electronics)

- EMC Publishing
  300 York Ave.
  St. Paul, MN 55101
  612-771-1555
  (comprehensive materials including
    computer software)

- Finney Co.
  3943 Meadowbrook Rd.
  Minneapolis, MN 55426
  612-938-9330
  (career exploration and awareness materials)

- Garrett Park Press
  P. O. Box 190
  Garrett Park, MD 20896
  (publishes Career Opportunities News)

- GBE Publishers, Inc.
  10900 N. E. 8th St., Suite 900
  Bellevue, WA 98004
  206-454-0724

- Guidance Associates
  Communications Park, Box 3000
  Mount Kisco, NY 10549-0900
  800-431-1242
  (career education catalog)

- J. G. Ferguson Publishing Co.
  111 E. Wacker Dr.
  Chicago, IL 60601
  (publishes The Encyclopedia of Career Guid-
    ance)

- JIST Works, Inc.
  720 North Park Ave.
  Indianapolis, IN 46202-3431
  800-648-5478 or 317-264-3720
  (excellent career resources catalog)

- Journal of Career Development
  Human Sciences Press, Inc.
  233 Spring St.
  New York, NY 10013
  (212) 807-1047

- Ken Cook Education Systems
  12855 W. Silver Spring Dr.
  Butler, WI 53007
  414-781-3080
  (interactive training system on life skills)

- Marsh Media
  5903 Main St.
  Kansas City, MO 64113
  800-821-3303
  (Apple software on health/wellness and
    careers)

- Meridian Education Corporation
  VC-91
  236 E. Front St.
  Bloomington, IL 61701
  800-727-5507

- Opportunities for Learning, Inc.–Career Aids
  941 Hickory Lane
  P. O. Box 8103
  Mansfield, OH 44901-8103
  800-243-7116
  (media/computer software, elementary to
    adult)

- Pesco International
  21 Paulding St.
  Pleasantville, NY 10520
  800-431-2040
  (assessment system for industry-education-
    employment and training and rehabilitation)

- Prakken Publications, Inc.
  275 Metty Dr., P.O. Box 8623
  Ann Arbor, MI 48107
  800-530-9673
  (publisher of Tech Directions magazine and
    books for vocational education)

- Psychological Assessment Resources, Inc.
  P. O. Box 996
  Odessa, FL 33556

- Publishers Test Service
  CTB/McGraw-Hill
  2500 Garden Rd.
  Monterey, CA 93940
  800-538-9547

- Software, Inc.
  101 Hill Rd.
  Aberdeen, WA 98520
  206-532-3392
  (computer software and videos for technology, health, and business careers)

- Target Marketing, Inc.
  115 Blue Jay Dr.–P. O. Box 217
  Liberty, MO 64068
  816-781-7557;
  or 221 Riverside Dr.
  Princeton, NJ 08540
  800-331-2496

- Teaching Aids Incorporated
  Attn: Customer Service
  P. O. Box 1798
  Costa Mesa, CA 92628-0798
  714-548-9321
  (workplace literacy and basic skills)

- United Learning, Inc.
  6633 W. Howard St.
  Niles, IL 60648
  800-424-0362
  (at-risk programs)

- U. S. Department of Labor
  Bureau of Labor Statistics
  Washington, DC 20212
  (publishes *Occupational Outlook Handbook, Occupational Projections and Training Data, Outlook 2000,* and *Occupational Outlook Quarterly;* available from Superintendent of Documents, U.S. Government Printing Office, Washington, DC 20402)

- VGM Career Books
  4255 W. Touhy
  Lincolnwood, IL 60646
  708-679-5500, ext. 204
  (described in *American Vocational Journal* as the foremost career information publisher)

- Video Training Resources, Inc.
  7900 W. 78th St.–Suite 250
  Edina, MN 55439
  800-828-8190 (450 video titles on video training with pre- and post-tests)

- *Vocational Aspect of Education*

Triangle Books, Ltd.
P.O. Box 65
Wallingford, Oxfordshire OX10 OYG
United Kingdom

- Vocational Biographies, Inc.
  P. O. Box 31, Dept. VEJ2
  Sauk Center, MN 56378
  800-255-0752
  (basic facts on more than 850 health, trade, and technical careers)

Rehabilitation Counseling

- Council on Rehabilitation Education
  185 North Wabash Ave., Rm. 1617
  Chicago, IL 60601

- Division of Resource Development
  Rehabilitation Services Administration
  U. S. Department of Education
  330 C St. SW
  Washington, DC 20202

- National Rehabilitation Counseling
  Association
  633 S. Washington St.
  Alexandria, VA 22314

- National Council on Rehabilitation Education
  c/o Maddux O'Malley, Inc.
  2921 Ermine Way
  Farmers Branch, TX 75234

Research Centers

- Ashiya University Center
  1117-A Kapahulu Ave.
  Honolulu, HI 96816
  808-735-0072; FAX: 808-737-0135
  (one research endeavor is Career Orientation and Planning Profile (COPP), a guidance tool)

- Far West Laboratory for Educational Research and Development
  1855 Folsom St.
  San Francisco, CA 94103

- U. S. Congress, Office of Technology Assessment
  OTA Publications
  Washington, DC 20510-8025
  202-224-8996

Safety/Consumerism

- Federal Communications Commission (FCC)
  Consumer Assistance Department
  1919 M St., NW–Room 254
  Washington, DC 20554

- U. S. Department of Labor-OSHO
  Publications Office, Rm. N3101
  200 Constitution Ave.
  Washington, DC 20210

Selecting and Using Career Education Systems

- ERIC Clearinghouse on Adult, Career, and Vocational Education. (no date). *Selecting and using career information systems. Practice application brief.* Columbus, OH: Author.

School-to-Work Transition

- Barton, P. E. (1990). *From school to work.* Princeton, NJ: Policy Information Center, Educational Testing Service.

- Feichtner, S. H. (1989). *School-to-work transition for at-risk youth.* Information Series No. 339. Columbus, OH: ERIC Clearinghouse on Adult, Career, and Vocational Education, Center on Education and Training for Employment, The Ohio State University. (ERIC Document Reproduction Service No. ED 315 666)

- Leach, L. N., & Harmon, A. S. (1987). *Annotated bibliography on transition from school to work. Vol. 2.* Champaign, IL: University of Illinois. (ERIC Document Reproduction Service No. ED 291 168, also see ED 279 115)

- School to work transitions. (13 classroom modules on work skills, such as Apply for jobs; Accept responsibility; Employer's choice; Career passport; Employment file; Dignity in the workplace; plus videotapes and other materials. Available from the Center on Education and Training for Employment, Publications Office, 1900 Kenny Rd., Columbus, OH 43210; 800-848-4815)

- Secondary Transition Intervention Effectiveness Institute
  College of Education
  University of Illinois
  110 Education Building
  1310 South Sixth St.
  Champaign, IL 61820
  217-333-2325

- William T. Grant Foundation, Commission on Work, Family and Citizenship. (1988, November). *Strategies to help non-college youth.* (Available from 1001 Connecticut Ave., NW, Suite 301, Washington, DC,

20036-5541)

Special Needs

- Association for Advancement of the Mentally Handicapped
  60 Prince St.
  Elizabeth, NJ 07208
  201-354-3040
  (serves severely mentally handicapped adults and emotionally disturbed adolescents)

- Council for Exceptional Children
  Division on Career Development
  1920 Association Dr.
  Reston, VA 22091

- Leach, L. N. (1986 to present). *Annual bibliography on secondary special education and transitional services.* Champaign, IL: Transition Research at Illinois. (ERIC Document Reproduction Service No. ED 279 115, ED 291 168, ED 303 026, ED 318 166, ED 332 428, ED 342 195, ED 353 718)

- National Association of the Deaf
  c/o Mr. Fred Schreiber
  814 Thayer Ave.
  Silver Spring, MD 20910
  (national clearinghouse and advocacy organization working to change attitudes and treatment of the deaf; also provides service contact and listing of publications)

- National Association of Vocational Education Special Needs Personnel
  P. O. Box 785
  Devils Lake, ND 58301
  RPM Press, Inc.
  P. O. Box 31483
  Tucson, AZ 85751
  602-886-1990

- Vocational Studies Center
  964 Educational Sciences Bldg.
  1025 West Johnson St.
  Madison, WI 53706
  608-268-2929

Standard References

- *Career information center* (3rd ed.). (1987). Mission Hills, CA: Glencoe/Macmillan. (Provides more than 600 occupational profiles that review the work characteristics, job entry, education, and training requirements, advancement possibilities, employment outlook, and earnings and benefits for 3,000 jobs)

- Gale, B., & Gale, L. (1982). *Discover what you're best at: The national career aptitude system and career directory.* New York: Simon and Schuster. (A self-administered and self-scored career aptitude evaluation system that discusses career strengths, setting career goals, evaluating job potential, and potential careers.)

- Handville, E. (Ed.). (1989-90). *Occu-facts.* (Available from Careers, Inc., P. O. Box 135, Largo, FL 34649-0135. Covers 565 careers; revised every two years.)

- Hopke, W. E. (Ed.). (1987). *The encyclopedia of careers and vocational guidance.* (7th ed.). Chicago: J. G. Ferguson Publishing Co.

- Hotchkiss, L., et al. (1979, January). *Theories of occupational choice: A critical assessment of selected viewpoints.* Columbus, OH: National Center for Research in Vocational Education. (ERIC Document Reproduction Services No. ED 197 111)

- *Military career guide. Employment and training opportunities in the military 1988-89.* (Available from U. S. Military Entrance Processing Command, 2500 Green Bay Rd., North Chicago, IL 60064; hotline: 800-323-0513.)

- *The encyclopedia of career guidance.* (Available from J. G. Ferguson Publishing Co., 111 E. Wacker Dr., Chicago, IL; 312-861-0666.)

- Toropon, B. (Ed.). (1987). *1988 national job bank.* (4th ed.). Boston: Bob Adams, Inc.

- *The career guide.* (1989). Parsippany, NJ: Dun's Employment Opportunities Directory. (Provides an overview of career opportunities, location of offices, benefits, addresses, and contact persons for U.S. companies with 1,000+ employees.)

- U. S. Department of Labor. (1977). *Dictionary of occupational titles.* (4th ed.). Washington, DC: U. S. Employment Service.

- U. S. Department of Labor. (1988, April). *Occupational outlook handbook.* (1988-89 ed.). Washington, DC: Author.

Systems
- OASYS
  VERTEK, Inc.
  555-116 Ave. N. E.

Ste. 118
Bellevue, WA 98004
206-455-9921

Technology Literacy
- *Tech Directions* magazine
  Prakken Publications, Inc.
  275 Metty Dr.–P.O. Box 8623
  Ann Arbor, MI 48107
  (teaching methods, projects for vocational and technology educators)

- *TIES* magazine
  Drexel University
  3219 Arch St.
  Philadelphia, PA 19104
  215-590-8861

Texts
- Baumgart, D. (1988). *Career education: A curriculum manual for students with handicaps.* Frederick, MD.: Aspen Publishers. (7201 McKinney Circle, P.O. Box 990, Frederick, MD 21701-9782; $95)

- Borchard, J. J., Kelly, J. J., & Weaver, N. P. K. (1988). *Your career: Choices, chances, changes. Vol. 4.* Dubuque, IA: Kendall/Hunt Publishing Co.

- Boyle, K. K. (1983). *Career information in the classroom: Workshop guide for infusing the occupational outlook handbook.* Columbus, OH: National Center for Research in Vocational Education. (ERIC Document Reproduction Services No. ED 321 985)

- Fredrickson, R. H. (1982). *Career information.* Englewood Cliffs, NJ: Prentice-Hall.

- Walsh, W. B., & Osipow, S. H. (1990). *Career counseling: Contemporary topics in vocational psychology.* Hillsdale, MI: Lawrence Erlbaum Associates, Publishers.

- Wircenski, J. (1988). *Employability skills for the special needs learner.* Frederick, MD: Aspen Publishers; $125.

- Wirt, J. G. (Director). (1990). *Evaluating guidance programs–A do-it-yourself approach for local school counselors.* (Available from Dr. John G. Wirt, Director, NAVE, U. S. Department of Education, 400 Maryland Ave., Washington, DC 20202.)

- Yost, E. B., & Corbishley, M. A. (1987). *Career counseling: A psychological approach.*

San Francisco, CA: Jossey-Bass Publishers.

Trends

- Bureau of Labor Statistics
Electronic News Release Service
441 G St. NW, Rm. 2822
Washington, DC 20212
technical information: 202-272-5381

- Halasz, I. M. (1988). *Trends and issues in career education.* Information Series No. 332. Columbus, OH: ERIC Clearinghouse on Adult, Career, and Vocational Education, Center on Education and Training for Employment.

- Hoyt, K. B., & Harmon, A. S. (1987). *Annotated bibliography on transition from school to work. Vol. 2.* Columbus, OH: ERIC Clearinghouse on Adult, Career, and Vocational Education. (ERIC Document Reproduction Service No. ED 290 933)

- Naylor, M. (1988). Trends and directions in career education. *ERIC Digest No. 79.* Columbus, OH: Clearinghouse on Adult, Career, and Vocational Education.

Women

- Equity Assistance Center
Metropolitan Center for Educational Research, Development and Training
New York University
32 Washington Pl., Suite 72
New York, NY 10003
212-998-5113.

- Women in technology videotapes and posters. Available from The Consortium for Educational Equity, Rutgers, State University of New Jersey, Kilmer Campus 4090, New Brunswick, NJ 08903, 908-932-2071.

- Women's Bureau. U.S. Department of Labor. *Directory of nontraditional training and employment programs serving women.* Washington, DC: U.S. Government Printing Office, $9. (To order, call (202) 783-3238.)

Work Ethic

- Naylor, M. (1988). Vocational education and the work ethic in a changing workplace. *ERIC Digest No. 78.* Columbus, OH: Clearinghouse on Adult, Career, and Vocational Education, Center on Education and Training for Employment.

Workplace Career Development

- Harrison, C. (1989). Career development in the workplace. *ERIC Digest No. 86.* Columbus, OH: ERIC Clearinghouse on Adult, Career, and Vocational Education, Center on Education and Training for Employment.

- Slavenski, L., & Buckner, M. (1988). *Career development programs in the workplace.* Information Series 333. Columbus, OH: ERIC Clearinghouse on Adult, Career, & Vocational Education, Center on Education and Training for Employment.

Youth Organizations

- Boys Club of America
Irving J. Seher Unit
Milwaukee Boys and Girls Club
2404 Rogers St.
Milwaukee, WI 53204

- Center for Community Change
1000 Wisconsin Ave.
Washington, DC 20007
202-342-0594
(a clearinghouse for information about unaffiliated community groups)

- Children's Aid Society
Director, Work Readiness Program
105 East 22nd St.
New York, NY 10010

- Future Business Leaders of America
1908 Association Dr.
Reston, VA 22091

- Jobs for Youth-Boston, Inc.
312 Stuart St., 3rd. Floor
Boston, MA 02116
617-338-0815

- National Urban League
Equal Opportunity Bldg.
500 East 62nd St.
New York, NY 10021
212-644-6500

- National Youth Employment Coalition
1501 Broadway, Rm. 1111
New York, NY 10036
212-840-1801
(an umbrella organization of more than 40 youth-serving agencies)

- OICs of America
  100 West Coulter St.
  Philadelphia, PA 19144
  215-849-3010

- Saint Louis County Juvenile Court
  Coordinator of the Educational-Vocational
    Program
  91501 South Brentwood Blvd.
  Clayton, MO 63105
  314-889-2968

- SER-Jobs for Progress
  1355 River Bend Dr., Suite 401
  Dallas, TX 75247
  214-631-3999

- 70001 Training and Employment Institute
  600 Maryland Ave., SW
  West Wing, Suite 300
  Washington, DC 20024

- William Penn Foundation
  Senior Program Officer
  1630 Locust St.
  Philadelphia, PA 19103
  216-732-5114

Major Occupational Curriculum Sources

Charles R. Doty

The following resources have been located over the past 23 years, during which I taught curriculum and career education courses and consulted in secondary vocational education schools, community colleges, and technical institutes.

- Adult, Career, and Vocational Education
  Educational Resources Information Center
    (ERIC) Clearinghouse*
  Ohio State University
  1900 Kenny Rd.
  Columbus, OH 43210-1090
  800-848-4815 or 614-292-4353;
  FAX 614-292-1260
  ERIC Reference and Referral Services:
    800-USE-ERIC
  (*There are 16 regional ERIC clearing
    houses.)

- Agency for Instructional Technology
  1111 West 17th S.
  Box A
  Bloomington, IN 47402
  800-457-4509 or 812-339-2203

- American Association for Vocational Instruc
    tional Materials (AAVIM)
  National Institute for Instructional Materials
  745 Gaines School Rd.
  Athens, GA 30605
  800-228-4689

- American Society for Training and Develop-
    ment (ASTD)
  1630 Duke St.
  Box 1443
  Alexandria, VA 22313
  703-683-8100

- American Vocational Association (AVA)

  Publications Dept.
  1410 King St.
  Alexandria, VA 22314
  800-826-9972 or 703-683-3111

- Annehurst Curriculum Classification System
  P. O. Box 85
  Lamoni, IA 50140
  515-784-7836
  (computerized program for curriculum
    materials)

- Arkansas Vocational Curriculum
    Dissemination Center
  115 Graduate Education Bldg.
  University of Arkansas
  Fayetteville, AR 72701
  501-575-6606 or 800-632-8754

- Aspen Publishers, Inc.
  1600 Research Blvd.
  Rockville, MD 20850
  800-638-8437
  (texts on career education, life skills, employ
    ability, etc., for special-needs students)

- Automated Cross Referencing Occupational
    System (ACROS)
  Vocational Technical Education Consortium
    of States
  Southern Association of Colleges and Schools
  1866 Southern Lane
  Decatur, GA 30033-4097
  800-248-7701 or 404-329-6543

- Business Council for Effective Literacy
  1221 Avenue of the Americas–35th Floor
  New York, NY 10020
  212-512-2415/2412

- Center for Occupational Research and
  Development (CORD)
  601 C. Lake Air Dr.
  Waco, TX 76710
  800-231-3015, 817-772-8756, or
  512-323-0779
  (The National Tech-Prep Network is located
  at CORD.)

- Center for Occupational and Professional
  Assessment (COPA)
  Educational Testing Service
  Princeton, NJ 08540
  609-734-5694 or 609-734-5686 (library)

- Center on Education and Training
  for Employment
  The Ohio State University
  Publications Office, Box P
  1900 Kenny Rd.
  Columbus, OH 43210-1090
  800-848-4815 or 614-292-4353;
  FAX 614-292-1260

- Consortium for the Development of Profes-
  sional Materials for Vocational Education
  Center on Education and Training for
  Employment
  The Ohio State University
  1900 Kenny Rd.
  Columbus, OH 43210-1090
  800-848-4815

Cooperative Education Centers

- National Commission for Cooperative
  Education
  360 Huntington Ave.
  Boston, MA 02115
  617-437-3778

- National Community College Center
  for Cooperative Education
  Chicago City-Wide College
  30 East Lake St.
  Chicago, IL 60601
  312-781-9430

- National Society for Internships
  and Experiential Education
  122 St. Mary's St.–2nd Floor
  Raleigh, NC 27605
  919-834-7536

- Counseling and Personnel Services
  ERIC Clearinghouse
  University of Michigan
  School of Education, Rm. 2108
  610 East University St.
  Ann Arbor, MI 48109-1259
  313-764-9492; FAX: 313-747-2425

- *Curriculum Product News* (a magazine for
  district level administrators, available from
  Educational Media, Inc., Six River Bend, Box
  4949, Stamford, CT 06907-0949; 203-358-
  9900)

- Curriculum Publications Clearinghouse
  Western Illinois University
  Horrabin Hall 46
  Macomb, IL 61455
  800-322-3905

- DACUM (Developing a Curriculum)
  Humber College of Applied Arts and
  Technology
  205 Humber College
  Etobicoke, Ontario
  M9W 5L7
  416-675-5061, 416-252-5571, or
  416-675-3111

- DACUM Resource Center
  Dundalk Community College
  7200 Sollers Point Rd.
  Dundalk, MD 21222
  301-285-9869
  Educational Development & Training Center
  East Texas State University
  Commerce, TX 75428-9990
  214-886-5624

- Educational Resources Information Center
  (ERIC)
  1600 Research Blvd.
  Rockville, MD 20850-3166
  ACCESS ERIC: 800-873-3742; ERIC Docu
  ment Reproduction Service: 800-227-3742

- Educational Testing Service
  Market Research/Test Collection/Library/
  or Center for Occupational Testing
  Princeton, NJ 08541
  609-734-5180

- Human Resources Research Organization
  Technical Education Center
  1100 S. Washington St.
  Alexandria, VA 22314
  703-549-3611

- Illinois Vocational Curriculum Center
  Sangamon State University
  E-22
  Springfield, IL 62708
  217-786-6375

- Industrial Training Board
  Kay Sians Rd.
  Singapore 10
  OFF, 639111 Ext. 346

- Instructional Materials Laboratory
  University of Missouri-Columbia
  2316 Industrial Dr.
  Columbia, MO 65202
  800-669-2465 or 314-882-2883

- Interactive Resources, Inc.
  P. O. Box 80
  Ft. Lauderdale, FL 33302-0080
  800-330-8988
  (Council for Exceptional Children career
  education materials)

International Sources

- Bildung und Wissenschaft
  Inter Nationes
  Kennedyallee 91-103
  D.5300 Bonn 2
  Federal Republic of Germany

- European Center for the Development
  of Vocational Training (Berlin)
  European Community Information
  Service
  2100 M St., NW-Suite 707
  Washington, DC 20037

- International Centre for Advanced
  Technical and Vocational Training
  C. SO Unita D'Italia 125
  V. Le Mastri Del Lavoro 10
  10127 Torino Italia
  telephone: (011) 633.733

- International Development Bank
  Publications
  1300 New York Ave., NW
  Washington, DC 20577

- International Federation of Training and
  Development Organizations
  923 State St.
  St. Joseph, MO 49085

- Organization for Economic Cooperation
  and Development (Paris)

OECD Publications
700
2001 L St., NW
Washington, DC 20036-4095

- Section of Technical and Vocational
  Education
  Division of Science, Technical, and Environmental Education
  7, place de Fontenoy
  75700 Paris;
  or B. P. 3.07
  1, rue Miollis
  75015 Paris
  telephone: national—(1) 568.10.00;
  international—+ (33.1) 568.10.00

- United Nations and U. N. Agencies
  United Nations Publications
  Rm. DC2-0853
  New York, NY 10017

- UNIPUB
  4611 F Assembly Dr.
  Lanham, MD 20706-4391
  World Bank
  World Bank Publications
  P. O. Box 37525
  Washington, DC 20013

- Job Skills Training Center
  William Rainey Harper Community College
  Northeast Center
  1375 S. Wolf Rd.
  Prospect Heights, IL 60070
  708-537-8660

- Junior Colleges
  University of California at Los Angeles
  Math-Sciences Bldg., Rm. 8118
  405 Hilgard Ave.
  Los Angeles, CA 90024-1564
  213-825-3931; FAX: 213-206-8095

- Marketing Education Resource Center
  (MarkED, Division of IDECC, Inc.)
  1375 King Ave.
  Columbus, OH 43212
  614-486-6708

- Materials Development Center
  Stout Vocational Rehabilitation Institute
  Job Analysis Exchange
  School of Education and Human Services
  University of Wisconsin-Stout
  Menomonie, WI 54751
  715-232-1342/1987/2419/2195

- Michigan Career Education and Vocational
  Education Resource Center
  Michigan State University
  College of Education
  133-E Erickson Hall
  East Lansing, MI 48824-1034
  517-353-4397; FAX: 517-292-1606;
  Michigan Vocational Education Information
  System: 800-642-2896
  (curriculum, career education, BIB notes)

- Michigan Occupational Information
  Coordinating Committee (MOICC)
  Victor Office Center
  201 N. Washington Sq.
  Box 30015
  Lansing, MI 48909

- Mid-America Vocational Curriculum
  Consortium
  Instructional Materials Lab—UMC
  908 Woodson Way—Basement
  Columbia, MO 65211

- Mid-America Vocational Curriculum
  Consortium (MAVCC)
  1500 W. 7th Ave.
  Stillwater, OK 74074
  800-654-3988 or 405-377-200

- Missouri LINC
  University of Missouri-Columbia
  College of Education
  401 E. Stewart St.
  Columbia, MO 65211
  314-882-2733; Missouri only: 800-392-0533;
  Special Education Dissemination Center
  (special-needs resources): 314-882-3594

- National Alliance of Community and
  Technical Colleges
  Center on Education and Training for
  Employment
  The Ohio State University
  1900 Kenny Rd.
  Columbus, OH 43210-1090
  800-848-4815

- National Association for the Exchange of
  Industrial Resources
  Dept. E, P. O. Box 8076
  540 Frontage Rd.
  Northfield, IL 60093
  312-446-9111

- National Association of State Directors of
  Special Education
  2021 K St., NW

Washington, DC 20006
National Center for Research in Vocational
  Education
University of California at Berkeley
2150 Shattuck Ave., Suite 600
Berkeley, CA 94704
415-642-4004; FAX: 415-642-2124

- National Consortium of State Career
  Guidance Supervisors (NCSCGS)
  Center on Education and Training for
  Employment
  The Ohio State University
  1900 Kenny Rd.
  Columbus, OH 43210-1090
  800-848-4815

- National Council on Occupational Education
  (NCOE)
  American Association of Community and
  Junior Colleges (AACJC)
  National Office
  National Center for Higher Education
  One DuPont Circle, NW, Suite 410
  Washington, DC 20036-1176
  202-293-7050; AACJC Publications:
  800-236-4776 or 703-823-6966

- National Employment and Training
  Association
  653 Eason Blvd.
  Tupelo, MS 38001
  601-842-5621
  National Entrepreneurship Education
  Consortium
  Center on Education and Training for
  Employment
  The Ohio State University
  1900 Kenny Rd.
  Columbus, OH 43210-1090
  800-848-4815

**National Network for Curriculum
Coordination in Vocational and
Technical Education (NNCCVTE)**
(a consortium that disseminates curriculum
resources; six centers located throughout the
nation, with affiliated curriculum centers)

  - East Center Curriculum Coordination
    Center
    Sangamon State University, F-2
    Springfield, IL 62794-9243
    217-786-6375

  - Midwest Curriculum Coordination
    Center
    Dept. of Vocational and Technical

Education
1500 W. 7th St.
Stillwater, OK 74074-4364
405-377-2000

- Northeast Curriculum Coordination
  Center
  Division of Vocational Education
  New Jersey State Department of Education
  Aberdeen, NJ 07747
  908-290-1900

- Northwest Curriculum Coordination
  Center
  Old Main–Rm. 478
  Saint Martin's College
  Lacey, WA 98503
  206-438-4456

- Southeast Curriculum Coordination
  Center
  Research & Curriculum Unit
  P. O. Drawer DX
  Mississippi State, MS 39762
  601-325-2510

- Western Curriculum Coordination
  Center
  University of Hawaii
  College of Education
  1776 University Ave., Wist 216
  Honolulu, HI 96822
  808-948-7834

- National Network of Employment and
  Resource Professionals
  Employment Management Association
  4101 Lake Boone Tr.
  Raleigh, NC
  919-787-6010; FAX: 919-787-4916

- National Occupational Competency Testing
  Institute, Inc. (NOCTI)
  409 Bishop Hall
  Ferris State University
  Big Rapids, MI 49307
  800-334-6283 or 616-796-4695

- National Occupational Information
  Coordinating Committee Training Support
  Center (NOICC)
  Oklahoma SOICC
  Dept. of Vocational & Technical Education
  1500 West 7th Ave.
  Stillwater, OK 74074
  800-654-4502 or 405-743-5197
  (coordinates NOICC's training programs and
  conferences nationwide; national career

development guidelines available)

- National Projects Branch
  Division of Innovation and Development
  Reporters Bldg., Rm. 519
  Washington, DC 20202
  202-732-2362

- National Tech Prep Clearinghouse
  NNCCVTE, East Central Region
  Sangamon State University, F-30
  Springfield, IL 62794-9243
  217-786-6173; FAX: 217-786-6036

- National Vocational Education Professional
  Development Consortium
  1420 16th St., NW
  Washington, DC 20036
  202-328-0216

- New Jersey State Employment and Training
  Commission
  Labor and Industry Bldg., Rm. 403
  CN 940
  Trenton, NJ 08625
  609-984-3534

- OCCUPJOBS
  Technical Education System
  Houston Community College
  4310 Dunlavy
  Houston, TX 77006
  713-868-0776
  (a computerized vocational tracking system)

- *Open Entries: A Competency-Based Education
  Information Exchange*
  Center on Education and Training for
  Employment
  The Ohio State University
  1900 Kenny Rd.
  Columbus, OH 43210-1090
  800-848-4915

- Quest International
  537 Jones Rd.
  P. O. Box 566
  Granville, OH 43023-0566
  800-446-2700
  (living skills, grades 9-12)

- Southern Regional Education Board–State
  Vocational Education Consortium
  (SREB–SVEC)
  Southern Regional Education Board
  592 Tenth St. NW
  Atlanta, GA 30318-5790
  404-875-9211

- Special Education Regional Center
HY RRC/400 Huntington Hall
Syracuse University
150 Marshall St.
Syracuse, NY 13210

- Supplemental Resource Instructors
Northeast Metro Technical College
3300 Century Ave.
North White Bear Lake, NM 55110-1894
612-770-2351
(special needs students)

- United States Office of Vocational and Adult
Education
U.S. Department of Education
Washington, DC 20202
202-732-2404

- U.S. Department of Education The National
Projects Branch Office of Vocational
and Adult Education
Washington, DC 20202

202-245-2614

- Vocational Instructional Materials Laboratory
1900 Kenny Rd.
Columbus, OH 43210
614-292-5001
(CAP, Ohio's Competency Analysis Profiles)

- Vocational Studies Center
University of Wisconsin-Madison
964 Educational Sciences Bldg.
1025 W. Johnson St.
Madison, WI 53706
608-263-3696

- Vocational Technical Education Consortium
of States
Commission on Occupational Education
Institutions
Southern Association of Colleges and Schools
1866 Southern Ln.
Decatur, GA 30033-4097
800-248-7701 or 404-329-6543

- Vocational & Industrial Training Board
Vocational Dr.
Singapore 0513
telephone: 7757800